90 0707843 X

D1756298

## 21 Day

# RESEARCH ETHICS COMMITTEES, DATA PROTECTION AND MEDICAL RESEARCH IN EUROPEAN COUNTRIES

# Data Protection and Medical Research in Europe: PRIVIREAL

*Series Editors*:
Deryck Beyleveld and David Townend
PRIVIREAL, Sheffield Institute of Biotechnological Law and Ethics

PRIVIREAL (Data Protection and Medical Research in Europe) is a European Commission funded project (Contract No. QLRT-2001-00056) examining the implementation of Data Protection Directive 95/46/EC in relation to medical research and the role of ethics committees in European countries. PRIVIREAL members and authors are national experts in their fields, and the project is coordinated by Professor Deryck Beyleveld, Faculty of Law at the University of Sheffield.

The PRIVIREAL series consists of five separate volumes following the development of the PRIVIREAL project, from first assessments of the implementation of the Directive with a particular focus on medical research, to consideration of the role of research ethics committees as regards data protection, leading to recommendations on the implementation of the Directive and the remit which should be given to RECs to protect research participants' rights.

The information collected in this series provides a valuable resource for those involved with data protection, medical research, and how they interact. The volumes work to present a comprehensive view of current proceedings right across Europe, including both New Member States and Newly Associated States.

*Other titles in the series*

**Implementation of the Data Protection Directive in Relation to Medical Research in Europe**
*Edited by*
D. Beyleveld, D. Townend, S. Rouillé-Mirza and J. Wright
ISBN 0 7546 2369 6

**The Data Protection Directive and Medical Research Across Europe**
*Edited by*
D. Beyleveld, D. Townend, S. Rouillé-Mirza and J. Wright
ISBN 0 7546 2367 X

# Research Ethics Committees, Data Protection and Medical Research in European Countries

*Edited by*

D. BEYLEVELD, D. TOWNEND AND J. WRIGHT
*Sheffield Institute of Biotechnological Law and Ethics*

ASHGATE

Published by
Ashgate Publishing Limited
Gower House
Croft Road
Aldershot
Hants  GU11 3HR
England

Ashgate Publishing Company
Suite 420
101 Cherry Street
Burlington, VT 05401-4405
USA

Ashgate website: http://www.ashgate.com

**British Library Cataloguing in Publication Data**
Research ethics committees, data protection and medical
    research in European countries. - (Data protection and
    medical research in Europe. PRIVIREAL)
    1. European Parliament. Directive 95/46/EC on Data
    Protection - Congresses 2. PRIVIREAL Project - Congresses
    3. Medical ethics committees - European Union countries -
    Congresses 4. Medicine - Research - Law and legislation -
    European Union countries - Congresses 5. Medical records -
    Access control - European Union countries - Congresses
    6. Privacy, Right of - European Union countries - Congresses
    7. Data protection - Law and legislation - European Union
    countries - Congresses 8. Medical policy - European Union
    countries - Congresses
    I. Beyleveld, Deryck II. Townend, D. M. R. III. Wright, J.
    344.4'041

**Library of Congress Control Number:**
Beyleveld, Deryck.
    Research ethics committees, data protection and medical research in European
countries / by D. Beyleveld, D. Townend and J. Wright.
        p. cm. -- (Data protection and medical research in Europe)
    Includes index.
    ISBN 0-7546-4350-6
    1. Medical records--Law and legislation--European Union countries. 2. Data
protection--Law and legislation--European Union countries. 3. Medicine--Research--Law
and legislation--European Union countries. I. Townend, D. (David) II. Wright, J.
(Jessica) III. Title. IV. Series.

    KJE6229.R43B49 2005
    342.2408'58--dc22

2005007238

ISBN 0 7546 4350 6

Printed and bound in Great Britain by MPG Books Ltd. Bodmin, Cornwall.

# Contents

# List of Contributors

*Rosalvo Almeida* Invited collaborator at the Biomedical Law Centre, Faculty of Law, University of Coimbra (Portugal).

*Stephen Baker* Director of Prescribing at Sheffield Teaching Hospitals NHS Foundation Trust, UK.

*Deryck Beyleveld* PRIVIREAL Director and founder of the Sheffield Institute of Biotechnological Law and Ethics based in the Department of Law at the University of Sheffield. He obtained his chair in 1995 and is an internationally acclaimed jurist and moral philosopher.

*Geneviève De Boeck* Sociologist and researcher, Centre de Sociologie de la Santé, Université Libre de Bruxelles, Belgium.

*Patrycja Bong-Połeć* Quality Services Auditor, conducting GXP audits for a contract research organisation.

*Dimitris Boukis* PRIVIREAL member for Greece and a lawyer specializing in civil, commercial law and litigation at Kremmydas-Doris & Associates law firm in Athens.

*Asta Cekanauskaite* PRIVIREAL member for Lithuania and Assistant Professor in the Department of Medical History and Ethics at the Medical Faculty of Vilnius University. She is a member of the Lithuanian Biomedical Ethics Committee.

*Octavian Doagă* PRIVIREAL member for Romania and M.D. based at the 'Carol Davila' University of Medicine and Pharmaceutics, Bucharest, Romania. He is also a member of the National Bioethical Committee, Ministry of Health, Romania.

*Brigitte Feuillet* PRIVIREAL member for France and Professor of Law at the University of Rennes, France.

*Sónia Fidalgo* Researcher at the Biomedical Law Centre, Faculty of Law, University of Coimbra (Portugal).

*Tina Garanis-Papadatos* PRIVIREAL member for Greece, a qualified barrister, and Research and Teaching Assistant, National School of Public Health, Athens. She has written extensively on confidentiality, data protection and ethics committees in Greece.

*Eugenijus Gefenas* PRIVIREAL member for Lithuania and Chairman of the National Committee on Biomedical Ethics. He is an Associate Professor at the Department of Medical History and Ethics, Medical Faculty of Vilnius University, and a Senior Researcher at the Institute of Culture, Philosophy and Arts.

*Jozef Glasa* PRIVIREAL member for Slovakia, and an Associate Professor, physician and clinical researcher, teaching at the Slovak Medical University in Bratislava. He is the present Chairman of the Slovak Central Ethics Committee and the Director of the Bratislava Institute of Medical Ethics and Bioethics (IMEB).

*Bert Gordijn* Doctor and lecturer at the Department of Ethics, Philosophy and History of Medicine in the University of Nijmegen, the Netherlands. He is also employed as a clinical ethicist at the Nijmegen University Hospital.

*Ritva Halila* PRIVIREAL member for Finland and a member of the National Advisory Board on Health Care Ethics at the Ministry of Social Affairs and Health in Finland.

*Matthias Kettner* PRIVIREAL member for Germany, teaches philosophy at the Private University of Witten/Herdecke.

*Lisbeth Knudsen* PRIVIREAL member for Denmark and Associate Professor at the Institute of Public Health, University of Copenhagen, Denmark.

*Josef Kuře* PRIVIREAL member for the Czech Republic and a research and development worker at the Faculty of Medicine, University Centre for Bioethics, Masaryk University, Brno.

*Vigdis Kvalheim* PRIVIREAL member for Norway and Assistant Director of the Privacy Issue Unit of the Norwegian Social Science Data Services (established by the Norwegian Research Council for Science and the Humanities), which covers medical research. She has written extensively on privacy and research.

*Roberto Lattanzi* PRIVIREAL member for Italy, holds a Ph.D. in Civil Law and is a legal adviser at the Italian Data Protection Authority, Rome. He is also a researcher at the Catholic University of Milan and has published numerous articles on data protection in relation to sensitive personal data.

*Guy Lebeer* PRIVIREAL member for Belgium, Professor of Sociology and Director of the Centre de Sociologie de la Santé (Centre of the Sociology of Health), Université Libre de Bruxelles.

*Lasse A. Lehtonen* PRIVIREAL member for Finland and Assistant Professor and Administrative Chief Physician at the Helsinki University Central Hospital, Laboratory Services.

*Paweł Łuków* PRIVIREAL member for Poland and Lecturer in Philosophy and Medical Ethics at Warsaw University. He specializes in moral philosophy and bioethics.

*Maeve McDonagh* PRIVIREAL member for Ireland and Associate Professor in Law at the University College, Cork. She is a member of the REC of the Irish College of General Practitioners.

*Deirdre Madden* PRIVIREAL member for Ireland and Lecturer in Law, University College, Cork. She is a member of the Legal Advisory Board of the European Commission and of the Editorial Board of *Freedom of Information Review*. She has written books and articles on freedom of information law and privacy.

*Pierre Mallia* PRIVIREAL member for Malta and a lecturer in the University of Malta, Faculty of Medicine. He is a family doctor and is also specialized in Medical Law and Bioethics, obtaining a doctoral degree from Nijmegen, Holland. Dr. Mallia is also President of the Malta College of Family Doctors.

*Jane Miller* PRIVIREAL coordinating co-worker and Doctoral student at the Sheffield Institute of Biotechnological Law and Ethics, UK.

*Helena Moniz* PRIVIREAL member for Portugal and Assistant Professor of Criminal Law at the Faculty of Law, University of Coimbra. Researcher in the Centre for Biomedical Law, University of Coimbra and collaborator on the *Portuguese Criminal Review*, she has published on data protection problems concerning medical data and medical confidentiality.

*Pilar Nicolás* A member of the Inter-University Chair and Research Assistant at the University of Deusto, Spain.

*Lukáš Prudil* PRIVIREAL member for the Czech Republic, a barrister and Senior Lecturer at the Medical Faculty of Masaryk University, Brno. He is a member of the Ethical Commission of the University Hospital and the Psychiatric Hospitals in Brno.

*Peter Rehak* PRIVIREAL member for Austria, Head of Division of Biomedical Engineering and Computing, Department of Surgery and Chair of the Ethics Committee, Medical University of Graz.

*Carlos Maria Romeo-Casabona* PRIVIREAL member for Spain, Professor of Criminal Law and Director of the Inter-University Chair BBVA Foundation-Provincial Government of Biscay in Law and the Human Genome, at the University of Deusto, Spain.

*Mary Rosenzweig* M.Sc., University of Copenhagen, Denmark.

*Laima Rudze* PRIVIREAL member for Latvia, Head of the European Issues Department at the Compulsory Health Insurance State Agency of Latvia, and Secretary General of the Central Medical Ethics Committee of Latvia.

*Elisabeth Rynning* PRIVIREAL member for Sweden and Professor of Medical Law at the Faculty of Law, Uppsala University. She is also the legal expert on both the Swedish Medical Research Council REC and the Swedish National Council for Medical Ethics.

*Judit Sándor* PRIVIREAL member for Hungary and Professor at the Faculty of Political Science, Legal Studies and Gender Studies at the Central European University in Budapest. She is also an expert in research ethics committees, and has helped UNESCO draft an international legal instrument on genetic data.

*Sylvia Tomova* PRIVIREAL member for Bulgaria, a lawyer and Chief Legal Advisor at the Medical University of Sofia. She is a member of the Council of Europe Steering Group on Bioethics.

*David Townend* PRIVIREAL coordinator, member of the Sheffield Institute of Biotechnological Law and Ethics, and Sub-Dean for Postgraduate Studies in the Faculty of Law at the University of Sheffield.

*Joze Trontelj* PRIVIREAL member for Slovenia, member of the National Medical Ethics Committee at the Ministry of Health of the Republic of Slovenia.

*Rafael Vale e Reis* Researcher at the Biomedical Law Centre, Faculty of Law, University of Coimbra (Portugal).

*Toomas Veidebaum* PRIVIREAL member for Estonia and Director of the Research Centre, National Institute for Health Development, Tallinn.

*Susan Wallace* Policy and Projects Officer (Humanities) at the Cambridge Genetics Knowledge Park, UK.

*Jessica Wright* PRIVIREAL coordinating co-worker and Doctoral student at the Sheffield Institute of Biotechnological Law and Ethics, UK.

# Chapter 1

# Introduction

Deryck Beyleveld, David Townend and Jessica Wright

This volume contains reports on the theoretical role and practical operation of research ethics committees (RECs) and in particular the impact of relevant international and national instruments on this area. The reports were prepared for the second workshop of the EC-funded 5th Framework Programme concerted action project, 'Privacy in Research Ethics and Law' (PRIVIREAL) (PL QLRT-2001-00056), which took place at the University of Helsinki from 14–17 August 2003. This volume is a companion to another volume (also published by Ashgate Publishing Ltd). The companion volume contains keynote papers given at the second workshop and a review of the operation of RECs in the different states, looking at the relevant regulation on the area, with a particular focus on data protection. That report was compiled from papers contained in the present volume. Reports were received from all the participating countries (see below) except Cyprus.

In this publication, the term New Member States (NMS) is used to indicate the Czech Republic, Cyprus, Estonia, Hungary, Latvia, Lithuania, Malta, Poland, Slovakia and Slovenia. The 'candidate countries' are made up of Bulgaria and Romania, whilst, as in previous editions, 'EU Member States' refers to pre-2004 Member States.

## Aims of PRIVIREAL

Protection of privacy of subjects in medical research depends as much on ethics review as on data protection law, but little is known about how this interacts with implementation of Directive 95/46/EC to protect privacy. PRIVIREAL brings together experts on relevant law and on ethics review of medical research from across all the EU Member States (except Luxembourg) and Norway (like Iceland and Liechtenstein, a member of the European Economic Area but not the EU, which has agreed to be bound by Directive 95/46/EC) as well as the NMS and candidate countries, to evaluate the interaction between implementation of the Directive and research ethics review in protecting Directive rights of research subjects, with a view to making recommendations to the Commission about how to optimize the protection provided by research ethics review (taking into account the background EU and domestic legal and ethical culture/s).

To carry out these aims, PRIVIREAL has three phases. In the first phase, which led to the first PRIVIREAL workshop (held at the University of Sheffield from 9–12 January 2003), what the partner countries have done, or plan to do, to implement Directive 95/46/EC in relation to medical research was ascertained, and the adequacy of this was evaluated in relation to the requirements of the Directive. In the second phase, which led to the second PRIVIREAL workshop (held at the University of Helsinki from 14–17 August 2003), the remit and practice of RECs in relation to legal requirements generally and those of data protection law in particular, were ascertained. This volume and its companion present the results of this phase. In the third phase, which was the concern of the final PRIVIREAL workshop (held at the University of Coimbra from 7–11 July 2004), the protection of privacy of medical research subjects resulting from the domestic implementation of Directive 95/46/EC, together with the remit and practice of RECs to protect data protection rights of medical research subjects, were evaluated in the context of domestic legal and ethical culture in relation to the objectives of Directive 95/46/EC. Recommendations will be made to the European Commission about what it might do to better protect privacy of medical research subjects where protection is judged to be inadequate. The results of the first phase have been published by Ashgate Publishing Ltd., as will be the results of the third phase.

**Methodology of PRIVIREAL**

The primary source of data is reports by experts in the partner countries. However, central to the project is a website (http://www.privireal.org). This contains relevant legislation and guidance on the topics of relevance to the project, with as much as possible being made available in translation to English as well as the original language. To assist with the second and third phases of the project, there was a questionnaire for RECs that could be completed on-line in English, French or German. There is also a public discussion forum in addition to sections that can only be accessed by the partners. The website is complementary to the published volumes, and readers of the volumes are invited to consult the website and use it actively.

The workshops have only been open to partners of PRIVIREAL. The purpose of the first two workshops was primarily to enable partners to discuss summaries and analyses of the material they submitted which form the basis of the reports prepared for the first two phases by the coordinating team. The purpose of the third workshop was to discuss and prepare recommendations for the European Commission. The first two workshops also provided for keynote papers given by invited partners or by persons from outside the project to comment on controversial, but crucially important, topics for the relevant phase of the project. These papers do not represent a consensus among the partnership; they are merely the views of their authors. Only in the recommendations, published in the third phase, will concerted statements and judgments (where possible) be made.

# Chapter 2

# Research Ethics Committees in Austria

## Peter Rehak[*]

### Establishment of RECs in Austria

*Development*

The system for ethical review in Austria was initiated by three medical faculties (in Vienna, Graz and Innsbruck) in the early 1980s with the establishment of research ethics committees (RECs) to evaluate clinical research projects on a voluntary basis. The formalization process started in 1988 when the amended Hospital Act[1] first stated that 'committees' are to be established in hospitals for the evaluation of medical research on medicinal products. A further amendment to the Hospital Act in 1993 renamed these committees 'ethics committees' and extended their responsibility to research on medical devices and the application of new medical methods.

In 1993, a major amendment to the Drug Act foresaw implementation of Directive 91/507/EEC,[2] the EU-GCP,[3] and the establishment of ethics committees by the federal states for the evaluation of research on medicinal products outside of hospitals. The Medical Devices Directive[4] resulted in a novel law in 1996, the Medical Devices Act, which also implemented the Active Implantable Medical

---

[*] Head of Division of Biomedical Engineering and Computing, Department of Surgery and Chair of the Ethics Committee, Medical University of Graz.

[1] The Hospital Act is not directly applicable but a skeleton law for the respective laws of the federal states. Thus, there is a considerable delay before amendments become effective in practice.

[2] Commission Directive 91/507/EEC of 19 July 1991 modifying the Annex to Council Directive 75/318/EEC on the approximation of the laws of Member States relating to analytical, pharmacotoxicological and clinical standards and protocols in respect of the testing of medicinal products.

[3] Good Clinical Practice for trials on medicinal products in the European Community, III/3976/88-EN, 1990.

[4] Council Directive 93/42/EC concerning medical devices.

Devices Directive.[5] Subsequently, an amendment implemented the In Vitro Diagnostic Medical Devices Directive.[6]

In 1997, an amendment to the Act on University Organization provided, for the first time, regulations for the ethics committees of medical faculties. This amendment established—among other things—the review of 'applied medical research on human subjects' as an additional responsibility.

## Present Status

The ethical review system in Austria is well regulated. The review of medical research on medicinal products and on medical devices is covered by law for research in and outside of hospitals. In hospitals, the application of new medical methods is also subjected to review by ethics committees. Thus, the ethical review of the vast majority of research projects on human subjects is regulated by law. The review of other medical research involving human subjects[7] is at present only covered by the Act on University Organization and therefore applies only to university hospitals.

In general, the system of review of medical research is separate from systems for clinical ethics advice. However, there may be some overlap regarding the persons involved.

## Membership and Accountability

An REC has at least the following members: a medical doctor (neither the medical director of the hospital nor the investigator); a medical specialist in the field of the given project; a nurse; a lawyer; a pharmacist; a patient advocate; a representative of handicapped persons; a theologian or other person with pastoral or ethical competence; a technical security officer/biomedical engineer (only in the case of research on medical devices); and a statistician or biometrician (in some federal states and in university RECs).

University RECs tend to have more medical doctors of different specialities as members. RECs may also consult external experts. Hospital RECs are accountable to the bodies responsible for the hospital, university RECs to the respective medical university, and RECs for trials outside of a hospital to the government of the respective federal state.

---

[5] Council Directive 90/385/EC on the approximation of the laws of the Member States relating to active implantable medical devices.
[6] European Parliament and Council Directive 98/79/EC on in vitro diagnostic medical devices.
[7] In the sense of Article 1 of the Declaration of Helsinki.

## General Powers of RECs

*Powers*

In the legal sense, RECs have only advisory powers.[8] Though the researchers or sponsors are obliged to seek the advice of the responsible REC, explicit approval is at present only necessary in special cases, for example, for trials on medicinal products involving patients who are not capable of giving informed consent.

Notification of trials must be given in advance to the competent authority and, if appropriate, to the medical director of the hospital. In practice, the competent authority and/or the medical director will not approve the research if the opinion of the REC is unfavourable.

*Non-compliance*

If researchers do not submit their research for review in advance or do not comply with the requirements of the review and this comes to the attention of the REC, it may notify the medical director of the hospital and/or the medical faculty, if appropriate. This may result in disciplinary actions taken by the hospital or the university (medical faculty).

If failures are brought to the public's attention, the Medical Association, the Federal Government, and/or the regulatory authorities may also take action.

## General Legal Responsibility of RECs

*Cognizance of Law*

That RECs must be cognizant of the law is at least implicitly indicated by the mandatory inclusion of a lawyer. Clearly, RECs may not approve unlawful research.

On the basis of the elements of review, for example the qualification and experience of the researcher, the suitability of the site, the study protocol (its scientific merit and benefit/risk ratio), the information provided to the trial subjects, the modalities of recruitment and obtaining informed consent, amongst others, RECs may reject research that is in principle lawful.

---

[8] After the implementation of the Directive 2001/20/EC a favourable opinion of an REC will be necessary for the commencement of a trial on medicinal products.

*Guidance*

RECs take into account, among other guidance, the Declaration of Helsinki,[9] the EC-GCP-Guideline,[10] and the International Conference on Harmonization Harmonized Tripartite Guideline on Good Clinical Practice.[11]

*The Impact of the Directive 2001/20/EC*

Since Directive 2001/20/EC is effective only for studies on medicinal products, it covers only a part of the work of the RECs, even though it is the largest part (in Austria nearly 70 per cent).

 The Directive does provide for substantial changes: a favourable opinion of the REC will be necessary for the start of a trial (this will also have an impact on the legal status and the responsibilities of RECs); a unique opinion will have to be provided for multi-centre trials; only a single request for additional information will be possible; and, last but not least, the paperwork will be improved (for example, the application form).

 There is already a time limit of 60 days for the decision in Austria, but the new limit of 35 days for the evaluation of amendments will be a challenge for RECs.

*Compliance to Law in Practice*

In general, RECs comply with the law and do not approve unlawful research projects. RECs have become increasingly aware of the data protection law. To disseminate information on data protection to applicants and RECs, the 'Forum of the Austrian Ethics Committees' posted a leaflet on data protection in clinical research projects on the website of the 'Forum' in 2002.[12] Furthermore, some relevant points on data protection have been added to the application form that may be used for applications to all Austrian RECs. Even so, there are still some differences from one REC to another. In special cases, RECs will also seek external advice, for example, from the Data Protection Commission.

*Legal Actions Against RECs*

There is no special law regarding actions against RECs. Legal actions are therefore only possible on the basis of non-specific law. To date, legal action has not been known to have been taken against an REC. At present, no legal action can be taken against a negative vote.

---

[9] Initially adopted during the 18th Assembly of the World Medical Association, 1964. The current text can be found at http://www.wma.net/e/policy/b3.htm (last accessed 16 May 2005).

[10] N. 3 *supra*.

[11] ICH-GCP-Guideline (CPMP/ICH/135/95).

[12] For more information, see the website at http://www.uni-graz.at/ethikwww/ index_dwnld.html (last accessed 16 May 2005).

**Specific Matters Related to Data Protection**

*Exemptions from Data Protection Rights*

In principle, RECs do not have the power to make exemptions from the subject's rights. RECs may approve data analyses without informed consent of the subjects from whom data were obtained when it would not be reasonably possible to obtain informed consent, or it would cause undue distress to the subjects, and provided that the data are processed anonymously. Such an approval has no effect on the applicant's responsibility for acting in compliance with laws and regulations.

*Anonymized Information and Genetic Information*

RECs consider that data are rendered anonymous for the purposes of processing only if the persons who process the data cannot identify the data subjects. This holds true even if the data subjects can be re-identified by those who obtained the data.

If data are legally obtained for a certain purpose and it is anticipated that the data will be used for other purposes after rendering them anonymous, RECs will demand informed consent from the data subjects.

RECs consider that DNA samples and genetic information are covered by data protection rights insofar as they are not covered by the law on genetic engineering.

Chapter 3

# Belgian Ethics Committees and the Protection of Personal Data

Guy Lebeer[*] and Geneviève De Boeck[†]

## Introductory Note

This report deals with the roles and responsibilities of Belgian hospital ethics committees with regards to the question of the protection of research subjects' personal data.

The report is based on two types of information. The first type comes from the few analyses produced in the last few years concerning the institutionalization of ethics committees in Belgium, as well as legal texts on this subject. There is currently very little data available in this area, on both the levels of academic research and legislation. The second type of information comes from basic research carried out within the scope of the PRIVIREAL project. To this effect, a questionnaire was sent out to around 30 of the hospital ethics committees involved in the evaluation of research protocols.[1] We also interviewed the presidents of medical ethics committees. As well as these interviews, the ethics committees replied to this questionnaire by post. In total, 17 ethics committees have responded to our request for information.

---

[*] Professor of Sociology and Director of the Centre de Sociologie de la Santé (Centre of the Sociology of Health), Université Libre de Bruxelles.
[†] Sociologist and researcher, Centre de Sociologie de la Santé, Université Libre de Bruxelles.
[1] This questionnaire was set up following guidelines issued by the PRIVIREAL project coordinators, keeping in mind the final results of national research reports on research ethics committees. The PRIVIREAL questionnaire can be found in Chapter 9 of the accompanying volume *Research Ethics Committees, Data Protection and Medical Research in Europe* (Aldershot: Ashgate Publishing Ltd, 2005).

## The Institutionalization of Ethics Committees

### *The Constitution of Ethics Committees in Belgium*

There are essentially three types of ethics committee in Belgium: a national committee created in 1993 called the Consultative Committee for Bioethics in Belgium; hospital-based committees, called Hospital Ethics Committees, which were legally established in 1994; and the Non-hospital Ethics Committees. The latter are referred to differently depending on which institution they are attached to (for example, faculties of medicine, scientific societies, pharmaceutical firms, professional associations, and health services such as the Belgian Red Cross).

*Hospital ethics committees*  The history of the institutionalization of hospital ethics committees has been studied in detail by Sylvie Carbonnelle.[2] The following data is taken largely from her research.

The first ethics commissions appeared in Belgium at the end of the 1970s, as the result of an initiative between the French-speaking and Dutch-speaking Academies of Medicine, under the indirect influence of various international organizations (such as the World Medical Association). The very first ethics commission was created in 1979 by the Foundation for Scientific and Medical Research (Fonds de la Recherche Scientifique Médicale—FRSM). These commissions developed rapidly and spontaneously, initially within medical faculties and university hospitals, soon spreading throughout medical institutions.

In 1984, the movement was strengthened by an impetus of the National Council of the Order of Doctors.[3] The council defined new ethics regulations in the area of human experimentation. These regulations mainly stipulated that all biomedical research involving human subjects should, first of all, be subject to a written protocol approved by an ethics commission. In addition to this, the Order of Doctors explicitly recommended the creation of ethics committees within hospitals, and it also specified the composition of such committees, with a concern for interdisciplinarity and independence. The function and role of ethics committees was clarified by the Order of Doctors in 1991. Where the evaluation of research protocols was concerned, the Order of Doctors recommended adding the function of analysing larger ethical questions about medical practice to the function of assessing research protocols. In so doing, it introduced in an informal way the concept of *mixed committees*, bringing activities suited to the *ethics of research* and also activities connected to *clinical ethics* to the same commission. From 1984 to 1994, the Order of Doctors registered nearly 120 ethics committees,[4] mainly

---

[2] S. Carbonnelle, 'Belgian Hospital Ethics Committees: from law to practice', in G. Lebeer (ed.), *Ethical Function in Hospital Ethics Committees* (Netherlands: IOS Press, OHMSHA, 2002), 19–35.

[3] The official body responsible for watching over the profession's regulation on ethics.

[4] National Council of the Order of Doctors, *Bulletin of the National Council of the Order of Doctors (Bulletin du Conseil National de l'Ordre des Médecins)* (no. 84, Brussels: National Council of the Order of Doctors, 1999), 5.

hospital-based but from outside hospitals as well. This rapid increase in the number of ethics committees was the result of a growing awareness in the medical world of the need to establish an authoritative body for the evaluation and regulation of medical research and hospital practices.

It was not until 1994 that the Belgian law was ratified, with the implementation of a law entitled *Royal Decree of the 12 August 1994 modifying the Royal Decree of the 23 October 1964, setting the standards with which hospitals and their services should comply.*[5] This law made it compulsory to create an ethics committee in every single hospital or group of hospitals. It also defined the aims, composition and function of such committees, and closely followed the recommendations listed in the Code of Deontology of the National Council of the Order of Doctors.

Ethics committees therefore operate at a local rather than a regional level. It seems that the intention of the legislation was to provoke health professionals into thinking clearly about the issues of medical ethics that they encountered on a daily basis. However, the creation of such ethics committees at a local level also fulfilled the need to safeguard the genuine plurality of ethical thought in Belgium:

> By establishing the committees at a local level, the legislative body aimed to avoid the centralisation of ethical thinking, and above all to ensure that the committees did not alter the balance of power between the main philosophical and religious opinions of the country.[6]

Where the ethics of research are concerned, the localization of ethics committees in hospitals is still a cause for criticism today. The main reasons for criticism are the risk of 'shopping around' by pharmaceutical companies (faced with a negative opinion on a protocol, is it not likely that the pharmaceutical company will just take their request to a more 'agreeable' committee?), and consequently the question of the independence of the committees in relation to the pharmaceutical companies.

There are currently more than 200 local ethics committees in Belgium, of which 20 are non-hospital based.[7] The following discussion only deals with hospital-based ethics committees. Furthermore, these committees will only be considered in their function as monitors of research. We intend to call these committees RECs, in order to aid comparison with the other participating countries. It is therefore necessary to bear in mind that RECs in Belgium also fulfil the function of clinical ethics committees.

---

[5] This law appeared in the *Moniteur Belge* on 27 September 1994 (Royal Decree of 27 September 1994). See the Public Federal Justice Service website, www.moniteur.be, for further information.

[6] S. Carbonnelle, n. 2 *supra*, 24.

[7] See the list of ethics committees on the National Council of the Order of Doctors website, at www.ordomedic.be/listecometh2002fr.htm (last accessed on 16 May 2005).

*The Consultative Committee for Bioethics in Belgium*  The Consultative Committee for Bioethics in Belgium (CCBB) was created in 1993 as the result of an agreement[8] between the federal state, the three linguistic communities, and the Common Community Commission.[9] The formation of this committee was the first intervention of public powers with regards to creating an opinion on bioethics in Belgium. It was not officially installed until 1996, however.

The aim of the CCBB is two-fold: *to formulate opinion* and *to inform the public*. It focuses on formulating opinions on the problems raised by research and its application in the fields of biology, medicine and health. These problems are examined with regard to their ethical, social and legal aspects, and in particular with regard to their respect for human rights. Its aim to inform the public applies as much to political authorities as to the public itself. The CCBB has no legislative power nor does it have the authority to implement regulations or set standards where ethics are concerned. Its role is strictly *consultative*.

The CCBB was created with a concern to preserve the multiplicity of ideological and philosophical trends within the country. The opinions it forms are not intended to establish a consensus on ethical questions, but rather to reflect different points of view. The composition of the CCBB also follows this concern for pluralism in ethical thought: there is a balance between Christians and non-Christians; French-speakers and Dutch-speakers; members with a scientific background and those with a background in philosophy, law and social sciences; and also between male and female members. The CCBB is composed of 35 actual members and the same number of substitutes, as well as eight members with a consultative voice. Their mandate lasts for four years.

The CCBB can decide to consider an issue either on its own initiative or following a request from the presidents of various parliamentary groups, a member of the government, a scientific research body, a higher education establishment, a healthcare provider, and finally from an REC. Since its creation, the CCBB has produced 23 opinions that deal as much with clinical ethics as with the ethics of research.[10]

It is equally important to note here that the RECs are totally independent of the CCBB. The CCBB only requires them to produce an annual report listing their activities (including the number of protocols dealt with and the number of opinions formulated) and to send a copy of it to the Order of Doctors.

---

[8] Co-operation agreement of 15 January 1993, which appeared in *Moniteur Belge* on 12 May 1993.

[9] The Common Community Commission is the representative political authority for the bilingual area of Brussels-Capital.

[10] As of September 2003, there have been 23 opinions of which opinion no. 13 of 9 July 2001 relates to human testing. These opinions can be viewed on the website of the Consultative Committee on Bioethics: www.health.fgov.be/bioeth (last accessed on 16 May 2005).

## The Legal Framework of RECs in Belgium

Where the legal framework is concerned, two royal decrees and a planning-law acted until recently as a frame of reference for the RECs. The first, as mentioned previously, is the Royal Decree of the 12 August 1994 setting the standards with which hospitals and their services should comply.[11] This Royal Decree made it officially compulsory to set up an REC in every hospital or group of hospitals. It also defined succinctly the function, composition and aims of these RECs taking ideas mainly from the ethical standards advanced by the Order of Doctors. These various elements will be discussed in more detail later on. We should note here, however, that this Royal Decree, which allows RECs to formulate their own opinions on experimentation protocols, does not in any way proscribe the methods of requesting, the procedures, or above all, the criteria to be used when evaluating research protocols. In the absence of guidelines and clear criteria for evaluating the protocols, deontological standards, as well as treaties and international guidelines, acted most frequently as a frame of reference at this time.

The second law is the Royal Decree concerning standards and protocols applicable in the area of clinical trials on medicinal products for human usage, modified on 22 September 1992, following the implementation into Belgian law of the provisions of the EC Directive of 19 July 1991.[12] In order to conform to the Directive, this Royal Decree requires the opinion of a suitable REC as a prerequisite for commencement of a human trial. The Royal Decree does not itself define what is considered 'a suitable REC' but rather it refers, in a very general manner, to the principles of *Good Clinical Practice* (GCP).

The planning-law of 24 December 2002[13] includes a paragraph in the Law on Drugs stating that the favourable opinion of an REC is mandatory before beginning any clinical trial.

Finally it should be emphasized that European Directive 2001/20/EC on the application of Good Clinical Practice in the conduct of clinical trials on medicinal products for human use,[14] has recently been implemented in Belgium. The Law relating to Experimentation on Humans[15] came into force on 7 May 2004 and concerns not only the clinical trials of drugs, but also medical experimentation in general. It is still difficult to evaluate its consequences, due to the newness of the legislation at the time of writing.

---

[11] See n. 5 *supra*.

[12] Commission Directive 91/507/EEC of 19 July 1991, which modified the annex of Council Directive 75/318/EEC on the approximation of the laws of Member States relating to analytical, pharmacotoxicological and clinical standards and protocols in respect of the testing of medicinal products.

[13] *Moniteur Belge* of 31 December 2002.

[14] Directive 2001/20/EC of the European Parliament and of the Council on the approximation of the laws, regulations and administrative provisions of the Member States relating to the implementation of good clinical practice in the conduct of clinical trials on medicinal products for human use.

[15] *Moniteur Belge* of 18 May 2004. In French, its title is the 'Loi relative aux Expérimentations sur la Personne Humaine'.

*The Aims of the RECs*

Article 1 of the Royal Decree of 27 September 1994, which introduced hospital ethics committees, assigned three aims to the RECs:

-    A duty to assist and advise on ethical and practical aspects of hospital care;
-    A duty to take part in decisions relating to individual cases in the area of ethics;[16]
-    A duty to formulate opinion on every protocol relating to human experimentation.

The RECs, therefore, are *mixed committees*, bringing together *research ethics* activities and *clinical ethics* activities. However, as is demonstrated by our field study, the way these activities are organized can vary considerably from one institution to another. In most hospitals there is just one committee that manages all the activities as set down in the law. However, several hospitals did decide to make a distinction between research ethics and clinical ethics by, for example, creating not only an REC responsible for the analysis of research protocols but also a commission dedicated to questions of clinical ethics. Depending on the circumstances, this commission is either totally autonomous with respect to the REC or it maintains very close links (principally in the way that the same people sit on both commissions).

In practice, the activities of the REC seem to be more concerned with the evaluation of research protocols than with the other two aims, which are more closely concerned with clinical ethics. Indeed, the report on the RECs' activities, published by the CCBB, states that, in 2001 90 per cent of the questions dealt with by RECs came within the area of processing the evaluation of experimental protocols.[17]

*The Composition of the RECs*

In Article 1 of the Royal Decree of 27 September 1994, which introduced hospital ethics committees, the composition of RECs is determined thus:

> The committee should be composed of between 8 and 15 members, made up of both sexes and should comprise:
> -    a majority of doctors connected to the hospital or group of hospitals;
> -    at least one general practitioner not connected to the hospital or group of hospitals;
> -    at least one member of nursing staff from the hospital or group of hospitals;
> -    a lawyer.
> Interested persons who may or may not be connected to the hospital or group of hospitals may be appointed as members of the committee.

---

[16] This aim of assistance with the decisions concerning individuals has been cancelled by a Decision of the Court of Arbitration on 30 October 2000 (*Moniteur Belge* of 21 November 2000).

[17] Y. Englert, *Rapport d'Activité des comités d'éthique locaux, Années civiles 1998–2001* (Brussels: The Consultative Committee of Bioethics in Belgium, 2003), 9.

The following persons may not be appointed to the committee:
- the director of the hospital;
- the head doctor;
- the president of the medical council;
- the head of nursing.

(...) Members are appointed to the committee by the manager of the hospital or group of hospitals.

By composing the RECs in this way, as is set down in law, it is possible to emphasize two points. Firstly, the wish to ensure a certain balance between members connected to the hospital—or group of hospitals—and those members from outside that institution. The second point is the decision to guarantee a multidisciplinary approach. However, as is emphasized by Sylvie Carbonnelle, one must ask oneself how the presence of only two non-doctors (a nurse and a lawyer) and two people from outside the hospital (a general practitioner and the lawyer again) is sufficient to ensure that the thought process is truly multidisciplinary and independent:

> Being composed mainly of doctors, and, it must be stressed, not allowing in any way for the presence of either the 'lay' person, of representatives from the community or even of patients, it appears that the model for the Belgian medical ethics committees would rather aim to favour agreement between doctors than to allow constructive debate between various points of view. However transparent it may appear, the hospital committee, as is composed by law, remains centred on the physician.[18]

In practice, the composition of the RECs is fairly variable. Some are limited to eight members, but most have more members than this. The physician-centred character of the RECs, relating to members from both inside and outside the hospital, was confirmed by our research. The members from outside the hospital, besides the general practitioner and the lawyer who are required by law, were in the large part people with a scientific or medical background: pharmacists or pharmacologists, sometimes retired doctors.

The law does not make any requirement in terms of education or ethical knowledge in order for a person to sit on an REC. It should also be noted that doctors in Belgium receive very little education in ethics in the course of their academic training and any information they do receive is more in the area of deontology. According to Carbonnelle's report, there is, however, a discrepancy between Catholic and non-religious institutions.[19] In Catholic hospitals, the tendency is to systematically surround oneself with ethics specialists (researchers, teachers from university research centres specializing in bioethics, for example). On the other hand, in non-religious hospitals, the tendency is to refuse to recognize the knowledge of an ethics expert. In their eyes, an understanding of ethics grows from the ordinary knowledge of everyone involved in care and comes with experience and from looking after people.

---

[18] S. Carbonnelle, n. 2 *supra*, 25.
[19] S. Carbonnelle, n. 2 *supra*, 28.

*The Legal Responsibility of RECs*

The Royal Decree of 27 September 1994, which introduced hospital ethics committees, provided the RECs with a legal framework. However, this law did not grant them any legal status. From that point on, the RECs could not be held responsible in any *civil action*. The Law relating to Experimentation on Humans, which came into force on 7 May 2004, has made the sponsor of the research assume responsibility for any damage caused by the investigation, even without fault, and to require him or her to have insurance covering this responsibility.

## Powers of the RECs

*From a Consultative to a Binding Opinion*

As mentioned previously, the Royal Decree concerning standards and protocols in the area of trials of medicinal products for human usage, which was modified on 22 September 1992, requires the opinion of an REC as a prerequisite to the initiation of any human trial. The opinion of an REC became, therefore, a legal obligation for any new experimental research on drugs for human use.

Article 1 of the Royal Decree of 27 September 1994, which introduced ethics committees by law into hospitals, states that:

> the opinions and the advice of the committee are confidential and non-binding, and are justified in a report that is provided only to the applicant, and which reflects the different points of view of its members.[20]

The planning-law of 24 December 2002 requires this opinion to be favourable, and the recent Law relating to Experimentation on Humans has confirmed this.

According to the people we surveyed, only about five per cent of research protocols were subject to amendments. It was highly unusual for an REC to refuse a protocol outright. According to some RECs, this is the result of an earnestness on the part of the pharmaceutical firms, who very often have at their disposal the knowledge necessary to ensure the legality of their protocol and who attest a concern for research ethics and a knowledge of the principal rules and guidelines.

*Disciplinary Action and Penalties*

Until recently, Belgian legislation did not make provision for the use of any kind of sanction against an investigator or study sponsor who do not fulfil the obligation of obtaining a favourable opinion from an REC.

Pharmaceutical companies who decided not to follow the REC's opinion on their research protocol were subject to no legal penalties. Having said this, it does seem that pharmaceutical companies, with their own interests in mind and with the

---

[20] S. Carbonnelle, n. 2 *supra*, 25.

desire to further their research, more often than not did take into account the opinions of RECs where amendments to their protocols were concerned, a fact supported by the majority of the committee presidents with whom we consulted.

The Code of Deontology of the Order of Doctors makes it clear that any doctor taking part in biomedical research involving the use of human subjects that was not submitted to an ethics committee in advance will be subject to disciplinary action. However, the Order of Doctors does not explain what sort of sanctions would be used against a doctor if such a situation arose. There are various disciplinary sanctions that the Order of Doctors could impose: a warning; censure; a reprimand; suspension from practising medicine (for up to two years); and being struck off the Order of Doctors. It should be emphasized that the main aim of disciplinary action is to maintain high working standards for certain professions or activities. In general, disciplinary law is not codified. The rules and principles of disciplinary action are not subject to detailed legal provisions, but rather are more often than not the result of custom and practice. The disciplinary powers of the Order of Doctors are entirely based on this idea.

Since May 2004, the Law relating to Experimentation on Humans provides a penalty of imprisonment from one month to two years and a fine of 500 to 250 000 Euros where a simple contravention of the law is concerned, as well as a penalty of three months to three years of imprisonment and a fine of 1000 to 500 000 Euros if the violation of the law resulted in either an apparently incurable illness or a physical or psychological permanent disability, or the complete loss of use of an organ.

## The Power to 'Render Lawful' Unlawful Research Activities

The RECs in Belgium do not have the power to legitimize a biomedical research activity that, in other circumstances, would be considered unlawful.

## RECs and Legal Responsibilities

### RECs and the Law

*Biomedical research and human experimentation: a legal vacuum recently filled*
The Royal Decree of 27 September 1994, which introduced hospital ethics committees, made it compulsory to include a lawyer on the committees, so demonstrating a desire to ensure the legality of research protocols. However, this Decree, which granted RECs the power to produce opinions on protocols concerning experimentation, did not in any way define the method of asking for advice, the procedures or, above all, the criteria for evaluating the protocols and the legal requirements with which every protocol must comply. Thus, until recently, the area of human experimentation was not satisfactorily regulated. Of course, the planning-law of 24 December 2002 requires the favourable opinion of an REC as a prerequisite to the setting up of any human trial. However, it does not define what the necessary criteria are for a research protocol to be accepted.

Therefore, RECs were faced with a legal vacuum where medical research and human testing are concerned. This legal vacuum has been filled by the implementation into Belgian law of European Directive 2001/20 on *Good Clinical Practice*, which lays down strict standards in the area of human testing and defines the criteria to which a protocol must subscribe in order to be accepted.

The Law relating to Experimentation on Humans mentions the main criteria for acceptance (Article 5):

1°   The experimentation is scientifically justified (…).
2°   The experimentation has the purpose of increasing human knowledge (…).
3°   There is no alternative methodology that has the same efficacy.
4°   The risks and foreseeable disadvantages on physical, psychological, social and economical levels have been evaluated in relation to the expected benefits for the participating person and for others, in particular regarding their rights to respect for their physical and mental integrity, for their private life and protection of personal data.
5°   The assessment reaches the conclusion that the benefits expected on a therapeutical basis and for public health justify the risks; (…) the interests of the patient always prevail over those of science and society.
6°   An ethics committee gave a favourable opinion to the protocol and, when the law requires it, an authorization from the Minister for Public Health has been provided.
7°   The participating person or his or her representative gave his or her free and informed consent (…).
8°   The care given to the participating person is the responsibility of a qualified doctor (…).
9°   The sponsor must be insured to cover his or her responsibility, even without fault, in case of damage caused by the experimentation.

*Legal reference texts used by RECs when evaluating protocols*   In practice, when faced with a Belgian law that up until recently has been severely lacking in the area of biomedical research and human experimentation, the RECs have referred to different legal texts, international treaties, and other sources of information both national and international, to aid in their evaluation of research protocols. In our field study, which took place before the recent law was enacted, we found that RECs demonstrated a distinct awareness of recent changes in legal texts that play a part, directly or indirectly, in the process of evaluating research protocols. Therefore, the majority of them were aware of the scope of European Directive 2001/20 and its implications for RECs. We should point out straight away that amongst the legal texts most frequently cited by the RECs was the Law on the Protection of Privacy.[21] It seems that this expressed a very real desire on the part of the RECs to ensure the confidentiality of research subjects' personal data. The

---

[21] Law which appeared in the *Moniteur Belge* on 3 February 1999, implementing Directive 95/46/EC of 24 October 1995 of the Parliament and of the Council on the protection of individuals with regard to the processing of personal data and on the free movement of such data.

main legal texts used by the RECs we surveyed are as follows (in order of importance):

- The Belgian Law on the Protection of Privacy;
- The Belgian Law of 22 August 2002 relating to the Rights of the Patient;
- The Royal Decree of 27 September 1994 introducing Hospital Ethics Committees;
- European Directive 2001/20/EC relating to Good Clinical Practice;
- The Royal Decree concerning standards and protocols applicable in the area of clinical trials on medicinal products for human usage, modified on 22 September 1992, following the implementation into Belgian law of the regulations of the European Commission of 19 July 1991;
- The Planning-Law of 24 December 2002;
- The Law of 22 May 2002 relating to Euthanasia.

Besides the various legal texts mentioned above, the RECs relied on other guidelines set down in national and international conventions. These 'codes of good conduct' still constitute a reference tool of prime importance to the RECs for their work. The results of our enquiry showed that the main national and international texts used by the RECs are:

- The Declaration of Helsinki;
- The Code of Deontology of the National Council of the Order of Doctors;
- The Good Clinical Practice Guidelines *(*purely as a guideline and without reference to Directive 2001/20/EC);
- The Nuremberg Code.

Finally, a certain number of RECs made use of opinions pronounced by the Consultative Committee on Bioethics of Belgium as much as those from the Order of Doctors in order to best carry out their work of protocol evaluation.

*Acceptability criteria for research protocols in practice*  The RECs defined, on an autonomous basis, their own acceptability criteria for research protocols, and made use of the legal texts, guidelines and other reference sources listed above. This situation was likely to lead to uncertainty and legal inequality for research subjects. In practice, however, it seems that the RECs all adopted similar criteria to use. However, due to this legal uncertainty, specific committees were seen as more conciliatory than others in their evaluation of research protocols. The main evaluation criteria cited by the RECs we questioned are:

- *The scientific relevance of the study*: the study should contribute to the advancement of scientific and medical knowledge for the good of society.
- *Research methodology*: the investigator must display a profound knowledge of the subject as well as the necessary qualifications; the scientific scope of the study should be appropriate.

- *Information provided to the patient*: the information given to the patient who has agreed to take part in the medical trial should be clear and complete. The information should always be presented in a written format but the REC often requires the doctor to explain this information verbally as well.
- *Free and informed consent of the research subject*: the free and informed consent of the research subject is indispensable for the initiation of any study. This consent should be revocable, thus allowing the patient to withdraw from the study at any time. Consent should be obtained without the use of any moral or financial pressure.
- *Confidentiality of data*: the gathering and handling of research subjects' data must be guaranteed the strictest confidentiality and should respect the provisions made in law for the protection of privacy.
- *Insurance*: the insurance contract must guarantee financial cover for any healthcare requirements resulting from the study in the case of side effects or accidents. This insurance cover should have no time limit. It should cover any undesirable effects experienced by the patient, including after the study has finished.
- *Benefit to the patient*: the study should present a medical benefit to the patient who agrees to take part in it. Where positive results are achieved, the research subject should be allowed to benefit from treatment from when the study ends to when the product is launched. Moreover, the protocol should respect the patient's autonomy and guarantee their rights.
- *Balance between risk and benefit*: the risks undertaken by the patient in the course of the research study should be in proportion to its estimated benefits.
- *Independence of the study*: the study should be carried out by an investigator who is independent from the study sponsor.
- *Publication of results*: the pharmaceutical companies cannot be granted ownership of the trial results. Where serious side effects are experienced by the research subjects, the pharmaceutical company must publicize these results.
- *The protocol should be clear, understandable and complete.*

These criteria, cited in practice, can be compared with those required in the Law relating to Experimentation on Humans. As the latter mentions (Art. 11 paragraph 4):

The ethics committee that is competent to hand down an opinion shall take the following elements into account when it formulates its opinion:

1°   relevance of the experimentation and its design;
2°   there is satisfactory evaluation made of the expected benefits and risks, as well as the reasonableness of the conclusions, especially regarding the therapeutic and public health aspects;
3°   the protocol;
4°   the competence of the investigator and his/her collaborators;
5°   brochure prepared for the investigator(s);
6°   quality of the research facilities;

7°    adequacy and completeness of the written information to provide, as well as the procedure to follow to obtain informed consent, and the justification for research on subjects who are not capable of giving their consent or whose consent cannot be obtained due to the urgent need for them to participate in the experiment;

8°    measures foreseen for amends and/or compensation in the case of harm to or death of a participant, imputable to the experiment;

9°    insurance or other guarantees covering the investigator's and promoter's liability; (...);

10°   any amounts and modalities for retribution/compensation to the investigators and participants, as well as the relevant elements of each contract drawn up between the promoter and the research site;

11°   methods to recruit the participants.

*The position of RECs when faced with a protocol that, even though ethical, does not conform to the law*   The RECs who were interviewed for our enquiry emphasized that their most important aim was to evaluate the *ethical nature* of a protocol. In so doing, they grant a certain *pre-eminence to ethics as opposed to the law*. This does not mean, however, that RECs are not interested in the legality of the protocol.

In practice, when faced with a research protocol that is ethical but not lawful, the majority of RECs have recourse to an amendment procedure. Any breach of law is pointed out to the sponsor of the study, with the need to guarantee the legal conformity of the research protocol and of the clinical trial being emphasized. Outright rejections from RECs are relatively rare. Furthermore, some RECs told us that pharmaceutical companies are generally highly knowledgeable in the area of legal expertise and are concerned that their protocols conform to the law.

All the RECs who we questioned had not yet come across a specific case of a research protocol being ethical but not lawful.

*The position of RECs when faced with a lawful but unethical protocol*   The RECs who we consulted unanimously agreed that if a protocol were unethical, for whatever reason, it would not receive a favourable opinion from the committee, even if it conformed entirely to the letter of the law. However, we have seen that research protocols are rarely rejected outright. Generally, protocols are subject to a process of amendments, which are agreed on by all the members of an REC and also by the sponsor of the study.

*Consequences of EC Directive 2001/20/EC*

The implementation of EU Directive 2001/20/EC into Belgian law has happened relatively recently. For this reason, it is currently difficult to evaluate the range of consequences of this new regulation. However, it can already be seen that the Law relating to Experimentation on Humans has confirmed or changed the function and responsibilities of RECs in the following ways:

-    *A compulsory favourable opinion*: it will become compulsory to receive a favourable opinion from an REC before the start of any clinical trial.

- *Multi-centre clinical trials*: in the case of a multi-centre clinical trial, the favourable opinion will be given by only one ethics committee, whatever the number of sites on which the experimentation is planned.
- *A time-limit for communicating the opinion*: the REC and the competent authority (which will only be competent for clinical trials and will only give an opinion on the issues in relation to the quality of the drug) will have a maximum time-limit of 15 days in the case of a trial of stage I and 28 days in the case of other experimentation, to communicate their motivated opinion to the investigator.
- *A single request for information*: the REC can only send one request for information to the requesting person.
- *Protocol evaluation criteria*: these criteria have been mentioned previously (pages 19–20).

*Legal Action Against RECs*

The Belgian legislation concerning hospital ethics committees did not grant the RECs any legal status. They cannot be held legally responsible if a subject is harmed in the course of the research study. The Law relating to Experimentation on Humans does not indicate that this will change in the future.

**RECs and the Protection of Personal Data**

*RECs and the Free and Informed Consent of the Research Subject and Public Interest in the Evaluation of Research Protocols*

*The Law on the Protection of Privacy and the question of the research subject's consent* According to Article 4 of the Belgian Law on the Protection of Privacy, two conditions have to be met in order to collect and process personal data: one must be pursuing a specific and legitimate purpose and must also be in compliance with one of the six hypotheses listed below.

To pursue a specific and legitimate purpose, personal data can only be collected for a specific reason. This reason must be legitimate, which means that there must be a balance between the interests of the person responsible for handling the data, and the interests of the data subjects.

It must also be in compliance with one of the following six hypotheses, which are that personal data can only be processed:

- if the person definitely gave their free (without being subjected to moral or financial pressure), specific (relating to a specific use of the data) and informed (the person should be given useful information about how their data is to be used) consent;
- *or* if the processing of the data is necessary to fulfil a contract, or to carry out pre-contractual obligations (an insurance contract, an invoicing service);

- *or* if the processing is required by law (for example, the obligation on an employer to provide the social security agency with particular information);
- *or* if the processing of the data safeguards the vital interests of the data subject—notably in the case of an unconscious accident victim about whom certain medical information needs to be gathered (mainly the results of blood tests), before treatment is possible;
- *or* if the processing of the data is necessary to carry out an aim which is in the public interest;
- *or* finally, if the processing of the data is necessary for a legitimate interest of the data controller or a third person, as long as the interest or rights of the data subject do not prevail.

According to the law therefore, the collection and processing of personal data does not necessarily mean that the subject has given their consent. However, the law deals much more strictly with the collection and processing of so-called *sensitive personal data*, which aims to find out information on a person's race (term to be understood in its juridical sense), political opinions, religious or philosophical beliefs, membership of a trade union, *health*, sexuality, if he or she is under suspicion for a crime, prosecutions or penal or administrative sentences. The law therefore prohibits the registration and use of such data, except under certain conditions. For personal data relating to health, the conditions are mainly as follows (Article 7 §1$^{er}$):[22]

- when the data subject has given their written consent for their data to be used; however, they are still allowed to revoke their consent at any time;
- when the processing of the data is necessary for the support and protection of public health, including screening;
- when the processing of the data is necessary to protect the vital interests of the data subject or of another person, in the situation where the data subject is physically or legally incapable of giving their consent;
- when the processing of the data is declared compulsory by law, decree or ordinance, on the grounds of important public interest;
- when the processing of the data is necessary for the purposes of preventative medicine, medical diagnoses, the administration of healthcare or treatment either to the data subject or a relative, where the management of the health service is acting in the interests of the data subject and the data are processed under the supervision of a health professional;
- when the processing of the data is necessary for specific research, and is carried out following conditions laid down by the King, by order of the Council of Ministers, following an opinion from the Commission on Privacy.

As a result therefore, Belgian law allows, in particular circumstances, the collection of medical data without the consent of the data subject, if the collection

---

[22] Please refer to Article 7 of the Law on the Protection of Privacy for a complete listing of specific cases enacted in law.

and processing of such data is in the vital interests of the data subject (the patient), for example, or if necessary for scientific research (public interest).

*The RECs and the question of the data subject's consent in the evaluation of research protocols*    The new law concerning the rights of the patient[23] specifies in Article 8 paragraph 1 that '[h]aving received the pre-requisite information, the patient has the right to give their free consent to any treatment by a medical professional'.

The Law relating to Experimentation on Humans, which implements European Directive 2001/20/EC, states: in Article 6 general provisions concerning the consent of persons participating in an experimentation (this consent would be written and if the person participating in the experimentation cannot write, he/she could give their oral consent in the presence of an adult witness who is independent of the sponsor and the investigator); in Article 7 'particular provisions for the protection of under age persons'; in Article 8 'particular provisions for persons of age unable to give their consent'; and in Article 9 'particular provisions for the protection of persons from whom consent cannot be obtained due to an emergency'.

The RECs who were questioned for our survey unanimously agreed that, when evaluating research protocols concerning human experimentation, it was essential to obtain the free and informed consent of the research subject if the protocol were to be accepted. However, several RECs did emphasize that, in certain circumstances, a research protocol could be accepted without the required consent of the patient (difficulties of re-contacting the patient, for example).

Faced with this type of protocol, the RECs seemed to generally believe that to require the free and informed consent of the patient would constitute an obstruction into medical research on particular diseases, research that could ultimately benefit the whole of society. Whatever the situation, however, the research must, primarily, be of benefit to the patient himself or herself before addressing a particular public interest, whether or not the patient's consent is required. Let us also add that in emergency situations, where it is impossible to obtain consent from either the data subject or their legal representative, the REC makes it a requirement to obtain the patient's agreement as soon as reasonably possible. Also, as soon as the patient is capable of giving their own consent, they should be informed of the methods and objectives of the study into which they have been enrolled and he or she is automatically entitled to withdraw their consent.

*RECs and Anonymity of the Subject's Data*

*Data anonymity criteria according to the RECs*    According to the members of the RECs consulted in the course of our enquiry, personal data is considered *anonymous* from the moment when it is no longer possible to identify the person who gave the sample. However, it is possible that the clinical data stay attached to

---

[23] Law of 22 August 2002 concerning the Rights of the Patient.

the sample, on the condition that they do not permit the identification of this person. Encoded data therefore are not considered to be anonymous data.

Finally, it is interesting to mention that one of the RECs questioned pointed out the recent creation within their hospital of a Privacy Commission. The main focus for this Commission was to strengthen the protection of personal data both within the hospital and when they are transferred to external agencies.

*RECs and the question of anonymity in the collection and processing of data*  In the course of our enquiry, we put the following question to the RECs:

> According to your REC, is coded data (a code is kept so individuals can be re-identified) considered to be anonymous data in the case where the data controller/sponsor, who processes the coded data, holds the code?

We should remind the reader that the members of the surveyed RECs considered that encoded data are not considered to be anonymous data, whoever has the code. Where these RECs are concerned, data that are encoded cannot be considered as anonymous. Moreover, for these RECs only the data collector/the investigator should be in possession of the code so that, if need be, he can give the rest of the information to the data controller/sponsor and can guarantee the patient's medical follow-up. Various RECs pointed out the difficulty of guaranteeing the confidentiality of a subject's data in relation to the pharmaceutical companies. These companies often actually want to be able to verify the accuracy of the data before they can guarantee that there has been no fraud on the part of the data collector/investigator. Certain RECs pointed out, however, that even if the data controller/sponsor has access to the code, the data are still confidential as they are protected by medical secrecy. We also posed the following question to the RECs:

> According to your REC, do RECs consider that when personal data is collected from data subjects, these data subjects do not have to be informed of anticipated or even intended processing that will occur only after the data is rendered anonymous?

The majority of the RECs responded in the negative. The patient must be informed of any secondary use of their data, even if this data is anonymous.

*RECs and Genetic Data*

In the course of our enquiry, many RECs pointed out the current legal vacuum in the area of genetic data and the importance of strict regulation in this matter. Certain RECs are currently discussing the subject of the collection and utilization of genetic data in biomedical research and have not yet adopted clear guidelines on this subject. However, the majority of RECs emphasized the importance of obtaining the subject's consent for any research carried out on their genetic data and also the importance of an increased vigilance with regards to the protection of such data, because genetic research, as is the case with pharmacogenetics, often allows for the possibility of being able to permanently re-identify the data subjects.

# Chapter 4

# Research Ethics Committees in Bulgaria

Sylvia Tomova[*]

## Introduction and Establishment of RECs

There are two systems for the ethical review of medical research in Bulgaria. The first is for clinical trials on human subjects, when the trial is initially approved by the Local Ethics Committee on drugs trials (LEC). In the case of phase I, II or III clinical trials it is further approved by the Department of Clinical Trials at the Bulgarian Drug Agency (BDA), and then by the Specialized Committee for Approval of Conducting Clinical Trials (SCACCT) based at the Ministry of Health. In the case of phase IV trials, approval is only required from the LEC and the BDA. The Ministry of Health defines the membership and operating procedures of the Central Ethics Committee on drugs trials (CEC), which controls the LECs based at regional hospitals. The LECs are therefore accountable to the CEC, and the CEC to the Ministry of Health.

The second system is the ethical review of research applications for funding by the National Science Fund or local funding bodies (for example, the Medical Research Council at the Medical University of Sofia), which is undertaken by local committees at the university or research institute in question. These committees are monitored by the Central Committee on Research Ethics at the Ministry of Education and Science.

These committees are formal, and are regulated by regulations of the respective ministries (Ministry of Health, and Ministry of Education and Science). For example, the activities of the CEC are covered by Regulation 26 of the Ministry of Health passed in 1995.[1] In 1995 the Law on Drugs and Pharmacies in Human Medicine[2] was also passed, which controls many aspects of clinical trials. In 2000 the new Law on Drugs and Pharmacies was passed, as well as Regulation 14 of the Ministry of Health (31 July 2000),[3] which introduced the guidelines of Good Clinical Practice (GCP) as being mandatory when conducting trials.

---

[*] Chief Legal Advisor at the Medical University of Sofia. Member of the Council of Europe Steering Group on Bioethics and a member of the Central Ethics Commission on drug trials at the Ministry of Health in Bulgaria.
[1] *State Gazette*, 1995.
[2] *State Gazette* No. 36, 1995.
[3] On the conditions and procedures for conducting clinical trials of medicines on human beings, *State Gazette* No. 73, 2000.

These systems are separate from that of clinical ethics, which involves commissions at the hospitals, and the Physicians' and Dentists' Unions, and which consider patient-doctor, doctor-doctor, and doctor-society relationships.

*Activities Covered by the Review*

The LECs at regional hospitals are independent bodies responsible for the protection of the rights and safety of participants, for providing a public guarantee for this protection through reviewing clinical trial protocols, and for the appropriateness of investigators, execution conditions, methods, and the materials for obtaining informed consent. According to Article 16(1) (Regulation No. 14, 2000) the local commissions: 'review scientific, medical and ethical aspects of the proposed clinical trial and give motivated opinion on these; execute regular monitoring of each clinical trial at appropriate intervals, but not less than once a year; require additional information about the safety of the participants in the trial if necessary'. The documents required for the review are: the plan for the clinical trial; the informed consent form; information on the recruitment procedures (for example, the announcement); written information about the participants; instructions for the investigators; the clinical card (a case research form) of the participant; available safety information; information about reimbursement and compensation of the participants; details on the insurance of the participants and the investigators; the investigators' CVs and/or other documents demonstrating their professional qualifications; and other documents deemed necessary.

*Membership Requirements*

The Central Ethics Committee on Drugs Trials includes at least nine members with medical and non-medical education (for example, a lawyer, priest, or teacher) from both genders. These membership requirements are stipulated in Regulation 26 of the Ministry of Health. Local commissions have a minimum of seven members, at least one of whom is from a non-medical profession, and at least one of whom is financially and administratively independent from the hospital where the clinical trial is going to be performed. These membership requirements are stipulated in Regulation 14 of the Ministry of Health.

**General Powers of RECs**

'Approval' from an REC is necessary for research to go ahead; however, it is not sufficient, and other bodies also have an input. The decision of an REC (Central or Local) is purely an opinion and they have no right to approve or reject applications.

As we see above, the other bodies consulted depends on the phase of the clinical trial—for phases I, II and III, two other bodies must approve the protocol; these are the Department of Clinical Trials at the Bulgarian Drug Agency (BDA) and then the Specialized Committee for Approval of Conducting Clinical Trials (SCACCT) based at the Ministry of Health. For phase IV trials, only the approval of the Department of Clinical Trials at the Bulgarian Drug Agency (BDA) is required. The GCP inspectors at the BDA check the study documentation and the compatibility of the protocol with the Law on Drugs and Pharmacies in Human Medicine and the relevant regulations (most often Regulation No. 14 of 2000).[4]

There are no consequences for researchers who do not submit their research or fail to follow what the review requires. In the first case, the ethical review is in all cases required for the decision-making body to allow the research to be conducted. In the latter case, the trial is monitored by the ethics committee at regular intervals.

There are no circumstances in which ethics committee approval will render activities lawful that would otherwise be unlawful

## General Legal Responsibility of RECs

According to Regulation No. 14 of 2000, the Central Ethics Committee (on Ethics in Drug Trials) makes its decisions on purely ethical considerations that are independent of legal ones. This also applies to the LECs.

The Central and Local Ethics Committees are entitled to give opinion on ethical issues only, and have no right to reject applications regardless of whether or not the proposals are lawful. The committee's opinion on ethical considerations is given to the body requesting it: the Minister of Health, the Specialized Committee for Approval of Conducting Clinical Trials, or the Bulgarian Drug Agency (Regulation No. 14 2000, Article 25). These bodies are empowered to reject the application, including on ethical grounds.

RECs may therefore advise against unlawful activities if they are also unethical, and at the same time, may approve of ethical but unlawful activities, as their only consideration is whether the project is ethical.

This leads logically to the position in Bulgaria that no legal action can be taken against an REC on the basis of its decisions.

## Specific Data Protection Matters

Consent is always obtained from the data subject. Public interest, in no circumstances, prevails over the interests of the subject in question. Data controllers are exempt from liability if they prove themselves not to be responsible for the damage (there is no explicit provision in the law, this is rather a general principle).

Data are considered to be 'anonymized' even when the clinical investigator holds the code. Explicit consent, being the free and informed agreement to data processing in a written form, is always given for the research. It appears as though these views are reasonably consistent across RECs.

---

[4] See, for more information, M. Vrabevski, 'Clinical Trials in Bulgaria' (2001) 1(3) *Clinical Medicine*, 197.

There are no explicit provisions in Bulgarian law as regards data protection rights in relation to DNA samples and genetic information. However, it is envisaged that separate informed consent is necessary, and required, in the case of genetic analysis.

Chapter 5

# Research Ethics Committees in the Czech Republic[1]

Lukáš Prudil[*] and Josef Kuře[†]

## The Establishment of RECs

At the moment there is no clear system of ethics committees reviewing medical research in the Czech Republic. According to Article 16 paragraph (iii) of the Convention on Human Rights and Biomedicine,[2] the duty to review medical research is governed by Czech law. However, in practice, proper legal regulation only exists for the establishment and work of ethics committees in the areas of pharmaceutical research, the research of medical devices and on transplantation matters. All other medical research, including the role of ethics committees and new methods in medicine, is not sufficiently regulated. New law is being prepared by the Ministry of Health; however, it is not clear when it will be proposed to Parliament. We will not discuss the role of ethics committees in transplantation matters below, because it is different from the role of ethics committees in medical research.

### Regulation

In reality, despite there not being—with regards to certain medical research—formal and clear rules for the establishment of ethics committees, particular healthcare facilities and other institutions involved in medical research do ask for approval from ethics committees when preparing to proceed with medical research. Formal and legally binding regulation on pharmaceutical research and testing is given by Act No. 79/1997 Collection on Pharmaceuticals;[3] whilst medical devices

---

[1] The situation is described according to the legal status in March 2004.
[*] Barrister and Senior Lecturer at the Medical Faculty of Masaryk University, Brno.
[†] Research and development worker at the Faculty of Medicine, University Centre for Bioethics, Masaryk University, Brno.
[2] Council of Europe, 1997, ETS No. 164.
[3] Most recently amended on 5 June 2003 by Act No. 129/2003, and has been issued as Collection of Laws No 269/2003. Other legislation on pharmaceuticals includes Decree No. 472/2000 on the Good Clinical Practice and more detailed conditions for Clinical Trials on Pharmaceuticals as amended.

are governed by Act No. 123/2000 Collection of Laws on Medical Devices and in the implementing regulations to the Act. In the following sections we will consider the regulations for the pharmaceutical (in particular) and medical device research ethics committees unless stated otherwise.

*Organization*

Ethics committees are established and managed, either by the single healthcare facility in which the research is to be processed, by a regional office, or by the Ministry of Health (MoH). The Ethics Committee of the MoH also works as an advisory body to the Minister of Health. These ethics committees can also give their opinion on other fields of biomedical research, not only for pharmaceuticals, unless legal regulations state otherwise. To what extent these opinions have to be accepted is not clear. The Ethics Committee of the MoH is not superior to the other ethics committees; however, it tries to produce materials and opinions helpful to the other committees. Despite this, the relationship of local ethics committees to the MoH, or with the MoH ethics committee, is not legally clarified.

Particular ethics committees can be named on the basis of the researcher's application, and after the approval of the State Office for the Control of Pharmaceuticals, may be nominated by the Ministry of Health as the ethics committee for the multi-centric clinical research (in pharmaceuticals). If there is multi-centric research, the application is received by a multi-centric ethics committee as well as other ethics committees, in particular healthcare centres. The application is reviewed by the multi-centric ethics committee and, after its approval, is discussed and approved or rejected by the ethics committee in the healthcare facility.

*Evaluation*

It is common that during the evaluation of proposed medical research, ethics committees will review the *ethical acceptability* of the research as well as its scientific background, *scientific feasibility* and acceptability. They also review the persons involved in the research; the suitability of the healthcare facility; the eligibility of the informed consents; insurance protection; eventual potential compensation; the enlisting of the persons involved in the research; contracts and remunerations. In situations where they may have some objections or doubts, they are entitled to invite experts to give opinions. Taking legal issues into consideration differs from case to case. According to Law 123/2000, RECs review scientific, medical and ethical issues; legal issues are not mentioned. One supposes, however, that the REC will consider legal issues as well.

*Membership*

Some basic rules are given for the *membership* of ethics committees. The members are nominated by the Head of the healthcare facility (or by the Minister of Health in the case of the Ethics Committee for the MoH). An ethics committee has to have at least five members including, amongst others, healthcare workers. The members should be qualified to review medical research from a scientific, medical and ethical point of view. At least one member must be a person without an education in healthcare or a scientific degree. At least one of the members cannot be in a position dependent on a research centre (healthcare facility). Members must agree with the terms of their membership, the publication of their membership and with the duty of confidentiality of information received during the proceedings of the ethics committee.

*Accountability*

No direct *responsibility* of the ethics committees to any person or authority exists; however, their members are nominated and recalled by the Head of the healthcare facility (or by the Minister in the case of the Ethics Committee of the MoH). No rules are given for recalling members; it is fully at the discretion of the person who nominated them.

## General Powers of RECs

Ethics committees are fully empowered by law to *approve* or *reject* applications. They can decide whether the project will be allowed to proceed or not. Applicants are not given the option to appeal against the decision of competent ethics committees. In certain situations, other bodies or authorities are also asked for their opinion, for example the State Office for the Control of Pharmaceuticals.

In the case where the research does not follow the approved conditions, the ethics committee can recall its approval and stop the research activity. The situation is more complex where the research proceeds without approval. In such cases fines can be imposed on the persons involved in the research by the Courts. Also, sanctions from the employer are applicable, the self-governing bodies (for example the Czech Medical Chamber) could apply their disciplinary power and, in certain circumstances, the Courts could apply regulations from penal law.

## General Legal Responsibility of RECs

In theory, nobody has to pay attention to the law. The situation of ethics committees is, in theory, similar. Of course they can reject activities that are unlawful or advise researchers that they are so. RECs, however, do not have legal responsibility.

As far as we know, research ethics committees pay attention to the *legal norms* that are in force. The main problem is that the law changes very frequently in the Czech Republic and therefore ethics committees, as with other institutions and bodies, sometimes struggle with knowing and thus following, valid legal regulation. In particular the Data Protection Act[4] is quite well recognized and, as far as we know, is followed by ethics committees.

The law in force does not contain any explicit sanctions applicable to cases where ethics committees fail during the decision-making proceedings. This means that any judicial action is hardly conceivable; rather the only sanction is the recalling of members of the ethic committee by its promoter (founder).

## Specific Data Protection Matters

Where it is not possible to obtain consent from the data subject, the situation is basically regulated by the Convention on Human Rights and the Biomedicine and Data Protection Act.[5]

As far as we know, ethics committees pay extra attention to DNA samples and any manipulation involving them. Even though there is no specific law concerning DNA samples, in practice they are treated like sensitive data.

---

[4] Act on the Protection of Personal Data of 4 April 2001, No. 101/2000, Coll.

[5] For more details, see M. Kocourkova and L. Prudil, 'Implementation of Directive 95/46/EC in the Domestic Law of the Czech Republic' in D. Beyleveld, D. Townend, S. Rouillé-Mirza and J. Wright (eds.), *Implementation of the Data Protection Directive in Relation to Medical Research in Europe* (Aldershot: Ashgate Publishing Ltd, 2004).

# Chapter 6

# Research Ethics Committees in Denmark

Mary Rosenzweig[*] and Lisbeth Knudsen[†]

## Establishment of RECs

There is an established scientific ethics committee system in Denmark, with seven regional scientific ethics committees and a Central Scientific Ethical Committee. It was started as a voluntary system in 1980 by biomedical scientists. For many years the system was regulated by recommendations from the central scientific committee. In 1992 it became a legally regulated system. The purpose of the law is to lay down the legal framework for the scientific ethical evaluation of biomedical research projects. There is also a separate ethical advisory committee whose purpose is to advise the public, the Danish Parliament and the Ministry of Health about ethical issues relating to biomedical technology. It also serves to support and promote public debate about these subjects.

## Laws Relating to RECs

The system of ethical review is regulated by the Act on a Scientific Ethics Committee System and the Processing of Biomedical Research Projects.[1] Directive 2001/20/EC is implemented through the Medicines Act[2] which took effect on 1 May 2004.

[*] M.Sc. University of Copenhagen.
[†] Ph.D. Associate Professor at the Institute of Public Health, University of Copenhagen, Denmark.
[1] Act no. 402 of 28 May 2003. This Act contains some provisions implementing aspects of Directive 2001/20/EC and came into force on 1 June 2003.
[2] Act no. 656 of 28 July 1995. Directive 2001/20/EC was party implemented when the Act was amended by Law 382 of 28 May 2003. The final stage of implementation was done through Executive Order no. 295 of 26 April 2004 on clinical trials of medicines on human individuals.

**Activities Covered by Ethical Review**

All biomedical research projects involving research on the following must be notified to the regional committee for the area in which the person responsible for the project works:

- human individuals;
- human germ cells intended to be used in fertilization, human fertilized eggs, embryos and foetuses;
- tissue, cells and genetic material from humans, foetuses or embryos; or
- deceased persons.

'Biomedical research' means any activity which has the purpose of gaining general knowledge about human biological and psychological processes as well as the origin, spread, prevention, diagnosis and treatment of human disease.

This also applies to research projects in which biomedical research constitutes a substantial part of the total project.

Projects based on questionnaires and registers are only to be notified to a regional committee if the project implies the use of human biological material, the substantial element of which has to be identifiable and stored in biobanks. 'Biobanks' is the general term for all collections of information arising from the clinical work of the health service with, or research into, human beings and their diseases, whether they are stored in the form of words, numbers, DNA codes, antigens, antibodies, morphological, biochemical or physiological characteristics. Research projects which make use of extracts from biobanks are, in general, to be regarded as register research.

The Central Scientific Ethical Committee may lay down regulations for the practical organization of the scientific and ethical assessment of projects being carried out at more than one research institution (multi-centre trials).

**REC Membership Requirements**

A regional committee consists of at least seven members, of whom three are nominated by the Danish Medical Research Council. If a County Council judges that the activities of a regional committee, the number of projects being reviewed, or other reasons, require an increase in number of members of the committee, they may do so up to 9, 11, 13 or 15 members. The number of persons nominated by the Danish Medical Research Council will rise also to four, five, six or seven respectively. The members nominated by the Danish Medical Research Council are active researchers within medical science. The remaining members are not from medical science and do not have an actual association to the medical profession. In cases where the committees do not have sufficient professional expertise to be able to judge submitted projects, they may use consultants.

The Minister of Research and Information Technology set up the Central Scientific Ethical Committee. This committee consists of two members appointed by and from each of the regional committees, plus two members appointed by the Minister of Research and Information Technology and two members appointed by the Minister of Health. Of the members appointed by the regional committees, one is chosen from amongst the members nominated by the Danish Medical Research Council, the other from among the other committee members.

## Accountability of RECs

The regional committees do not have binding rules with the central committee, but decisions taken by a regional committee on research projects can be appealed to the central committee, the highest Court of Appeal. The central committee is an independent unit which cannot be instructed and their decisions cannot be brought before other administrative authorities. The central committee issues recommendations to the RECs on pertinent issues, for example genetic testing.

## General Powers of RECs

RECs can approve or reject applications and an approval from the REC is always necessary for the research to go ahead. In the case of projects which include the clinical trials of medicines covered by the Medicines Agency, the regional committee will submit a scientific and ethical evaluation of the project to the Danish Medicines Agency. The evaluation must be submitted no later than six weeks after the regional committee has had an opportunity to carry out the evaluation. The Danish Medicines Agency gives the final permission for the initiation of the project.

In accordance with the law on personal data, all research projects including sensitive personal information must be notified to the Data Surveillance Authority (Danish Data Inspectorate). Projects being carried out for persons responsible for private data handling must have consent from the Danish Data Inspectorate before initiating the project, as do projects being carried out for public institutions. Substantial changes in projects must be notified to the Danish Data Inspectorate and may require their advance permission or opinion.

In the case of register research in public health (linkage of different registers), permission must be obtained from the National Board of Health.

## Penalties for Not Submitting Research for Review or Failing to Follow Review Requirements

Anyone initiating a project covering one of the above activities that require review, and without permission from an REC or other required authorities such as the Danish Medicines Agency or Data Surveillance Authority, will be punished by a fine or imprisonment. In directives issued in pursuance of the Act the penalty may be determined as a fine.

If contraventions are committed by a limited company, a co-operative society or similar, the company or society may be fined. Similarly, if a contravention is committed by the state, a municipal authority or a municipal co-operative, they too may be fined.

The legal action can be taken by the patient themselves, the control system within the central committee, a regional ethics committee or anyone else who notices an infringement and informs the police about it.

## RECs and the Law

RECs can reject or advise against activities that are lawful if they judge they are unethical. Unlawful activities will never be approved. The REC must pay attention to the law and all the members at the secretariat have a degree within law. RECs have a high knowledge of the law and take it into account in practice.

The Danish ethical system is regulated by the Act on a Scientific Ethics Committee System and the Processing of Biomedical Research Projects. The Helsinki Declaration has been integrated into Danish law.

The implementation of Directive 2001/20 EC has had the following impact on the system of ethical review:

- multi-centre clinical trials—a unique opinion is required;
- the time-limit for a decision will be 60 days; and
- protocol evaluation criteria—use of expert consultation in relation to incapable persons will occur. For instance, if the trial subjects are small children, then an expert in paediatrics will be consulted.

Data protection law is about the collection, registration, storage, transfer and destruction of personal data. It distinguishes between sensitive and non-sensitive data. Health data are sensitive data and cannot be examined without consent. But the law implies that these data can be examined if it is necessary in relation to prevention of disease, medical diagnosis, nursing, treatment of patients or administration of health services, and the treatment is undertaken by a person bound to professional secrecy.

## RECs and Public Interest Decisions

RECs have the power to decide on an exemption from consent in the public interest and to decide on an exemption from other data protection requirements for public interest.

If a research project that has to be reviewed for reasons of inclusion of biological material does not involve any health risk or under other circumstances is a load on the person concerned, the committee can decide that consent is not necessary for the beginning and proceeding of the trial. This concerns adults, minors and incapacitated adults. Furthermore, this is the case if informed consent is impossible or inordinately difficult. The Data Surveillance Authority assesses the balance between the difficulty of obtaining informed consent and the public interest. RECs also make this assessment, but have more focus on the protection of the subject.

If the project can only be carried out in an emergency situation where the subject is not in a position to give consent and it is not possible to obtain a surrogate consent, then it may go ahead if it will lead to an improvement of the patient's condition in the long term. The researcher must try to obtain consent from the patient as soon as possible. This does not apply in clinical trials with medicine.

## RECs, Coded Data and DNA Samples

RECs assess the need for anonymization of personal data on each project as part of their review process. They would not consider coded data to be anonymous if the data controller still has the possibility of identifying individuals. However, if a third party who cannot identify the data subjects processes the data, then RECs may consider this data anonymous, although with certain restrictions. When personal data are collected from data subjects they should be informed, where reasonable, of any anticipated or intended processing that may occur after anonymization. DNA samples and genetic information are considered by RECs on the same level as their other assessments with regard to data protection rights.

Chapter 7

# Research Ethics in Estonia

Toomas Veidebaum[*]

## Establishment of Research Ethics Committees

In Tallinn official ethics committees for research started in 1992, although from 1989 there were ad hoc committees created just for clinical trials at different hospitals. Currently in Tallinn, there is one ethics committee located at the National Institute for Health Development (previously the Estonian Institute of Experimental and Clinical Medicine). Similarly, in Tartu University Hospital, the location of the only medical faculty in Estonia, an ethics committee for clinical trials started in 1990 which has extended its approval to other research projects with human subjects when needed. There are thus two independent research ethics committees (RECs). A special REC for the Estonian Genome Project (EGP) was established according to the Human Genes Research Act that entered into force on 8 January 2001. All three RECs are independent bodies coordinated by the Council of Ethics located at the Ministry of Social Affairs. Projects are reviewed by only one REC so that if it was rejected by an REC, it should be resubmitted to the same committee.

REC activities are regulated by decrees of the Ministry of Social Affairs[1] and the Ministry of Education and Science. RECs deal only with research projects and clinical trials. Local ethics committees based in hospitals deal with clinical practice.

RECs work with documents which are mandatory for the principal investigator to submit for review: the complete project; study protocol; researchers' CVs; informed consent forms for patients; insurance certificates; data protection issues. All changes to the protocol during the study must be approved by the REC that gave initial approval. Another task of the REC is to look through all serious adverse events during the trials or research and consultation of patients. All REC documents are archived.

---

[*] Director of the Research Centre, National Institute for Health Development, Tallinn.
[1] For example, Regulation No. 77 of 9 July 2001 on the Requirements for Membership of Medical Ethics Committee for Clinical Trials, Rules of Procedure of Committee, Rate of Fee for Evaluation of Clinical Trials and List of Information to Be Submitted in Order to Obtain Approval. Also, see Regulation No. 79 of 9 July 2001 on the Procedure for Conduct of Clinical Trials of Medicinal Products.

Membership of RECs is determined by a decree of the Ministry of Social Affairs. They have at least seven members from different medical institutions and it is also compulsory to have a layperson, a theologian and a lawyer. All members are nominated by the institution itself (hospitals, municipalities, churches, research units). RECs are funded from the state budget but are independent bodies and not accountable to anyone. Each committee must submit an annual report which is discussed by the Council of Ethics at the Ministry of Social Affairs.

## General Powers of RECs

The REC approves or rejects the project, and indicates why it was rejected. Approval of research projects or clinical trials by an REC is mandatory for the funding (external or internal) and conducting of the research project. A written consent from the head of the research institution where the study is planned to be conducted must be submitted as part of the documentation to the REC. For clinical trials, permission from the National Drug Administration must also be obtained. Approval by an REC is absolutely mandatory for any research to go ahead.

If a principal investigator does not submit their research for review or fails to follow what the review requires, RECs have an obligation to inform the administration of the research institution to stop the study. All illegal activities of researchers or physicians are covered by civil or criminal law and dealt with in Court. A situation in which REC approval contradicts the law is impossible.

## General Legal Responsibility

RECs pay attention to the law generally—lawful activities may be approved as well as rejected, unlawful ones only rejected. REC review is based on the Helsinki Declaration, Good Clinical Practice and Directive 2001/20/EC. The Medicinal Products Act[2] states in Section 13(4) that ethical review by, and approval from, an REC is necessary for clinical trials.

The Data Protection Act regulates all matters concerning individual data: their collection, coding/decoding, the informing of subjects, amongst others. For medical research, as well as for clinical trials, specific permission must be obtained from the Data Protection Inspectorate. The requirements for applying for this permission are set out in the Data Protection Act. The Data Protection Inspectorate (DPI) gives permission to institutions that can then handle all delicate individual data, keep them in databases and process them. Written permission is given for five years and new permission is needed for each linkage of the dataset with different registries or databases or follow-up of cohorts. The objective of the Act is to regulate the collecting and processing of personal data and supervise these procedures. It also determines the penalties when personal data are misused.

---

[2] Passed on 19 December 1995, and most recently amended by the Act of 12 February 2003.

The Act determines all definitions, such as: What are personal data? What are delicate personal data? It sets out the principles of collecting and processing the data, archiving study protocols and questionnaires, and determines all security issues for institutions that collect, process and keep personal data. Processing of delicate personal data must be registered at the DPI.

The new Personal Data Protection Law was adapted by the Estonian Parliament on 12 February 2003 and came into force on 1 October 2003. The law precludes any use of personal identifiable health and other sensitive (for example, nationality) data unless the subject has given explicit written consent for this. In the law, the expression 'public health' is mentioned only once and there is no mention of 'research', 'scientific', 'preventive medicine' or 'statistics'. The law is more restrictive than the European Directive 95/46/EC or the previous Estonian Personal Data Protection Act that was adapted on 12 June 1996. It actually carries the spirit of the 1990 and 1992 versions of the European Directive. In fact the law prohibits all registry-based epidemiological research where record-linkage has been based on a personal identification number and/or names because obtaining an informed consent is logistically impossible. All this has been widely discussed, for example, in the UK.

The law places in jeopardy existing national medical registries. It is still not clear whether an informed consent has to be received from persons whose data will be sent to registries (for example cancer notification). The DPI has begun to apply strong pressure even to the Statistical Office of Estonia to remove all personal identifiers from the National Mortality Database. Use of names and identification numbers in this database is being criticized as violating individual privacy. All these bureaucratic obstacles have prevented the Estonian Cancer Registry from linking its database to the National Mortality Database. This results in losing about five per cent of cases annually, distorting national cancer incidence, survival and prevalence statistics, and excluding Estonia from the global cancer-monitoring network. This is only one case demonstrating the consequences of the new Data Protection Act.

RECs have to follow the Data Protection Act. Coded data are taken as anonymous and researchers do not normally have access to personal identifiers. All biological samples (including DNA) must be coded and stored in a depository under codes. Informed consent from donors or patients must be obtained if probes are studied. People whose samples are in a depository have the right to remove them and destroy the sample.

Chapter 8

# The General Legal Responsibility of Research Ethics Committees in Finland

Lasse A. Lehtonen[*] and Ritva Halila[†]

## Background

The Declaration of Helsinki was issued by the World Medical Association at its meeting in Finland in 1964. Shortly after that the first Finnish research ethics committees (RECs) were established. In the 1970s there were ethics committees in at least every university hospital in Finland and by the 1980s in most large hospitals. Initially, however, the committee's status was unofficial. Often the members of the local REC were closely linked to the institution whose research they were reviewing. The activity of RECs was, indeed, more to nominally satisfy the requirements of peer-reviewed medical journals than to protect the rights of the research subjects.

Finland joined the Council of Europe in 1992 and since then has implemented several conventions on human rights into the national legislation. The Convention on Human Rights and Biomedicine in 1997 has, however, not yet been ratified by Finland. Nevertheless, this Convention was the impetus for new biomedical legislation in the late 1990s. The existence of RECs is based on the Medical Research Act 488/1999. The organization of ethics committees in Finland is essentially a regional system, since every healthcare district (which is the local authority running the hospital service) must have at least one ethics committee in its area. In addition, there is one national committee (the sub-committee on medical research ethics of the National Advisory Board on Health Care Ethics) which is located in the Ministry of Social Affairs and Health.[1]

[*] Helsinki University Central Hospital, PO Box 720, HUS-00029, Helsinki, Finland (e-mail: lasse.lehtonen@hus.fi).
[†] National Advisory Board on Health Care Ethics, Ministry of Social Affairs and Health, PO Box 33, FIN-00023, Helsinki, Finland (e-mail: ritva.halila@stm.fi).
[1] L. Lehtonen, 'Sairaanhoitopiirin eettinen toimikunta ja sen oikeudellinen asema' (The legal status of the research ethics committee of a healthcare district, in Finnish) (1999) 35 *Finnish Medical Journal*, 4421–4426.

## Nomination and Composition of the Committees

Regional research ethics committees in Finland act within a healthcare district. A healthcare district is formed by the communities of the area and the city councils nominate the council for the district, which in turn nominates the board of the district. The board consists of politicians from political parties that are represented in the district council. It nominates the members of the research ethics committees for the district. In theory, the members of the RECs can be politically selected. In practice, however, even the most lay persons on the committee are individuals that are merely interested in clinical research and the protection of research subjects, even though some might have links to political parties.

The National Advisory Board on Health Care Ethics (ETENE) is appointed by the Ministry of Social Affairs and Health for four years on the basis of amendment 333/1998 to the Act on the Status and Rights of Patients (785/1992). It guides and discusses issues related to ethics in healthcare. It also has a sub-committee on medical research ethics (TUKIJA) that evaluates protocols on medical research. According to Article 17 of Act 488/1999, TUKIJA evaluates those pharmaceutical trials that require a single national opinion, unless it is delegated for evaluation to one of the hospital district RECs.

Article 18 of Act 488/1999 requires that the REC has a chairperson and at least six members. Disciplines other than medicine should always be represented on the committee. In addition, the REC should include at least two lay members (for example, persons that are not healthcare professionals). A quorum is reached when the chairperson or vice-chairperson and half of the other members are present. There must, however, always be one lay member present.

## Procedural Requirements

Since RECs in Finland are maintained by either regional authorities that are also running the hospital system or the ministry, they are considered as public bodies and are bound by the legislation that regulates decision-making in the local government (communities) or in the central administration. The RECs have to follow both procedural and material norms of administrative law, of which the regulations on bias (see also Medical Research Act, Act 488/1999, §19) and the publicity of proceedings, are of major importance. Therefore, RECs in Finland can only approve studies that are considered lawful. As a matter of fact, Article 17 of Act 488/1999 states explicitly that an ethics committee must take into consideration all laws and regulations concerning medical research in its decision-making and pay special attention to the Personal Data Act (523/1999).[2]

The regulations on bias in administrative decision-making are in Article 10 of Act 598/1982 on Administrative Procedures (replaced from 1 January 2004 onwards by Act 434/2003 on Public Administration). According to Article 10,

---

[2] L. Lehtonen 'Henkilötietolaki ja lääketieteellinen tutkimus' (The data protection law and medical research, in Finnish) (2000) 31 *Finnish Medical Journal*, 3015–3019.

anybody who has, or whose relatives have, personal interests in the matter is biased in relation to the decision-making and should abstain from all preparation and decision-making concerning it. Therefore, no investigator or study subject can themselves be involved in the decision-making of the ethics committee. Otherwise there are no specific procedural regulations in Act 488/1999 on the handling of research protocols, but the healthcare districts can give their own instructions and regulations for their committees in this respect.

Ethics committees in Finland do not usually approve (or reject) protocols before the principal investigator has submitted to them all clarifications asked for by the committee. The difference made by the time limits of GCP Directive 2001/20/EC will influence the decision-making process of the RECs, since it mandates that an opinion must be given within 60 days of submission.[3] This might lead to a greater rejection rate of the protocols since the time for further inquiries is limited.

In Finland, as in Sweden, there is a strong tradition of openness in public administration. Only matters specifically stated in the law can be kept secret. Therefore the decisions made by the ethics committees are in principle public, even though the commercial secrets in research protocols are to be kept secret according to Article 24 of Act 621/1999 on the Publicity of Administrative Actions (and on the basis of similar regulations of Article 23 of the Act 488/1999). In addition, the persons whose rights or duties depend on the decision are entitled to receive information on most documents considered non-public or even secret. On the basis of a decision of the Finnish Supreme Administrative Court, however, the research subject is not entitled to receive copies of confidential study documents just on the basis of his or her participation in a study.[4] On the other hand, he or she always has the right to receive copies of his or her own case record forms when he or she is participating in a medical study.

### Decision-making in a Research Ethics Committee

The main function of the regional ethics committees is to review the medical research protocols submitted to them. The functions of RECs in Finland are, however, not limited to assessment of research protocols. On the basis of paragraph 17 of Act 488/1999, ethics committees may also give general advice on research ethics in their area.

The definition of medical research is rather wide in Finland and covers all research activities that infringe personal integrity and intend to increase knowledge on health or disease states. There are some difficulties in drawing the line between medical and other research. For example psychological, educational or social studies might sometimes include health-related issues and must then go through ethical review. Furthermore, nursing studies might include issues that need evaluation by an ethics committee prior to the initiation of the study.

---

[3] See Amendment 295/2004 of the Medical Research Act.

[4] Finnish Supreme Administrative Court decision KHO 31 December 2001 T 3346.

If the REC gives a negative opinion on a protocol, the investigator may ask for a second opinion from the sub-committee on medical research ethics (TUKIJA). The regional ethics committee must then follow the advice given by the national committee. In practice, however, the investigators follow the opinion of the regional committee and change their protocol accordingly. The opinion of an ethics committee is not considered as an administrative decision that could be re-evaluated by the administrative Courts. However, since the members of a committee are considered civil servants, their actions can be evaluated by general Courts and in extreme cases even sanctioned (for example in cases of gross negligence of the handling of administrative affairs or in cases of breaching confidentiality).[5]

## Unlawful Research

Act 488/1999 requires that no medical research is started prior to the favourable opinion of an ethics committee.[6] Therefore doing medical research without an opinion of an ethics committee is unlawful in Finland and might be punished by a fine.[7] This requires that a Public Prosecutor deems it appropriate to sue the investigator and a general Court convicts him or her. However, there have not been any such cases in the Courts yet. In addition, the hospitals or other healthcare units may take disciplinary action (for example give an official warning) if they find out that some of their personnel are doing medical research without appropriate authorization or against the regulations of that hospital.

There are no further legal restrictions on initiating a study than to have the favourable opinion of an ethics committee and the consent of the study subject. If the study is carried out in public hospitals, then permission from the body governing the hospital is usually needed in addition to the ethical approval by an REC. Furthermore, studies with pharmaceutical products or medical devices have to be notified to the National Agency for Medicines.

Any patients suffering harm because of research that violates regulations might also be entitled to compensation for damage. As a matter of fact, recently some patients received compensation from the Finnish patient insurance system on the basis of the fact that the principal investigator did not follow all the requirements set by the ethics committee (for patient information and consent) in his studies with neurological drugs. Finally, the National Authority for Medicolegal Affairs that issues the licences for medical doctors and other healthcare professionals may restrict or revoke the licence if it finds out that the

---

[5] Act 488/1999, Article 23.
[6] L. Lehtonen, J-J. Himberg and A. Bardy 'Kliinisen lääketutkimuksen etiikka, normit, ohjeet ja valvonta' (The ethics, regulations, guidance and supervision of clinical research, in Finnish) in Huupponen *et al* (eds.), *Kliininen farmakologia* (Jyväskylä: Kandidaattikustannus Oy, 2002), 918–931.
[7] Act 488/1999, Article 27.

activities are in contradiction of the obligations of the Medical Research Act, the Health Care Professional Act (559/1994) or violate patients' rights (Act 785/1992).

## Evaluation of Public Interest

The RECs in Finland must, in their evaluation, weigh the need for protection of the study subject against the public interest of society.[8] According to Article 4 of Act 488/1999, the benefit and well-being of the research subject must always prevail over the interests of society. In this respect the formulation of the Finnish Act is identical to Article 2 of the Bioethics Convention of the Council of Europe. Research ethics committees can give a favourable opinion on the study only if this requirement is fulfilled. Furthermore, the ethics committee has to verify that the possible risks and disadvantages for the study subject are minimized and that the subject is only exposed to procedures that will clearly result in greater scientific merits than risks or disadvantages to the research subject.

## Data Protection Issues in Ethical Evaluation of Medical Research

Article 17 of Act 488/1999 specifically requires that the REC takes into consideration data protection regulations when it gives its opinion on a study protocol. It is, however, noteworthy that research that only utilizes patient data is not covered by the Medical Research Act.[9] This type of research can be carried out on the basis of permission by the authority that has the patient's files is it's possession[10] and there is no need for consent of the data subject for the further processing of the data if this permission is granted.[11,12] However, permission to use confidential data for research may not be given if the research violates an important private interest. In practice there is no requirement to inform the data subjects of the fact that their data are used for medical research. The data subject does not even have access to data that are processed only for research purposes.[13]

If any biological samples are used in addition to the patient data, the research falls under the Medical Research Act and must be reviewed by an ethics committee

---

[8] S. Lötjönen, 'Ihmiseen kohdistuva lääketieteellinen tutkimustoiminta ja siihen soveltuvat oikeussäännöt' (Human subject research and its legal regulation, in Finnish) (1997) 6 *Lakimies*, 856–879.

[9] L. Lehtonen, 'Government Registries Containing Sensitive Health Data and the Implementation of the EU Directive on the Protection of Personal Data in Finland' (2002) 21 *Medicine and Law*, 419–425.

[10] Act 621/1999, 28§.

[11] Act 523/1999, Article 12, exemption number 5.

[12] L. Lehtonen, *Potilaan yksityisyyden suoja* (The patient's right to privacy, in Finnish with an English summary) (Vammala: Suomalainen Lakimiesyhdistys ry, 2001).

[13] Act 523/1999, Article 27.

prior to the initiation of the study.[14] In this case the ethics committee has to evaluate whether there is sufficient public interest to justify the research. Furthermore, biological material can be used for medical research only if the patient has expressly consented to this, or if anonymous data are used.[15]

In other studies involving human subjects, the ethics committee has the power to weigh the public interest against the need for protection of the research subjects. They can decide if and how the consent of the patient will be obtained or if the law allows the initiation of the study without the prior written informed consent of the research subject (as in the case of emergency medicine studies). They can also consider to what extent the intrusions into patient privacy are acceptable in the name of public interest for scientific research.

## Summary

The organization of research ethics committees in Finland was revised by the Medical Research Act 488/1999. From November 1999 onwards the RECs are maintained by the hospital districts that also organize the specialized medical care. In addition, there is one national committee in the Ministry of Social Affairs and Health. Research ethics committees in Finland are public administrative bodies and are thus bound by the law. In their assessment they have to take into consideration the data protection principles as stated in the Personal Data Act (523/1999). For a summary of the general legal responsibilities of RECs in Finland, see Table 8.1 below.

---

[14] L. Lehtonen *Terveydenhuollon ammattihenkilön salasaspitovelvollisuus* (The duty of confidentiality of a medical professional, in Finnish) (Saarijärvi: Gummerus Oy, 2003).
[15] Act 101/2001, 20§.

**Table 8.1 Summary of the General Legal Responsibilities of RECs in Finland**

| Question | Status in Finland |
| --- | --- |
| *Is there a system or systems for ethical review of medical research in Finland?* | Yes. |
| *If there is, then is it formal (regulated) or informal (purely voluntary)?* | It is regulated. |
| *If it is formal, is it regulated by law or other means, and in the latter case, by what means?* | The activity of RECs is regulated by Medical Research Act 488/1999. |
| *If there is a system of review, is it separate from any system for clinical ethics advice or guidance or do the same committees do both kinds of review?* | The same committees review both research protocols and give general advice. |
| *What kinds of activities are covered by the review?* | The definition of medical research is rather wide in Finland and covers all research activities that infringe personal integrity and are intended to increase knowledge on disease. All of this is covered by the review. |
| *What membership requirements are there for RECs?* | RECs should have a chairman and at least six members. In addition to medicine, other disciplines should be represented. The REC should have at least two lay members (Act 488/1999, Article 18). |
| *To whom are RECs responsible or accountable?* | Most RECs are organized by the hospital districts and the committee is therefore also responsible to it (the board of the hospital district is elected by the political bodies of the member cities and consists of politicians). In addition, there is one national committee that is responsible to the Ministry of Social Affairs and Health. |
| *Do RECs approve or reject applications or do they have only advisory, recommendatory powers? Specifically:*<br>*A. Is 'approval' by an REC sufficient for the research to go ahead, or do other bodies also have a say?*<br>*B. Is 'approval' by an REC necessary for the research to go ahead?* | The Act on Medical Research requires that the favourable opinion of an REC is a prerequisite to medical research. So, if the research gets a negative opinion, the study cannot be carried out. Permission from the institution or hospital is also required before the study can begin. In addition, pharmaceutical trials have to be notified to the National Agency for Medicines. |

| Question | Status in Finland |
| --- | --- |
| *What are the possible consequences (penalties, disciplinary actions or other) for researchers who do not submit their research for review or fail to follow what the review requires? Please discuss whether such action is taken by the REC, the Courts, or possibly another body.* | The Act on Medical Research makes it a criminal offence to carry out research without ethical approval (it is punishable by fines). The RECs do not have any power to punish anybody but they can notify the Public Prosecutor, if necessary. |
| *Are there any circumstances in which REC approval will render activities lawful that would otherwise be unlawful? If so, please elaborate.* | As stated above, medical research cannot be carried out without the favourable opinion of an ethics committee. In that sense, the approval makes the activities lawful. However, if something is prohibited by the law, approval by an REC will not amend this. |
| *In theory, what attention must RECs pay to the law generally? In particular:* <br> - *May RECs reject or advise against activities that are lawful?* <br> - *May RECs approve activities that are unlawful?* <br> *Please answer this question from the points of view of any laws or guidance.* | RECs have to follow the Finnish law. They may reject activities that are lawful, if they consider them unethical. They cannot approve activities that are unlawful. There is explicit law on this (Act 488/1999 on Medical Research, Article 17). In addition, there is a lot of guidance on different topics from the hospital district and the national body. |
| *What impact has the implementation of Directive 2001/20 EC on Good Clinical Practice had?* | The Directive requires that ethics committees more closely monitor that their advice and opinions are implemented in practice. Furthermore, decision deadlines have been implemented. REC activities in Finland are in accordance with the requirements of the Directive. |
| *Regardless of the theory, what attention do RECs actually pay to the law in practice? Please tell us specifically about data protection law.* | Most RECs in Finland pay close attention to the data protection law. |
| *What forms of legal action, if any, can be taken against an REC on the basis of its decisions?* | A new opinion can be requested from the national body if the REC gives a negative opinion. The individual members of the REC can be prosecuted as any civil servant can in Finland for criminal misconduct (for example, for the breach of confidentiality). |

| Question | Status in Finland |
|---|---|
| *Do RECs have the power to make decisions about when research is justified in the public interest, when it means that:*<br>*A. consent does not have to be obtained from the data subject,*<br>*B. or other exemptions are created from the data protection rights of the data subject, or from the duties of data controllers?* | RECs can weigh the public interest against the need for protection of the study subjects. They can decide whether the requirements when not obtaining explicit consent (as regulated by Act 488/1999) are met. They can also consider if the requirements for exemption from the data protection rights (as presented in the Act on Personal Data 523/1999) are met. |
| *What view is taken by RECs concerning 'anonymized' information? In particular:*<br>*- Is coded data considered to be rendered anonymous in the case where the data controller, who holds the code, processes the coded data?*<br>*- Do RECs consider that when personal data are collected from data subjects, these data subjects do not have to be informed of anticipated or even intended processing that will occur only after it is rendered anonymous?*<br>*- Do RECs consider that data are rendered anonymous for processing by those who cannot identify the data subject, even though it still exists in personal form in the hands of those who obtained the data?* | Coded data are not considered as 'anonymous'. However, in practice RECs may think that adequate data protection measures are taken if the data are coded, and accept the use of the data for medical research without the consent of the data subject as an exemption from the data protection principles. The Finnish Act on Personal Data makes an exemption to informing data subjects in cases where the data are used for research. Therefore, RECs do not have to require that the data subjects should be informed (RECs follow the data protection law). |
| *To what extent and in what circumstances do RECs consider that DNA samples (biological materials) and in particular genetic information are covered by data protection rights?* | DNA samples and biological materials are not data, but are covered by a separate law (Act on the Use of Human Organs and Medical Samples 101/2001). However, the data derived from them falls under the data protection law when a person can be identified from them. |

Chapter 9

# The Role of Ethics Committees in Relation to French Biomedical Research: Protection of the Person and Personal Data

Brigitte Feuillet*

## Introduction

Biomedical research in France has been globally regulated since the implementation of the *Huriet-Sérusclat* Law on 20 December 1988.[1] This law has been reviewed several times[2] and has recently undergone important changes with the introduction of the Law of 9 August 2004 relating to the policies of public health. The purpose of the recent review was notably to implement Directive 2001/20/EC of 4 April 2001 on Good Clinical Practice, which devotes some of its text to the role of ethics committees.[3]

As well as this legislation relating to research, France has also introduced laws that ensure the protection of data subjects when their personal data is being processed. The Law of 6 January 1978 on 'Informatics and Freedom' is the text at the heart of this legislation.[4]

This legislation led to the establishment of authorities responsible for ensuring the protection of any person participating in a biomedical research project and of his or her personal data, complying with the requirements of the Directive of 4 April 2001 on Good Clinical Practice. Indeed, this Directive requires that the Member States introduce 'the measures necessary for establishment and operation of Ethics Committees'. However, the nature and the powers of the authorities created by the French legislation ought to be clarified, in particular as to what constitutes an 'ethics committee'.

---

* Professor of Law at the University of Rennes, France.
[1] This law was introduced in Articles L.1121-1 and followed the Code of Public Health.
[2] In particular by Law No. 94-630 of 25 July 1994, *Official Journal* of 26 July 1994.
[3] *Official Journal of the European Communities*, 1 May 2001-L 121/34 to 121/44.
[4] Law No. 78-17, *Official Journal*, 7 January 1978. This law has been vastly altered by Law no. 2004-801 of 6 August 2004, *Official Journal* of 7 August 2004, on the Protection of Data Subjects as regards the Processing of Personal Data.

## The Establishment of Committees

The European Directive of 4 April 2001 requires the intervention of an ethics committee before any clinical trial. The objective of this committee is essentially to ascertain the seriousness of the project[5] and the protection of each person participating in the research.[6] Thus, it appears that the committee concerned is actually an authority responsible for ensuring the protection of the person and of his or her fundamental rights rather than an ethics committee *stricto sensu*.

Indeed, the role of an ethics committee should rather be to lead a discussion on ethical issues relating to a particular situation. However, the protection of the person, which includes obtaining his or her consent, is more a matter of defence of fundamental rights than an ethical issue.

The problem of the definition of ethics and its relation to the law is at the heart of the European comparative research project, PRIVIREAL. It seems that an essential distinction has to be made to be able to establish a connection between the systems adopted in the different Member States of the European Union. In states like France, which has legislation that guarantees the protection of the person participating in research, the committees that have been set up are not actually able to give a verdict on ethical issues but are rather authorities responsible for ensuring that basic human rights are respected. On the other hand, states that do not have specific legal arrangements relating to biomedical research have created authorities called 'ethics committees', but which are actually responsible for monitoring the protection of persons involved in the research. The ambiguity of the European Directive stems from its calling these 'ethics committees' whilst affording them the remit of acting as 'legal committees'.

The case of France provides an example of the importance of this distinction. Indeed, before 1988, research protocols were not submitted to the control of any legal committee. In practice, however, some investigators did submit their projects to a local ethics committee.[7]

Since the adoption of the 1988 Act on Biomedical Research, one can distinguish, on the one hand, authorities whose remit is to enforce the legal rules protecting the person participating in the research and his or her personal data and, on the other hand, ethics committees that are only concerned with the ethical issues related to the intended research.

---

[5] The committee must review the relevance of the trial and its design, the suitability of the investigator and of his or her colleagues, and the quality of the facilities.

[6] The committee must assess the balance between risks and benefits, the methods for informing participants and the procedure for receiving the consent of the person participating in the research, and the methods and processes established for ensuring the responsibility of the investigator and the indemnification of the victim.

[7] B. Le Mintier, 'Les comités régionaux d'éthique en France: réalités et perspectives', Rapport Mission de recherche (MIRE) *Droit et Justice*, Ministère de la Justice, Ministère du travail et des affaires sociales, October 1998, 18.

*The Institutionalization of Committees for the Protection of Persons*

Biomedical research on humans is mainly regulated by the Law of 20 December 1988, which was amended by the Law of 9 August 2004.[8] The aim of this text is to authorize research on humans,[9] whilst ensuring the protection of the people who participate in it (notably, the protection of physical integrity). This safeguard is reached by the investigator's obligation to obtain the opinion of a Committee for the Protection of Persons. Before the Law of 9 August 2004, these authorities were known as 'Consultative Committees for the Protection of Persons Participating in Biomedical Research' (CCPPRBs). These Committees are still in use whilst we wait for the application decrees of the Law of 9 August 2004. This legislation safeguards the protection of the person participating in research rather than protecting the processing of his or her personal data. The specific texts relating to this issue grant the Commission Nationale de l'Informatique et des Libertés (CNIL) the task of controlling the use of personal data, notably in relation to biomedical research, once it has received an opinion from the National Consultative Committee on the Processing of Information in the Health Sector (Comité Consultatif National sur le Traitement de l'Information en matière de Santé).

*The Committees for the Protection of Persons*

Where biomedical research is concerned, French Law provides for the systematic submission of research to a Committee for the Protection of Persons. These committees were created by the Huriet Law in 1988 and were given the name 'Consultative Committees for the Protection of Persons Participating in Biomedical Research' (formally known as CCPPRBs).[10] They are now going to be replaced by Committees for the Protection of Persons.

These committees will have a legal nature. There are currently 48 CCPPRBs in France.[11] These committees are responsible for any trial or experiment organized

---

[8] Law relating to the policies of public health, *Official Journal* no. 185 of 11 August 2004, 14277.

[9] The Law of 9 August 2004 removed the distinction between research that had a direct benefit and that which had no direct benefit for the person participating in the research. The law also retained the logic of the European Directive, which encourages the evaluation of the balance between benefits and risks.

[10] The PRIVIREAL Questionnaire on the role of Ethics Committees in biomedical research was addressed to these CCPPRBs (committees that existed before 2004). A total of 13 of them replied: the CCPPRBs of Basse-Normandie, Limousin, Nancy, Rennes, Alsace, Toulouse, Guadeloupe and Ile de France: Créteil-Henri Mondor, Paris-Cochin, Boulogne-Billancourt, Bicêtre, Pontoise, Saint-Germain en Laye. One of them did not answer the questionnaire but provided some notes.

[11] Most (44) of these CCPPRBs are organized as a National Conference (CNCP) which ensures the education of its members. It favours the diffusion of good practice and enables the committees to be represented before public authorities.

and carried out on humans with the intention of developing biological and medical knowledge, whether or not such experimentation has a therapeutic aim.

The remit of the new Committees for the Protection of Persons is more important than that which was initially granted to the CCPPRBs.

There is a time-limit of five weeks after the submission of the research protocol by the investigator for the committee to provide a 'reasoned opinion' on the conditions of validity of the research with regards to the protection of persons. In this framework, the committee must verify that the written information to be provided is suitable, exhaustive and intelligible. The committee must also ensure that the procedure for obtaining consent is clear, that there is justification provided for any research carried out on people who are unable to give consent, that there is a possible requirement for 'thinking time' or to allow for the prohibition of simultaneous participation in another research project, the general relevance of the research, the suitability of the project's aims and the means set up to pursue them, as well as the qualifications of the investigator(s), the amounts and methods for compensation and the means of recruiting participants.[12] This remit corresponds to that which was assigned to ethics committees introduced by the European Directive of 4 April 2001.

The field of competence for the protection committees was extended in so far as the protection of the person basically rests on the appreciation of risks in relation to benefits. The remit of the committee is therefore quite subtle. In order to be able to provide an opinion on the risks involved, the committee members must possess a certain degree of knowledge. Thus, in the near future, there will be a danger of transforming these committees into panels of experts. Such a move would be regrettable and would negate the original purpose of the Committees for the Protection of Persons.

However, if the opinion of a protection committee is obligatory, then this formality is not sufficient. Indeed, the law anticipates that 'biomedical research can only be initiated having received a favourable opinion from a committee for the protection of persons ... and authorization from the competent authority...'.[13] The latter must either be the French Agency for the Sanitary Security of Health Products (l'Agence Française de Sécurité Sanitaire des Produits de Santé—AFSSAPS) if the research focuses on drugs, contraceptives or progesterone-inhibiting products,[14] or the Minister for Health if other types of research are concerned. These two steps do not necessarily have to be carried out at the same time; the latter can be postponed. *In fine*, depending on the situation, either the AFSSAPS or the Ministry of Health can prohibit the research.[15]

---

[12] Article L.1123-7 of the Code of Public Health.

[13] Article L.1121-4 of the Code of Public Health

[14] The AFSSAPS is responsible for any research relating to the products mentioned in Article L.5311 of the Code of Public Health.

[15] Article L.1123-8 of the Code of Public Health states that 'if ... the competent authority informs the research sponsor that there are objections to the establishment of the research project, the sponsor can modify the contents of their project and submit a new request .... If

As agreed by the Minister for Health, Committees for the Protection of Persons should be multidisciplinary and independent. The Government's representative (le Préfet) in the region where the committee has its headquarters[16] appoints members of these committees for six years. These committees are composed of 12 members[17] including specialist doctors and General Practitioners, pharmacists, nurses, psychologists, an ethicist, a social scientist, and a person qualified in legal matters. The Law of 9 August 2004 introduced 'representatives of patients' associations or groups using the health service'.[18] In practice, this multidisciplined nature does not seem to be effective due to an important lack of attendance by members of the Committees for the Protection of Persons, namely the 'non-medical representatives'.

The independence of the committees is guaranteed by a law that requires members to declare on nomination 'their associations, either direct or indirect, with the research sponsors and investigators'. Any declaration is made public and is updated on the member's initiative whenever any change arises relating to these associations or when new associations are made.[19] In practice however, this issue of independence is difficult. It requires that members of a protection committee can operate freely in relation to the institutions that nominate them, but also in relation to themselves. They must be fully aware of the responsibilities that they shoulder. Independence is a gamble.

Even if the law provided that these committees be composed in such a way as to 'guarantee their independence and diversity of knowledge in the field of biomedicine and in relation to *ethical*, social, psychological and legal issues' (emphasis added),[20] these authorities cannot be considered as ethics committees. Rather, they are groups with a multidisciplinary composition responsible for verifying that the legal rules relating to the protection of the person involved in a research project are respected. The opinion they provide is not of an ethical nature but rather concerns the verification, in each research protocol, of the respect of the rules on the protection of the person involved in the research (essentially the rules relating to consent).

The law does not provide that these protection committees have any role in the protection of data subjects with regards to their personal data. However, in practice, a sponsor can appeal to such a committee in order to ascertain its opinion on the intended processing of personal data in the research protocol that he or she is submitting.

---

the sponsor does not modify the contents of their request, then this final request is considered to be rejected'.

[16] There can be one or several committees per region.

[17] With 12 substitutes.

[18] Article L.1123-2 of the Code of Public Health.

[19] Article L.1123-3 of the Code of Public Health.

[20] Article L.1123-2 of the Code of Public Health.

Examination of the PRIVIREAL questionnaires addressed to the CCPPRBs[21] demonstrates that these committees believe that the legal conformity of the research protocol with regards to data protection is a necessary condition for the approval of the research project. Nine of these CCPPRBs declared that they would prohibit any research activity that does not comply with the law, and three of them stated that they would only validate a proposal if certain conditions as defined in law were met. Half of the CCPPRBs that responded to the PRIVIREAL questionnaire believed that a research project could be refused solely on the basis of the consideration by members of the CCPPRBs that the law was not being respected. It would not be necessary for them to obtain advice from their institution's lawyers or from the lawyers in their group. Generally, most of the CCPPRBs believe that they are authorized to appeal to the Data Protection Authority.[22] These different observations show that the committees consider themselves to be responsible for the decisions they take.

All of the replies demonstrated a real desire on the part of the protection committees to play an effective role in the verification of research projects requiring the processing of personal data. Nevertheless, doubts can be expressed concerning the effectiveness of this remit. Indeed, knowledge of the law applicable to the processing of such data is indispensable in order to be able to respond to a research project that does not fulfil its legal obligations. However, it is unlikely that the members of the Committees for the Protection of Persons, who are mainly all scientists, would possess such legal knowledge. Only the lawyer or lawyers sitting on the committee could provide such knowledge. Furthermore, it is necessary for the lawyer on the protection committee to have a sound understanding of the laws relating to the protection of personal data in the health sector, and he or she should at least attend the committee meeting!

Generally speaking therefore, in order to carry out biomedical research on humans in France, the sponsor must first receive an opinion from a Committee for the Protection of Persons and then authorization from the French Agency for the Sanitary Security of Health Products or of the Ministry of Health. The role of the Committee for the Protection of Persons has been increased. All that used to be required was the consultation. The Law of 9 August 2004 anticipates that this committee issues 'an opinion'. This law therefore implements a change in the legal nature of the remit of these committees.

This guaranteed protection prior to the research now exists during the research itself. The 2004 law anticipated several interventions by the committee during the course of the research.[23] Firstly, 'any modification to this [the research] must receive a favourable opinion from the committee and authorization from a competent authority, preferably before it is put in place'. The committee must therefore ensure that new consent is obtained from those persons participating in

---

[21] The questionnaires were sent to the CCPPRBs not the Committees for the Protection of Persons, as the legal reform is recent (August 2004).

[22] However, a third of the CCPPRBs seems to be unwilling to do this.

[23] Moreover, in their protocol, the research sponsor must indicate whether or not the constitution of an independent surveillance committee is anticipated.

the research 'if this is necessary'.[24] Secondly, the committee must be informed when the research is over as well as the reasons for stopping the research when this has been anticipated.

The Law of 9 August 2004 also anticipated the creation of a national database of people participating in biomedical research. This will identify the volunteers and patients who are taking part in research without any reference to their state of health. However, whilst taking into account the risks and constraints of certain types of research, the Committee for the Protection of Persons can decide to register other people.

Examination of this legislation shows that the committee that intervenes is not really an 'ethics committee', that is to say, a committee that gives opinions on the ethical nature of a research project.

In parallel to this system of authorization for the research itself, the law also allows for specific protection of a person's personal data. Other authorities are responsible for this.

*The National Consultative Committee on the Processing of Information in the Health Sector and the Data Protection Supervisory Authority, the Commission Nationale de l'Informatique et des Libertés*

In France, some texts provide for the protection of personal data in the case of biomedical research. Where the Law of 6 January 1978[25] is a text of general application concerning 'informatics and freedom', the Law of 1 July 1994 is specific to health issues.[26] The Law of 6 August 2004 relating to the protection of personal data did not introduce any important changes into the particular area of health.[27]

The law states that 'the processing of personal data[28] for the purpose of research in the health sector'[29] is submitted to a particular procedure. Thus, any research into health that gives rise to the processing of personal data[30] must receive

---

[24] Article L.1123-9 of the Code of Public Health

[25] Law No. 78-17 of 6 January 1978 *Official Journal* of 7 January 1978.

[26] Law modifying No. 78-17 of 6 January 1978 on 'Informatics and Freedom', *Official Journal* of 2 July 1994.See also Decree No. 95-682 of 9 May 1995 (*Official Journal* of 11 May 1995). In parallel, the rules on professional secrecy apply.

[27] See new Articles 40-2 to 40-4 of the Law of 6 January 1978.

[28] Whether this is in the Public Sector or not.

[29] The processing of health data for statistical purposes or for the purpose of analysis of practices and activities of care and prevention is also regulated. Law No. 99-641 of 27 July 1999 on the creation of the 'Universal Health Cover' introduced new provisions in the 'Informatics and Freedom' legislation by submitting the processing of this data to authorization of the CNIL in the case of a transfer of indirectly nominative data. Decree No. 99-919 of 27 October 1999 provides the procedure and investigation methods which enable the CNIL to appreciate 'the safeguards taken by the plaintiff', 'the conformity of his/her request to its aims and its business', and 'the necessity to use personal and nominative data'.

[30] Research can concern a person and his or her personal data or only the processing of nominative data.

an authorization from the Supervisory Authority, the Commission Nationale de l'Informatique et des Libertés (CNIL), after having received the opinion of a committee (The National Consultative Committee on the Processing of Information in the Health Sector).[31]

Firstly, the National Consultative Committee on the Processing of Information in the Health Sector must be appealed to as soon as the computerized processing of personal data is linked to a particular piece of research.[32] Unlike the CNIL, which has general responsibility for supervising the use of personal data, this authority has specific responsibility for health. However, this committee is only concerned with research studies that use computerized methods during the processing of nominative data. It does not deal with the use of automated files that are intended to provide an individual therapeutic or medical follow-up for the patient, nor are they concerned with internal studies that are set up using information in these files by the people who need to ensure the medical follow-up and who will be the only people to use the data.[33]

The aim of this appeal is to formulate an opinion on 'the methodology of the research' with regards to the law on 'informatics and freedom' and also on 'the necessity of using personal data and the relevance of such data with regards to the aims of the research'.[34] The legal remit assigned to this committee, that is to say the supervision of the legal rules on the protection of personal data, shows that this authority does not constitute an 'ethics committee'.

The National Consultative Committee for the Processing of Information in the Health Sector is composed of 14 members and one president who are all appointed following a joint agreement between the Minister for Research and the Minister for Health 'due to their abilities in the area of research into health, epidemiology, genetics, and biostatistics'. It is notable that no lawyers are included on the committee. Indeed, the committee members are all scientists. Their mandate is for

---

[31] See I. de Lamberterie, 'Protection of the Private Life in Relation to Medical Research in French Law' in D. Beyleveld, D. Townend, S. Rouillé-Mirza and J. Wright (eds.), *Implementation of the Data Protection Directive in Relation to Medical Research in Europe* (Aldershot: Ashgate Publishing Ltd, 2004), 97–119, for the conditions of this authorization.

[32] The PRIVIREAL Questionnaire on 'the role of Ethics Committees' has been addressed to this committee.

[33] Submissions are made to the National Consultative Committee on the Processing of Information in the Health Sector for research projects that intend to use computerized methods for processing nominative data, with the exclusion of automated files whose aim is the therapeutic or medical follow-up for individual patients (as in the case of computerized medical files) nor are they concerned with internal studies that are set up using information in these files by the people who need to ensure the medical follow-up and who will be the only people to use the data. Manual research files do not seem to be covered by the Law of 1 July 1994. For guidance on the regulation of the processing of health data for statistical purposes or for the purpose of analysing the practices and activities of care and prevention, see Law No. 99-641 of 27 July 1999 on the creation of Universal Medical Cover and Decree No. 99-919 of 27 October 1999.

[34] Article 40-2 of the Law of 1 July 1994. Decree No. 95-682 of 9 May 1995 provides the practical methods of control.

three years, with the possibility of one renewal. The committee's opinion is based on the views of the majority of attending members, and in cases where the vote is split, the president has the deciding vote.

A person qualified to represent the public or private body that initiated the data processing operation must make the request for an opinion. The request must consist of a dossier that, principally, should include the research protocol and the sample group, the intended observation method, the origin and nature of the collected nominative data and justification for the use of this data, the duration of the research, and the methods of organization, amongst other things. The law states that 'opinions formulated by "scientific and ethical"[35] authorities must be included in the file'. The reference to a possible ethics committee shows that the legislator is making a distinction between the National Consultative Committee on the Processing of Information in the Health Sector and an ethics committee.

The consultative committee has one month from the receipt of the request to give its opinion on the project. After this time-limit, the opinion is taken to be favourable. In an emergency situation, this time-limit can be reduced to 15 days following a request from either the Minister for Research or the Minister for Health.

Secondly, the CNIL is appealed to and must give its authorization for the processing of personal data[36].

The CNIL is an independent administrative authority that has been granted some important responsibilities, such as checking the legal compliance of projects and providing information and advice.[37] It is composed of 17 members appointed for five years, of which 12 are appointed by their peers: two deputies, two senators, two members of the Economic and Social Committee, two members or former members of the Cour de Cassation, the Council of State and of the Court of Auditors, three persons qualified for their knowledge of computer science applications or issues relating to personal freedoms, two people qualified by their knowledge of data processing techniques and who are appointed by the President of the National Assembly and the President of the Senate respectively. The President is elected by the CNIL's members.

In our area of interest, the procedure for the CNIL's supervisory function is as follows. The opinion of the National Consultative Committee on the Processing of Information in the Health Sector, together with a breakdown of envisaged measures for informing each data subject individually, must be included in the file presented to the CNIL. The following must be outlined:

> The measures taken to ensure the security of data processing and of the information, as well as the safeguards in place for secrets protected by law, and scientific and technical

---

[35] See below on 'the factual recognition of the Ethics Committees' and, more precisely, the role of the 'Local Ethics Committees'.

[36] The powers of the CNIL were strengthened by the Law of 6 August 2004 implementing European Directive 95/46/EC of 24 October 1995 on the protection of individuals with regard to the processing of personal data and on the free movement of such data.

[37] The Law of 6 August 2004 strengthens the CNIL's powers.

justification for every request for exemption to the prohibition of the conservation of data in a nominative form beyond the required time needed for the research.

The CNIL is allowed two months, with the possibility of one extension, to give notification of its decision. Silence from the CNIL beyond this time-limit signifies an authorization.

It is important to note that the supervision carried out is not of an ethical nature but rather a legal one. The general aim of the CNIL is to make sure that the law entitled 'Informatics and Freedom' is complied with, notably where health is concerned,[38] rather than to lead 'ethical' reflection.

Thus, France established committees responsible for supervising the application of legal rules both for the protection of persons participating in research and also of his or her personal data. Together with these legal procedures, real ethics committees can, in practice, be induced to intervene.

*The Establishment of Ethics Committees*

In France, ethics committees are authorities that are responsible for leading reflection on ethical issues relating to biomedicine. The only ethics committee that has a legal existence is the National Consultative Ethics Committee (CCNE). The others, which are linked to main research organizations or to hospitals, are not institutionalized. These different committees can only play a minor role in biomedical research.

*The legal acknowledgement of the National Consultative Ethics Committee (CCNE)* On a national level, the National Consultative Ethics Committee (CCNE) was created to reflect on ethical issues in the fields of biology, medicine and health.[39] The Law of 6 August 2004 relating to bioethics extended this competence to 'societal issues'. For a long time, the CCNE was the only ethics committee that was legally recognized.[40] The Law of 6 August made it an 'independent administrative authority',[41] as the CNIL already was. It is induced to provide opinions and, since the 2004 law, recommendations.[42] However, these standards possess no legal value. The CCNE has provided general opinions on biomedical research[43] but does not intervene in concrete cases. Therefore, the CCNE was set

---

[38] In application of the Law of 1 July 1994.

[39] Article L.1412-1 of the Code of Public Health.

[40] The CCNE was created by Decree No. 83-42 on 23 February 1983. The Law of 6 August 2004 established the composition of the CCNE into the legislative programme, however it also created 'spaces' of ethical reflection (see *infra*).

[41] As such, the CCNE ought to benefit from financial independence (the committees' funds are registered in the Prime Minister's budget).

[42] Article L.1412-3 of the Code of Public Health.

[43] The CCNE has had the opportunity to give its opinion on the role of the ethics committees in the case of research; see Opinion of 9 October 1984 on the ethical issues resulting from the trials of new drugs on humans. Recommendation of 7 November 1988 on Local Ethics Committees, of 27 January 1992.

up to lead a general reflection, but it does not intervene in the review of research protocols.

*The factual recognition of ethics committees*  Firstly, ethics committees that are linked to the main research organizations should be mentioned.

The INSERM (the only public organisation entirely devoted to biomedical research and health) and the CNRS (National Centre for Scientific Research) set up their own ethics committees as a result of the acceleration of scientific progress, where the researcher can find him or herself caught between two different logics: the logic of the researchers that would have him continue with his work, and the logic of the society that would control it.

The INSERM's ERMES Committee[44] (Ethics in Medical Research and Health), set up on 11 October 2000, leads reflection on ethical issues in biomedical research and would like to play an active role in the dialogue between the biomedical research community and general society. This committee does not have a remit to intervene in each research protocol, but rather only to favour the integration of ethical reflection into biomedical practice. This authority seems to have more of a general remit and does not seem to play a role where research protocols are concerned.

The CNRS' Ethics Committee, formerly known as COMETS,[45] also only has a general remit and does not intervene in research protocols. It leads reflections on ethical issues that arise out of the practice of research. Nevertheless, it can give opinions to researchers. However, as well as the COMETS, another authority was created in the Department of Life Sciences at the CNRS: the COPE (Operational Committee for the Ethics of Life Sciences[46]). This authority aims to establish a new kind of dialogue between the Department of Life Sciences and its laboratories. It intends to make a list of the ethical issues with which the researchers are confronted and to give advice to these researchers, either by putting them in touch with the appropriate authorities (CNIL, CCNE), or by helping them to comply with the current regulations in their field.

The COPE, with the assistance of its internal ethical unit, helps the researchers to steer themselves through the jungle of laws and regulations. This committee demonstrates the ambiguity between ethics and law: it is known as an 'ethics committee', however its main occupation is essentially informing its researchers of the legal rules regulating research.

---

[44] It is composed of 17 members (one President, 12 INSERM members, four external to INSERM).

[45] The Ethics Committees for Sciences of the CNRS (COMETS) was created by a decision of the CNRS on 29 June 1994. COMETS created the Ethics Committee of the CNRS by a decision of 20 August 2002.

[46] The COPE was created in November 1991. The president of the COPE is a member of the Ethics Committee of the CNRS.

Secondly, local ethics committees were born. Hospitals created their own internal ethics committees.[47] These ethics committees are linked to healthcare establishments or created within sections of hospitals that are seen as being particularly 'sensitive', such as neonatal or palliative care services.[48]

These committees do not have any legal recognition but exist in practice. Generally, the aim of these committees is to provide opinions, essentially on clinical ethics issues that are encountered in practice by medical professionals.[49] Their opinions can be considered as an aid in the decision-making process; however they have no legal value. Before the Huriet Law of 20 December 1988 on Biomedical Research, the coordinators of research projects sometimes submitted their projects to these ethics committees. The creation of the CCPPRBs put an end to this practice.

However, these ethics committees can be consulted by project coordinators before appealing officially to a Committee for the Protection of Persons (formally known as a CCPPRB). The aim could be to obtain an opinion on the *ethical aspects* of the intended research. However, it seems that a submission relating to the protection of a person's personal data is unlikely, since the law provides the legal procedure to be followed. As far as we are aware, no regional ethics committee has ever been consulted on the processing of personal data. If this were to happen, the ethics committees should encourage the sponsor of the research to comply with the legal procedure. Once again, however, such reasoning requires the members of this committee to understand the legal rules. Yet the presence of lawyers in these committees is small and sometimes non-existent.[50]

The law relating to bioethics that was introduced on 6 August 2004 anticipated the creation of spaces for ethical reflection on a regional and inter-regional level.[51] These authorities must be 'places for training, information, meetings or inter-

---

[47] Beyond the ordinary ethics committees, Ethical Spaces have been created near healthcare establishments. For example, the Ethical Space of the Public Assistance of the Paris Hospital, Ethical Mediterranean Space.

[48] A. Cordier, 'Ethique et Professions de santé', a report delivered to the Minister of Health, May 2003, available at http://www.ladocumentationfrancaise.fr/BRP/034000226/0000.pdf; C. Byk and G. Mémeteau, *Le droit des comités d'éthique* (Paris: Eska, 2000).

[49] B. Mathieu, 'Les comités d'éthique hospitaliers' (2002) January–March *Revue de droit sanitaire et social*. In May 2002, a Clinical Ethics Centre was created within the Cochin Hospital, on an exceptional basis, on the anglo-saxon template. See S. Druelles, 'Evolution récente de l'éthique clinique en France', DESS dissertation, University of Law of Rennes under the supervision of B. Feuillet-Le Mintier, Rennes 2003. J. C. Mino, 'Les comités hospitaliers d'éthique clinique sont-ils des lieux de production de nouvelles normes de pratique? Etude sur le champs institutionnel hospitalier de l'éthique clinique en Amérique du Nord et en France', Rapport Mission de recherche (MIRE), July 1999.

[50] B. Le Mintier, 'Les comités régionaux d'éthique en France: réalités et perspectives', Rapport Mission de recherche (MIRE) *Droit et Justice*, Ministère de la Justice, Ministère du travail et des affaires sociales, October 1998.

[51] Article 1412-6 of the Code of Public Health. Rules governing the constitution and function of these spaces must be defined in a decree by the Minister for Health after having received an opinion from the National Consultative Committee for Ethics (CCNE).

disciplinary discussions on ethical issues in the field of health'. They must act as 'regional observation centres for practices relating to ethics'. These spaces must not be induced to play a role in biomedical research.

## Powers of the Committees

In order to understand the mechanism of protection concerning biomedical research and, more precisely, the use of personal data within a research project, it is important to understand the conditions for applying to committees, the type of decisions they can take, the powers of these authorities and the possibilities for contesting their decisions.

### Application to the Committees

It is compulsory to apply to institutionalized committees ensuring the protection of the person participating in research and the processing of his or her personal data. However, applying to an ethics committee is not enforced.

*Obligation to apply to Committees for the Protection of Persons*  In order to carry out biomedical research on humans, it is compulsory to consult first of all a Committee for the Protection of Persons and then to receive authorization from the French Agency for the Sanitary Security of Health Products or from the Ministry of Health.[52] Carrying out research without obtaining a favourable opinion from a Committee is punishable by an imprisonment of one year and a fine of 15 000 Euros.[53]

   As for the processing of personal data, it is also compulsory to receive authorization from the CNIL, after having received an opinion from the National Consultative Committee for the Processing of Information in the Health Sector. Article 226-16 of the Penal Code provides a sanction of five years' imprisonment and a fine of 300 000 Euros for anyone who conducts, or allows others to conduct, any automated processing of nominative information without respecting the preliminary formalities required for such work, including through negligence.

*The rare application to an ethics committee*  Concerning ethics committees *stricto sensu*, since they do not have an official role in research on humans or in the supervision of the processing of personal data, they will be applied to only if, in parallel to the legal procedure, the coordinator of the research project wishes to consult an ethics committee.[54]

   However, within the CNRS, the laboratories seem to have to submit their protocol to the COPE to first ensure that the laws protecting persons participating

---

[52] Depending on the type of research carried out, see *supra*.
[53] Article L.1126-5 of the Code of Public Health.
[54] For example, consultation of a regional ethics committee (committee linked to a Regional Hospital Centre).

in the research, or whose personal data is used, are respected. If there was no consultation by the COPE and no compliance with the current laws, the CNRS could decide not to renew the Research Unit.

## Powers of the Committees

The main aim of the different committees created by law (the committees for biomedical research, the National Consultative Committee for the Processing of Information in the Health Sector and the CNIL for the protection of personal data) is to verify the legal compliance of the research project. Consequently, these authorities cannot authorize an unlawful research project. For example, they cannot accept a research project, even if it were in the public interest, which would be carried out without the consent of the subject or would dismiss the protection of personal data, except in the cases defined by law.[55]

With regards to the Committees for the Protection of Persons involved in research, the answers provided by the CCPPRBs to the PRIVIREAL questionnaire demonstrate this point. Even if the research project were interesting from a scientific point of view, if the express consent of the research subject were not sought, or if the project led to a violation of confidentiality, then all the Committees for the Protection of Persons[56] would reject such a project.

The CNIL authorizes the use of personal data only if it follows the conditions defined by law and, in particular, the law relating to the consent of the data subject.[57]

Local ethics committees that would be consulted in practice by a sponsor also have to comply with the law. It is true that these authorities lead reflection on ethical issues. However, these committees are subject to legal principles, in particular the obligation to respect the fundamental rights of a person. In practice, knowledge of the legal rules demonstrated by these committees is not obvious due to the small number of lawyers in these authorities.

If respect of the laws is the principle, the question of the interpretation of these rules by the committees is not obvious and can lead to differences. This is demonstrated by studying the PRIVIREAL questionnaire results on anonymization.

The French law provides that data enabling the identification of the persons concerned must be encoded prior to their transmission.[58] However, this obligation can be ignored when the processing of the data is linked to studies of pharmacovigilance, or to research protocols carried out within international or national cooperative studies, or if a particularity of the research requires it. The

---

[55] On the exemptions provided in the case of processing data, see I. de Lamberterie, n. 31 *supra*.

[56] Only two CCPPRBs say they would approve such a project subject to the opinion of competent persons. Another CCPPRB considers that this violation could be justified in the public interest on a case-by-case basis and following its own judgment!

[57] See Articles 40-4 and 40-5 of the Law of 6 January 1978.

[58] Article 40-3 paragraph 2 of the Law of 6 January 1978.

presentation of the results of the data processing operation must never enable the direct or indirect identification of the data subjects.[59]

The National Consultative Committee for the Processing of Information in the Health Sector considers that data are anonymized when a person cannot directly or indirectly identify the data subjects.[60] As for the CCPPRBs, four of them consider that even under this assumption, data cannot be considered anonymized. However, all of the CCPPRBs who replied to the PRIVIREAL questionnaire believe that data are anonymized when researchers cannot identify the data subject, even if the medical staff who obtained this information can still identify them.[61] The committees also believe that when a researcher obtains personal data concerning the treatment of a patient, he or she must comply with the principle of protection of these data even if they are anonymized.

However, all the surveyed committees believed that as soon as there is a risk of discovering the identity of the human source, either directly or indirectly, then the processing of human biological samples for genetic research must comply with the protection of personal data.[62]

## Impact of the Committees' Decisions

In the area of biomedical research on humans, the intervention of the CCPPRBs was purely consultative. These opinions had to be conveyed to the French Agency for the Sanitary Security of Health Products or to the Ministry, who are the authorities responsible for authorizing the research. The Law of 9 August 2004 gives greater importance to the Committees for the Protection of Persons since it is compulsory to receive their opinion and also to receive authorization either from the French Agency for the Sanitary Security of Health Products or from the Minister for Health.

If the French legislator anticipated this double method of control, he or she remained silent on the possible conflict between this opinion and authorization from the administrative authority. The laws only state that 'in the situation of an unfavourable opinion from a Committee, the research sponsor can request that the Minister for Research submits the research project for a second opinion to a different Committee, as designated by the Minister.[63]

However, careful reading of the Law of 9 August 2004 seems to demonstrate the determining nature of the single authorization from the administrative authority.[64]

---

[59] For more information, see I. de Lamberterie, n. 31 *supra*.

[60] Information found in the PRIVIREAL Questionnaire answered by the National Consultative Committee on the Processing of Information in the Health Sector.

[61] Only one CCPPRB answered no to this question in the PRIVIREAL questionnaire.

[62] Questionnaire answered by the Committees. Also, see I. de Lamberterie, n. 31 *supra*.

[63] In the conditions defined by regulatory means. See Article L.1123-6 of the Code of Public Health.

[64] Article L.1123-8 paragraph 1 of the Code of Public Health states that 'no one can initiate a biomedical research project without authorization from the competent authority …'.

Moreover, in the case of processing personal data for the purposes of research in the health sector, the National Consultative Committee for the Processing of Information in the Health Sector provides nothing more than an opinion. Only the CNIL is entitled to authorize this use. The Law of 6 August 2004, which modified the Law of 1978, increased the CNIL's powers in relation to the sanctions that it can issue against persons who do not respect the measures relating to the processing of personal data.[65]

*Recourse Against the Committees' Decisions*

With relation to Committees in the area of research, the CCPPRBs were already independent before the reforms of 9 August 2004 and, as such, did not answer to any regulatory authorities. Moreover, their opinions could not, in principle, be appealed to for annulation of administrative acts, since this is limited to Acts considered to be 'holding a grievance', that is to say, those producing direct legal effects. However, as the opinions of the CCPPRB were purely consultative, authorization for the research ultimately rests with the French Agency for the Sanitary Security of Health Products or with the Minister for Health.

The legislator expressly regulated on the issue of possible responsibility for the Committees for the Protection of Persons. 'Where a Committee makes a mistake in the execution of its remit, the State assumes responsibility'.[66]

Where the National Consultative Committee for the Processing of Information in the Health Sector is concerned, this Committee is accountable to the Ministry of Research; however, its role is only optional. Only the CNIL has the power to authorize projects. It is an independent administrative authority and as such does not have any legal status and its decisions are purely of an administrative nature. However, as it is also an independent authority, it has no regulatory authority and is not involved in the hierarchy of the State. Its members are independent and receive 'instruction from no authority'. The law states that:

> the ministers, public authorities, managing directors of public or private companies, leaders of various groups and, more generally, those in possession of or using nominative files cannot oppose any action taken by the Commission or by its members for whatever reason but must, on the contrary, take all measures to help facilitate the Commission's work.[67]

However, the decision of the CNIL can constitute a grievance and be considered as an act that can be appealed to the administrative judge.[68]

---

[65] See the new Articles 44 to 52 of the Law of 6 January 1978; Article 45.I provides the possibility for the CNIL to issue a warning, to order a breach in the law to stop, to impose a financial sanction, to inform the Prime Minister in order for him to stop the violation or to appeal to the competent authority to order any necessary security measures.

[66] Article L.1123-7 of the Code of Public Health.

[67] Article 21 of the Law of 6 January 1978.

[68] See 'Les fichiers informatisés dans le domaine de la santé' in M. Gobert (ed.), *Médecine, Bioéthique et Droit: Questions choisies* (Paris: Economica, 1999), 237.

## Conclusion

In conclusion, it appears that the comparison of the systems of protection of the person or of the use of personal data in the different European countries firstly requires some reflection on the definition of ethics committees. Indeed, the essential underlying element to this study is the risk of granting these ethics committees the aim of protecting what should be a matter of law.

Indeed, if the intention of the European Directive is to generalize protection of persons in the field of biomedical research, it seems limited. Ensuring the effective protection of persons and of the use of personal data can only happen through legal protection. If not, it will be nothing more than an illusion, as it will be described as real protection, whereas, in fact, it will have a very small impact. It must be hoped that the additional protocol to the Convention on Human Rights and Biomedicine that has just been implemented will lead to such legal protection.[69]

---

[69] Protocol on Biomedical Research passed by the Council of Ministers of the Council of Europe on 30 June 2004.

# Chapter 10

# Research Ethics Committees in Germany

Matthias Kettner[*]

## The Landscape of RECs in Germany

In 2003, there were 52 public law-based 'Ethics Commissions' (RECs) operating in Germany. These RECs were set up according to state law and have a task defined by both the legislature and the specific body of law that governs the medical profession. These committees specifically regulate the moral integrity of research on human subjects, although their popular German name of 'Ethics Commission' misleadingly suggests that their competence covers medical ethics in general.

If one bears in mind the scandalous history of despicable medical experiments in Germany and elsewhere, one can easily be convinced that these discreetly operating committees successfully fulfil an important control function, making the world of medical research considerably safer for test-subjects.[1]

The RECs in Germany have developed into a stable and recognized integral part within the system of medical research on human subjects.[2] Their achievements in the regulation of medical experimentation on humans have meant that test-subject and patient protection, as well as the quality of medical research in Germany, has improved. However, the practice of RECs encounters criticism, often voiced by scientists and representatives of business interests (for example, pharmaceutical enterprises), that they are an obstacle to research.[3]

---

[*] Teaches philosophy at the Private University of Witten/Herdecke. In 2000–2003 he conducted the first research project in Germany on clinical ethics committees; and was funded by the National Research Agency (Deutsche Forschungsgemeinschaft).
[1] G. Maio, *Ethik der Forschung am Menschen* (Ethics of Research on Humans) (Stuttgart: Frommann-Holzboog, 2002), 212–291.
[2] H. Rosenau, 'Landesbericht Deutschland' (State Report for Germany), in E. Deutsch and J. Taupitz (eds.), *Forschungsfreiheit und Forschungskontrolle in der Medizin. Zur geplanten Revision der Deklaration von Helsinki* (Freedom of Research and Research Controls in Medicine. On the Planned Revision of the Declaration of Helsinki) (Berlin: Springer, 2000); U. Wiesing, 'Zur Geschichte der Ethik-Kommissionen in Deutschland' (On the History of Ethics Commissions in Germany) in J. Ach and A. Gaidt (eds.) *Herausforderung der Bioethik* (The Challenge of Bioethics) (Stuttgart: Frommann-Holzboog, 1993).
[3] E. Schwendler-Haffke, U. Reinken, H. Hüttmann and K. Schick, 'Ethikkommissionen in Deutschland aus der Sicht der forschenden pharmazeutischen Industrie' (RECs in Germany

## The Composition of RECs

In Germany considerable differences have arisen (and will continue to arise) between different RECs.[4] Some are structural. These include variations in the membership composition of RECs.[5]

Most RECs have between 5 and 19 members, and at the extreme this can range from as few as four, up to one REC with 32 members. The majority of RECs are made up of medical practitioners with the involvement of a lawyer. Often philosophers and/or theologians are also members. Biometricians are represented in barely a third of RECs, which is surprising in view of the necessary and difficult calculations for testing the scientific content of the design. Only in a handful of cases are patient representatives or those who care for patients included in an REC consultation, which seems counter-productive to the desired authorizing effect of this procedure upon the general public.

The empirically well-demonstrated likelihood of divergence of votes by RECs—a noticeable inconsistency between RECs advising on the same thing—can certainly be traced back not only to the ethical factor of moral diversity but also to the organizational factor of the differing composition of RECs.

## Diversity in Fees Charged

RECs also vary considerably with regard to the fees they charge for their work. The processing fees, which RECs demand from applicants, are between 400 and 2 700 Euros. It is strange how there can be a difference in fees of over 2 000 Euros for the same application.

Even for secondary votes, which sometimes only entail the adoption of primary votes from other RECs, RECs often charge fees. On REC fees alone, pharmaceutical firms who want to carry out a normal clinical trial must pay out between 25 000 and 50 000 Euros.

In general, members work in an honorary capacity, which means their work for the REC is not a source of income. A few RECs, for example the RECs that pertain to the professional organizations of medical doctors ('Landesärztekammer') in each of the states that make up the Federal Republic of Germany, pay their members an 'attendance allowance'. Financial reimbursement is often paid by RECs to any expert consulted in the course of an REC procedure.

---

From the Point of View of the Research Pharmaceutical Industry) (1999) 1 *Pharmind*, 11 onwards.

[4] A. Wilkening, 'Zur aktuellen Praxis der Ethik-Kommissionen—Verbreitung, Besetzung und Beratungsinhalte' (On the Current Practice of Ethics Commissions—Expansion, Composition and Contents of Consultation) (2001) *Medizinrecht* (MedR), 301 onwards.

[5] G. Neitzke, 'Über die personelle Zusammensetzung von Ethik-Kommissionen' (Who are the members of Ethics Committees?) in U. Wiesing (ed.), *Die Ethik-Kommissionen. Neuere Entwicklungen und Richtlinien* (Ethics Commissions: New Developments and Guidelines) (Köln: Deutscher Ärzteverlag, 2003), 104–123.

**The Workload of RECs**

The following picture is formed from 2000 and 2001 survey data: the number of applications that RECs had to process varied between 19 and 600 per year. On average that makes 244 applications per REC per year. In addition each commission receives around 100 protocol amendments and a high, but not exactly ascertainable, number of reports on side-effects which have occurred in the course of a study. Slightly less than half (on average, 138 applications per REC per year) of the research protocols advised upon are concerned with multi-centre studies.

**Historical Development of RECs**

The development of RECs in Germany goes back to the 1960s. When the German Research Foundation established a new medical research programme in 1972 it required the introduction of a corresponding REC. This was the first time that RECs figured as an obligatory element in research. The decisive point for the development of RECs in Germany, however, was the re-wording of the Declaration of Helsinki by the World Medical Association in 1975, which made the conduct of research involving human subjects conditional on prior consultation by an independent body.[6] At this point, RECs became part of the normative force of the most known and important document on medical ethics regulating medical research. In Germany the Declaration of Helsinki is, of course, also accepted as a leading ethical guideline for medical doctors who are active in research.

In 1978 the Westphalian Wilhem-University in Münster was the first university to establish an independent and general REC in Germany. From 1979 onwards, the Professional Organization of German Doctors (German Medical Association)[7] recommended the introduction of independent RECs to the different Medical Associations at state level. This recommendation was motivated by the prior initiative of the German Research Foundation.

This initiated a phase when RECs were established with neither explicit legal regulation nor public scrutiny; for example, they were only governed by the framework of professional self-regulation that is represented by the German Medical Association, and by the medical faculties of university hospitals. The function of RECs was to impose self-regulation on the professional conduct of medical research and to keep externally imposed legal regulation at bay. In parallel with the rise of RECs tied to professional self-regulation, an increasing number of 'free' RECs evolved—that is RECs based not on the law governing the medical

---

[6] A. A. Kollwitz, *Kontrolle medizinischer Forschung durch RECs* (Control of Medical Research by RECs) (Dortmund: Humanitas-Verlag, 1999); W. Van den Daele and H. Mueller-Salomon, *Die Kontrolle der Forschung am Menschen durch Ethikkommissionen* (The Control of Human Research by Ethic Commissions) (Stuttgart: Enke-Verlag, 1990).

[7] In German, Bundesärztekammer (the website is available at: www.bundesaerztekammer.de). The National Medical Organization represents, at the federal level, almost 400 000 medical doctors and comprises 17 state-level Medical Organizations.

profession but on private law. These 'free', or private, RECs gradually came to play a significant role in surveying the pharmaceutical industry's clinical drug trials. Moreover, some big medical research institutes established their own RECs in order to deal with their medical research projects on the basis of in-house regulations and contractual agreements.

In 1985 RECs gained explicit legal recognition on the level of medical professional law when their establishment was made obligatory in the Model Professional Guidelines for Medical Practitioners.[8] According to these guidelines, then, every medical doctor must be advised by an REC before carrying out clinical research on human subjects. The peculiar normative force of this obligation is that as a norm, professional self-regulation—on the basis of a self-imposed duty, and in that sense, on a voluntary basis—researchers consult a body that is comprised chiefly of medical colleagues and lawyers and has no further legal sanctioning power. The obligation to submit clinical research to the scrutiny of RECs was strengthened and made more binding in 1988,[9] and is now a regular part of the official Model Professional Code for Medical Practitioners.[10] Corresponding resolutions are found in the Constitutions of the 17 Medical Organizations at the state level.

Legal recognition of RECs advanced further when in 1994 a role for RECs was fixed in the Medicinal Products Act[11] and the fifth amendment to the Law on the Trade in Drugs (Drug Law, 'Arzneimittelgesetz (AMG)').[12]

Furthermore, in 2001 a role for RECs was written into the Radiation Protection Act ('Strahlenschutzverordnung (SSVO)'). In addition, RECs are also included in paragraph 8, section II, number 7 of the Transfusion Act of 1998, and in this context they play a role in the supervision of immunization programmes.

## RECs and Clinical Ethics Committees

Any history of ethics committees in Germany must mention the fact that from 1997 clinical ethics committees are increasingly found to be an attractive form of ethics in healthcare. In 2003 there was ethics consultation in the form of clinical ethics

---

[8] (1985) *Deutsches Ärzteblatt*, A-3371.

[9] (1988) *Deutsches Ärzteblatt*, A-3601.

[10] (1997) *Deutsches Ärzteblatt*, A-2354, cf. paragraph 15 on 'Forschung' (research). (The 1997 version of the code is available in the archive at www.aerzteblatt.de.)

[11] Gesetz über Medizinprodukte (MPG) of 2 August 1994 (This Act is available online at http://bundesrecht.juris.de/bundesrecht/mpg/, last accessed 16 May 2005).

[12] The requirement to include the opinion of an REC in the process of pharmacological-toxicological tests is contained already in the original 1976 version of the Drug Law (cf. paragraph 40, 'Allgemeine Voraussetzungen', at http://bundesrecht.juris.de/bundesrecht /amg_1976/index.html; an English consolidated version is available at http://www.bmgs. bund.de/downloads/AMG-englische_Fassung.pdf, cf. section 40, both last accessed 16 May 2005).

committees in 67 hospitals, 51 of which are confessional (Catholic or Protestant).[13] RECs and clinical ethics committees have been implemented as two functionally distinct advisory bodies. While the evolution of RECs has its roots, so to say, in the process of the Helsinki Declaration, the recent rush towards clinical ethics committees in Germany has quite different motives. These committees were promoted in 1997 in a memorandum that was published jointly by the Association of Catholic Hospitals and the Association of Protestant Hospitals. According to this memorandum, an important goal of establishing clinical ethics committees is to strengthen the profile of the religious and moral values of the hospitals in question. Rhetorically the paramount goal, as one would expect, is to empower the patients in the medical system.

## The Complex Legal Status of RECs in Germany

Statutory regulations for RECs are found on different levels and in different legal domains, as described in the previous sections. Since in Germany a unified legal regulation for medical research is still lacking (although this lack has been observed and deplored various times in the past), standardized legal recognition of RECs has only succeeded in the already mentioned special statutes of the Medicinal Products Act, the Law on the Trade in Drugs, and in the law regulating medical trials with radioactive material and protection against radiation. A wider scope of REC review is to be found only in the law regulating the medical profession, in the medical professional codes at the state level, and in some regulations that exist in big research institutes.[14] Again and again, problems encountered in the ongoing practice of medical research attest to the fact that the normative pattern of these various regulations is as yet not fully coherent.

In the past the legal governance of RECs in Germany has been heterogeneous and complex. A factual heterogeneity corresponds to this normative heterogeneity of RECs.[15] Empirical surveys reveal a remarkably disorderly picture of RECs in practice relating to their composition, their procedures, and their decision-making practices. Already in the early 1980s, under the auspices of the National Medical Association, a task force was formed with the aim of making the practice of the existing public law-based RECs more consistent by creating common procedural

---

[13] M. Kettner, 'Ethik-Komitees. Ihre Organisationsformen und ihr moralischer Anspruch' (Ethics Committees: their Organization and their Moral Claims) (2005) Nr.1 *Zeitschrift für Erwägungskultur*. In 2003 about 800 confessional hospitals and 1 500 non-confessional hospitals were operative in Germany.

[14] In 1999, for example, the German National Research Agency (Deutsche Forschungsgemeinschaft (DFG)) instituted the 'Senatskommission für klinische Forschung' (see http://www.dfg.de/dfg_im_profil/struktur/gremien/senat/kommissionen_ausschuesse/ senatskommission_klinische_forschung/index.html, last accessed on 16 May 2005).

[15] J. Czwalinna, 'Ethik-Kommissionen für medizinische Forschung am Menschen' (Ethics commission for medical research on human subjects) (1986) *Medizinrecht* (MedR), 305 onwards.

guidelines.[16] However, as recent investigations show, the desired standardization of, and comparability across, RECs has not yet been achieved.[17]

## Critique of the Legal Over-Regulation of the Review Process in RECs

Among the many voices that comment on the development of the 'landscape' of RECs in Germany there is substantial criticism of relevant EU guidelines, such as Directive 2001/20/EC, in particular from medical doctors. Critics fear that such guidelines engender an excessive legal over-regulation ('Verrechtlichung') of RECs' monitoring and counselling activities.

Arguably, this development serves to strengthen the role of RECs, which can be seen positively. Moreover, the trend towards formulating ever more detailed instructions for applications to RECs will strengthen the decision-making role of RECs. In the area of medicinal drugs it is already evident that RECs will distance themselves from their historical roots in the medical profession's self-regulation and, through increasing over-regulation of the law, turn into an instrument of external legal control.

This trend towards legal over-regulation is also very clear in the EU Directive on Good Clinical Practice (GCP), which includes the need for '[d]etailed guidance on the application format and documentation to be submitted in an application for an Ethics Committee opinion on the clinical trial of medicinal products for human use'.

## The Supremacy of Public RECs over Private RECs

At present, the complex legal status of RECs described in the previous sections as heterogeneous tends to diminish the former importance of 'free' RECs registered according to the Medicinal Products Act. For researchers and industrial sponsors there is less incentive to ask a private REC for advice when its advice is likely not to be fully recognized from the point of view of professional public law-based RECs.[18]

---

[16] E. Deutsch, *Medizinrecht: Arztrecht, Arzneimittelrecht, Medizinprodukterecht und Transfusionsrecht* (Medical Law: The Law of the Medical Profession, Medicinal Drugs Law, Medical Products Law, and Transfusions Law) (5th edn., Berlin: Springer, 2003).

[17] The 2001 study by Wilkening shows, as did some previous studies, a surprising amount of diversity in the practice of the RECs that are operative in Germany. Cf. also M. Hirtle, T. Lemmens and D. Sprumont, 'A Comparative Analysis of Research Ethics Review Mechanisms and the ICH Good Clinical Practice Guidelines' (2000) 7 *European Journal of Health Law* 3, 265 onwards.

[18] W-R. Schenke, 'Verfassungsrechtliche Probleme einer öffentlich-rechtlichen Monopolisierung der ethischen Beratung bei klinischen Versuchen am Menschen' (Constitutional Problems of a Public Law Monopoly on Ethics Consultation for Clinical Trials on Human Subjects) (1996) *Neue Juristische Wochenschrift* (NJW), 745 onwards.

On the part of the 'free' RECs, the professional regulations are interpreted as an infringement of their basic right to freedom of profession in Article 12 I GG (Grundgesetz). They consider the attempts by the Medical Associations to entrust only public law-based RECs with the review of clinical trials as a strategy to monopolize this professional activity, and hence as unconstitutional.

In agreement with the published views from representatives of 'free' RECs, the Administrative Court of Stuttgart accepts that a public law monopoly for RECs cannot be justified by reference to an overwhelming public interest, since legislation on the federal level has expressly authorized in the Medical Products Law (MPG) the activities of 'free' RECs and federal law must not be subverted by state law. On the other hand, only a few years before the Administrative Appeal Court in Baden-Württemburg had decided that the existing regulation does not unduly infringe the rights of 'free' RECs by state legislation.

In the juridical literature concerning this controversy there is also the interesting opinion that the public law-based organization of RECs in no way guarantees that the review process is qualitatively superior, nor that the process is fair and independent. Rather, these desired procedural qualities correlate with an REC's number of qualified experts and the rational form of the deliberative processes in its routine procedures. So-called 'free' RECs could even be in a better position than the public law RECs. In addition, some commentators mention positive experiences with 'free' RECs in other Member States to the effect that the independence of 'free' RECs appears not to be endangered by commercialization.

On the other hand there are other commentators who argue that monopolizing clinical trial oversight by public law-based RECs is not only constitutionally acceptable but even mandatory, considering the importance of legally protected rights of the participating patients and research subjects.

The main argument critical of admitting 'free' RECs is the admonition that the commercial orientation to which they are prone is likely to create conflicts of interest between their clients (for example pharmaceutical enterprises) and the protection of the legitimate interests of patients and test-subjects. In particular, these critics expect that strategically acting industrial sponsors or medical researchers seek out RECs which are positively biased towards them, or that they manage to buy favourable opinions ('hopping and shopping').[19]

## Problems with Multi-Centre Studies in the Past

In the past, multi-centre medical research projects had to undergo a multitude of examinations by different RECs. Study designs were to be reviewed not only by the principal investigator's local REC but in addition, on the basis of professional

---

[19] E. Doppelfeld, 'Funktionen und Arbeitsweise der Ethik-Kommissionen' (Functions and Procedures of Ethics Commissions) in E. Deutsch and J. Taupitz (eds.), *Forschungsfreiheit und Forschungskontrolle in der Medizin. Zu geplanten Revision der Deklaration von Helsinki* (Freedom of Research and Control of Research in Medicine: On the Planned Revision of the Declaration of Helsinki) (Berlin: Springer, 2000), 341 onwards.

rights, by every relevant REC that was locally situated within the respective research network. In consequence, simplifications of the review process made possible on the legal level of special statutes (such as the MPG) have tended to be outrun by complexity at the legal level of professional regulations. This tendency has been massively criticized in particular by the pharmaceutical industry.[20]

Some critics argue that this complexity endangers the quality of clinical testing in Germany and that the actual variation in the assessments that are issued by different RECs in a multi-centre design mocks the ideal of rational and comparable decision-making. Furthermore the enormous workload and the resulting increasing costs of a clinical trial are heavily criticized. They might result in considerable disadvantage depending on the location of the clinical research in Germany. Against these critics, others hold that RECs cannot sufficiently guarantee the protection of patients and test-subjects by a centralized assessment. They argue that a central REC, distant from the diverse local milieus where the study is to be carried out, is not in a good enough position to take the morally and legally relevant circumstances of these milieus into consideration as it properly should.

Attempts to counteract the negative effects of the juxtaposition of simplifying special statute supervision and multiple professional consultation are made in practice by distinguishing between 'primary' and 'secondary' opinions of RECs. Only primary opinions require a complete examination of the research plan, whereas secondary opinions make do with a simplified assessment that can build on the primary opinion where feasible. The REC task force—as yet non-binding, suggested procedures for RECs involved in multi-centre studies (of 1986)—make it clear that any positive opinion at some level in no way excludes a re-examination of the entire research design if needs be.

### The Minor Role of Ethics in German Ethics Committees

Between medical law and medical ethics, the normative force of positive law is more powerful than the normative force of moral judgments. The legal enforcement of normative standards that are primarily backed by, and derived from, medical ethics is dependent on their legal recognition. As published reports on the practice of RECs show, RECs for the most part take up and apply existing legal regulations. Ethical considerations are factored into the application of such regulation to concretize circumstances, but there is very little ethical assessment on its own grounds beyond this.

There is evidently much leeway in the moral as well as the legal scope of review as carried out by RECs at present. It is an open question how this leeway cashes out in terms of the overall aim of protecting patients and research subjects. A corollary to this question is the problem of how to rationally deal with the factual diversity of judgments encountered across different RECs. If the review and

---

[20] In this context it must be pointed out that in a study on three multi-centre clinical trials, the number of the participating ethics commission members almost corresponded to the number of participating subjects of research. E. Schwendler-Haffke *et al* (1999), n. 3 *supra*.

the corresponding assessments remain within a purely moral sphere of validity, then a plurality of votes appears to be less problematic, owing to the undisputable fact of moral diversity. If the diversity of assessment issues is in discrepant *decisions* with different *legal* consequences, however, then it would appear that the bounds of acceptability of such diversity are much stricter. This, at least, seems to be the majority opinion.

The diversity of normative judgments on clinical trials that has been critically observed in the past, especially concerning multi-centre studies, could develop not only into an obstacle to medical research; it could also grow into a danger for patients and research subjects. It is sometimes argued that *moral* pluralism—the leeway of judgments based on standards of medical ethics—threatens the overall aim of protecting patients and research subjects even more than the greater homogeneity of a legally regulated and, to a large extent, demoralized control process. This assumption provides a strong motive in favour of the progressive legal regulation of RECs, threats of over-regulation (see above) notwithstanding— a process that has recently been pushed along by the 12th amendment of the Medicinal Drugs Act (AMG).[21] This is explained in the next section.

## Current Problems with the EU Homogenization of RECs

Since summer 2004 the European regulations on pharmaceutical vigilance for human and animal medicinal drugs, as well as the guidelines on the use of standards for good clinical practice of clinical trials with human medicinal drugs, were legally implemented into German law through the 12th amendment of the Medicinal Drugs Act. The amendment stipulates that only RECs which are constituted in accordance with state law, for example RECs situated in university clinics and RECs pertaining to state Medical Associations, should assess clinical trials for medicinal drugs.[22] For multi-centre clinical trials the application must be submitted to the REC associated with the principal investigator responsible for the study. If the opinion of the corresponding REC is favourable then the legal requirements are met.

The Working Party of Health Care Ethics Commissions ('Arbeitskreis medizinischer Ethikkommissionen') has criticized this centralization of the assessment procedure. The working party is not principally opposed to a single assessment procedure for multi-centre studies but favours participation in the assessment procedure of all co-responsible local RECs within the network of the intended multi-centre study. They argue that a shared and integrated consultation process of many local RECs is necessary for the construction of a single opinion

---

[21] The amendment came into force on 6 August 2004. The text of the amendment can be found at www.bmgs.bund.de/deu/gra/gesetze/index.cfm, click on the entry 'zur Gesundheit' and then on 'zu Arzneimitteln', last accessed 16 May 2005. The amendment is particularly concerned with the implementation of Guidelines 2001/83/EC, 2001/20/EC and 2002/98/EC.

[22] Cf. paragraph 42 as modified in the AMG of 2004, n. 12 *supra*.

with nationwide legal validity. The National Medical Association ('Bundesärztekammer (BÄK)'), the German Union of National Health General Practitioners ('Kassenärztliche Bundesvereinigung (KBV)'), and the Medicinal Drugs Commission of the German Medical Profession ('Arzneimitellkommission der deutschen Ärzteschaft (AkdÄ)') maintain a similar position.[23]

The Working Party of Health Care Ethics Commissions, the BÄK, the KBV and the AkdÄ, all also agree that for all clinical trials of medicinal drugs the principal investigators must be medical doctors. This used to be so in the past. The new legal situation, however, no longer recognizes this constraint. Instead, all that is required now is that the clinical trial be responsibly carried out by 'an appropriately qualified' investigator. For instance, would-be principal investigators count as qualified when they have at least two years' experience in clinical trials of medicinal drugs. Therefore, a biologist meeting this requirement could figure as the principal investigator. This new, weaker, requirement is not sufficient, in the view of many medical doctors, to guarantee a high enough level of protection to patients and research subjects.

## Current Data Protection Issues in German EU-Homogenized RECs

The 12th amendment of German Medicinal Drugs Act (AMG) says the following about data protection:[24]

> Test-subjects are, in the course of informed consent, also to be informed about the purpose and scope of the extraction and use of person-specific data, especially for data relating to health. They are particularly to be informed that the extracted data as far as necessary:
>
> 1.  will be inspected by the supervising authorities or representatives of sponsors for checking that the clinical trial is being properly carried out,
> 2.  will be made anonymous by the use of pseudonyms before it is given to sponsors or representatives of the authorities for the purpose of scientific evaluation,
> 3.  in the case of an application for authorisation the names will be made anonymous in order for it to be passed on to the applicants and the authorities responsible for authorisation,
> 4.  in the case of unwanted effects from the tested drug will be made anonymous for sponsors and the responsible Federal Authorities as well as for the information which is passed on to the European Databank.

Test-subjects must also be informed that, even if they withdraw their consent, the data already collected may be used as far as is necessary to ascertain the effects of the drug in question, or to make sure that the rights of the person concerned that

---

[23] H. Korzilius, '12. Novelle zum Arzneimittelgesetz: Mehr oder weniger Ethik?' (12th Amendment to the Medicinal Drugs Act: More or Less Ethics?) (2004) 101 *Deutsches Ärzteblatt*, A-309.

[24] Cf. paragraph 40 as modified in the AMG of 2004, n. 12 *supra*.

are worthy of legal protection are not damaged, or to fulfil the duty of presenting documents of authorization. In the case of a withdrawal of informed consent, the authority responsible has to examine immediately how much of the saved data could still be necessary. Data that are no longer necessary must be deleted immediately.

## Conclusion: Perspectives for the Future of RECs in Germany

According to the concurring views of many commentators, RECs in Germany will develop over the next few years into strong controlling mechanisms capable of effective safeguarding. Their agreement will be necessary for a study protocol to be carried out, whilst their refusal to agree will effectively be a veto. Moral deliberation will recede into the background even further, whilst juridical deliberation will dominate the characteristic field of normativity staked out by RECs more and more.

This tendency towards legal over-regulation (at the expense of medical ethics) is being criticized but will prove inevitable if only because the due implementation of EU guidelines into national law unequivocally encourages such over-regulation by the law.

A milestone in this process, and a vehicle for the homogenization of the practice of RECs in Germany, is the 12th amendment to the Medicinal Drugs Act (AMG). According to many critics, on the one hand the AMG in its present state will strengthen the normative authority of RECs because now the agreement of an REC is a necessary condition for the realization of a trial. On the other hand, though, the protection for patients and research subjects in clinical trials for medicinal drugs—the core area of RECs' work—is weakened because the principal investigator may now be a person without strong ties to the medical profession and its inherent medical ethical standards and virtues.

In addition the applicants, big pharmaceutical firms, can indirectly exert pressure on the RECs. The 12th amendment of the AMG allows for pharmaceutical enterprises to sue (or threaten to sue) an REC for economic disadvantages that arise if the REC rejects the application, or if the REC does not process the application within a specified time limit.

At present a parliamentary commission, 'The Select Committee for Law and Ethics in Modern Medicine',[25] has, so to speak, 'discovered' the unruly practices of RECs as an issue worth parliamentary scrutiny. The patchwork of RECs which has developed in Germany is likely soon therefore to be made the object of more systematic study. The Select Committee would be well advised to make the emerging legal regime of RECs a major subject on its agenda.

---

[25] See the website of the German Bundestag (www.bundestag.de/parlament/kommissionen/ethik_med/aktuell/index.html, last accessed 16 May 2005).

Chapter 11

# Research Ethics Committees in Greece

Tina Garanis-Papadatos[*] and Dimitris Boukis[†]

## Introduction

For the reader who is not familiar with the Greek system, a brief introduction could help the understanding of the conditions under which the development of research ethics committees (RECs) is taking place.

Traditionally in Greece, physicians have enjoyed considerable paternalistic authority over their patients and society.[1] This way of thinking had, in the past, left little room for the expansion of other values and notions, such as the concept of autonomy on which the protection of the research subject is mainly based. Autonomy, however, is a central notion in Greek jurisprudence[2] which provides fundamental directions regarding respect for human beings and self-determination, but despite the underlying common fundamental values, cultural differences and ethical relativism may occasionally lead to a different interpretation and application of certain values.

International developments regarding the ethical framework of medical research have had a considerable impact on the Greek situation—the need to establish research as well as clinical ethics committees has over time become more obvious and steps have been gradually taken towards this direction. Moreover, the rapid progress of technology and the growing awareness of individuals regarding their rights as well as the need to abide by relevant international regulations, have played an important role in this issue.

## Establishment of RECs

According to Article 16 of the Greek Constitution, the freedom of research is protected as an individual and functional liberty at the institutional level, so that

[*] Lawyer, Teaching and Research Assistant, National School of Public Health, Athens, Greece.
[†] Specializes in civil, commercial law and litigation at Kremmydas-Doris & Associates, Athens.
[1] I. Granitsas, 'Medical Deontology' (December 1991) *Iatriko Vima* (the second part was also published in *Iatriko Vima*, in February 1992) (in Greek).
[2] Greek Constitution of 1975 (2001).

interference of the state in the process of acquiring and transmitting knowledge is avoided. This right, however, cannot be enjoyed against other constitutionally protected rights and remains subject to certain limitations, which have to be justified by the state.

Towards this aim, many attempts have been made in Greece regarding the establishment of ethics committees; the first took place in 1965 at the Institute of Child Health. This committee suspended its function in 1981 due to political instability and restarted in 1990.

Other attempts were made in 1973 with Legislative Decree 97/1973 (Section 2, paragraph 6), which mainly concerned the approval of clinical drug research, and in 1978 with a Ministerial Circular,[3] which imposed establishment of ethics committees at a local level.

In the early 1990s a National Council of Medical Ethics and Deontology was established.[4] The Council's main objectives included participation in formulating the general policy of the Ministry of Health and Welfare on issues of medical ethics and deontology, in particular, handing down opinions on all such issues, settling disagreements in local ethics committees by consultation, and establishing a Centre of Medical Ethics.

The same Law 2071/1992 also provided for the establishment of local ethics committees in both public and private hospitals and clinics. The tasks of these committees—which by law have five members—includes consultation on issues of medical ethics to the Governing Board of the hospital or the clinic, as well as monitoring the respect of relative rules and principles.

It is only very recently that this Council has actually been activated, and until now it has not dealt with ethics committees as other pieces of legislation have addressed this issue.

A comparatively recent law[5] has been enacted in order to decentralize the management of the health system and to ensure the public focus of the National Health Service. Under this law the country is split into healthcare regions corresponding to the existing administrative regions. At the *regional level*, Section 2 paragraph 6 states that a Scientific Council established at each Regional Health Service is responsible, amongst other things, for the foundation of an Ethics and Deontology Committee. At the *hospital level, Section 5 paragraph 11 states that in each hospital the established Scientific Council* also has the responsibilities of an ethics and deontology committee.

Although at the local level the progress which has been made is far from spectacular, at the national level some new Bioethics Committees have emerged, stimulating the general interest in this field.[6]

---

[3] Ministerial Circular A2/oik3061/5 June 1978.

[4] Law 2071/1992 on the Modernization and Organization of the National Health Service, *State Journal* A' 123/15 July 1992.

[5] Law 2889/2001 on the Improvement and Modernization of the National Health Service, *State Journal* A' 37/2 March 2001.

[6] T. Garanis-Papadatos and P. Dalla Vorgia, 'Clinical trials in Greece: ethical review proceedings' (2000) 7 *European Journal of Health Law* 441–447.

The National Committee on Bioethics was established in 1998. Its remit is to explore the ethical and legal impact of the possible applications of biological sciences. This Committee does not examine research protocols; however, a part of its role consists of outlining proposals of general policy in collaboration with the respective ministries, whilst also providing specific recommendations on related issues.

The Bioethics Committee of the General Secretariat of Research and Technology was established in 1997. It also has a general role with respect to giving opinions to the Ministry of Development, public debate on biomedical issues, and research funding.

### General Powers of RECs

In Greece RECs only have advisory powers. The approval of an REC is necessary for the research to go ahead; however, the project also has to be approved on its scientific merit by a Scientific Committee. A new Ministerial Decision, analysed below in relation to Directive 2001/20/EC, provides for the creation of a National Deontology Committee with decisive powers.

As RECs have only recently been established in Greece, sufficient follow-up does not exist regarding their functional experience. Nevertheless, it is a fact that researchers who do not submit their research for review cannot get approval for their work. Moreover, they cannot publish their work, since scientific journals ask for the approval of an ethics committee as a prerequisite for publication.

### General Legal Responsibility of RECs

In Greece no specific detailed legislation exists regarding the function of RECs, their terms of reference or issues of membership, access or independence. The above-mentioned legislation provides for the establishment of these bodies but not for their working methods, regulations or restrictions. Thus, the remit and practice of such committees is still being developed. Moreover, neither the Greek Medical Association nor other relevant bodies have issued any guidelines regarding ethics committees. Thus, the responsibilities of these committees cannot be defined accurately. In general, however, taking into account the existing civil penal and constitutional law, RECs have to function within the limits of legitimacy. They can, therefore, neither reject lawful activities, on the basis of the legal status, nor approve unlawful activities, for example activities which violate general rules of law or specific regulations enacted by law, either provisions imposed by *jus cogens* or by contractual obligations. The notion of *activity* also includes omitting to act, especially where the person concerned is under a specific obligation to act in a particular way. In the Greek legal order the Courts are the appropriate bodies for defining when a legal regulation comes into conflict with the Constitution.

Any natural or legal person whose legal interest can be affected by a decision of an REC has the right to bring an action against the Committee. The evaluation of possible harm, however, can only be carried out by the Courts. The rules of the Greek civil procedure define which Courts have this jurisdiction.

Another piece of legislation which should be mentioned here concerns the rights of the patients. According to Law 2071/1992, Article 47.4, the patient has the right to be *a priori* informed about the risks entailed in any experimental or research procedure for which the patient must give explicit consent. This consent can be revoked at any time and the patient must feel completely free in his or her decision to accept or reject his or her cooperation regarding research or education. Law 2519/1997[7] has extended these rights to all users of healthcare services.

Despite the lack of detailed regulations regarding the role and practice of RECs, the willingness of Greece to abide by international regulation and the extent of international collaboration in research projects has obliged researchers in Greece to abide by internationally established and accepted protection standards regarding the rights, safety and well-being of trial subjects. Thus, the role of international regulation is very important, in particular the Declaration of Helsinki, which, being a declaration and not a convention, is not legally binding on Greece, but nevertheless remains the fundamental text regulating research.

Another important international document is the Convention for the Protection of Human Rights and Dignity of the Human Being with regard to the Application of Biology and Medicine (Council of Europe), which Greece has signed and ratified, incorporating it into domestic legislation through Law 2619/1998, and as a consequence Greece is obliged to create committees which have to follow the rules included in the Convention.

The Convention sets the minimum required standard for the protection of the individual, allowing the state to impose stricter domestic regulations. It should also be noted that unlike other international conventions, this Convention obliges the member states 'to furnish an explanation of the manner in which its internal law ensures the effective implementation of any of the provisions of the Convention'.[8] Greece recently also signed the Additional Protocol to the Convention concerning Biomedical Research; a subsequent ratification of this Protocol will lead to further obligations regarding the establishment and the functioning of ethics committees.

Another important piece of international legislation affecting national regulation is Directive 2001/20/EC, regarding laws and regulations relating to the implementation of good clinical practice in the conduct of clinical trials on medicinal products for human use.[9] It provides that the Member States are obliged to apply the provisions at the latest with effect from 1 May 2004. The most

---

[7] Law 2519/97 on the development and organization of the National Health Service, organization of medical services, drug regulations ..., *State Journal* A' 165/21 August 1997.
[8] Council of Europe 1997 Convention for the Protection of Human Rights and Dignity of the Human Being with regard to the Application of Biology and Medicine, ETS No. 164, Article 30: Reports on the application of the Convention.
[9] Directive 2001/20/EC of the European Parliament and of the Council on the approximation of the laws, regulations and administrative provisions of the Member States relating to the implementation of good clinical practice in the conduct of clinical trials on medicinal products for human use, Article 22.

important innovation of this Directive is the establishment of a control mechanism of the 'ethical appropriateness' of a clinical trial. This mechanism is vested within the power of approval or rejection which will function independently from the control of their scientific validity. This Directive has now become domestic law in Greece, with a Ministerial Decision issued by both the Ministries of Health and Finance[10] regarding the harmonization of the Directive with national law. This decision applies to clinical trials including multi-centre studies on human subjects. Its scope does not include non-interventional studies.

According to this Ministerial Decision, the ethics committees of the Regional Health Councils will provide expert opinion regarding every proposal put forward to the newly established 'National Committee of Deontology of Clinical Trials' that will finally approve the project. It is the first time that Greek legislation has recognized a bioethics institution vested with decisive and not only advisory power. The Committee will make its final decision taking into account the following additional factors:

- the appropriateness of the clinical trial and its design;
- the risk/benefit analysis;
- the protocol;
- the method of selection of participants;
- the appropriateness of the researcher, the research team, and the premises;
- the researcher's curriculum vitae;
- the accuracy and completeness of the written information provided to the participants, the consent procedure, and the justification of including individuals who are not capable of consent in the research;
- the measures in place in case of death or damage caused by the clinical trial;
- insurance and compensation covering the researcher's and sponsor's responsibility;
- the amount and the way of payment of any compensation or indemnity of the researchers and the participants, as well as the content of the contract between researchers and sponsors.

This Committee, an independent body based in the National Drugs Organization (EOF), will be appointed by the Minister of Health after consultation with EOF and will be composed of six members of the health sciences, a lawyer, a theologian and a scientist specializing in bioethics. A new ministerial decision will provide for the by-laws of this Committee, and this was supposed to begin proceedings on 1 May 2004.

Until now, the main legislative text regarding the conduct of clinical trials has been a Ministerial Decision of 1984.[11] Since 1997, researchers are also obliged to follow the rules laid down by Law 2472/1997 regarding Data Protection.

---

[10] Ministerial Decision DYC3/89292, *State Journal* B' 1973/31 December 2003.
[11] Ministerial Decision A6/10983/1/12 December 1984, *State Journal* 886 B' 20 December 1984, regarding clinical trials.

## Specific Data Protection Matters

During the examination of research proposals submitted to them, committees have the power to decide whether research is justified in the public interest, and in particular whether it is justified not to obtain consent in a particular situation or whether an exemption exists. This decision, however, must comply with the provisions of all the legislative texts mentioned above and especially with the provisions of the Biomedicine Convention of the Council of Europe. These provisions show particular concern for research on persons not able to consent or related situations, and the conditions under which this kind of research may be carried out.

The application of the law regarding data protection in research and health matters remains open to interpretation as there have been no studies yet evaluating the national situation. As far as 'anonymized' information is concerned, the Committees have to follow the regulations laid down by Law 2472/1997 'on the protection of individuals with regard to the processing of personal data'. This law does not specify when personal data have to be rendered anonymous nor does it specify what exactly is meant by the term *anonymization*. A possible interpretation could be that the data subject is rendered anonymous when he or she can no longer be identified.[12] The law also states:

> personal data, in order to be lawfully processed must be… (d) kept in a form which permits identification of data subjects for no longer than the period required, according to the Authority, for the purposes for which data were collected or processed.

It seems that the law cannot give a clear-cut answer regarding processing occurring after the anonymization of the data; however, in practice RECs tend to accept that this is permitted and they tend to consider that the data are rendered anonymous when they are codified in a way which prevents access and identification of personal data, even if a particular controller can have right of access. These, however, are vague estimations which are not based on systematic comparative studies of the way in which RECs work. The experience in Greece is still limited and there exist no detailed guidelines concerning this issue.

It is not possible to answer how in practice each REC views the issue of DNA samples (biological material) but it is generally accepted that genetic information is covered by the data protection law. This protection should be read in conjunction with the Greek Constitution (especially Article 5) and the Convention of Biomedicine of the Council of Europe.[13] According to Greek constitutional theory, genetic data are considered to be a special kind of information and are constitutionally protected as belonging to the sphere of the private life of the individual. Thus collection of genetic information can only be carried out in cases

---

[12] Law 2472/97 on the Protection of Individuals with regard to the Processing of Personal Data, Article 2(c).
[13] I. Kriari–Katrani, *Bioethical Developments and Constitutional Law* (Thessaloniki: Sakkoulas, 1994) (in Greek).

specified by the law for civil or penal reasons, and an REC which did not follow these principles could be found liable for breaching the law.

# Chapter 12

# Research Ethics Committees in Hungary

Judit Sándor[*]

## Introduction

According to Hungarian health administrators, the monitoring of public health and medical activities within the Hungarian health system is one of the oldest models of its kind in Europe. The history of the Health Science Council,[1] the main review body operating at the national level, goes back to the nineteenth century. Questions of medical ethics, of course, were interpreted differently at that time than today: concerns about the public good had higher priorities in designing and implementing new medical services than, say, focusing on the rights of the patient. Nevertheless, issues of consent already appeared in the lectures of a famous medical doctor at the beginning of the twentieth century.[2]

Though the current model of ethical supervision of medical activities was first adopted in 1951 when the Health Science Council was established in its present form, this body may be considered as a legitimate successor to the National Public Health Council, which was formed in 1868.[3] Since then the composition, name and function of the Council has been through numerous changes. After the Second World War, the main function of the body was to provide professional guidelines and opinion in important matters of health and science and to provide education in health. However, explicit reference to ethics in science appeared in 1977, when a

---

[*] Professor at the Faculty of Political Science, Legal Studies and Gender Studies, Central European University (CEU), Budapest.
[1] In Hungarian this is the Egészségügyi Tudományos Tanács, hereinafter the ETT. In 2001 the chairman of the Council was Prof. Szilveszter E. Vizi, Chair of the Hungarian Academy of Sciences. Since 2002, the chairman of the ETT has been Prof. Péter Sótonyi, a pathologist and rector of the Semmelweis University of Medical Sciences. More information on the Council can be found in Hungarian at the website http://www.ett.hu (last accessed on 16 May 2005).
[2] A Professor of medicine, Dr. József Imre, collected and published his lectures on medical ethics in 1925. The Professor studied Hungarian and German legal literature, and it is surprising even today to see the degree to which the necessity of informing the patient, and receiving his or her permission before carrying out medical procedures, was recognized and considered ethical at the start of the twentieth century.
[3] The King appointed the first members of this Council in 1868. See the brief history of the Health Science Council, available in Hungarian at the website http://www.ett.hu (last accessed on 16 May 2005).

new committee was established within the Council—the research ethics medical committee (Tudományos és Kutatásetikai Bizottság, ETT TUKEB).

The first specific law on biomedical research was adopted in the form of a Ministry Decree in 1987.[4] In the same year the text of the Helsinki Declaration was published in the Official Gazette.

The general rules for conducting biomedical research were laid down in the Health Care Act of 1997, while conditions for research on human beings were specified in a Ministry Decree issued in 2002.[5]

Today research ethics committees operate on three levels in Hungary: on the national level, the regional level, and the level of healthcare institutions (such as hospitals).

## Institutions

*Definition of Ethics Committees under the Hungarian Law*

Under the Ministry of Health Decree on Medical Research on Human Beings, ethics committees are defined as 'independent bodies that are responsible for protecting the human rights, safety, and well-being of the research subjects, by means of, among other things, evaluating and assessing, from a scientific and ethical perspective, the research plan, conditions of the research, the methods applied in the research, and the information given to the participants'.[6]

As the above citation reveals, these ethics committees safeguard not only human rights and safety concerns, but are also responsible for assessing the scientific and professional merits of newly proposed research plans or protocols. Thus, these committees have the combined function of evaluating both the ethical and scientific aspects of new research proposals in a single procedure.

As already mentioned, these ethics committees operate at national, regional, and institutional levels.

*Central Research Ethics Committees*

The Health Science Council is the advisory, opinion making, and policy preparing body of the Minister for Health, Social and Family Affairs. The Council consists of seven board members (medical doctors and academic scholars), two chairmen emeriti, five chairmen of the committees (see below) operating within the ETT,

---

[4] Ministry of Health Decree No. 11 of 1987 (VIII.19) on Biomedical Research (EüM rendelet az orvosbiológiai kutatásokról), amended by the Ministry of Welfare Decree No. 31 of 1998 (VI.24).

[5] Act No. CLIV of 1997 on Public Health (also referred to as the Health Care Act) and Ministry of Health Decree No. 23 of 2002 (V.9) on Medical Research on Human Beings (EüM rendelet az emberen végzett orvostudományi kutatásokról).

[6] Ministry of Health Decree on Medical Research on Human Beings, n. 5 *supra*, Article 2(h).

and eleven *ex officio* members (as specified by the law). The members of the Council are appointed for three years.

The Law on the Health Science Council[7] specifies five committees of the Council:

- Scientific and Research Ethics Committee (with the Hungarian acronym, ETT TUKEB);
- Clinical Pharmacology Ethics Committee (ETT KFEB);
- Human Reproduction Committee (ETT HRB);
- Forensic Committee; and
- Research and Development Committee.

Members of the Council and the Committees are appointed by the Minister for Health. There is no rotation, though the appointment has a fixed term.

The Scientific and Research Ethics Committee (ETT TUKEB) plays a principal role in the ethical review of new medical technologies based on a protocol submitted to the Council. Most members of this Committee are prominent medical professors.[8] As the Committee operates within the Health Science Council, formally an advisory body for the Minister of Health, it is not entirely independent from the government.[9]

The ETT TUKEB provides ethical and professional opinion on:

- the introduction of new preventive, therapeutic or diagnostic methods and procedures in Hungary, if those involve invasive treatment of the patient;
- the clinical applicability of medical technologies and equipment, and the effectiveness of them in the treatment of the patient;
- research projects concerning the development and characteristics of genetically determined illnesses, research in the fields of population genetics, somatic genetics and genetic epidemiology;
- research that does not belong to the categories described in the previous points but falls under the competence of more than one regional research ethics committee due to its multi-centred organization;
- any other research where the regional ethics committee forwards the application to the highest authority.[10]

---

[7] Ministry of Health, Social and Family Affairs Decree No. 34 of 2003 (VI.7) on the Health Science Council (ESzCsM rendelet az Egészségügyi Tudományos Tanácsról).

[8] The head of the Commission is Prof. Zoltán Papp, a gynaecologist and obstetrician. Among the members of this Commission, there are two legal scholars: Ágnes Dósa and Judit Sándor.

[9] Béla Blasszauer and Eszter Kismődi, 'Ethics Committees in Hungary', in Josef Glasa (ed.) *Ethics Committees in Central and Eastern Europe* (Bratislava: Charis–IMEB Foundation, 2000), 190–193.

[10] Ministry of Health Decree on Medical Research on Human Beings, n. 5 *supra*, Article 9(2).

The Committee on Human Reproduction (ETT HRB)

> provides professional and ethical opinion on specific procedures that are targeting human reproduction; on research and invasive treatments involving the use of embryos and embryonic stem cells; and on research and treatments involving a study of the human genome in relation to reproduction.[11]

The Committee on Clinical Pharmacology (ETT KFEB) 'provides professional and ethical opinion on medicinal products and on the clinical applicability of pharmacological products'.[12] Evaluation of procedures and protocols before the KFEB are based on the Law on Clinical Trials of Medicinal Products for Human Use.[13]

*Regional Research Ethics Committees*

There are 13 regional research ethics committees (Regionális Kutatásetikai Bizottság, RKEB) in Hungary.[14] The main role of the regional ethics committees is to formulate ethical and scientific opinion on any research that does not fall within the special competence of the central or national committees (TUKEB, KFEB, HRB).

The composition and procedures of the regional ethics committees are subject to the approval of the Scientific and Research Ethics Council. Members of the regional ethics committees are appointed by the heads of the health institutions involved.

---

[11] Ministry of Health Decree on Medical Research on Human Beings, n. 5 *supra*, Article 9(3).

[12] Ministry of Health Decree on Medical Research on Human Beings, n. 5 *supra*, Article 9(4).

[13] In full: Ministry of Health Decree No. 24 of 2002 (V.9) on The Implementation of Good Clinical Practice in the Conducts of Clinical Trials on Medicinal Products for Human Use (EüM. rendelet az emberi felhasználásra kerülő vizsgálati készítmények klinikai vizsgálatáról és a helyes klinikai gyakorlat alkalmazásáról).

[14] In addition to the six geographic-administrative regions (grouping two or three counties), the Semmelweis University of Medical Science and its institutions together with three central counties form one region; the health institutions under the direct supervision of the Ministry of Health, Social Affairs and Family form another; the health institutions in Budapest are grouped into two additional regions (the health institutions on the Buda and Pest sides of the Danube are separated); hospitals of the Hungarian Military Forces form their own region; the health institutions of the Ministry of Internal Affairs form yet another region, and the hospitals of the National Railways form the last one. See Annex to the Ministry of Health Decree No. 23 of 2002 (V.9) on Medical Research on Human Beings, amended by the new Ministry of Health, Social Affairs and Family Decree No. 34 of 2003 (VI.7) on the Health Science Council (see n. 7 *supra*).

## Research Ethics Committees at Health Institutions

Every health institution in which biomedical research is conducted has to have an institutional research ethics committee (Intézményi Kutatásetikai Bizottság, IKEB).[15] The composition and procedural rules of the committee have to be approved by the competent regional ethics committee. The main task of these local research ethics committees is to check whether the personal and technological conditions at the health institution are adequate for organizing and conducting research and to monitor the research procedure once the research protocol is approved.

The chairman, the secretary, and the members of the institutional research ethics committees are appointed by the head of the health institution. The chairman of the committee may nominate the members. The committee has to have at least five members including the chairman and the secretary. It is recommended that the membership include professionals who do not have a labour contract with the health institution. It is also recommended (thus, unfortunately, not mandatory) that there is a member in the committee who has some legal expertise in the field of research on human beings.[16]

## Procedures

### Meetings of the Committees

The Central Research Ethics Committees (TUKEB, KFEB, HRB) have regular meetings at least once every two months. The meetings are organized on the invitation of the chairman of the committee. An irregular meeting can be initiated by two thirds of the members. The chairmen, deputy chairmen, and members of the committees are based on the nomination of the Council Chairman appointed by the Minster for Health. Selection should take into account the age and gender composition of the committees.

The agenda for meetings is drafted by the secretary of the given committee. Members of the committees should receive the invitation at least ten days prior to the meeting.

On the level of hospitals and health institutions, ethics committees review research protocols. Each healthcare institution where research is conducted has to set up a research ethics committee. In addition there are some institutions where regional research ethics committees have to be established as well.

---

[15] Ministry of Health Decree on Medical Research on Human Beings, n. 5 *supra*, Article 12.

[16] See Guideline Number 2 on the 'Operation of the regional and institutional health committees', included in the Annex to the Ministry of Health, Social Affairs and Family Decree No. 34 of 2003 (VI.7) on the Health Science Council (see n. 7 *supra*).

*Conflict of Interest[17]*

Based on Article 11 of the ETT Decree,[18] if any member of the research ethics committees has a conflict of interest for either legal, ethical or economic reasons, the person has to reveal this fact to the committee. Members of the committee may also claim that another member has a conflict of interest. In the latter case the committee decides on the conflict of interest by vote.

## Basic Rules of Biomedical Research[19]

General rules and the content of research protocols are regulated in a Ministry Decree.[20]

Biomedical interventions can only be carried out with authorization and with the research purpose of developing diagnostic, therapeutic, preventive and rehabilitation procedures, for working out new procedures, and for a better understanding of the aetiology and pathogenesis of illnesses.

Within the meaning of this decree the term biomedical intervention covers the following: human genetic research carried out on living human beings and human genetic material, or other human genetic research; trying new, not yet applied, medical and treatment procedures, interventions, tools, equipment, applying medicines on the basis of new recommendations, or using other substances; for public health purposes—epidemiology and environmental healthcare research carried out on human beings; and research carried out on embryos and stillborn foetuses.

Biomedical intervention has to be based on appropriate and satisfactory laboratory and animal experiments and a deep understanding of relevant professional literature. Biomedical intervention can only be carried out in the institutions defined in the Health Care Act. In the process of biomedical intervention, the scientifically proven diagnostic and therapeutic procedures accepted in practice must be provided for the persons participating in the intervention, including those in the control group.

---

[17] For more on this topic, see Imre Szebik, 'Masked Ball: Ethics, Laws and Financial Contradictions in Hungarian Health Care' (2003) 9 *Science and Engineering Ethics* 109–124.

[18] Ministry of Health, Social Affairs and Family Decree No. 34 of 2003 (VI.7.) on the Health Science Council (see n. 7 *supra*).

[19] For more details on Hungarian medical law and research ethics, see Judit Sándor, 'Hungary, Medical Law' in the *International Encyclopedia of Laws* (Medical Law, Supplement 31, April 2003) (The Hague: Kluwer Law International, 2003).

[20] Ministry of Health Decree No. 24 of 2002 (V.9.) on The Implementation of Good Clinical Practice in the Conducts of Clinical Trials on Medicinal Products for Human Use (see n. 13 *supra*).

The biomedical intervention—including the interventions not carried out for therapeutic and preventive reasons—can only be carried out within the framework of Chapter VIII of the Health Care Act (Act CLIV of 1997) if:

- it is in the public interest and is scientifically sustainable;
- the expected results can be verified;
- the professional, personal and material circumstances necessary for careful preparation and verification of the evaluation are satisfied.

The health and the personal rights of the healthy person or the person under medical treatment involved in the biomedical intervention (in the following: the person involved in the research) must be secured. The biomedical intervention cannot endanger, without justification, the health condition of the person involved in the research.

The head of the research has the obligation to put together a detailed research plan and individual data-files about all the persons involved in the research. The data-file has to contain all data, facts, and events that are connected to the intervention and that may respectively influence the outcome of the research. The head of the research must send the research plan and the data-file to the director of the institute—non-affiliated doctors must send them to the director of the capital or county hospital with responsibility for their area.

If the authorization for the biomedical intervention[21] is not from the director of the institution, then, before starting the intervention, the consent of the director of the institution is required as well. Biomedical intervention—unless laws provide differently—can only be carried out on patients or healthy persons who undertake it voluntarily. Carrying out biomedical intervention requires the preliminary written consent of the person involved in the research.

Biomedical intervention can, even if ethical-scientific approval is given, only be started if the person involved in the research or respectively his or her legal representative has been informed in detail, by the director of the research or based on his or her authorization, by another doctor participating in the research, about all the facts, circumstances or events that are connected or could be connected to the intervention.

Information has to be provided especially about the purpose and the course of the research, the interventions necessary for the research, the frequency of the interventions, the possible and expected effects and side effects connected to the research, possible advantages and risks and possible consequences. Information must also be given concerning the fact that the consent to participate in the research can be withdrawn any time, including orally, and that in case of any damage to their health condition, they may ask for compensation of damages. This information has to include explanation of any medical terminology.

Such information has to be included in the document referring to the consent, including withdrawal of consent. Reimbursement of expenses can be given to the

---

[21] Health Care Act, Article 161(4), see n.5 *supra*.

person involved in the research—unless the intervention was made for therapeutic purposes.

The interests of the persons involved in the research are represented—for medical purposes—by a doctor who is not participating in the research and is appointed by the director of the institution (appointed doctor of the institution). If more than one doctor is needed, he or she can be appointed. In selecting the appointed doctor of the institution, the preference of the patient has to be considered. The appointed doctor of the institution has to be informed regularly—without special request—about the standing of the biomedical intervention, and any occurring problems. Information must be given immediately if the appointed doctor requests it.

It is the task of the appointed doctor of the institution to monitor the health condition of the research participants. For this purpose they keep in touch regularly with them, provide information for them, initiate professional help, examine them regularly, in the case of a complaint immediately report this to the director of the institution, and take part in the supervision and evaluation of the research.

## Ethical Monitoring of Research Projects

Biomedical intervention is continuously supervised from a professional, scientific and ethical point of view by the director of the institution and by the chief doctor of the department professionally in charge. The appointed doctor of the institution also has to be involved in the supervision.

The health condition of the person involved in the research has to be observed and documented carefully before starting the research, continuously during the research and after the research.

### Informed Consent Process

Written information required under the Decree[22] should include the following elements:

- data on the scope of the research;
- the experimental nature of the research;
- the object of the research;
- the expected duration of the research;
- the number of research subjects;
- biomedical interventions and their frequency;
- other available treatments;
- information about changes in therapy and its impact on the research subjects' health;
- the expected consequences of the research;

---

[22] Decree of the Minister of Health No. 23 of 2002 (V.9) on Biomedical Research on Human Beings, n. 5 *supra*, Article 4(4).

- the benefits of the research (if no benefit is expected then it has to be stated why the research is necessary), the method of selecting different research groups, compensation for potential damages and a statement describing any compensation for study participation (including expenses and access to medical care) must be given to research participants;
- data protection; and
- the name of the ethics review committee.

Research subjects should receive special information on the handling of their personal data.[23]

*Minimal Content of the Consent Form*

The written consent form that should be signed by each of the research subjects should include at least the following elements:[24]

- the name of the health institute where the research will be conducted;
- the name of the head of the research and names of the staff members who will provide information on the research;
- personal data of the research subject (name, mother's maiden name, date and place of birth, social security number, address);
- statement of the consent;
- date of signature;
- signature of the researcher who provided the information;
- list of any relevant research conducted on animals.

*Mandatory Elements of the Research Project*

The following data are considered as data of public interest:

- the purpose and relevance of the research including a description of the expected results;
- the background and justification of the scientific research;
- an evaluation of the anticipated benefits and requirements, including bibliography;
- arrangement for the recruitment of the research subjects, selection criteria, projected number of research subjects and their distribution by gender and age;
- research methodology and the medical interventions to be applied;
- procedures in case of adverse events and injuries, provisions for indemnity or compensation in the event of injury;

---

[23] Ministry of Health Decree on Biomedical Research on Human Beings, n. 5 *supra*, Article 4(2)(j).
[24] Ministry of Health Decree on Biomedical Research on Human Beings, n. 5 *supra*, Article 4(5).

- the protocols on processing the personal and health data of the research subjects;
- guidelines for the statistical processing of research data;
- a statement made by the chief researcher on the compatibility of the research with the Hungarian laws and with the Helsinki Declaration.[25]

Data related to scientific hypotheses and the pre-clinical trial are not considered data of public interest.

*Termination and Suspension of the Research*

The researcher has to terminate the biomedical intervention immediately if he or she perceives that its continuation could be damaging to the person involved in the research.

In the case that an adverse effect occurs that justifies the interruption of the biomedical intervention, or an important change occurs in the circumstances on which the ethical-scientific opinion was based, the director of the institution must immediately suspend the intervention and notify the committee which gave the ethical-scientific opinion. The director of the institution must also suspend the research if more than one fifth of the persons involved in the research withdraw their consent.[26]

## Criminal Sanctions

A new sub-section of the Criminal Code, effective from 1 July 1998, concerns biomedical ethics.[27] Criminal activity classified here includes interference with the human genome,[28] human gamete usage,[29] the use of techniques that aim to select the sex of the unborn child,[30] human experiment research protocols,[31] embryo and

---

[25] Ministry of Health Decree on Biomedical Research on Human Beings, n. 5 *supra*, Article 8(3)(a)(i).
[26] Ministry of Health Decree on Biomedical Research on Human Beings, n. 5 *supra*, Article 15(1).
[27] 'Crimes Against the Order of Medical Interventions and Medical Research, and Against Self-Determination Related to Health Issues', Criminal Code, Title II, Chapter XII, Crimes Against Persons.
[28] Criminal Code, n. 27 *supra*, Section 173/A.
[29] Criminal Code, n. 27 *supra*, Section 173/B.
[30] Criminal Code, n. 27 *supra*, Section 173/C.
[31] Criminal Code, n. 27 *supra*, Section 173/D.

gamete research protocols,[32] violation of the rules of self-determination in the field of healthcare, and the sale for transplantation of human body parts and cadavers.[33]

Violations of these legal rules and norms is punishable by up to five years' imprisonment, with the exception of when the right to self-determination has been violated or a human body or corpse used, where the punishment is up to three years. In some cases attempting to commit these crimes is also punishable.[34]

Any intervention in the human genome, including alteration of a human embryo, is punishable by up to five years' imprisonment. If the alteration resulted in a change to the genome, the punishment is two to eight years' imprisonment.[35] Reproductive use of cadaver gametes, including the gametes of the dead embryo is punishable by up to five years' imprisonment. Sex selection is punishable by up to five years' imprisonment.[36] The only exception to this is the case where the sex selection of the human embryo is conducted in order to avoid an inheritable disease (Health Care Act 1997 No. CLIV, Article 182).

Violation of the rules on human research is punishable by up to five years' imprisonment.[37] Research conducted on an embryo or gametes without permission issued on the basis of the Public Health Act is punishable by up to five years' imprisonment.[38]

## Data Protection in Biomedical Research

Research subjects have to receive information about the methods of data protection before consenting to research. A general rule of data protection can also be applied here. Under Article 16/A(1) of the amended Data Protection Act,[39] the data subject may object to the data processing if the processing only serves the interests and rights of the data processor, except where it is prescribed by the Parliamentary Act.

Furthermore, the data subject may protest against processing or transfer of the data if it serves the purposes of marketing, opinion survey or scientific research. In addition to these instances, data subjects may protest against data processing if the law prohibits it in other cases.

---

[32] Criminal Code, n. 27 *supra*, Section 173/E–G. These Sections basically prohibit all forms of cloning for any reason except if done by, and strictly according to, a permission issued in line with the law on healthcare.

[33] Criminal Code, n. 27 *supra*, Section 173/I. This Section prohibits the unlawful obtaining and any kind of sale of all parts of the human body from the genes to the whole body.

[34] Criminal Code, n. 27 *supra*, Sections 173/B, E, F, G and I. Preparation is either a misdemeanor punishable by up to two years' imprisonment, or a crime in itself, punishable by up to three years' imprisonment.

[35] Criminal Code, n. 27 *supra*, 173/A (1).

[36] Criminal Code, n. 27 *supra*, Section 173/C (1).

[37] Criminal Code, n. 27 *supra*, Section 173/D.

[38] Criminal Code, n. 27 *supra*, Section 173/E.

[39] Parliamentary Act No. XLVIII of 2003 on the amendment of the Act on the Protection of Personal Data, Article 16/A(1).

**Conclusions**

As we have seen above, the ethical and professional review of medical research and the implementation of new protocols operates on three different levels in the Hungarian health system. Ethics committees, due to the composition of their members and the by-laws regulating their operation, generally focus on the parallel aspects of scientific merit and ethical acceptability.

On the national level, specialized committees monitor new and particularly sensitive research, such as genetic research on either human reproduction or the human embryo.

One of the most problematic issues that may arise on all three levels is how to ensure professional and political independence.[40] The law declares independence as a principle on which the operation of the ethics committees should be based. In practice, however, the ethics committees often neglect this principle by not involving patient rights representatives, ethicists, or other non-medical professionals in their work. There has been some change recently on the higher, national and regional levels—the committee membership now also includes highly educated professionals, often with two degrees, usually in medicine and law. This is very useful in many respects, but it may still be problematic in the case of representing the interests of research subjects. On the level of local ethics committees the problem is quite the opposite—there is a striking lack of expertise in ethics and ethical issues.

Ethics committees at the national level have a high prestige and they are often considered as the bearer of ultimate knowledge on almost any issue. This is partly due to the fact that the majority of the members are heads of university hospitals and senior professors who represent a variety of medical fields. Although ethics committees, even at the national level, may provide only scientific and ethical opinions on the implementation of new research projects, their opinions are often regarded as ultimate decisions in administrative licensing of the various new medical procedures and research protocols.

This widespread perception of the authority of the Health Science Council led to a rather unusual legal procedure in 2003. In this case, the Health Science Council was sued by a private company, and its clients, for the adverse consequences of the statements of the Council that collecting umbilical cord blood for storage and the future use of haematopoietic cells for the purposes of the therapy of the child constitutes research.[41] Although the Council does not have an independent legal personality, it had to act as the defendant in the civil proceeding.

---

[40] According to the World Health Organization (WHO) *Operational Guidelines for Ethics Committees that Review Biomedical Research* (Geneva: World Health Organization, 2000), independence is understood as independence from political, institutional, professional and market influences.

[41] The use of umbilical cord blood stem cells for transplantation treatment holds exciting promise, but this area of medical science is still largely investigational. It was only in 1988 that French researchers performed the first successful stem cell transplantation using

During recent years three Health Ministry Decrees on biomedical research on human subjects have been adopted. These Decrees have improved the quality of ethical review by providing new and detailed provisions on mandatory elements of the research protocols. Due to time pressure and many protocols on the agenda of the committees, however, it is often difficult to conduct serious and careful discussions on the scientific merits and ethical aspects of the research.

Issues of data protection are discussed together with other legal and ethical conditions for lawful research in the ethical review process.

In the future a new Parliamentary Act will be adopted on the protection of genetic data in biomedical research and in the operation of biobanks. The conceptual framework of the law is currently being circulated among all interested and relevant public and professional bodies.

---

umbilical cord blood. The transplant was taken from a newborn and given to a five-year-old sibling with a severe anaemia syndrome that included skeletal defects.

# Chapter 13

# Research Ethics Committees in Ireland

Deirdre Madden[*] and Maeve McDonagh[†]

## Establishment of RECs

The system for ethical review of medical research in Ireland was streamlined in 2004 with the introduction of the European Communities (Clinical Trials on Medicinal Products for Human Use) Regulations (S.I. No. 190 of 2004). Under these regulations the Minister for Health shall be the Ethics Committees Supervisory Body, which is the body responsible for recognizing and monitoring ethics committees in the State. The 2004 Regulations apply only to investigations or studies of medicinal products and do not cover non-interventional trials. Non-interventional trials are defined as those involving trials of licensed medicines that are used within the terms of the licence.

Under the Regulations a clinical trial may only be started or conducted in Ireland if:

- the ethics committee has issued a favourable opinion;
- the Irish Medicines Board (IMB) has granted an authorization;
- and the sponsor or legal representative of the sponsor is established within the European Community.

Clinical trials are defined in the 2004 Regulations as studies on clinical, pharmacological, pharmacodynamic or pharmacokinetic effects or studies to identify adverse reactions to investigational medicinal products. Investigational medicinal products include placebo products and both authorized and unauthorized medicines with any type of active substance, including herbal and homeopathic products.

The Regulations stipulate that ethics committees must be established by appointing authorities. Appointing authority is defined as the institution on whose behalf application for recognition of an ethics committee is made. It includes a health board, hospital, university, or other similar higher education body. The ethics committee must consist of expert and lay members, the latter being defined as a member who is not and never has been a registered medical practitioner or registered dentist, and who does not in the course of his or her employment provide

---

[*] Lecturer in the UCC Law Department, Cork, Ireland.
[†] Associate Professor in the UCC Law Department, Cork, Ireland.

medical, dental or nursing care, or participate in the promotion or conduct of clinical research. An ethics committee must consist of not more than 21 members, of which one third shall be lay members.

## General Powers of RECs

As described above, approval by a recognized ethics committee is an essential part of the statutory scheme. Where IMB approval is granted for a clinical trial, it may not proceed until the ethics committee for the trial has given approval under the 2004 Regulations. IMB approval remains a statutory requirement. Under the 2004 Regulations an ethics committee must have issued a favourable opinion in relation to the trial, and the IMB must have granted an authorization, before commencement of the trial.

Part 8 of the 2004 Regulations provides penalties for contravention of the provisions of the Regulations. Any alleged offence may be prosecuted by the IMB. Section 44(7) of the Regulations provides that a person guilty of an offence under these regulations shall be liable on summary conviction to a fine not exceeding 3 000 Euros or to imprisonment for a term not exceeding six months, or both. Defences of due diligence and reasonable precautions are available.

## General Legal Responsibility of RECs

All trials must be conducted in accordance with current legislation and good clinical practice. Ethics committees must have regard to specified matters under the legislation such as the objectives of the trial, qualifications of investigators, selection of participants, confidentiality, consent, payments, and any other matters that may be prescribed. Therefore ethics committees could reject a trial that was considered to be unethical even if lawful.

The issue of disclosure of information may have to be re-visited as the Clinical Trials Directive 2001 (2001/20/EC) requires that the research subject be given the opportunity to understand the objectives and risks of the trial. The 2004 Regulations provide for the subject to have had an interview with the investigator, or a member of the investigating team, in which he or she must be given the opportunity to understand the nature and objectives of the trial. Also in relation to minors and legally incapacitated adults, the issue of provision of information and indication of refusal is important and may impact on the current regulatory system. The 2004 Regulations provide that the explicit wish of a minor not to participate must be taken into consideration by the investigator, while the minor must receive information about the trial commensurate with his or her maturity and capacity to understand. Similar provisions apply to incapacitated adults.

It is difficult to know the attitude of ethics committees in practice, as there is no collective REC or umbrella body from which such information can be gleaned.

A recent guide published by the Irish Council of Bioethics[1] advises ethics committees and investigators to be aware of the Data Protection Acts 1988–2003 and their obligations under those Acts. It specifically sets out the considerations that should be taken into account in this regard as the following:

- who will have access to personal data of the research subject;
- what provisions are in place to ensure the confidentiality and security of personal information concerning research subjects;
- the extent to which data will be anonymized;
- how samples or data will be obtained, and the purposes for which they will be used;
- how long samples or data will be kept;
- to which countries the samples or data will be sent.

---

[1] *Operational Procedures for Research Ethics Committees: Guidance 2004* (Dublin: The Irish Council for Bioethics, 2004). Available online at http://www.bioethics.ie/pdfs/guide.pdf, last accessed 16 May 2005.

# Chapter 14

# Research Ethics Committees in Italy's Legal System[*]

Roberto Lattanzi[†]

## Research Ethics Committees and Italy's Delay in Regulating Them

Authoritative scholars have long been remarking on the delay with which Italy's legal system is shifting its focus of attention to the '"concrete" concept of individual, relating no longer to a qualification, i.e. the capacity to have rights, but to the individual as such in all its components, starting from his or her life'.[1]

The effects of this lack of attention have also influenced the approach to the protection of individuals in medical and scientific research, both at its broadest scope, and in connection with clinical trials—which is actually the most studied area, though narrower in scope. Indeed, despite significant exceptions,[2] this is one of the least favoured topics in literature, partly because it has long been regulated exclusively via secondary legislation—and at times, even by provisions of an administrative nature.[3]

---

[*] I wish to thank Mr. Antonio Caselli for his help in translating this text.

[†] Legal adviser at the Italian Data Protection Authority, Rome. Researcher at the Catholic University of Milan.

[1] L. Mengoni, 'La tutela giuridica della vita materiale nelle varie età dell'uomo' (1982) *Rivista trimestrale diritto processuale civile*, 1117, 1136.

[2] Some of the first considerations can be found in M. Barni and G. Segre, 'La sperimentazione dei farmaci sull'uomo' (1970) *Politica del diritto*, 285; F. Bricola, 'I problemi giuridici relativi alla sperimentazione dei farmaci', in *Regioni e ordinamento farmaceutico* (Bologna: Cooperativa libraria universitaria editrice, 1973) and now in *Scritti di diritto penale* (I, Milano: Giuffrè, 1997), 844; F. Mantovani, *I trapianti e la sperimentazione umana nel diritto italiano e straniero* (Padova: Cedam, 1974), 758; A.M. Sandulli, 'La sperimentazione clinica sull'uomo' (1978) *Diritto e società*, 507, 511; the need for social control mechanisms concerning research by means of 'the health care organisation as a whole' was stressed by P. Perlingieri, *La personalità umana nell'ordinamento giuridico* (Napoli: ESI, 1972), 330.

[3] See, however, the studies by A. Bellelli, *Aspetti civilistici della sperimentazione umana* (Padova: Cedam, 1983); S. Sica, *Sperimentazione umana, disciplina francese e esperienza italiana* (Napoli: ESI, 1990); and L. Chieffi, *Ricerca scientifica e tutela della persona. Bioetica e garanzie costituzionali* (Napoli: ESI, 1993).

In any case, the cultural backwardness of our legal system with regard to these issues[4] prevented the development of autonomous regulatory standards, so that currently our legal experience draws inspiration from derivative (statutory) rules, that is, imported rules, and few or no significant contributions could be lent to their development.[5]

The discussion on bioethics should be credited with having kept this seemingly peripheral sector of the legal system 'in the limelight',[6] which applies particularly to the role played by research ethics committees—which is addressed here.[7] However, a key factor accounting for the implementation of standards

---

[4] This is the view held by Italy's CNB (Comitato nazionale per la bioetica), *Orientamenti per i comitati etici in Italia* (2001), and published online at http://www.palazzochigi.it /bioetica/testi/130701.html (last accessed: 16 May 2005): 'undoubtedly, neither the healthcare sector nor civil society felt the need for setting up ethics committees at that time. In the literature of those days as well as in the document drafted by the CNB in 1992, reference was made to this "lack of interest" and several possible explanations were mentioned [...]'. Major doubts on ethics committees were raised by M. Portigliatti Barbos, 'I comitati etici tra urgenza e disincanto' (1995) *Diritto penale e processo*, 1246.

[5] There are several well-known documents available at international level. To quote only the most important ones, reference can be made to the so-called Nuremberg Code (of 1946), followed by the Helsinki Declaration of 1964 (repeatedly amended). More generally, the main outline of 'biolaw' was developed outside Italy's legal system, which was tardier in catching up with international standards. See, with regard specifically to informed consent in connection with clinical trials, P. Zatti, 'Il diritto a scegliere la propria salute (in margine al caso S. Raffaele)' (2000) II *Nuova giurisprudenza civile commentata*, 1, 11. This is also shown by the comparative analysis carried out in Camera dei Deputati—Servizio Studi, *I comitati di bioetica*, X Legisl. (Roma: Camera dei Deputati, 1989), 307; updated information is available in Camera dei Deputati, Materiali di legislazione comparata, *I comitati etici nei principali paesi europei* (Roma: Camera dei Deputati, 1999).

[6] The establishment of ethics committees in connection with research activities is one of the first examples of an institutional mechanism created to cope with the relationship between science and society, which is nowadays of paramount importance—in particular having regard to their 'mixed' composition, which does not only include experts.

[7] See, in particular, P. Cattorini, 'I comitati d'etica negli ospedali' (1988) *Aggiornamenti sociali*, 415; S. Spinsanti, *I comitati di etica in ospedale* (Milano: Edizioni paoline, 1988); V. Ghetti (ed.), *I comitati etici* (Milano: F. Angeli, 1988); G. Dalla Torre, 'Profili giuridici dei Comitati etici (fra ius conditum e ius condendum)' (1989) *Iustitia*, 381, 386 (and in G. Dalla Torre, *Bioetica e diritto. Saggi* (Torino: Giappichelli, 1993), 139) starts his analysis by stating that: 'in Italy there is no national legislation concerning "medical ethics committees"', and reports on the first initiatives in this sector, in particular at regional level; see also F. D'Agostino, 'I Comitati etici. Riflessioni preliminari' (1989) *Iustitia*, 75; more recently, interesting considerations can be found in D. Neri, 'La bioetica: storia e problemi' (1999) *Ragiusan*, 162; R. Mordacci, *Bioetica della sperimentazione. Fondamenti e linee-guida* (Milano: F. Angeli, 1997), 683; a historical perspective on RECs can be found in V. P. Benciolini, R. Pegoraro and F. Cadelli, 'Il servizio di bioetica dell'azienda ospedaliera di Padova: un'esperienza italiana di consulenza e formazione etico-clinica' (1999) *Medicina e morale*, 61. Legal scholars did not fail to take part in the bioethical discussion: see P. Pajardi, 'I comitati etici ospedalieri: che cosa potrebbero essere e che cosa non devono essere' (1987) *Iustitia*, 315 (and in Unione giuristi cattolici italiani, *Problemi giuridici della*

developed elsewhere has quite likely been the risk of being excluded from international multi-centre research.[8]

It is true that nowadays one can safely maintain that Italy's legal system has finally 'caught up' with the most advanced systems worldwide, at least based on the *'black letters of law'*;[9] still, this is not enough to allay the misgivings concerning effectiveness of the existing regulations.[10] Indeed, it looks as if some measure of distrust is hovering over the whole sector of so-called 'biolaw'. Only in this way can one account for the accusation made by authoritative scholars in respect of the 'Italian paradox', that is the 'blatant dissociation between solemnly affirmed principles and absent or clearly inadequate regulations'.[11]

## Ethics Committees in Domestic Law

The role of ethics committees—in the broadest sense of the term—only started being outlined more precisely in the 1990s via several regulatory measures that laid down their institutional features at different levels. This process can basically be said to have been finalized; it started when the 'National Bioethics Committee' was set-up,[12] which served as a model subsequently reproduced at a regional level.[13]

---

*biomedicina*. Atti del XXXVIII Convegno nazionale di studio, Roma, 4–6 dicembre 1987 (Milano: Giuffrè, 1989); G. Caselli, 'I comitati d'etica: alcune notazioni giuridiche' (1991) *Diritto di famiglia e delle persone*, 355; G. Gerin (ed.), *Funzione e funzionamento dei comitati etici* (Padova: Cedam, 1991).

[8] See CNB (2001), n. 4 *supra*.

[9] The first steps made by our legal system concerning clinical trials, partly in order to bridge the existing gaps, date back to Act no. 519 of 7 August 1973 (see Sandulli, 'La sperimentazione clinica sull'uomo' (1978) *Diritto e società*, 507, 511); a detailed survey of the regulatory measures adopted over the years also concerning the drug industry can be found in G. Scuderi, 'Storia della normativa italiana in materia di medicinali fino alle norme più recenti sulla valutazione bioetica della sperimentazione clinica' (2001) *Medicina e morale*, 509.

[10] That these doubts are grounded is shown quite clearly by the Circular Letter issued by the Ministry of Health on 12 October 1999 concerning Irregularities in Authorization Proceedings and Implementing Measures Related to Drug Clinical Trials (in *Gazzetta Ufficiale* 29 October 1999, no. 255), in which researchers and sponsors were called upon to abide by the applicable legislation concerning research.

[11] F. D. Busnelli, *Bioetica e diritto privato. Frammenti di un dizionario* (Torino: Giappichelli, 2001), 222.

[12] This was done via a Prime Minister's Decree of 28 March 1990; the National Committee is not specifically competent as regards trials.

[13] Based on the tasks committed to regions in the healthcare sector as also related to medical and scientific research (see the Constitutional Court's decision of 21 December 2000, no. 569, (2001) *Foro italiano*, I, 1082), regional bioethics committees were set up. They act as links and coordinating entities in respect of the individual ethics committees at local level as well as between the latter and the National Committee. If requested, they provide advice to regional bodies; see, for instance, the regional law of Abruzzi region no. 100 of 18 May 2000 (Setting up the Regional Bioethics Committee). However, in some regions only the

However, a major step was made as regards human experimentation following the 'incorporation' into our legal system of the 'good clinical practice rules', which were initially implemented by the Ministerial Decree of 27 April 1992[14] and subsequently by the Decree of 15 July 1997.[15] Thanks to these measures—both resulting from the enactment of Community law—the legal status of local ethics committees could ultimately be recognized within Italy's legal system, even though they already existed in some areas after decisions made voluntarily by some research bodies. These ethics committees are independent, mixed-composition bodies,[16] in charge of supervising experimentation. They are to be set up within healthcare units and/or authorized research institutes[17] and supervised by the

---

regional ethics committee has been set up so far, which is therefore also in charge of approving research protocols.

[14] *Disposizioni sulle documentazioni tecniche da presentare a corredo delle domande di autorizzazione all'immissione in commercio di specialità medicinali per uso umano, in attuazione della Direttiva no. 91/507/CEE*, in *Gazzetta Ufficiale,* 15 June 1992, no. 139, S.O. This decree transposed Directive 91/507/EEC, of 19 July 1991, published in the *Official Journal of the European Communities* no. L 270 of 26 September 1991, which replaced the annex to Directive no. 75/318/EEC Concerning Approximation of Member States' Legislation Applying to Rules and Analytical, Pharmacological-toxic and Clinical Protocols in Respect of Drug Testing.

[15] Decree by the Minister of Health no. 162 of 15 July 1997 on Transposing EU Good Clinical Practice Guidelines to Perform Drug Clinical Trials, in the *Gazzetta Ufficiale* of 18 August 1997. See, in this regard, P. Preziosi, 'La valutazione del protocollo di sperimentazione' (1998) *Medicina e morale,* 731.

[16] Based on the Ministerial Decree of 18 March 1998 (Reference Guidelines Applying to the Establishment and Operation of Ethics Committees), the membership of ethics committees should be such as to ensure, on the whole, the necessary skills and experience to assess ethical and scientific and methodological issues related to the trials at stake. To that end, ethics committees should preferably include a core set of experts, that is, two clinicians with documented experience in and knowledge of controlled and randomized clinical trials, a bio-statistician with documented experience in, and knowledge of, controlled and randomized trials, a pharmacologist, a pharmacist from the Pharmaceutical Service of the hospital and/or territorial institution where the clinical trial is expected to take place, the healthcare director and, where applicable—for example, in the case of Istituti di Ricovero e Cura a Carattere Scientifico (IRCCS)—the scientific director of the institution where the trial is expected to be performed, and an expert in legal matters. The other members will have to be skilled in and/or competent for the following sectors: general medicine, bioethics, nursing, voluntary assistance and/or associations for patients' support. It is appropriate for a significant portion of the members not to be dependent upon the institution that avails itself of the committee and not to have medical and/or related technical skills.

[17] Whose organization and operation are regulated by regions and Trento and Bolzano autonomous provinces, having regard to the indications and minimum requirements set out at national level as well as by setting up a register of the ethics committees in their respective geographic areas (Section 12-*bis*, paragraph 9, Legislative Decree no. 502 of 30 December 1992, *Riordino della disciplina in materia sanitaria, a norma dell'articolo 1 della legge 23 ottobre 1992, n. 421*, in *Gazzetta Ufficiale* 30 December 1992, no. 305, S.O.); see also Decreto Ministeriale 19 Marzo 1998, *Riconoscimento della idoneità dei centri per la sperimentazione clinica dei medicinali*, in *Gazzetta Ufficiale* 28 May 1998, no. 122.

Ministry of Health.[18] Detailed regulations concerning them are set out in two Decrees issued by Italy's Minister of Health on 18 March 1998, of which one contains Guidelines Concerning the Establishment and Operation of Ethics Committees.[19]

The regulatory framework applying to experimentation was recently completed in Italy by Legislative Decree no. 211 of 24 June 2003,[20] which transposed EC Directive 2001/20—even though one might more appropriately say that the Community legislation was materially translated—into Italian law.

To provide the full picture concerning research ethics committees, reference should be made to the 'National Ethics Committee for Research and Clinical Trials', which was set up by paragraph 10 of Section 12-*bis* of Legislative Decree no. 502 of 30 December 1992[21] and regulated in detail via a Ministerial Decree of 23 November 1999.[22] In addition to advising on ethical and technical and scientific issues within the framework of the Ministry of Health, this committee is in charge

---

[18] Under Section 7(6) of the Ministerial Decree of 18 March 1998 (Mechanisms to Exempt the Drugs Used in Clinical Trials from Assessment), the Ministry of Health is to perform supervision on a sample basis as regards setting up and operation of ethics committees. In particular, a Ministerial Decree of 30 May 2001 concerning Inspections on Compliance with Good Manufacturing and Clinical Practice Rules, published in *Official Journal* no. 216 of 17 September 2001, provides that the assessment is to be aimed at evaluating compliance of ethics committees' activities with the procedures in force as well as compliance of the opinions issued by local ethics committees with scientific positions at national and Community level (Section 2). See also Ministero della Salute—Direzione generale della valutazione dei medicinali e della farmacovigilanza, *La sperimentazione clinica dei medicinali in Italia*, 1° Rapp. Nazionale, 2001, online at http://oss-sper-clin.sanita.it (last accessed on 16 May 2005).

[19] Ministerial Decree of 18 March 1998, Reference Guidelines Applying to Setting up and Operation of Ethics Committees; reference should also be made to a Ministerial Decree of 18 March 1998, Mechanisms to Exempt the Drugs Used in Clinical Trials from Assessment, and to the Ministerial Decree of 19 March 1998 concerning Recognition of Centres Qualifying for Drug Clinical Trials (all of these were published in *Official Journal* no. 122 of 28 May 1998). See also Circular Letter no. 8 by the Ministry of 10 July 1997—Drug Clinical Trials and Comitato Nazionale per la Bioetica, *La sperimentazione dei farmaci*, (Roma, 1992). As for jurisprudence, see P. Zavatti, A. Trenti and C. Salvioli, 'Drug Trials and Good Clinical Practice in Italy: Legal and Ethics-Deontological Aspects' (1996) 3 *European Journal of Health Law* 301, 303; an earlier text is N. Silvestri, *La sperimentazione sull'uomo* (Padova: Liviana, 1990).

[20] Implementing Directive 2001/20/EC on Application of Good Clinical Practice in Performing Drug Clinical Trials, in *Gazzetta Ufficiale* 9 August 2003, no. 184, S.O. As regards preparatory work, see Camera dei Deputati—Servizio Studi, Pareri al Governo, *Attuazione della direttiva 2001/20/CE sulla sperimentazione clinica di medicinali ad uso umano*, schema di decreto legislativo (Article 1, legge no. 39/2002), no. 171, XIV *Legislatura*, 9 Aprile 2003 (Roma: Camera dei Deputati, 2003).

[21] Reorganization of the Provisions Concerning Health Care Pursuant to Section 1 of Act no. 421 of 23 October 1992, in *Gazzetta Ufficiale* 30 December 1992, no. 305, S.O.

[22] Setting up and Tasks of the National Ethics Committee for Drug Clinical Trials, pursuant to Legislative Decree no. 229 of 19 June 1999 as published in *Gazzetta Ufficiale* 27 January 2000, no. 21.

of coordinating ethical and scientific assessment of multi-centre clinical trials of substantial national interest.

## The Tasks Entrusted to Research Ethics Committees

Research ethics committees are required 'to verify that the research subject's safety, integrity and human rights are protected, thereby affording public safeguards'.[23] This is quite broad wording which is focused mainly on the protection of bodily integrity, that is, health, as well as on fostering the research subjects' self-determination by checking the information provided with regard to the specific research protocol(s).

The wording used in good clinical practice rules to refer to the tasks entrusted to ethics committees, basically reproduced in Legislative Decree no. 211/2003,[24] is quite broad and somewhat blurred; however, the tasks were specified more precisely in Section 6(2) of the aforementioned Legislative Decree, modelled on Article 6 of Directive 2001/20/EC. The items an ethics committee is required to take into consideration in providing its opinions are mainly of a technical and scientific nature, as well as being focused on the quality of the information provided to research subjects in order for the latter to consent to participation in a trial on the basis of the highest possible degree of information and awareness.[25]

---

[23] See Section 3(1) of Ministerial Decree of 15 July 1997, and point 1.27 of GCP. The provision contained in Section 2(1) (m), of Legislative Decree no. 211/2003 is no different. This same principle was upheld by the Constitutional Court in its decision no. 569 of 21 December 2000 (2001) *Foro italiano* I, 1082.

[24] See n. 20 *supra*.

[25] In particular, ethics committees are required to assess:

a.   relevance and importance of the clinical trial and study design;

b.   whether the analysis of expected benefits and risks fulfils the requirements set out in Section 3(1), letter a), and whether the relevant conclusions are justified;

c.   the protocol;

d.   trial researcher's and co-operators' qualifications;

e.   the researcher's file;

f.   adequacy of the healthcare institution;

g.   adequacy and completeness of the written information to be communicated to research subjects and the procedure to be followed for them to provide their informed consent, and fulfilment of the conditions allowing enrolment of research subjects unable to provide their informed consent;

h.   provisions applying to payment of damages and/or compensation in case of death resulting from the clinical trial;

i.   provisions on insurance against damage affecting research subjects to cover tort liability in respect of researchers and sponsors;

l.   amounts and payment mechanisms concerning fees and/or compensation and/or sums to be paid to researchers, and the allowances, if any, to be paid to research subjects as well as the relevant items in the agreement between trial sponsor and trial centre;

In the light of the above premises, the uncertainty surrounding the functions entrusted to these committees can be said to have been significantly reduced. Indeed, the technical and scientific components as well as the preventive assessment of the prerequisites for deciding that a given trial is reasonably safe, would appear to prevail over exclusively ethical considerations.

### The Value Conferred on Opinions Rendered by Ethics Committees— Towards 'Professional' Research Ethics Committees?

Taking account of the aforementioned contents, one might reasonably argue that 'ethical' as an adjective applying to the context of drug testing can be misleading; indeed, although the committees in charge of approving research protocols continue to be referred to as 'ethics committees', one of the functions traditionally fulfilled by ethics committees is being considerably downsized.[26] Rather than being fora hosting cultural debates and ethical discussions,[27] they tend to give priority to tasks that mostly require technical and professional skills.[28] This trend can be actually accounted for by one of the original—therefore fundamental—tasks committed to these bodies, that is, the protection of research subjects. Supervision and safeguards are no longer a matter of prevention, as they tend to go hand in hand with the whole research activity via the monitoring of its progress.[29]

---

m. enrolment mechanisms of research subjects and the information procedure implemented to disseminate knowledge of the trial by complying with the provisions laid down in the good clinical practice rules as well as with the legislation in force.

[26] See, in this regard, the documents published by CNB, *I comitati etici*, adopted on 27 February 1992 (published in http://www.palazzochigi.it/bioetica/testi/270292.html, last accessed on 16 May 2005); CNB, *I Comitati Etici in Italia: problematiche recenti*, adopted on 18th April 1997 (published at http://www.palazzochigi.it/bioetica/testi/ 180497.html, last accessed on 16 May 2005), and CNB, '*Orientamenti per i comitati etici in Italia*', adopted on 13 July 2001 (see n. 4 *supra*).

[27] The diminished importance of ethical issues in the regulatory framework is also pointed out by A. Loreti Beghè and L. Marini, 'Il ruolo dei Comitati etici tra regole internazionale, disciplina comunitaria e normativa italiana sulla sperimentazione clinica dei farmaci' (2000) *Iustitia*, 51, 53 ss. and 69 ss.

[28] See the contributions collected with particular regard to clinical ethics by M. Picozzi, M. Tavani and P. Cattorini (eds.), *Verso una professionalizzazione del bioeticista: analisi teorica e ricadute pratiche* (Milano: Giuffrè, 2003), *passim*.

[29] As for the expected changes in the *modus operandi* of RECs, S. Holm, 'Ethics Committees in Northern Europe' (2002) XVIII *Politeia* 67, 54, 57 wrote that 'RECs will begin to monitor whether researchers perform the research according to the approved research protocol and with the approved patient information. A number of cases have indicated that some researchers do not adhere to the approved research protocol or do not inform the committees of changes'. The guidelines set out in the Ministerial Decree of 18 March 1998 committed additional tasks to ethics committees, that is, a) assessing trial progress reports, b) assessing adverse events and inadequate progress of the clinical trial, also in view of reviewing the approved protocol, and c) supervising the communications which sponsors are required to provide.

However, these regulatory developments are resulting in what has been termed the crisis of ethics committees seen as 'single multi-functional bodies',[30] which accordingly raises the issue of whether it might be appropriate to distinguish at least between the tasks entrusted to such committees—if not between different types of committee.[31] In this way, one would distinguish between ethical assessment of clinical practice and dissemination of bioethical culture on the one hand, and the markedly technical functions related more specifically to assessing and monitoring drug testing protocols on the other.[32]

Indeed, the increased importance that is attached to the upstream and—as explained above—downstream supervision functions fulfilled by ethics committees, is mirrored by the value conferred by our legal system on the opinions rendered by these committees with regard to research. As to this issue, one may no longer maintain that the opinions of research ethics committees are not binding.[33] The Decree by the Minister of Health of 15 July 1997 already provided expressly—further to similar requirements laid down in the GCP (Good Clinical Practice) such as those in points 1.27, 1.31, 2.6, 4.4.1—that 'the independent ethics committees referred to in Annex 1 to this Decree shall be in charge of *approving performance* of the individual trials in accordance with the mechanisms set out therein …. No clinical drug trial may be carried out failing approval by the competent ethics committee as per paragraph 1' (emphasis added).[34] This conclusion is supported further by Legislative Decree no. 211/2003.[35]

---

[30] See CNB, *I comitati etici in Italia*, n. 26 *supra*.

[31] See CNB, *I comitati etici*, n. 26 *supra*; this stance was supported, in particular, in CNB, *I comitati etici: problematiche recenti*, n. 26 *supra*; and in CNB, *Orientamenti per i comitati etici in Italia*, see n. 4 *supra*; see also R. Celesti, G. Mara and E. Profumo, 'I Comitati etici come strumento di verifica dell'attività medica' (1990) I *Rivista italiana di medicina legale*, 401; this distinction is also drawn in F. Freni, *Biogiuridica e pluralismo etico-religioso: questioni di bioetica, codici di comportamento e comitati etici* (Milano: Giuffrè, 2000), 270.

[32] This is also the prevailing orientation resulting from the overview carried out by Camera dei Deputati, Materiali di legislazione co Celesti mparata, *I comitati etici nei principali paesi europei*, (Roma: Camera dei Deputati, 1999), 1 ss.; as for jurisprudence, see M. Franzosi, 'Clinical trials' (2001) *Rassegna di diritto farmaceutico*, 1; A. Manna, 'Sperimentazione medica', in *Enciclopedia del diritto* (Milano: Giuffrè, 2000), Agg., vol. IV, 1120 and, specifically with regard to the REC members' liability, 1136 ss.; see also M. Portigliatti Barbos, 'Sperimentazione medica', in *Digesto* IV edition, *Discipline penalistiche* (Torino: Utet, 1997), vol. XIII, 543, which includes wide-ranging bibliographic references.

[33] L. Eusebi, 'Profilo giuridico dei Comitati etici', in C. Viafora (ed.), *Comitati etici. Una proposta bioetica per il mondo sanitario* (Padova: Gregoriana libreria editrice, 1995), 225 and 227.

[34] L. L. P. Tronconi, 'La disciplina del Comitato Etico per la sperimentazione dei farmaci nelle aziende sanitarie e negli IRCCS' (2002) *Rassegna di diritto farmaceutico*, 451, 455 considers that ethics committees are 'administrative bodies that are hierarchically independent both in discharging the required procedural tasks as regards intra-company clinical trials …, and in respect of other Committees by having regard to their hierarchical competence in this sector …, further to what is expressly provided for in secondary legislation (point 2.6, letters a) and b), Annex 1 to Ministerial Decree of 18 March 1998)'. This entails 'a change in the role played by Committees—being no longer merely advisory

**Unresolved Issues A: The (Ir)Responsibility of Ethics Committees**

One of the issues as yet unresolved relates to the liability, if any, of ethics committees with regard to research subjects for any damage incurred by the latter on account of the trial; this is actually compounded by the decision-making power conferred on their advisory activities, the increasingly technical features of their tasks as described above, and the watchdog role committed to them under the law.

Initially the liability of ethics committees was rejected by jurisprudence exactly on account of the non-binding nature of their opinions;[36] however, several doubts started being raised after the good clinical practice rules were introduced.[37] Of late, failing commented case law on this subject matter, it was considered desirable by several scholars that this issue should be solved by the legislation

---

fora, but veritable administrative bodies entitled to operate in accordance with specific regulatory criteria' (*ibid.*, 456). In the author's view, the administrative nature of the instruments issued by ethics committees is also supported by the contents of Circular Letter no. 6 of 2 September 2002 from the Ministry of Health, concerning the Activities Performed by Ethics Committees with Particular Regard to the so-called Observational Studies.

[35] See point 1.6, letter b), Annex 1, Ministerial Decree of 27 April 1992; see also Section 108 of Legislative Decree no. 230 of 17 March 1995, on the Implementation of Directives 89/618/Euratom, 90/641/Euratom, 92/3/Euratom, and 96/29/Euratom Concerning Ionizing Radiations (in *Gazzetta Ufficiale* 13 June 1995, no. 136, S.O.), providing that, as regards clinical trials, 'exposure of individuals for clinical trial purposes may only take place with said individuals' written consent after providing information on the risks related to exposure to ionizing radiation as well as exclusively within the framework of programmes notified to the Ministry of Health at least thirty days prior to their start. The documents to be transmitted shall include the binding opinion issued by the ethics committee, which shall be acquired in pursuance of the legislation in force'.

[36] Liability is disputed by G. Gualdi, 'La rilevanza giuridica dei comitati etici: considerazioni sul tema' (1992) *Iustitia*, 446, 454; the same applies to L. Eusebi, 'Controllo etico e tutela penale nella sperimentazione in ambito sanitario' (1993) *Rassegna italiana di criminologia*, 47, 64 ss., where the underlying assumptions are related to the features of the regulatory provision setting out the relevant obligations, and to L. Eusebi, 'Profilo giuridico dei Comitati etici', see n. 33, at 225; this view is also shared by P. Benciolini and C. Viafora, 'I comitati etici', in G. Giusti (ed.) *Trattato di medicina legale e scienze affini* (vol. I, Padova: Cedam, 1998), 683, 695; F. Freni, n. 31 *supra*, 280.

[37] This is the main problem, especially following 'incorporation' into our legal system of the 'good clinical practice rules' via the Ministerial Decree of 27 April 1992, containing an Annex with the 'Good Clinical Practice' rules of the Directive. In this regard, see Zanchetti, 'Profili etici e giuridici in tema di sperimentazione clinica', in P. Cattorini, R. Mordacci and M. Reichlin (eds.), *Introduzione allo studio della bioetica* (Milano: Europa scienze umane, 1996), 385; M. Zanchetti, 'La responsabilità giuridica del comitato etico di etica ospedaliera', in P. Cattorini (ed.), *Una verità in dialogo—Storia, metodologia e pareri di un comitato di etica* (Milano: Europa scienze umane, 1994), 78; this is in agreement with A. Manna, 'Sperimentazione medica', see n. 32, at 1137. However, a seemingly contrary view is supported by the Ministerial Decree of 15 July 1997, point 4.4.1. Provisions, whereupon Freni, see. n. 31, considered it appropriate to distinguish between bindingness of the opinions concerning ethical vs. scientific issues (284). However, only tort liability will be taken into account herein.

enacted to transpose Directive 2001/20/EC—which actually had not coped with this issue.[38]

This was not the case. Thus, the issue at stake—though tabled long ago[39]—is bound to remain unresolved. However, it could be argued that one should refrain from hastily recognizing the liability of RECs as such. Firstly, account should be taken of the overall framework laid down by Parliament in respect of research activities, whereby the insurance-based model was preferred over that based on tort liability with a view to holding research subjects harmless against any damage. An additional consideration to be made is that it would be inappropriate to provide for the liability of REC members—who could not but be jointly liable, unless provided otherwise by the law—without taking account of their different areas of competence; in short, one should re-consider the whole system for assessing research protocols,[40] which is obviously to be left to law-makers.

Furthermore, providing for some sort of liability in the absence of its clear-cut definition under the law would not appear to be desirable either. On the one hand, this would affect the 'alliance relationship' established between research subjects and RECs, and on the other hand it would run the risk of jeopardizing the performance of research activities because RECs might be tempted to follow an excessively cautious approach—in view of disclaiming any future responsibility. One should also wonder whether providing for this type of liability might not result in hampering participation in an REC—which is not usually compensated on the basis of professional fees.

### Unresolved Issues B: Prerogatives of RECs and Data Protection Laws

The research subject's confidentiality is commonly included among the safeguards to be afforded to participants in medical and scientific research. This is unanimously agreed upon.

However, the issue to be addressed here relates to the mechanisms allowing for this to occur as well as—in the light of the enactment of data protection legislation—the role, if any, to be played in this regard by ethics committees.[41]

---

[38] As to the need for the legislation transposing the Directive to clarify the legal status of ethics committees as well as their competence in connection with performance of clinical trials, see A. Loreti Beghè, 'Considerazioni sulla recente normativa Comunitaria sui Comitati etici nella sperimentazione clinica dei medicinali' (2002) vol. XVIII *Politeia* 67, 145, 151.

[39] See G. Ferrando, 'La sperimentazione sull'uomo' (1995) *Politica del diritto*, 485, 500 and 502 respectively.

[40] G. Umani Ronchi, G. Bolino and L. Bonaccorso, 'La responsabilità professionale nella sperimentazione farmaceutica' (2000) *Rivista italiana di medicina legale*, 733; F. Massimino, 'La responsabilità nelle sperimentazioni cliniche' (2000) *Danno e responsabilità*, 953.

[41] Further to the considerations made so far, as well as failing specific regulations applying to ethics committees apart from those concerning human clinical trials, my analysis will only focus on this issue.

This sector is sometimes considered to fall within the scope of competence of RECs, as shown by point XIV of the Appendix to the Additional Protocol to the Convention of Human Rights and Biomedicine concerning Biomedical Research (30 June 2004)[42]—where the information to be made available to ethics committees when assessing research is required to include 'arrangements to ensure respect for the private life of those persons who would participate in research and ensure the confidentiality of personal data'. Indeed, this provision is quite similar to the arrangements laid down in Italian legislation, although data protection is not expressly mentioned as one of the items to be taken into consideration by RECs with a view to forming their opinions (see, in this regard, Section 6(2) of Legislative Decree no. 211/2003). Section 8 of the latter decree lays down the mechanisms to request an opinion from an REC, and reads as follows: 'Having regard to the detailed guidelines published by the European Commission, the Minister of Health shall set out, in a decree, the form and documents that are necessary to submit a request for opinion to the ethics committee by also specifying, in particular, the information to be provided to research subjects and the appropriate safeguards for protecting personal data'.

This provision can be considered to transpose the requirement set out in Article 8 of Directive 2001/20/EC by making room for a mechanism according to which our legal system would be continuously (and automatically) adjusted to Community Law. At the same time, this raises the issue of whether any measure aimed at safeguarding the research subjects' personal data may be subjected to review by ethics committees.

The implied recognition that RECs would be empowered to perform this type of assessment insofar as they are the addressees of communications describing the adopted safeguards—as per Section 8 of Legislative Decree no. 211/2003—can be arguably challenged. In fact, point 2.11 of the GCP as adopted by Ministerial Decree of 18 March 1998 requires that 'any documents identifying the research subjects should be kept confidential by complying with privacy and confidentiality provisions contained in the applicable legislation'; however this obligation is imposed on researchers rather than on the REC, whose tasks are regulated by point 3.

This conclusion would appear to be supported, albeit indirectly, by the wording used in the legislation transposing the relevant Directive, as well as in the previous legislation. Personal data protection would appear not to fall under the scope of the assessment committed to RECs, it being entrusted to the Data Protection Authority (Garante per la protezione dei dati personali) on account of the explicit reference to the data protection provisions set out in Act no. 675/1996 (now superseded by Legislative Decree no. 196/2003) which are contained in Section 3(1), letter c), of Legislative Decree no. 211/2003.

In the light of data protection legislation, as well as based on the assumption that the basic decisions concerning processing operations are left to the individual data controller—that is, the individual researcher—only the latter can be said to be

---

[42] CETS No. 195, published online at the Council of Europe Treaty Office, http://conventions.coe.int/ (last accessed on 16 May 2005).

liable for the mechanisms implemented in using any personal data.[43] From this viewpoint, no role would appear to be committed to RECs failing a provision to this effect. Indeed, if RECs were required to advise on this issue, and the approval of a research programme were dependent upon compliance with their decisions—including possibly measures on data protection[44]—researchers could not but abide by such decisions on account of the binding nature of the opinion rendered, short of refraining to continue their research. Thus, it might happen that the data controller (that is, the researcher) would be liable for any unlawful feature of the processing as established by the Garante's subsequent audit, even if he or she were not directly responsible for the relevant decisions.

Thus, partly on account of the above reasons,[45] it would not appear to be appropriate for ethics committees to be empowered to issue advice on data protection issues within the framework of the opinions they are required to render in connection with trials. In fact, RECs are supervised by the Ministry of Health, which is not the entity in charge of, under law, deciding on personal data protection issues.

This view is further supported by the provisions contained in Section 110(1) of Legislative Decree no. 196/2003, whereby (in addition to other cases provided for by specific legislation[46]) the data subject's consent to the processing of his or her own medical data for scientific research purposes in the medical, biomedical and/or epidemiological sectors 'shall not be necessary if data subjects cannot be informed on specific grounds and the research programme has been the subject of a reasoned, favourable opinion by the geographically competent ethics committee as well as being authorised by the Garante' also via a general authorization pursuant to Section 40 of said Legislative Decree. As regards the issue at stake, this provision—which can be criticized from several viewpoints[47]—leaves it to the Garante to assess and authorize processing of data, obviously with regards to data protection requirements. In particular, the relevant authorization may only be

---

[43] Indeed, sponsors—most often pharmaceutical companies—usually have no contact with the research subject and only receive the personal data relating to the samples in an aggregated form.

[44] For instance, as regards re-wording the information notice for data subjects.

[45] Account should also be taken of the possible lack within the ethics committee of adequate skills in this sector, which may play an especially important role with regard to some specific trials.

[46] The data subject's consent to process data which refer to health with a view to scientific research purposes in the medical, biomedical or epidemiological sectors is not required if the research is provided for expressly in legislation and the latter expressly requires the processing to take place, or else if the research is part of a biomedical and/or healthcare research programme pursuant to Section 12-*bis* of Legislative Decree no. 502 of 30 December 1992 as subsequently amended—on condition that 45 days have elapsed following the relevant communication to the Garante as per Section 39.

[47] It would not be appropriate to carry out a detailed analysis of this instrument. However, it should be pointed out that, apart from the interpretive difficulties related to the 'in specific cases' wording, the provision at stake is meant to lay down additional cases in which it is allowed not to inform data subjects—and, accordingly, not to obtain their consent—in connection with processing medical data for research purposes.

granted if the research project is approved by the competent ethics committee. This interpretation is supported by the wording of the above provision; however, it should also be stressed that it would be meaningless for RECs to assess data protection requirements, as they could be reviewed in any case by the Garante thereafter.[48]

Therefore, the *en passe* seemingly incurred by our legal system might be overcome by arguing that the safeguards aimed at protecting personal data are to be communicated to RECs exclusively with a view to *informing* RECs rather than in order for said safeguards to be assessed. In any event any assessment, once performed, would not be binding on researchers.[49]

### Final Considerations: Which Model for Data Protection in Medical and Scientific Research?

In light of the above considerations, it can be stated that in Italy's legal system it is still necessary to clearly specify—first and foremost, in the researchers' interest—which entity among those taking part in a research activity is to say the last word on processing of the research subjects' personal data, and how to unambiguously set out the scope of competence as regards supervision—even though the latter is committed, in general, to the Garante per la protezione dei dati personali.

Indeed, it can reasonably be argued that the opacity of the interpretation resulting from an analysis of Italy's legislation cannot be accounted for exclusively by the 'inattentiveness' of our lawmakers; in fact, there are deeper reasons, which are probably related to the differences in the 'spirit' underlying Directive 2001/20/EC—which are bound to be mirrored in the national laws transposing the Directive itself as well as in any future regulations modelled after the Directive in the broader area of biomedical research. Indeed, the main body of the Directive is grounded on GCP rules. As mentioned above, adoption of this instrument was a major step forward with a view to the harmonization of the procedures implemented in medical trials not only at European level, but worldwide—by approximating the European, Japanese and US models.[50]

---

[48] It might be interesting to consider whether the authorization in question could be drafted by using general, all-purpose wording in pursuance of Section 40 of Legislative Decree no. 196/2003, rather than by taking account of the concrete circumstances.

[49] Indeed, this solution would not rule out the supervision of data protection issues by the committee, which might subsequently notify the Garante—also pursuant to the requirement laid down in Section 17 of Legislative Decree no. 196/2003—of any components in a research project that would appear questionable, in the committee's view, as for their compliance with data protection legislation.

[50] This objective is referred to in the *incipit* of GCP ICH E6: *Good Clinical Practice: Consolidated Guideline*, CPMP/ICH/135/95, which reads as follows: 'The objective of this ICH GCP Guideline is to provide a unified standard for the European Union (EU), Japan and the United States to facilitate the mutual acceptance of clinical data by the regulatory authorities in these jurisdictions. The guideline was developed with consideration of the current good clinical practices of the European Union, Japan, and the United States, as well

Keeping this consideration in mind—which is really indispensable—it may be easier to realize why informational privacy (or data protection) and confidentiality issues were bound to be taken into account, at least to some extent, by ethics committees. These issues are not regulated specifically in some legal systems that were the addressees of the GCP rules—first and foremost, the US and Japanese legal systems—nor are there independent authorities in charge of ensuring respect for such regulations in those countries.

On the other hand, the model developed by the GCP rules (once it was transposed into the European context, which happened when Directive 2001/20/EC was adopted) was bound to face personal data protection requirements, that is, Directive 95/46/EC, as well as the scope of competence related to national supervisory authorities.

In short, transposing GCP rules into the Directive would have required redefinition of the context of the by then 'globalized' rules with regards to the regulatory framework set out for personal data protection in Europe. In order to achieve this target, Directive 2001/20/EC leaves unprejudiced, on the one hand, the provisions laid down in Directive 95/46/EC by expressly referring to it in Section 3(2), letter c) and Recital no. 17; on the other hand, it requires the European Commission to issue common rules applying to data protection in the research sector (Section 8); that is, it provides that this sector is not to be regulated by the Data Protection Directive (and by the national laws transposing it).

This attempt would not appear to have been successful so far. As for the provision leaving data protection legislation unprejudiced, this has simply shifted the burden of 'squaring the circle'—that is, reconciling the provisions on research with those concerning data protection—onto national lawmakers transposing the Directive. In Italy this objective could not be achieved, as explained above. From this viewpoint, it appears that 'hybrid' models are more successful, at least theoretically; I am referring to the models in which the attempt has been made, in different ways, to coordinate the two bodies of legislation.[51]

The above remarks have to do with issues that are absolutely in need of clarification from a regulatory viewpoint; however, they concern a subject matter that is already 'obsolete'. Apart from the desirability of bridging some, partly long-standing, gaps such as those affecting observational[52] and epidemiological

---

as those of Australia, Canada, the Nordic countries and the World Health Organisation (WHO)'.

[51] These solutions have been adopted in other legal systems, for example in France, Switzerland, and—with regard to genetic testing—Iceland and Estonia.

[52] Also with regard to this area of research one should consider the advisability of requesting an opinion from an ethics committee. The only definition that can help construe the 'observational' qualification can be found in Section 2(1) of the Circular Letter no. 6 of 2 September 2002 from the Ministry of Health, concerning the Activities of the Ethics Committees Set up Pursuant to Ministerial Decree of 18 March 1998 (published in *Gazzetta Ufficiale* 12 September 2002, no. 214), which reads as follows: 'Observational studies shall refer to studies focused on problems and diseases for which drugs are prescribed in the standard manner pursuant to the conditions set out in the relevant marketing authorisation. Enrolment of a patient into a given treatment strategy is not decided upon in advance based

research, it is to be pointed out that it is indispensable to build up, at least in Italy, a clear-cut regulatory framework applying to genetic research. This is a sector where one has to take account of another, as yet unregulated, issue, in addition to data protection; that is to say the legal status of biological samples in medical and scientific research.[53]

---

on the experimenting protocol, being actually a matter of standard clinical practice, and the decision on prescription of the drug at stake is wholly independent of the one concerning the patient's enrolment'. Italy's legal system also contains legislation seemingly pointing to the involvement of ethics committees in observational studies. This applies, in particular, to the therapeutic applications of drugs that are the subject of clinical experiments, where the physicians requesting said drugs—failing any other treatment alternatives—should have obtained the competent ethics committee's approval (see Section 4(2) of Ministerial Decree of 8 May 2003, Therapeutic Use of Drugs Undergoing Clinical Experiments, in *Gazzetta Ufficiale* 28 July 2003, no. 173). Under Section 4(1) of said Decree, *inter alia*, 'data collection arrangements' should be made 'according to the logic of an observational study'.

In fact, no obligation to request the ethics committee's opinion with regard to these studies—where the most important issues are related not so much to ensuring the research subject's well-being, as to safeguarding his or her personal data—can be found, in general, in our legal system. The aforementioned Circular Letter from the Ministry of Health provides that 'drug clinical trials of "observational" nature shall have to be notified to the local ethics committees [competent for the area] where the relevant researcher operates. Based on the specific by-laws adopted in setting up the individual ethics committees, the latter shall either approve the trial(s) officially *or only take note of said trial(s)*' (emphasis added).

[53] In this regard, it should be pointed out that the *Guidance* referred to in Article 8 of Directive 2001/20/EC actually regulates these issues, albeit in very general and far from clear-cut terms. A detailed analysis of the matter cannot be carried out here; however, it would appear that the provisions in question go beyond the scope of the implementing powers conferred by Article 8 in the Directive. Generally speaking, one should also stress that the whole subject matter has been left outside the framework of data protection legislation, and that the European Commission did not consider it appropriate to seek the advice of the Article 29 Working Party as per Articles 29 and 30 of Directive 95/46/EC— whereas the latter Working Party might have provided useful guidance upon adoption of Directive 2001/20/EC, that is, in the upstream phase.

# Chapter 15

# Research Ethics Committees in Latvia[1]

## Laima Rudze[*]

### Ethics Committees that Review Biomedical Research in Latvia

These are the main ethics committees involved in reviewing biomedical research in Latvia:

- Central Medical Ethics Committee of Latvia;
- Two independent ethics committees for the clinical trials of drugs;
- Ethics committee of the Latvian Institute of Cardiology for clinical and physiological research, and drug and pharmaceutical product clinical investigation;
- Ethics Committee of the Medical Academy of Latvia;
- Ethics Committee on Laboratory Animal Use in Biomedical Research.

### Central Medical Ethics Committee of Latvia

This committee was set up by the Republic of Latvia's Cabinet of Ministers on 25 March 1998. Its legal basis is a Statute of the Cabinet of Ministers of Latvia. The committee consists of 14 members—doctors, nurses, scientists, pharmacists, lawyers, a religious representative, a representative of disabled people and a representative of the retired. The Statute of Ethics Committees governs the recruitment of committee members. Members are proposed by the Ministry of Welfare and appointed by the Cabinet of Ministers. They serve a term of four years with a possible extension for a further four years. The committee is a standing body and is independent.

All matters referred to the committee must be in writing. Its resolutions are adopted by a majority vote and take into consideration the rights of minorities and divergent opinions. The debates within the committee are open to the public. These resolutions are issued in writing in the form of recommendations. The committee also organizes events for the general public and makes recommendations on television, radio and in the newspapers. The main topic the committee considers is

---

[1] This report is based on the situation as of February 2004.
[*] Head of the European Issues Department, Compulsory Health Insurance State Agency of Latvia. Secretary General, Central Medical Ethics Committee of Latvia.

biomedical research. Issues on which the committee has given its views are: the evaluation of research projects; the evaluation of devices for medical procedures; and recommendations to refine experimental techniques.

The committee convenes at the request of the chairman once a month, and more often if necessary. The Cabinet of Ministers appoints a chairman and members of the committee. The members of the committee elect a Vice-Chairman who executes the authorities of the Chairman in his or her absence. The Chairman presents cases for consideration verbally. The committee is legally competent when the Chairman or Vice-Chairman, and more than half of the members, are present. The committee may obtain additional information from the investigator during consideration of a project or summon the investigator to a meeting with the committee. Each case is decided by a majority vote, with the chairman having the decisive vote. Members shall inform the committee of circumstances that may raise doubts about their competence; for example, a member cannot participate in the handling of a project that concerns his or her personal or commercial interest. The committee decides whether a member has such an interest in a case and if so, they are excluded from participation in the handling of the case. In cases where the committee is without the necessary professional expertise, they obtain relevant expert opinion. The decisions of the committee are given in writing within four weeks. The secretary of the committee registers the cases received and takes minutes of the committee's meetings.

The aims of the committee are to secure that:

- The risks that might be connected with the implementation of a project have been judged;
- The patients or healthy volunteers participating in the project will be informed in writing about its content, foreseeable risks and advantages, and then their free and explicit consent will be obtained and given in writing;
- Information will be given to, and consent obtained from, the closest relatives, guardian or donor in cases where the patient cannot give their consent;
- It is obvious from the information sheets that patients and healthy volunteers or relatives, guardian or donor can at any time retract their consent;
- The committee follows up individual projects and ensures that the final scientific report or publication is submitted to them.

## Other Ethics Committees

The procedures concerning the clinical trials of drugs and pharmaceutical products are set out by the Cabinet of Ministers of the Republic of Latvia through the 1997 Pharmaceutical Law (updated on 16 April 2003). The Minister of Welfare confirms the Statutes of the ethics committees for the clinical trials of drugs, and coordinates the personnel on the above-mentioned committees. According to the Statute of Ethics Committees (enacted by the Minister of Welfare on 6 August 1998) and the Pharmaceutical Law, there are independent ethics committees to give ethical assessment prior to a clinical trial. These ethics committees must include both medical and non-medical laypersons.

The Ethics Committee on Clinical Trials of Drugs consists of 14 members including physicians, a pharmacist, a journalist, a lawyer and a computer specialist. The Ethics Committee on Clinical Trials of Drugs at the Latvian Institute of Cardiology has nine members—six physicians, a biologist, a biochemist and a laboratory assistant.

The Independent Ethics Committee for the Investigation of Drugs and Pharmaceutical Products consists of 12 members including physicians, economists, pharmacologists, lawyers, a psychologist and laypersons.

A clinical trial of drugs and pharmaceutical products may start only after a written approval from the independent ethics committee for clinical trials and drugs and written permission from the State Agency of Medicines are obtained. Documents can be submitted to the State Agency of Medicines and the independent ethics committee for clinical trials of drugs at the same time. An application together with supporting documentation submitted to the independent ethics committees for clinical trials of drugs must include the following: signed protocol and amendments (should be translated into Latvian); investigator's brochure; information given to trial subject and informed consent form (should be translated into Latvian and Russian); insurance statement; curriculum vitae of investigators and sub-investigators; advertisement for subject recruitment; and the agreement of the Head of Hospital (clinic or centres) to perform the clinical trial. In order to obtain an authorization from the State Agency of Medicines for commencing a clinical trial, the sponsor or the person authorized by the sponsor shall submit the above-mentioned documents, and:

1. a sample of the Case Report Form;
2. Investigator's Brochure *and Summary of Product Characteristics* in Latvian, *(for foreign applicants, the referred documents shall be submitted in compliance with the requirements stipulated by Language Law)*;
3. documentation attesting the chemical-pharmaceutical quality of the investigational product and the comparator product (certificate of quality);
4. sample of labelling of the investigational product packaging;
5. written confirmation from the investigator and the sub-investigators that the clinical trial will be conducted in conformity with the protocol and normative deeds;
6. an authorization issued by the sponsor, if the documents are submitted by a person authorized by the sponsor;
7. reference values for the laboratory tests used at the clinical trial laboratories;
8. a favourable opinion by an Ethics Committee.

## Ethics Committee on Laboratory Animal Use in Biomedical Research

The Ethics Committee on Laboratory Animal Use in Biomedical Research acts under the auspices of the Committee of the Latvian Council of Science and in accordance with their regulations. Its activities touch all aspects connected with the use of laboratory animals in biomedical and veterinary medical investigations, including sources supplying laboratory animals, laboratory animal breeding, transportation, housing and use in experiments. The ethics committee's task is to consider, from the ethical point of view, all new scientific projects which plan the use of laboratory animals and have applied for funding to the Latvian Council of Science or any other expert committee.

*Goals and Field of Activities*

The aims are to assist the certified and competent specialists, as well as all the others involved in the breeding and use of laboratory animals, to implement in their work the recommendations, directives and regulations of the European Convention of 1986 'Protection of vertebrate animals used for experimental and other scientific purposes', and also:

- to cooperate with corresponding laboratory animal-breeding facilities and research institutions in any field connected with laboratory animals;
- to give recommendations and consultations to the researchers who apply for funding to the Latvian Council of Science or any other expert committee and whose research projects plan the use of laboratory animals.

It also ensures that the scientific projects planning the use of laboratory animals:

- limit as far as possible the number of laboratory animals used and their suffering, as well as the unnecessary use of animals or their organs, on the basis of the high quality of the scientific experiments;
- use laboratory animals economically and in a humane way;
- promote development and use of alternative methods;
- use thoroughly researched methods in experiments with laboratory animals, including appropriate analgesia, anaesthesia and euthanasia, providing the implementation of improvements in routine practice.

It participates actively in the development of legislation concerning the protection of laboratory animals used in biomedical and veterinary medical research and works to optimize the welfare conditions of laboratory animals by:

- cooperating with the State Veterinary Department to develop regulations on the inspection of laboratory animal breeding facilities and the research laboratories where laboratory animals are used for the investigations, in order to control routine conditions and improvements of the environment;
- supplying the scientific community with information concerning today's situation in laboratory animal science in order to give an opportunity to the researchers to evaluate the level of welfare of laboratory animals;
- regularly organizing training and practical workshops towards obtaining the basic competence to work with laboratory animals.

Lastly, it also publicizes information about the welfare of laboratory animals:

-	to ensure that every researcher who uses laboratory animals in a direct or indirect way is informed about the problems of laboratory animal welfare;
-	to assist in the dissemination and understanding of information about laboratory animals by organizing constructive discussions on ethical problems;
-	to ensure that every researcher who works with laboratory animals has an opportunity to express his or her concern, thoughts or ideas about this work.

The Latvian Council of Science approves the list of members of the ethics committee and appoints the Chairperson. There are 13–15 members who are:

-	representatives of the Latvian Council of Science;
-	laboratory animal breeders;
-	representatives of the State Veterinary Department;
-	representatives of the Ministry of Welfare;
-	laboratory animal users from different research institutions;
-	representatives of the environment protection organizations;
-	representatives of the Baltic Laboratory Animal Science Association.

## General Powers of RECs

RECs can approve or reject applications, and approval by an REC is necessary for the research to go ahead. However, they only have recommendatory powers.

There are no consequences for researchers who do not submit their research for review or fail to follow what the review requires for medical research except in the case of medical trials.

## General Legal Responsibility of RECs

When reviewing, RECs follow Latvian laws and regulations, WHO Guidelines for Ethics Committees that Review Medical Research, The Convention for Human Rights and Dignity in Biology and Medicine and Good Clinical Practice for Trials on Medicinal Products in the European Community.

*Laws Relating to the System for Ethical Review of Medical Research in Latvia*

*Law on Medical Treatment*[2]	Article 15 states that the Central Medical Ethics Committee shall operate in accordance with Cabinet regulations and it shall examine ethical issues of biomedical progress relating to social problems.

---

[2] Adopted 12 June 1997, amendments on 26 February 1998, 1 June 2000 and 20 June 2001. Published in *Vēstnesis* No. 167, 1 July 1997.

Members of the Central Medical Ethics Committee shall be approved by the Cabinet upon recommendation from the Minister for Welfare.

*Law on Pharmacy*[3] Section 6 states that

The Minister for Welfare shall, within the scope of his or her competence:

1.  implement the policy of the Government in the field of pharmaceuticals, organise the preparation of draft regulatory enactments, necessary for the regulation of pharmaceuticals, and the control of compliance with the requirements of the regulatory enactments in force, and approve the systems of classification and coding of medicaments in the pharmaceutical sector;
2.  determine the procedures pursuant to which medicinal products shall be evaluated and registered, and the procedures pursuant to which the list of medicinal products registered in the Republic of Latvia (hereinafter – the Medicinal Product Register of Latvia) shall be formed, as well as the register of certified pharmacists and licensed pharmacies, medicinal product wholesalers and medicinal product manufacturing undertakings;
3.  organise the attestation of inspectors of the State Pharmaceutical Inspection and coordinate the preparation of pharmaceutical specialists, issue permits for conducting the training process, for students of higher educational institutions or pupils of secondary specialised educational institutions, in pharmacies, medicinal product wholesalers and medicinal product manufacturing undertakings, based on recommendations from the higher or secondary specialised educational institutions;
4.  regulate the conditions for the manufacture, storage, control and distribution of particular medicinal products or groups of medicinal products;
5.  ensure that the special permits (licences) provided for in the regulations of the Cabinet are issued;
6.  [17 December 1998];
7.  approve the model by-law for the medicinal products clinical trials ethics committees and the membership of such committees;
8.  determine the requirements for good manufacturing practice, good distribution practice, good clinical practice of medicinal products, for the monitoring of sideeffects caused by the use of medicinal products and the requirements for co-ordination of the advertising of medicinal products;
9.  determine the auxiliary substances to be indicated in the labelling and instructions for use of medicinal products and the requirements for legibility of the labelling and instructions for use of medicinal products; and
10. determine the requirements for pharmaceutical care.

---

[3] Also called the Pharmaceutical Law, it was approved on 10 April 1997, with amendments on 19 March 1998, 17 December 1998, 1 June 2000, 14 June 2000 and 16 April 2003. In force since 5 August 1997 and published in *Vēstnesis* No. 103, 24 April 1997. The Law with full amendments can be found through the Latvian State Agency of Medicines at: http://www.vza.gov.lv/english/pdf/1EDFFD30.pdf (last accessed on 16 May 2005).

*Regulation on clinical trials of medicines*[4] A clinical trial shall only be initiated in the case where the anticipated benefits from the clinical trial justify the risk to the healthy person or patient who voluntarily participates in the clinical trial (hereinafter the 'trial subject') and receives the investigational product, or participates in the control group and receives comparator product (product with a known effect or pharmaceutical form without an active substance used as a control for the clinical trial data) (paragraph 2).

The medical care given to, and all medical decisions made on behalf of, subjects shall be the responsibility of an appropriately qualified healthcare practitioner with a certificate proving their rights to perform treatment without assistance in the field associated with the specified clinical trial (hereinafter the 'investigator'). An investigator shall be selected by the sponsor having regard to his or her qualification and experience. The sponsor shall ensure further training for the investigator if required (paragraph 7).

Prior to the initiation of the clinical investigation, the investigator shall inform the trial subject in writing of the trial objectives, methods to be used, the anticipated benefits and risks, trial duration, compensation for participating in the clinical trial, if any, as well as of the treatment expenses that will be covered in the event of a trial-related injury. Written information and other materials to be provided to the trial subject shall be in a language of which he or she has a good command (paragraph 8). Written information for the trial subject shall state that the trial subject may withdraw from the trial at any time without mentioning motives, as well as ensure that the withdrawal from the trial will not negatively affect the further medical care of the trial subject (paragraph 9).

When deciding about participation of a child in a clinical trial, if the child has reached seven years of age, the child's own desire shall be taken into account (paragraph 11). Inclusion of unconscious persons or persons without legal capacity in a clinical trial is possible only in cases where the investigator justly believes this to be in favour of the respective person and in the event that the Medicines Clinical Trial Ethics Committee (hereinafter an 'ethics committee') gives its consent. In the event of the person being unconscious, written consent for participation in the clinical trial shall be obtained from the closest relatives of the person, with priority to the spouse's, parent's or children's opinion. In the case of the person being without legal capacity, priority is given to a legally acceptable representative's opinion (paragraph 12). Clinical investigation is forbidden in women during pregnancy and lactation, except in cases when clinical investigation otherwise is impossible and the risks during clinical investigation are proportional to the anticipated benefits to the embryo, foetus or infant (paragraph 13).

Any trial subject in need of active disease treatment shall not be included in the control group where the trial subject receives a reference product without the active substance (paragraph 14).

To ensure protection of the trial subject's identification data, the investigator must assign an identification code to each trial subject, which is used instead of the

---

[4] Cabinet of Ministers No. 312, 12 September 2000. Amendments on 9 September 2003 (No. 506) and on 15 June 2004 (No. 542).

trial subject's name when the sponsor reports to the State Agency of Medicines and the ethics committee (paragraph 17). To ensure the trial subject's rights and protection in the clinical trial, the sponsor is responsible for the insurance of the trial subject covering possible injury and damages during the trial when administering the investigational product or performing other procedures in accordance with the protocol (paragraph 20).

The sponsor shall ensure supply of investigational product necessary for the clinical trials which has been manufactured and the quality of which has been controlled in accordance with good manufacturing practice (paragraph 22).

In order to obtain the favourable opinion of an ethics committee, the sponsor or the person authorized by the sponsor should submit the following documents:

1.  Application for the clinical trial signed by the sponsor (hereinafter: 'application');
2.  protocol *and* amendments to the protocol, if any, in Latvian signed by the sponsor and the investigator (for foreign applicants *the referred documents shall be submitted in compliance with the requirements stipulated by Language Law*);
3.  trial subject's informed consent form laid down by the sponsor in Latvian, and also in other languages if required;
4.  other written information regarding the specific clinical trial to be provided to the trial subjects, in Latvian, and also in other languages if required;
5.  description of the trial subjects involvement activities in Latvian, *(for foreign applicants, the referred document shall be submitted in compliance with the requirements stipulated by Language Law)*;
6.  compilation of data from previous investigational product studies (hereinafter: 'Investigator's Brochure') in Latvian, *(for foreign applicants, the referred document shall be submitted in compliance with the requirements stipulated by Language Law)*;
7.  Descriptions of experience and qualification of investigators and other persons involved in the clinical trial (selected and supervised by the investigator at the trial site) (hereinafter 'subinvestigator');
8.  documents regarding compensation for the trial subject for participation in the clinical trial, if provided, as well as insurance conditions and a copy of the policy, *or a certificate confirming* insurance of the trial subject in the case of a possible injury related to the clinical trial;
9.  consent of the medical institution for performing the clinical trial;
10. authorisation issued by the sponsor, if the clinical trial documents are submitted by a person authorised by the sponsor (paragraph 31).

The ethics committee must provide an opinion in writing within 30 days of receipt of the documents referred to above (paragraph 33). If the ethics committee decides during examination of the application that the submitted documentation is incomplete or additional information on the planned clinical trial is required, it has the right to require supplementary documents (paragraph 34).

To ensure that the clinical trial is conducted in compliance with the regulations, the activities of everyone involved in the clinical trial is subjected to adequate quality control *and surveillance*. This surveillance is performed by the State Agency of Medicines as one of its terms of its reference (paragraph 43).

## Specific Data Protection Matters

*Law on Medical Treatment*

According to Article 20, patients have the right to receive information from a doctor in a way that they can comprehend regarding the diagnosis of his or her illness, examination and medical treatment plans, as well as other medical treatment methods and the prognosis.

A patient has the right to refuse, in full or in part, examination or medical treatment offered, by certifying such refusal with his or her signature. If a patient is a minor or a person who due to his or her state of health is unable to understand the consequences of his or her actions, family members, but if such do not exist, the closest relatives or lawful representatives of the patient (trustees, guardians) have such rights and liability for the decisions taken. The doctor has a duty to explain the consequences of a refusal to these individuals. If a patient has accepted a treatment plan, he or she is responsible for observing all instructions of the medical practitioner related to the medical treatment and care (Article 23).

Article 50 requires that information regarding the medical treatment of a patient, the diagnosis and prognosis of a disease (hereinafter—information regarding a patient), as well as information obtained by medical practitioners during the medical treatment process regarding the private life of a patient and his or her closest relatives, is confidential. Information regarding a patient may be provided to:

1. other medical practitioners for the purpose of achieving the objectives of the medical treatment;
2. the Medical Commission for Expert-Examination of Health and Working Ability (MCEEHWA);
3. the Quality Control Inspection for Expert-Examination in Medical Care and Ability to Work;
4. a Court, the Office of the Prosecutor, the police, the State Centre for the Protection of the Rights of the Child (inspectors), an Orphan's Court (a Parish Court) and to investigative institutions only at the written request of such institutions and if there is a permission signed by the head of the medical treatment institution.
5. it may be used in scientific research if the anonymity of the patient is guaranteed or his or her consent has been received.
6. State military service administrations of the Ministry of Defence are entitled to request from medical treatment institutions information regarding the state of health of conscripts, reserve soldiers and reservists in accordance with the procedures prescribed by the Cabinet.

*Latvian Human Genome Research Act*[5]

The objectives of this Act are:

- to regulate the creation and function of the Genome Database and genetic research connected with the database;
- to ensure the voluntary nature of gene donation and the confidentiality of the identity of gene donors;
- to protect gene donors from misuse of their data and from discrimination based on interpretation of their DNA (Section 2).

The Council of Ministers authorizes the main processor of the Genome Database (Section 4). The main processor organizes the taking, coding and storage of tissue samples, and prepares, stores, codes and destroys descriptions of the state of health (hereinafter 'health descriptions') and genealogies. It performs genetic research, and collects, stores, destroys and issues genetic data. The main processor has the right to delegate the rights of processing, except for coding and decoding, to an authorized processor. The State Genome Register under the supervision of the Ministry of Welfare was founded to create the database of personal data of gene donors. Gene donors shall receive:

- information about the aims and content of the Genome project;
- information about the taking of tissue samples, the questionnaire and medical records;
- information about potential risks;
- information about the right to withdraw his or her consent and the right to apply for the destruction of tissue samples or data which enables decoding;
- information about the fact that there will be no personal financial benefits for gene donors; and
- information about the data protection system.

A written informed consent from the gene donor is to be prepared in two copies and signed by the gene donor and main processor. One copy is to be stored in the State Genome Register and the other copy given to the gene donor.

The main processor gives each tissue sample, DNA description, health description and genealogy a unique code. The code is indicated on the written informed consent of the gene donor. Specific persons are appointed to perform the coding and to issue coded tissue samples, DNA descriptions or health descriptions. The State Data Inspection approves the methods of generating the codes. The main processor delivers the written consent together with the code indicated thereon to the State Genome Register and this is the only possible key for decoding. The State Genome Register appoints specific persons who perform decoding and have access to the written consents of gene donors. Coded tissue samples, DNA descriptions

---

[5] Approved by Saeima (the Latvian Parliament) on 3 July 2002, and in force from 1 January 2004.

and health descriptions shall be stored by the main processor within the territory of the Republic of Latvia. The Central Medical Ethics Committee may grant permission for a limited number of tissue samples to be stored abroad if appropriate research methods are not possible in Latvia.

Supervision over the collection, coding and decoding, and processing of tissue samples, descriptions of DNA, health descriptions and genealogical data is exercised by the State Data Inspection. The Central Medical Ethics Committee supervises ethical issues during the creation of the Genome Database and processing of the data according to generally recognized ethical rules and international conventions. Gene donors have the right to access their data stored in the Genome Database and the right to have genetic counselling. Gene donors have the right to submit additional information on themselves to the main processor, as well as the right to prohibit the supplementation, renewal and verification of the health descriptions stored in the Genome Database. Any gene donor has the right at any time to withdraw their consent to be a gene donor for the Latvian Genome Database.

*Law on Data Protection[6]*

The Personal Data Protection Law outlines the conditions for personal data processing in Section 7:

Personal data processing is permitted only if not prescribed otherwise by law, and at least one of the following conditions exist:

1. the data subject has given his or her consent;
2. the personal data processing results from contractual obligations of the data subject, or observing request of the data subject, the data processing is necessary for conclusion of the corresponding contract;
3. the data processing is necessary to a system controller for performance of his/her obligations established by the law;
4. the data processing is necessary to protect vitally important interests of the data subject, including life and health;
5. the data processing is necessary in order to ensure that the public interest is complied with, or to fulfil functions of public authority for whose performance the personal data have been transferred to a system controller or transmitted to a third person; and
6. the data processing is necessary in order to, complying with the fundamental human rights and freedoms of the data subject, exercise lawful interests of the system controller or of such third person as the personal data have been disclosed to.

It also prohibits the processing of sensitive personal data in Section 11, except in cases where:

---

[6] The Personal Data Protection Law of 23 March 2000, amended by the Law of 24 October 2002.

1. the data subject has given his or her written consent for the processing of his or her sensitive personal data;
2. special processing of personal data, without requesting the consent of the data subject, is provided for by regulatory enactments which regulate legal relations regarding employment, and such regulatory enactments guarantee the protection of personal data;
3. personal data processing is necessary to protect the life and health of the data subject or another person and the data subject is not legally or physically able to express his or her consent;
4. personal data processing is necessary to achieve the lawful, non-commercial objectives of public organisations and their associations, if such data processing is only related to the members of these organisations or their associations and the personal data are not transferred to third parties;
5. personal data processing is necessary for the purposes of medical treatment, rendering health care services or administration thereof and distribution of medical remedies;
6. the processing concerns such personal data as necessary for the protection of lawful rights and interests of natural or legal persons in court proceedings;
7. processing of personal data is necessary for rendering social aid and is performed by a provider of social aid services;
8. processing of personal data is necessary for establishment of the Latvia State Archives Fund is performed by state archives and institutions having the right of a state depository approved by the Director General of the State Archives;
9. processing of personal data is necessary for statistical research carried out by the Central Statistics Board;
10. processing relates to personal data published by the data subject him/herself.

A data subject has the right to request that his or her personal data be supplemented or rectified, as well as that their processing be suspended or that the data be destroyed if the personal data are incomplete, outdated, false, unlawfully obtained or are no longer necessary for the purposes for which they were collected. If the data subject is able to substantiate that the personal data included in the personal data processing system are incomplete, outdated, false, unlawfully obtained or no longer necessary for the purposes for which they were collected, the system controller has an obligation to rectify this inaccuracy or violation without delay and notify third parties who have previously received the relevant processed data (Section 16).

The protection of personal data shall be carried out by the State Data Inspection, which is subject to the supervision of the Ministry of Justice (Section 29).

## Laws on Research Involving Human Biological Material

Laws on human biological material include the Law on the Protection of Dead Human Beings and the Use of Human Organs and Tissues[7] together with the Regulations of Cabinet of Ministers on Kidney Transplantation,[8] the Act on the Use of Human Organs and Tissues[9] and the Regulation of Ministry of Welfare of Latvia on Blood Safety.[10]

### *Laws on Research Involving Human Embryos and Stem Cells*

The Law on Reproductive and Sexual Health[11] states that cells capable of development may be used for medically assisted reproduction. Frozen embryos may be stored for a maximum of ten years and in order to reduce the risk of multiple births, only three embryos may be transferred to an individual patient and any remaining embryos cryopreserved.

Confidentiality of all records will be maintained relating to cryopreserved embryos as with all medical care and other procedures performed at the Reproductive Health Centres of Latvia.

The creation of human embryos for research purposes is prohibited, as is human cloning. The human biological material or embryo shall not, as such, give rise to financial gain and the use of the techniques of medically assisted procreation shall not be allowed for the purpose of choosing a future child's sex, except where serious hereditary sex-related disease is to be avoided.

---

[7] 15 December 1992, modified on 21 September 1995 and 6 December 2001, in force since 1 January 1993.

[8] The object of the regulations is to protect the dignity and identity of everyone and guarantee, without discrimination, respect for his or her integrity and other rights and fundamental freedoms with regard to transplantation of organs and tissues of human origin. Live organ donation is currently confined primarily to kidneys.

[9] Cabinet of Ministers, Rules No. 398, 15 July 2003. This Act covers the relevant professional obligations and standards in accordance with which all interventions in the transplant and storage process must be performed.

[10] No. 260, 20 September 1995. These regulations cover blood and the products derived from blood for use in transfusion medicine, the preparation, use and quality assurance of blood components.

[11] Approved 31 January 2002, in force on 1 July 2002.

# Chapter 16

# Research Ethics Committees in Lithuania

Asta Cekanauskaite* and Eugenijus Gefenas[t][t]

## Introduction

The process of the development of ethical review for biomedical research in Lithuania (and probably many other Central and Eastern European countries), comparable with that in Western countries, was strongly facilitated by foreign pharmaceutical companies. It was due to multi-centre clinical trials, which involved healthcare research institutions in Lithuania, that two Institutional Review Boards (one in Kaunas Medical University, and the other in the Lithuanian Oncology Centre) started ethical review in the country about ten years ago. In general, research ethics committees in Lithuania follow international requirements and guidelines and respect the Constitution and procedural framework for the ethical review of biomedical research. This paper provides an overview of the ethical review of biomedical research in Lithuania.

## Establishment of RECs

*The System for Ethical Review of Medical Research in Lithuania—Laws and Regulations*

When the Law on Ethics of Biomedical Research came into force (in 2001) with provisions concerning the establishment of regional committees, the foundations for the current two-level system of ethical review of biomedical research were laid down in Lithuania. According to the law, there are two kinds of institutions which have legal responsibility for biomedical research. The Lithuanian Bioethics Committee represents the first type of institution, namely, the national one. The second type of institution is the Regional Biomedical Research Ethics Committee. Biomedical research in Lithuania may be performed only subject to an approval

* Assistant Professor, Department of Medical History and Ethics at the Medical Faculty of Vilnius University.
[t] Associate Professor, Department of Medical History and Ethics at Medical Faculty of Vilnius University and Senior Researcher at the Institute of Culture, Philosophy and Arts.
[t] The authors express their gratitude to the Lithuanian State Data Protection Inspectorate for its consultations on data protection issues.

obtained from the Lithuanian Bioethics Committee or the Regional Biomedical Research Ethics Committee. Conducting biomedical research without prior approval is unlawful.

According to the Procedure to Issue Approvals to Conduct Biomedical Research:[1]

> The Regional Biomedical Research Ethics Committee shall have the right to accept and examine the application and documents of the sponsor and/or principal investigator of the biomedical research and issue approval independently from the Lithuanian Bioethics Committee just in the case where the biomedical research project shall be carried out only in the region which has been assigned to the mandate of the corresponding Regional Biomedical Research Ethics Committee by the Lithuanian Bioethics Committee.
>
> Should biomedical research be carried out in more than one region, the Lithuanian Bioethics Committee shall issue the approval. In this case, the Lithuanian Bioethics Committee shall decide upon the necessity to get the approval of the Regional Biomedical Research Ethics Committees of the regions where the biomedical research will be carried out. The Lithuanian Bioethics Committee shall inform the Regional Biomedical Research Ethics Committees about biomedical research to be carried out in their respective regions.
>
> The approvals to conduct clinical research on medical instruments or substances shall be issued upon a recommendation of the State Health Care Accreditation Agency.
>
> Before May 2004, the approvals to conduct clinical research of medicinal products were issued upon a recommendation of the State Drug Control Agency. This practice has been changed because of the implementation of the Directive 2001/20/EC. Since May 2004, a reasoned opinion is issued by RECs and the final approval is given by the State Drug Control Agency in the case where the application has received both a positive opinion from the REC as well as the competent authority (which is the State Drug Control Agency in Lithuania).

Therefore the procedure of ethical review in Lithuania is formal, regulated by the Law on Ethics of Biomedical Research and other normative documents. This *review* covers evaluation of the research protocol and its amendments, issuing approvals and monitoring ongoing (approved) research.

*RECs' Accountability*

Both types of RECs are accountable to their constitutors: the Lithuanian Bioethics Committee to the Ministry of Health, and, for example, the Kaunas Regional Biomedical Research Ethics Committee is accountable to both the Kaunas Medical University and the Lithuanian Bioethics Committee.

---

[1] Minister of Health, *Decree on Procedure to Issue Approvals to Conduct Biomedical Research* (23 October 2000).

*Clinical Ethics vs. Research Ethics*

Generally speaking, there are two kinds of biomedical ethics institutions in the country—institutions involved in clinical ethics, namely, hospital ethics committees and institutions; and then those responsible for the ethical review of biomedical research—Regional Biomedical Research Ethics Committees. The activity of the Lithuanian Bioethics Committee covers both of these fields.

*Membership Requirements for RECs*

The group of biomedical research experts on the Lithuanian Bioethics Committee is formed in compliance with an order given by the Chairman of the Lithuanian Bioethics Committee. The members of this group (not less than nine members) are elected by the members of the Lithuanian Bioethics Committee on the basis of a regular majority of the vote, for a period of one year. Regional Biomedical Research Ethics Committees are to be composed proportionally of representatives of the degree-holding academic community, healthcare specialists and the general public. The establishment and functioning of Regional Biomedical Research Ethics Committees is specified in the Model Operating Procedures for Regional Biomedical Research Ethics Committees.

## General Powers of RECs

*The Authority of RECs*

RECs are enabled to approve and reject applications for biomedical research projects except when they involve research on medicinal products (see section above on 'Establishment of RECs'). Approvals to conduct clinical research on medical instruments or substances are issued upon recommendation of the State Health Care Accreditation Agency. RECs could in principle approve the application despite the negative opinion given by the mentioned authority. However, these cases are very rare.

*Possible Consequences for Researchers who do not Submit their Research for Review or Fail to Follow what the Review Requires*

According to Article 18 of the Law on Ethics of Biomedical Research:

> Carrying out biomedical research without an approval or not in conformity with the requirements of this Law and other legal acts provided the research has not damaged the research subject's health shall be treated as an act of malpractice.

Penalties from the Court or administrative authority are not specified in the law, and there were no precedent lawsuits of such kind in Lithuania at the time of writing.

Article 29 of the Law on Legal Protection of Personal Data states that the extent of material and non-material damage for any person who has sustained damage as a result of the unlawful processing of personal data or other acts or omissions by the data controller or data processor shall be determined by the Court.

## General Legal Responsibility of RECs

*Attention Paid to the Law by RECs*

There are no circumstances in which REC approval will render activities lawful that would otherwise be unlawful. According to the current legislation it seems that RECs may neither reject nor advise against activities that are lawful nor approve activities that are unlawful. These are the relevant legal documents that RECs consider:

- Law on Ethics of Biomedical Research;
- Health Care Ministry Decree on the Procedure to Issue Approvals to Conduct Biomedical Research;
- Health Care Ministry Decree on the Procedure for the Estimation and Covering of Expenses Incurred by Research Subjects;
- Health Care Ministry Decree on the List of the Documents to be Presented by the Sponsor of Biomedical Research and (or) by the Principal Investigator in Order to be Authorized to Conduct Biomedical Research.

*The Impact of Implementation of Directive 2001/20/EC on Good Clinical Practice*

The implementation of Directive 2001/20/EC on Good Clinical Practice has influenced a number of relevant laws, in particular the Law on Ethics of Biomedical Research. This law deals with a much broader scope of research than clinical trials on medicinal products. The Health Care Ministry Decree on the Implementation of the Rules of Good Clinical Practice came into force on 11 May 2004. This legal document enforces the basic principles of the Directive. As mentioned above, the most significant change in the system of issuing approvals to conduct biomedical research was the fact that the right to issue approvals to conduct research on medicinal products was assigned to the State Drug Control Agency after a positive opinion has been given by the relevant REC.

*RECs' Practice and the Law*

RECs are obliged to follow all laws which are enforced in the country, including data protection laws. However, when there are difficult situations, RECs can approach the Data Protection Authority for consultation. Unfortunately, the practice of communication between RECs and data protection authorities has so far been rather limited.

*Forms of Legal Action that Can be Taken Against an REC on the Basis of its Decisions*

The research subjects or their representatives have the right to appeal the actions of the sponsor, the principal investigator and other persons involved in carrying out biomedical research to an institution which has issued an approval and to Court in the manner prescribed by law and other legal Acts. The decision made by the regional committee could be appealed to the Lithuanian Bioethics Committee and the latter's decision to the Court.

## Specific Data Protection Matters

*The Powers of RECs to Make Decisions About when Research is Justified in the Public Interest*

The Law on the Legal Protection of Personal Data[2] says that while carrying out scientific research, personal data shall be processed with the consent of the data subject. Personal data could be processed for research purposes without the consent of the data subject only after reporting this to the State Data Protection Inspectorate, which should conduct a prior check. However, according to the current legislation (Law on Ethics of Biomedical Research) the Lithuanian Bioethics Committee or Regional Biomedical Research Ethics Committee has the power to decide whether the subject's informed consent is necessary for carrying out biomedical research on medical documents and tissues, a foetus, cell or genetic material which had been obtained from the person for other purposes.

The subject might not be informed if the provision of such information proves impossible or would involve disproportionate effort (there is a large number of data subjects, the data is old, or the expenditures would be very high).

*The View Taken by RECs Concerning 'Anonymized' Information*

*Coded data* Article 2, Paragraph 1 of the Law on Legal Protection of Personal Data of the Republic of Lithuania defines personal data as any information relating to a natural person.[3] Paragraph 1 of Council of Europe Recommendation No. (97)5 on the Protection of Medical Data states that:

> an individual shall not be regarded as 'identifiable' if identification requires an unreasonable amount of time and manpower. In cases where the individual is not identifiable, the data are referred to as anonymous.

---

[2] 21 January 2003, No. IX-1296.
[3] '[t]he data subject who is identified or who can be identified directly or indirectly by reference to such data as a personal identification number or one or more factors specific to his physical, physiological, mental, economic, cultural or social identity'.

Personal data could be rendered anonymous when those who process it cannot identify the natural person directly or indirectly. If the data controller processes the personal data and he or she is able to identify the natural person in any possible way (for example he or she holds the code that can decode coded data)—such data cannot be considered as anonymous data.

*Informing the data subject, when data is collected, about processing to take place after anonymization* Article 18, Paragraph 1 of the Law on Legal Protection of Personal Data of the Republic of Lithuania states that:

> The data controller must provide to the data subject from whom data relating to himself are collected directly the following information, except where the data subject already has it:
>
> 1.    the identity of the data controller and his representative if any, and his permanent place of residence where the data controller or his representative is a natural person, or other particulars, and the registered office where the data controller or its representative is a legal person;
> 2.    the purposes of the processing of the data subject's personal data;
> 3.    any other additional information—the recipient of the data and for what purposes the data of the data subject are disclosed; what personal data the data subject is supposed to provide and the consequences of his failure to provide data, the right of the data subject to have access to his personal data and the right to request rectification of incorrect, incomplete and inaccurate personal data, necessary for ensuring a proper processing of personal data without violation of the data subject's rights.

Therefore the data subject does not have to be informed if the data controller processes only anonymous data. However, when the data controller collects data knowing they are to be used for a further purpose (even if these data would be anonymized), the data controller should inform the data subject about this other purpose.

*Is data considered as anonymous when the original data controller still holds it in personal form?* This question is closely related to the question on coded data. If the data controller who processes personal data makes the data anonymous and transfers such data to another data controller, it should be considered that for the first data controller (who still has the primary set of data and can identify the data subject) this set of data is not anonymous and for another data controller (who has received only a set of data, not allowing to identify a natural person directly or indirectly) this set is anonymous.

### DNA Samples (Biological Materials) and Genetic Information as a Subject of Data Protection Rights

Lithuanian laws do not single out genetic information as a distinct data group. It seems that genetic information is covered by regulations covering health information. Biomedical research on genetic material should be conducted under all of the general provisions for biomedical research laid down in the Law on Ethics of Biomedical Research. Whether the subject's informed consent is necessary for carrying out biomedical research on genetic material—which has been obtained from the person for other purposes, for example, during medical interventions performed before the project was submitted for ethical review—shall be decided by the Lithuanian Bioethics Committee or the Regional Biomedical Research Ethics Committee giving the approval.

Chapter 17

# Research Ethics Committees in Malta

Pierre Mallia*

### Establishment of RECs

The ethical review of research is a relatively new introduction into Maltese academia. The Maltese medical school has the longest established research ethics committee (REC) in Malta, and until recently all research proposals produced at the University of Malta had to pass through this committee. In summer 2003 another REC was set up in the Institute of Health Care (the IHC) to look into students' research projects within this institute. There are also plans to introduce an REC at university level; currently other faculties do not have established RECs that are recognized by the University Senate. Therefore all proposals go through faculty boards in such cases.

It should be noted that most research is done at undergraduate level, whilst postgraduate research is also usually work or theses towards higher degrees or diplomas. Any research done outside the medical school aegis does not have to undergo any form of review by an REC. With the introduction of the Data Protection Act (DPA),[1] however, most researchers are aware that they should have some form of approval before carrying out the trial. This way of thinking provides a false sense of security however, as it is not felt that RECs should be responsible for the implementation of data protection, other than to see that adequate informed consent and confidentiality rules are being regulated. Recently in fact, more emphasis is being given to video recordings, and guidelines are being written by the author with regard to this development.

### Legal Regulation

There is no legal requirement for research to go through any form of REC. However, there are two important regulatory stages which will at least prevent the University's research from being published without any form of review. The first is that the faculties within the University now recognize that research must have

---

* M.D., M.Phil., Ph.D., Hon. President of the Malta College of Family Doctors and lecturer at the University of Malta.
[1] *Government Gazette of Malta No. 17,* 175—14 December 2001, Chapter 440, by virtue of Act No. XXVI of 2001.

some form of ethical review, and therefore students or researchers are obliged to submit their proposals to these committees. Secondly, if there is to be any publication of the research, the editors are usually keen on asking about ethical review. Some would see this as evidence of an increased awareness of the ethical review process. Having said this, everything is at an initial stage and considerable research, especially in faculties such as philosophy and psychology, may go undetected and only receive approval at the faculty level.

Therefore there is no regulatory obligation to undergo review, although this is most likely to change in the near future. Indeed this is why it was felt that the IHC needed its own REC. This change followed certain problems of a logistical nature, whereby the medical school (which oversees research done at St. Lukes' Teaching Hospital) was also reviewing research done within the paramedical teaching institute (the IHC). This was despite most research within the IHC being done by nursing and other paramedical students doing diplomas and first degrees. The REC at the IHC recognizes that the research must meet strict criteria, as all research must do; however, it has been suggested by the author during a meeting of the REC that research here should be recognized for what it is—a statement showing that the student has learned how to conduct research and has fulfilled the criteria for their diploma or degree. It has therefore been recommended that no student should be able to publish his or her work without the permission of the REC, and that all research that is carried out is to be the property of the University and not of the student. It must be emphasized that this was only discussed at committee level and stills needs formal approval through Senate. It is envisaged, however, that this situation will be remedied soon. This would be an important milestone, as occasionally newspapers get to know the results of a student's research, making interesting news. This research is then published as fact by the media when most of these studies may not have undergone the rigorous standards of research necessary for the more professional analyst. For example, a student may not have taken certain factors into consideration. The limits of the studies would have been recognized at faculty level; however, it would still be approved for the project's purposes as having met the needs required by the student—that being the capability to understand and carry out research.

Continuing along this line of thought, one may also point out that any research of an important nature may actually not pass through any REC, especially if this is done outside the aegis of the University. Submitting a project to the REC is therefore done purely on a voluntary basis, especially if the researcher needs this approval for submitting his or her work for publication in a journal. There is therefore still considerable controversy about research done in the field of genetics, an important research field in the University. There are ample samples of DNA available and researchers feel that an REC may not sufficiently understand the nature of genetic research, leading to the continual refusal of genuine research. Geneticists in Malta have often pointed out that it is not technically feasible to return to the persons from whom the samples were obtained for informed consent each and every time research—which will not identify people—is carried out. They recommend some form of middle ground, whereby the REC decides the nature of the research and whether it may be offensive to any category of patients or people.

## Membership and Powers of RECs

There are no strict criteria by which members are chosen to form an REC. The Dean of the Faculty of Medicine and Surgery selects the chairperson and the members of the board of an REC. These would usually range from a suitable Professor, to act as chairperson, to members drawn from the ethical and professional sphere. In this regard many members are more knowledgeable on the area of methodology than that of ethical issues; this works well for the REC as the methodology is in itself of high ethical value as to the nature and quality of the results. If, for example, a student does not have a large enough sample, a qualitative research approach may be more appropriate. Conversely the REC may recommend that the sample is too small to have validity and that this is reason enough *not* to put the small number of patients through the trouble of research.

Whilst the REC has only recommendatory powers, the faculty is approving less and less research which has not gone through any ethical review process. Also the REC definitely retains the power to disapprove of the research, this being shown recently when a research proposal requested an invasive procedure to patients who would otherwise not have undergone that procedure. The patients were therefore being subjected to an invasive method carrying some risk, without a clear medical reason for undergoing that investigation. Although the answer to the question was a legitimate one—it was envisaged that this group of patients would have benefited from this research if it could be proven to be statistically relevant—the fact that this had not yet been established on reasonable grounds led the REC to disapprove entirely of the whole research project.

Projects are usually not rejected in their entirety; rather recommendations are made to the researcher on what is necessary to make the research ethically valid. The REC may want to review a questionnaire or have a discussion of the informed consent process which has not been adequately presented or adequately proposed. A research project would thus be accepted on certain provisos. The REC is not in a position, nor is it required to, overlook the actual research. Although theoretically any complaints can be referred to the REC, it is unlikely that people would know about this. To the author's knowledge there have been no formal complaints so far, nor has any research case been referred to Court.

There is a general feeling, therefore, that RECs are experts with regard to methodology. When papers are quoted, rebuttals are often made on a methodology question—even if this has not been proven. Once an REC can prove the methodology to be sound, researchers could say that ethically it was viable and therefore there would be no grounds to argue against the research. Despite this, methodology is criticized even with regards to the best research, and therefore this is highly unlikely to occur.

## Addendum

It is relevant now, after the main paper was written, to add that the Data Protection Commissioner has asked the University of Malta to see that all research in Malta is undertaken in accordance with the data protection laws. Presumably this is legal as the Commissioner has, in effect, appointed a body to do its work. As a result the University has set up yet another REC, which is still in its infancy, to start doing this work. This would mean that private companies, such as a genetics company, doing any form of research which handles patients' data would have to go to the University to gain approval. Moreover, laboratories have a condition on the back of their licences stating that all research must be approved by the University before going ahead. Therefore, if previously there was a question as to the legality of this request, it now seems to be an official requirement from the Data Protection Commissioner.

Chapter 18

# Medical Research on Human Subjects and RECs in the Netherlands

Jessica Wright[*] and Bert Gordijn[†]


## Introduction and Background

Ethics committees have been accepted and incorporated with ease in the Netherlands due to its 'natural affinity to deliberative structures and consultative bodies' arising from its political structure.[1] The Netherlands was therefore one of the first European countries to have developed and implemented ethics committees. These were mainly hospital-based clinical ethics committees, which are now present in almost every hospital and nursing home in the Netherlands. Medical Ethics Review Committees (METCs) are separate to these clinical ethics committees, and were formally established in 1999 by the Medical Research Involving Human Subjects Act (WMO). The METCs are overseen by the Central Committee on Research Involving Human Subjects (CCMO), also set up by the 1999 WMO. All medical research involving human subjects must be assessed by an ethics committee in advance, and whether it is an METC or the CCMO depends on the type of research. The CCMO itself is responsible for some of the more 'controversial' techniques and research, such as gene therapy, xenotransplantation and any research involving embryos or gametes. What follows in this report is an exploration of the establishment and powers of RECs in the Netherlands, followed by detailed consideration into some of the legal and, specifically, data protection issues of the REC's deliberations.

---

[*] Doctoral researcher and PRIVIREAL co-worker, Sheffield Institute of Biotechnological Law and Ethics.
[†] Dr, Department of Ethics, Philosophy and History of Medicine, University of Nijmegen, Nijmegen, The Netherlands.
[1] See B. Gordjin, 'Ethics Committees in the Netherlands' in J. Glasa (ed.), *Ethics Committees in Central and Eastern Europe* (Strasbourg: Council of Europe, 2000), 205—208.

**Establishment of RECs**

There is an established system of ethical review of medical research projects involving human subjects in the Netherlands. This is a formal system since the 1999 WMO. This system of review is separate to the well-established Netherlands system of clinical ethics review. A separate clinical ethics committee exists in many hospitals and nursing homes in the Netherlands.

*Activities*

Activities covered by this review are firstly only those that involve medical research on human subjects. This includes both observational and interventional medical research. Whether the research protocol is reviewed by an METC or the CCMO is then dependent upon the type of medical research in question. The METCs are responsible for research where the subjects are capable of giving consent, for therapeutic research where the subjects are not capable of giving informed consent, and non-therapeutic research where subjects are not capable of informed consent but it is not interventional (observational research).[2] The CCMO is responsible for approving medical research protocols involving gene therapy, xenotransplantation and other research areas specified by the CCMO. The CCMO also considers research protocols where there are additional ethical problems to consider. These split into two areas, both involving non-therapeutic research. The first involves interventional non-therapeutic research where the subjects are not capable of giving informed consent. The second is observational non-therapeutic research that the CCMO has ruled itself competent to review. It also advises on research involving embryos or gametes.

In the case of multi-centre research, there is a specific formal procedure attached, and the Multicentre Research Review Procedure Directive[3] has been effective since 1 January 2001. Under this a reviewing METC should forward questions regarding local feasibility to the management of another institution where part of the research will take place. The management may in turn forward this question to the institution's associated accredited or non-accredited METC.

*Membership*

There are different membership requirements for an METC and the CCMO. The membership requirements of an METC are regulated by the WMO (16(2) a–e)

---

[2] Useful information about the remit of METCs and the CCMO is available on the CCMO's webpage: www.ipfier2.nl (last accessed 16 May 2005).

[3] Published in the Netherlands Government Gazette of 13 December 2000, no. 242, this has recently been replaced by the External Review Directive, effective from 1 May 2004, available online at http://www.ipfier2.nl/hipe/uploads/downloads/RET-eng(1).pdf (last accessed 16 May 2005). Following this, the applicant must have obtained statements on the local feasibility of the trial from the management of each participating centre before submitting the project for multi-centre review.

which includes both obligatory and non-obligatory, or preferable, members. The obligatory members are at least one physician, a lawyer, an expert in medical research methodology, an ethicist and a person sympathetic to the patient's viewpoint. A judgment of the METC is only lawful if the meeting has been attended by at least these five members, and if supported by a majority. The remaining preferable members are an expert in nursing or nursing science, and experts in clinical pharmacology or clinical pharmacy (if the committee is to review medical product trials). If the METC is attached to an institution there is a request that at least one member should be independent of the institution.

Membership requirements for the CCMO are also mentioned in the WMO, and Section 14 states that:

1.  There shall be a central committee for medical research; it shall have at most thirteen members.
2.  The members of the central committee shall include at least one doctor, persons with expertise in pharmacology, nursing, behavioural science, the law, research methodology and ethics, and a person charged with the task of examining protocols specifically from the subject's point of view.
3.  A deputy shall be appointed for each member of the central committee.
4.  The members of the central committee, including the chairperson and the deputies, shall be nominated by Our Minister and appointed by royal decree for a term not exceeding four years. Our Minister shall appoint a person to act as an observer at committee meetings.

As is obvious from the section above, the expertise which must be present in members of the CCMO is a little more varied than for METCs, for example it includes a behavioural scientist. The CCMO members also have the luxury of having deputies who can attend committee meetings in their name. An observer is also appointed by the Minister of Health, Education and Sport to attend the CCMO meetings, indirectly ensuring governmental supervision.

*Responsibility and Accountability*

METCs can be part of a hospital or other body, but in general they are part of the national government and are not hierarchically answerable to any other government body.[4] Decisions taken by METCs are forwarded to the CCMO, but the CCMO has no power to change a decision, and instead acts as an ethical appeal body with regard to these decisions. The CCMO has the authority to both recognize METCs and stop them from functioning. The Minister of Health, Education and Sport (VWS) has ultimate responsibility for the way METCs and the CCMO fulfil their statutory roles.[5] The CCMO is answerable to both the

---

[4] De Centrale Commissie Mensgebonden Onderzoek (CCMO), *Manual for the Review of Medical Research Involving Human Subjects* (Netherlands: 2002), 15, available from the webpage: http://www.ccmo.nl/download/toetsingshandleiding-2002_ENG.pdf (last accessed on 16 May 2005).

[5] *Ibid.*, 16.

Minister and to Parliament. The CCMO also provides annual and four-yearly reports on its work to the Minister for Health, Welfare and Sport.

## General Powers of RECs

In general, METCs and the CCMO approve or reject medical research protocol applications submitted to them. The CCMO does offer an advisory role for medical research involving gametes or embryos. An approval from an METC or the CCMO is required by law before medical research on human subjects can go ahead. Depending on the specific research project, there can be additional legal requirements that must be met and so approval by a committee is not always sufficient.

As this area is governed by law, there are penalties in place for those who do not follow it. In Section 33(5) of the WMO, it is stated that if any person '...performs research for which no protocol has been approved, or contrary to the protocol approved for it...' they shall be imprisoned for up to six months or receive a fourth category fine (12 500 Euros). These are summary offences. There are stricter penalties for those persons who, for example, contravene Section 6(1) of the WMO, which relates to consent conditions for research. For this a person would receive imprisonment for up to one year or a fourth category fine (Section 33(1) of the WMO), an indictable offence. There are also other possible summary offences outlined under Section 33 of the WMO.

Compliance with the WMO is monitored by public health inspectors appointed by the Minister for Health, Welfare and Sport (VWS), and the civil servants who work under the inspectors at the Public Health Supervisory Service. These inspectors are empowered by Sections 28 and 29 of the WMO. They have the power to require the provision of information and the production of documents, and all parties have a duty to cooperate with them.

## General Legal Responsibility of RECs

METCs are independent administrative agencies which conduct reviews on the basis of statutory criteria, rather than their own thinking. This means the committees pay great attention to the law. These laws include the WMO, the Multicentre Directive (now the External Review Directive), the Decree on Compulsory Insurance, and General Administrative Regulations on Gene Therapy and Xenotransplantation. The CCMO has recommended that all protocols related to medicinal product trials, and to some extent all research, should take into account the GCP Guidelines.[6] However, Article 55 of the Decree on Manufacturing and Delivering Medicinal Products (BBA), issued pursuant to the Medicines Act (WOG), requires compliance with the guidelines for all medicinal

---

[6] N. 4 *supra*, 38.

product trials involving human subjects.[7] Naturally, the Statement of Helsinki also applies.[8]

*Implementation of the Good Clinical Practice Directive*

Due to the mention of the GCP Guidelines in the law, there should not be too great an impact when the 2001/20/EC Directive on Good Clinical Practice is fully implemented. To achieve this, the WMO has been amended, and first approved by the Lower House of Parliament on 16 December 2003. Approval by the Upper House of Parliament is pending as of December 2004, when the discussions were scheduled to recommence in 2005, with implementation postponed until March 2005 at the earliest.

Following the amended WMO, there will be changes both to the overall system of review and specifically to the system for those trials researching medicinal products.[9] Changes to the overall system of review include: that METCs will be referred to as accredited ethics committees (aECs); that 'approval' of the protocol by a 'Competent Authority'[10] as well as the aEC will also take place; timelines are specified for decision-making; a hospital pharmacist and clinical pharmacologist must now be on the aECs; and there will be a network of experts established, contactable through the CCMO if needed. The appeal structure will be changed, and the aEC will also be able to revoke a positive decision if it has grounds to suspect trial continuation could lead to unacceptable risks for subjects.

Specific changes relating to research with medicinal products will affect gene therapy trials (which will not be allowed to modify the germ-line), and trials involving either incapacitated adults or children under 18—where appropriate experience will be needed on the REC. The Health Care Inspectorate of the Ministry of Health, Welfare and Sport will be able to inspect before, during or after a clinical trial to ensure that the standards of GCP are followed, inspecting data, information and documents.

As from 1 May 2004, sponsors may submit trials under this new system, but there will be no review by the 'Competent Authority' until the new law is properly implemented.

---

[7] N. 4 *supra*, 48.

[8] N. 4 *supra*, 7.

[9] This information has largely been taken from: The Working Party for the Implementation of Directive 2001/20/EC, *'Clinical Research with Medicinal Products in the Netherlands'* (The Ministry of Health, Welfare and Sport, June 2004).

[10] The Competent Authority will—in the case of an aEC—be the CCMO, and when the protocol is reviewed initially by the CCMO, the Ministry of Health, Welfare and Sport. This second review will decide if there are any grounds for 'non-acceptance', check documentation, and see if there are any adverse reactions not reported to the aEC present on the EudraCT database. These assessments may be sequentially or in parallel, according to the applicant's wishes.

*Rejection of Lawful Activities*

The results of a brief survey of both METCs (nine) and the CCMO conclude that the vast majority, including the CCMO, would be permitted to prohibit a lawful activity, for example, if it were unethical. Two local METCs, however, indicated they would not be permitted to prohibit an activity which was lawful. This shows there is not agreement on this issue.

*Approval of Unlawful Activities*

The results conclude that committees would never approve an unlawful activity (even if otherwise ethical). This supports the assertion that they pay great attention to the law.

*Attention to the Law in Practice, and Specifically Data Protection Law*

In relation to law, at least in theory, Sections 3 and 6 of the WMO set out the criteria for review of a research protocol, including medical, ethical and other considerations.[11] Within the ethical review, it is stated that the proposed arrangements for obtaining consent should be assessed to ensure they are consistent with legal requirements.[12] The Personal Data Protection Act (WBP) is one such source mainly addressing the issue of consent and consent forms. It is advised that other questions should also be addressed: who has access to the data? How will it be stored? Who needs to access the data? Will the data be anonymized? Researchers should answer these questions on application for research review. These questions appear to be asked in light of the WBPs confidentiality provisions.[13]

Indeed all ethics committees surveyed, including the CCMO, and except for one local METC, stated that complying with data protection law is a necessary condition of approval. Two of these stated it could also be seen as a recommendation. Seven METCs stated that if the protocol was ethical but did not comply with data protection law, they would prohibit it. The CCMO and one local METC would approve the research but make it conditional on getting legal advice. All METCs and the CCMO stated that they individually interpret the law and guidance in order to decide on data protection issues. All of these committees, except two, would also rely on other guidance—but often from different places. The CCMO would also ask for advice from legal academics or from the Data Protection Authority. Of the other METCs, two would ask legal academics, two would ask practising lawyers and one would ask the Data Protection Authority to help them decide on data protection issues. The CCMO is permitted and prepared to draw a breach of data protection law to the attention of the Data Protection Authority. The other METCs are divided on this question; only three of eight

---

[11] See n. 4 *supra*, 35.
[12] *Ibid.*, 38.
[13] *Ibid.*

believe they are permitted to (and prepared to) do the same. Two METCs would reject a breach of Data Protection Directive 95/46/EC even if the research were otherwise ethical and lawful. These results show that on the main issues—such as complying with data protection law—the committees are agreed. However, there is variation on how this is done in practice, including who they would ask for advice about data protection law.

## *Legal Action Against RECs*

In practice, all ethics committees, except one local METC, believe they have liability at law in relation to their decisions or opinions regarding research proposals. The decision made by an METC is legally binding on the researchers, and the WMO prohibits medical research with human subjects unless it has been approved. All decisions of an METC must be submitted to the CCMO, and the CCMO can only reverse these decisions on administrative appeal. The CCMO can also revoke the METC's accreditation. Appeal against a CCMO's decision can be made to the administrative law division of the Appellant's High Court, see Part 8 of the General Administrative Law Act.[14]

## Specific Data Protection Matters

### *Public Interest Judgments*

Essential to REC approval is that the research itself is important and needed, and that this outweighs the risks and burdens for the subjects. Alongside this, whilst reviewing protocols, it is important how consent is obtained.[15] The ethics committees were asked what action they would take if scientifically interesting research, that promises to benefit future patients, requires breaches of privacy or confidentiality? Of the responses received none believed it was automatically justified in the public interest, four of ten (including the CCMO) would see it as justified on a case-by-case basis, and four would reject it. Three of the committees (including the CCMO) would also consider approval subject to an external legal opinion. This shows that although the actions the ethics committees would take are different, they would still never view acceptance as automatically justified.

Consent is a very important consideration in relation to research protocols in the Netherlands; the WMO includes provisions relating directly to it. The WMO states that no one may be used as a research subject in medical research until he or she has signed a statement giving his or her informed consent (Section 6.1). Without such written consent participation is against the law. The only exemptions to the need for consent, and the linked right to be informed, can be those provided in law. The only exemption provided for by the WMO is where the research needs to be performed in an emergency situation, when written consent is unobtainable,

---

[14] N. 4 *supra*, 50.
[15] *Ibid.*

and where the results may be of direct benefit (Section 6.2). This law makes no mention of being able to forgo consent where in the public interest, and would view such research as unlawful. However, other laws stipulate certain exceptional situations that would allow a more liberal management of data in view of the public interest.

*Anonymized Information*

*Is coded data considered to be rendered anonymous when the code is kept?* Coded data can only be seen as indirectly identifiable, as normally the person undertaking the processing cannot identify the data subject—only clinicians or high-level researchers will hold the code to the personal data. As seen below, a narrow majority of ethics committees believe the data are anonymous even though they are indirectly identifiable, showing that coded information could be seen as anonymous.

*Informing patients that their data will be further used for research after anonymization* The CCMO responded that it is necessary to inform the patients of this type of processing, and all METCs except one (seven out of eight) agreed with this position. The vast majority would therefore feel it is necessary to inform patients, when their data are collected, if it will be further used for the purposes of research even after it has been anonymized.

*When is data anonymized?* The ethics committees answered questions about when they consider data are anonymous and therefore the data protection principles do not apply. Four METCs consider they are *only* anonymous when it is no longer possible for anyone, directly or indirectly, to identify who the data are about. Three METCs and the CCMO think that data are anonymous both in this event, and when the researchers cannot directly or indirectly identify who the data are about, even if those from whom the researchers have obtained the data (for example, the clinicians) still can. One METC only mentions it considers data anonymous in the second case. These views show that thoughts on anonymization clearly differ between ethics committees, perhaps due to a lack of clear guidance. The WBP would appear to insist that data are only anonymous when no one can identify the data subject either directly or indirectly. However, the WBP does not apply when encryption or agreements regarding access to data 'reasonably' excludes identification of an individual.[16]

*DNA Samples and Genetic Information*

Six METCs and the CCMO consider that, at least when the identity of the human source is directly or indirectly knowable, the processing of human biological material for genetic research falls within the scope of data protection law. Two

---

[16] Ministry of Justice, *Guidelines for Personal Data Processors (Personal Data Protection Act)* (2001), 14.

METCs consider that it does not. There is no provision in the data protection law which states whether human biological materials do fall under its remit.[17] The Medical Treatment Contracts Act mentions that the use of anonymous body materials, such as blood, in scientific research is only allowed if at the very least the person involved made no objection.[18] The *Manual for the Review of Medical Research* also adds that blood and body tissues may not be retained at the end of research without the subject's informed consent, and they may only be retained for a purpose directly related to the research for which it was originally obtained.[19] Further consent must be obtained for a new purpose. RECs therefore appear to regard such material as data and, where traceable, as personal data.

---

[17] Some relevant guidelines concerning the further use of body tissues for medical research are the *Gedragscode Goed Gebruik Lichaamsmateriaal 2001* [Good Practice in the Use of Body Tissues] (Federation of Medical Associations (Stichting FMWV), 2001), available from the webpage: http://www.fmwv.nl (last accessed on 16 May 2005).

[18] T. Hooghiemstra, 'The Implementation of Directive 95/46/EC in the Netherlands, with Special regard for Medical Data' (2002) 9 *European Journal of Health Law* 219–227, 222.

[19] See n. 4 *supra*, 115.

Chapter 19

# The Norwegian Model
# for Ethical Review of Medical Research[*]

Vigdis Kvalheim[†]

## Introduction

Norway was relatively late, compared to other European countries, to establish formal ethical review procedures in biomedical research. Whereas the USA and Europe saw the development of a formal research ethics committee (REC) system in the late 1960s and 1970s, the Norwegian system for the ethical review of medical research was only organized during the late 1980s. In 1985 five regional committees for medical research ethics were established, followed in 1990 by three national committees covering all scientific disciplines.

Given the focus of PRIVIREAL on the data protection rights of participants in research, it is interesting to note that contrary to this slow start in formalizing a system of ethical review, Norway was very early if not the first to establish a formal system for the legal review of (medical) research. Norway enacted its Personal Data Register Act in 1978 and was thus part of the first wave of data protection laws passed in Europe in the 1970s and early 1980s. Responding to the requirements of the new legal framework, the Research Council of Norway established the Secretariat for Data Protection Affairs in 1981, a national interdisciplinary body. The mandate being to review research projects against the requirements of the Personal Data Register Act. The agreement made the Secretariat a mandatory broker reviewing, against the legal requirements, all

---

[*] By kind permission of the National Committee for Medical Research Ethics (NEM), this paper relies on material published on the internet pages of NEM and the regional committees for medical research ethics. In particular, parts of the section on terms of reference are by and large copied from an article written by H. C. Guldberg and K. W. Ruyter in 1997 on 'Research Ethical Review in Norway', published on the NEM's website: http://www.etikkom.no/Engelsk (last accessed 16 May 2005).

[†] Assistant Director, Norwegian Social Science Data Services (NSD). NSD is a national research infrastructure, its principal mission being to facilitate empirical research. NSD is currently one of the largest social science data archives in the world, providing a variety of services to researchers in Norway as well as internationally. Besides being a gateway to rich data holdings, NSD serves as a resource centre assisting researchers with respect to data gathering, questionnaire design, social science data analysis, methodology and privacy issues.

projects where research involved the collection, use, storing and re-use of personal data, giving recommendations to the Data Inspectorate. At present the Data Protection Official for Research,[1] or the Ombudsman for Privacy in Research (the Norwegian title for the office), carries on the activities of the Secretariat.[2]

The focus of this paper is primarily on the system of ethical review of medical research by the five regional research ethics committees (RRECs). In order to understand the role and functions of the RRECs, it is essential to have at least some knowledge of the broader system of review of medical research in Norway. After a more detailed description of the organization and function of the RRECs, the paper will briefly describe the independent bodies that review medical research from a legal perspective. In this context the Data Protection Official for Research, set up specifically to guarantee the data protection rights granted by the Data Directive in (medical) research, is seen as being particularly important. Before this, however, the role and functions of the National Committee for Medical Research Ethics (NEM) merit discussion.

## The National Committee for Medical Research Ethics (NEM)

In 1989 the Norwegian Government proposed the establishment of three national committees for research ethics. This proposal was approved by Parliament and the Ministry of Education, Research and Church Affairs, which set up the NEM in 1990.

The NEM has 12 members with different professional backgrounds. Traditionally a physician has chaired the committee. Pursuant to its charter the committee, in addition to having medical competence, shall include members with competence in ethics, law, psychology and genetics. The committee also has lay representatives who have often been persons with experience in politics or media.

Members of the committee are appointed by the Ministry of Education and Research upon recommendation from the Research Council of Norway. They are appointed for terms of three years and may not sit on the Committee for more than two terms. All members are selected on the basis of personal qualifications, not as a reflection, or as a result, of their membership of a specific interest group.

The committee has a permanent Director, who attends to the day-to-day business. The three national research ethics committees also have a common secretariat with shared public relations and administrative functions.

A characteristic feature of the Norwegian model is that the national committees do not only deal with issues within the more narrowly defined field of

---

[1] The role and functions of this position are described in more detail in: Vigdis Kvalheim, 'Implementation of the Data Protection Directive in Relation to Medical Research in Norway' in D. Beyleveld, D. Townend, S. Rouillé-Mirza and J. Wright (eds.), *Implementation of the Data Protection Directive in Relation to Medical Research in Europe* (Aldershot: Ashgate Publishing Ltd, 2004), 289–305.

[2] This article uses the title Data Protection Official to prevent confusion and ensure comparability to the Directive.

research ethics, but also include the broader field of ethics of science. This includes issues of scientific responsibility for wider social concerns.

It is important to emphasize that even though Norway has a national medical research ethics committee in addition to the regional committees, this does not mean that the NEM is an appeal body for the RREC system, as they are not organized in a hierarchical system. NEM is an advisory and coordinating body for the five regional committees for medical research ethics. These committees evaluate all concrete medical research projects, while the NEM gives its opinion on issues that are more a matter of principle. Most importantly, the NEM should bring current and potential questions on medical research ethics to the attention of the scientific community, politicians, civil servants, relevant professions, organizations and the general public. Consequently the NEM should in particular:

- be a resource of competence in ethics in all fields of scientific research;
- function as a watchtower and an adviser at the national level;
- inform and advise scientific communities, governmental authorities and the general public;
- coordinate relevant national activities, and cooperate with other national and international research ethics committees.

Bi-annual meetings attended by the chairs and secretaries from each of the five regional committees deal with issues on which they need to collaborate. Furthermore, all members of the NEM and the regional committees attend a two-day joint meeting each autumn, for professional replenishment and discussion.

## The System of Regional Research Ethics Committees (RREC)

In line with development in Scandinavia, the Norwegian model for ethical review of medical research was formed on a regional basis. In 1985, medical research ethics committees were set up, one for each of the five health regions.

Law does not regulate the Norwegian system for ethical review of medical research. The role and function of the RRECs is formally regulated through the terms of reference laid down by the Ministry of Education and Research.

The Ministry appoints both the Chairperson of the committee and its members. Each committee has eight members with the following multidisciplinary backgrounds:

- a medical professional from the faculty of medicine in the region;
- a medical professional from the official health authority of the region;
- a member with qualifications in psychology from the department or faculty of psychology in the region;
- a member with officially recognized nursing qualifications;
- a representative of the regional hospital owners;
- a member with professional expertise in ethics;

-    a lawyer.

Administratively, RRECs are located in the medical faculties of one of the universities that are funding the RREC. This funding includes the secretary's salary, current expenses and payment of members on the basis of the workload.

## The Terms of Reference[3]

RRECs have two main responsibilities: they shall provide guidance and advice on matters of research ethics, and information on the principles of research ethics.

All relevant biomedical research in the respective region shall be reviewed by the RREC. This encompasses both therapeutic and non-therapeutic research on patients and healthy subjects and, analogously, research on cadavers and aborted foetuses, including foetal tissue.

The official comments issued by the Ministry on the terms of reference for RRECs for medical research ethics emphasize that biomedical research is interpreted more widely than has traditionally been the case. It may also embrace research that *applies* psychological, social scientific or biotechnological *methodology*. The criteria for requiring the submission of such research projects are that they deal with the physical or mental health of human beings and that they involve the use of therapeutic or non-therapeutic methods on human beings. Such research projects must be submitted for review if they deal with the physical or mental health of patients. Thus, in this context, biomedical research is interpreted more widely than has traditionally been the case. This has caused some frustration within the social sciences, which argues that the committees do not have the composition and thus the necessary knowledge to assess the ethical implications of a social science project, nor to balance the interest in the research against ethical considerations.

## General Powers

The Norwegian RRECs have advisory power. The terms of reference state that if a project is subject to prior evaluation by an RREC, the project cannot start before the regional committee has reviewed it. This means that the committees approve and reject applications despite their formal power being clearly recommendatory. It also means that approval by one of the committees is, although not formally, necessary for the research project to go ahead.

## Review Procedure

The main purpose of the review procedure is to ascertain that human subjects participating in research are protected according to ethical norms, thereby giving

---

[3] Norwegian Ministry of Education and Research, *Terms of Reference for the Regional Committees for Medical Research Ethics*, Norway, 1 July 2003.

the public assurance and trust in the process. Thus the advice given by the regional research ethics committees for medical research should be based on generally accepted principles of research ethics with due attention to guidelines established by national or international bodies. Special reference is made to the Declaration of Helsinki, the Vancouver Convention, and International Guidelines for Review on Epidemiological Studies.[4]

Some examples of generally accepted principles of research ethics are mentioned, such as: the freely given informed consent requirement, the distinction between therapeutic and non-therapeutic research, and the weighing up of the potential risk and discomfort to the subjects as opposed to the medical benefits of the research project, for the subject and/or others.

In the case of clinical trials, the evaluation is also based on regulations relating to clinical testing of drugs on humans and on the Guidelines for Good Clinical Practice. Norway has accepted these guidelines through the EEA collaboration on the basis of EU Directive 2001/20/EC.

Law and legal requirements are not explicitly mentioned in the terms of reference except with regard to the new Biobank Act.[5] However, it is acknowledged, in line with the Helsinki Declaration, that all research involving humans or information about humans must comply with national legislation. Thus, committees may not recommend or approve of unlawful activities, and compliance with current law must be considered.

In practice, RRECs do play an important role ensuring the rights and freedoms as granted by Data Protection Directive 95/46/EC, both in general and more specifically with regard to the use of biological material as defined by the Biobank Act of 2003 and described in their mandate. RRECs pay attention to the law on two levels. Firstly they provide information on laws and regulations such as the obligation to notify the Data Protection Official for Research, and/or the Data Inspectorate, if the research project involves the processing of personal data. Secondly they review research projects and consider the legal requirements whilst reviewing these projects. From July 2003, the new Biobank Act plays a particularly important role in the committees' decisions.

*The Review Process*

The first step is to evaluate the study, its scientific soundness in terms of chosen methodology and its originality. Such an evaluation requires scientific competence, which may not be inherent among the committee members; however, consultative help or advice can be sought from such parties as the grant-giving bodies.

The main consideration is to ensure that research below a minimum standard, which is not going to give valid results and is therefore clearly unethical, is not recommended. A more difficult, and in this sense challenging, task is to apply the

---

[4] National Committee for Research Ethics in Science and Technology, *Standard Operating Procedures for the Regional Committees for Medical Research Ethics* (SOP), Norway, 2 July 2002.

[5] Ministry of Health, *Lov om biobanker, Med merknader* (2003) Rundskriv I-10.

concept of utility to distinguish between ethical and unethical research. To applied research one should always ask: what is the need and possibly the benefit of the actual project? This may be difficult to assess or represent, at times providing an ethical dilemma for committee members.

The second step is to assess the aspects of the proposed research design that directly concern the protection of research subjects. The subject's informed consent is of paramount importance in order to protect the autonomy of the individual; that being the right to receive detailed, understandable and honest information about the project alongside the individual's freedom to consent. It is also important that the cultural values prevalent in the population are given due consideration. The insurance of study subjects is, by Norwegian law, in most instances, taken care of on objective grounds.

The final step is to arrive at a decision in order to recommend the project or not. In the Norwegian committee system this is achieved by consensus through a process of solving issues in a discussion on medical, legal and common sense grounds, projecting the opinions on the normative spectrum of accepted ethical standards.

## Changing and Extending the Terms of Reference

The mandate or terms of reference of the committees have been changed in the past and are presently under deliberation by the Ministry of Education. In this context it is important to note that in July 2001 the terms of reference for the RRECs were changed to open the committee's business to public scrutiny. The Freedom of Information Act 1971 shall apply in full to the activities of the committees, and furthermore the operating procedures must also be in accordance with the Public Administration Act 1967.

The committees, however, are not administrative bodies, therefore they do not make individual decisions within the meaning of the Public Administration Act. The result of this is that decisions cannot be appealed and the committees continue to recommend or advise against projects. Any 'appeal' may only be addressed to the committee by which the case was first reviewed. Another consequence is that the committees have no formal power to impose penalties or enforce sanctions for researchers who do not submit their research for review, or fail to follow the committee's requirements and recommendations. In practice, however, the committees have substantial power. Failure to follow their recommendations may have serious consequences for the project and the scientists involved. It may result in the withdrawal of funding and institutional support, the lack of possibilities to publish in internationally prestigious magazines, resulting in the loss of prestige and status. Additionally in cases involving processing of personal information, the Data Inspectorate may stop the project.

Both the NEM and RRECs have questioned if the formal status of being advisory or consultative bodies is consistent with the application of the Freedom of Information Act, and in part the Public Administration Act, and the work of the regional committees. The working committee, which represents the national and five regional committees, have recommended a practice ensuring a second opinion to be provided. The established practice implies that the project leader will first be invited to converse with the committee responsible for reviewing the project. If it turns out to be impossible to reach an agreement, the project leader will then be offered a second opinion from one of the other regional committees. The NEM is sometimes asked for advice, but will normally not comment on a specific project. The NEM may, however, choose to comment on the ethical questions involved on a general level.

## Regulation of the System for Ethical Review of Medical Research

In July 2003 the Ministry of Education and Research appointed a committee with a mandate to assess the need for, and consequences of, legal regulation of the Norwegian system of research ethics committees. It was implied that the Norwegian system, with one national and five regional committees for medical research ethics, will continue to exist in its present form. It was also implied that there will be no major changes in terms of reference and operating procedures of the RRECs. The regional committees should continue to be free and independent with no formal sanctions at their disposal.

It was, however, expected that the Ministry would propose to make the Norwegian system of research ethics committees part of the legal system, therefore regulated by law like our neighbouring Scandinavian countries. The committee was mandated to draft a new act regulating the entire system of RECs, including the national committees. It was also expected that the uncertainties and confusion with regard to the extent to which the rules of the Public Administration Act apply to the work of the committees would be clarified. It was, however, more uncertain whether the proposal would include the possibility to appeal or not, and if so, how the appeal procedures would be organized. The NEM had proposed to formalize the current practice of offering a second opinion from a different committee.

The Ministry delivered its proposal on 17 June 2004. The proposal includes a draft law regulating the system for ethical review, including the national (NEM) and the regional (RRECs) committees reviewing medical research. The proposed act by and large codifies the existing system for ethical review in Norway. Establishing that the RRECs are indeed public administrative bodies solves the former ambiguity in relation to the Public Administration Act. The RRECs will, however, continue to be advisory boards exempted from the rules on decision-making in the Public Administration Act.

## Case Load and Type of Projects

Applications to the Norwegian RRECs are dealt with in around 30 days, with each RREC meeting ten times a year on average. In 2002 the five committees reviewed 929 projects of which nine projects (one per cent) were rejected. The number of protocols referred each year has gradually increased from an average of 600 projects in the mid 1990s to above 900 in the last four years.

Clinical research studies account for 71 per cent of all proposals submitted to the RRECs while pharmaceutical products account for 21 per cent. Most projects involve adult patients. Ideally the ethical committees should be responsible for establishing a review procedure for tracing progress and the final outcome of all studies. Following up approved proposals is not practised by the Norwegian RRECs unless there is a significant deviation from the agreed protocol, or matters affecting the safety of the subjects arise during the study. For the RRECs in Norway, a mandatory project follow-up would result in a tremendous increase in workload.

Other bodies that review medical research with regard to the Personal Data Act and the Health Data Filing System Act, such as the Data Inspectorate, follow up and control medical and health projects. The Data Inspectorate announced in 2004 that the processing of health information for scientific purposes would be one of the priorities for their controlling activities.

## Biological Material and Research Biobanks

The terms of reference were amended on 1 July 2003 to include the new role and responsibilities of RRECs as set out by the Norwegian Act on Biobanks (the 'Biobank Act').[6] According to this Act the establishment of research biobanks is possible only after permission from the Ministry of Health and after being reviewed by one of the five RRECs for medicine. This is reflected in Chapter 3 of the terms of reference for the committees:

> The committees shall evaluate the establishment of all research biobanks in relation to section 4 of the (Norwegian) Act on biobanks (the 'Biobank Act') p. 4.

> The committee will recommend or not recommend the establishment of the research biobank on the basis of the information about the biobank submitted to the committee on a special form.

> In the event of changed, extended or new use of previously collected biobank material, queries shall be submitted to the committee regarding exceptions from the main rule about new freely-given, explicit and informed consent from the donor of the material. After evaluating whether it is impossible or very difficult to obtain new consent, the committee will recommend or not recommend that the Ministry of Health grants a dispensation from the new consent requirement, cf. Biobank Act p. 13 first and second paragraphs.

> In the case of changed, extended or new use of anonymous biobank material, the committee will recommend or not recommend such changed, extended or new use.

The RRECs should be consulted and make recommendations about when scientific use is justified in the public interest without prior consent from participants. This

---

[6] See n. 5 *supra*.

could be the case if material in diagnostic and therapeutic biobanks is used for research purposes, or when a research biobank is used for a new and changed purpose. The committees should also, on a more general level, assess the public interest in the research biobank as compared to a reasonable use of resources, whilst considering if there are commercial purposes involved in the project.

The recommendation by the committee is sent to the Ministry of Health, which decides on the establishment of research biobanks, or the Directorate of Health and Social Affairs, which decides on changed, extended, or new uses of biobank material. The Ministry and the Directorate shall consider the recommendation, but may decide against it on the basis of important ethical considerations or public interest. This is contrary to standard procedures with regard to ethical review of medical research where the Ministry has no power to override recommendations made by the RRECs.

## Definitions and Scope of the Biobank Act

According to the Biobank Act, a research biobank is a collection of human biological material *and* information that is directly produced through analysing that material where it is used for scientific purposes. Therapeutic and diagnostic biobanks, on the other hand, are defined as a collection of biological material.

The legal definition of a research biobank is narrow but at the same time wide ranging. It is narrow as it encompasses even one single blood sample, temporarily stored for the purpose of research; wide as it not only covers biological material but also information produced whilst analysing the material. Also in relation to the provision on access to information for research participants, the definition extends to related and otherwise collected information. It is important to note at this stage that the Biobank Act also regulates the information produced even after the biological material is deleted.

Consequently the Biobank Act will apply to a majority of research projects already reviewed by the RRECs against generally accepted ethical standards. It will also apply to a large amount of projects reviewed by the Data Inspectorate and the Data Protection Official for Research. Research projects that process personal information, as defined by the Directive and national legislation, must follow the established procedures for notification and prior licensing.

In the context of PRIVIREAL, it may also be interesting to note that the Biobank Act strengthens the rights of participants involved in research as compared to the Personal Data Act and the Data Protection Directive. It may even be the case that the Act does not comply with the Data Protection Directive and the Personal Data Act with regard to the provision on withdrawal of consent. Depending on how this section of the law is interpreted and practised, the right of research participants to object to further participation by demanding the biological material be deleted and the information (produced by analysing the biological material or collected in relation to the material) be deleted or handed over, may have some unintended and severe consequences on medical research. The National Committee for Research Ethics in Medicine (NEM), among others, have pointed to the possible problems of a participant's rights of access to research data.

According to the Ministry of Health's comments on the Biobank Act, the projects should be reviewed and if necessary licensed prior to their making a decision. In practice, however, the Ministry will make its decision earlier and notify the project leader prior to licensing by the Data Inspectorate. The Biobank Act sets a time limit of 45 days, meaning that the biobank could be legally established if the Ministry does not react within this time limit.

An important argument for including *information* in the legal definition of a research biobank has been the lack of adequate regulation in the Personal Data Act and the Personal Health Data Filing System Act, for the potential commercial use of research biobanks. It is interesting to note that the Norwegian Data Inspectorate advocated against the Biobank Act in its comments on the draft. The Data Inspectorate has argued that the Biobank Act is redundant and that the Personal Health Data Filing System Act of 2002, with minor amendments, would provide adequate protection of biological material. The Inspectorate pointed to the fact that the now-enacted Biobank Act contributes to fragmented and sometimes overlapping regulations, as well as unclear division of responsibilities and labour between the different authorities enforcing the different acts. The NEM has supported this view, stressing that the new Act adds to the complexity and inaccessibility of the legislative framework within which health personnel and researchers operate. Lack of compliance with existing legislation is seen to add to this as a source of ambiguity and confusion for medical and health personnel and researchers.

The debate on the Biobank Act aside, the fact remains that the RREC system is given very important tasks in relation to the enforcement of the new Biobank Act. The new and extended tasks and responsibilities are reflected in the manner in which the 'decisions' or recommendations are made. Whereas the Helsinki Declaration, the Vancouver Convention and other national and international guidelines constitute the basis for the general ethical review and recommendations made by the RRECs, the Biobank Act is the main basis for deciding on the establishment and use of research biobanks. This must be said to represent a major change with regard to the *raison d'etre* behind the system of ethical review of medical research, shifting the focus from ethical standards to legal requirements when reviewing research projects. The legal definition of research biobanks adds to the potential impact of the law on the operation of the committees in general. A research project based on data material including one single blood sample qualifies as a research biobank. Therefore it must comply with the regulation and procedures established for the review and authorization of projects involving the establishment, use, changed use, extended use, re-use, and deletion of research biobanks. This means that a large volume of the projects already reviewed by the committees on the basis of ethical considerations will be defined as research biobanks.

It remains to be seen if and how the new role and responsibilities of the RRECs in relation to the Biobank Act will impact the balance between the attention the committees pay to internationally accepted ethical principles as compared to legal standards. Critical voices fear that vital ethical considerations and research values will suffer as the attention of the committees will gradually focus more on the law and the Ministry may overrule decisions. On the other hand, review processes based on ethical standards and legal principles clearly involve overlapping considerations, for example, in relation to issues of informed consent, necessity, public interest and risk. The fear is that moving from an ethical to a legal review process may involve a shift in balance or appreciation of different values. This could result in different conclusions and recommendations, for example with regard to passive consent being acceptable or not.

## Other Bodies Reviewing Medical Research

The Norwegian System of Review of Medical Research is based on a division of labour between different bodies reviewing legislation and guidelines on law and ethics respectively. Thus approval by an RREC is normally not sufficient to go ahead with the project. Usually several other bodies will have a say, assessing different legal aspects of the projects.

### The Data Protection Official for Research

The Data Inspectorate and Data Protection Official for Research have a special responsibility in ensuring rights and freedoms as granted by the Data Protection Directive and implemented in the Personal Data Act 2000 and the Personal Health Data Filing System Act 2001. If a research project involves the processing of personal data, these two Acts apply irrespective of whether the project is approved by an RREC, the Ministry of Health or the other authorities reviewing medical research.

In the context of PRIVIREAL, where the data protection rights of participants in research are the main focus, the Data Protection Official for Research at NSD is of particular interest.[7]

As mentioned in the first part of this paper, the Official carries out the functions of the Secretariat for Data Protection Affairs, which was established in 1981 to review research projects against the requirements of the newly enacted Personal Data Register Act of 1978. Drafting the Personal Data Act of 2000, it was widely agreed that both privacy and research have benefited from the close collaboration and the mutual trust that have developed between the Data Inspectorate and the research milieus. The research community has benefited by having an institution that provided counselling and guidance on the use of personal data, and by having a qualified and legitimate broker representing the research interests to the protectors of privacy. The interest in privacy has resulted in gaining regulation in an important area, and having a system of mandatory legal review has contributed significantly to raising the level of awareness of privacy protection within the Norwegian research community. Consequently, it was seen as important that the

---

[7] The role and functions of this position are described in more detail in: Vigdis Kvalheim (2004), see n. 1 *supra*.

regulations replacing the Personal Data Registers Act 1978 were conducive to developing and enhancing existing collaboration.

In line with these views, the Norwegian legislators took advantage of the possibility offered by the Data Protection Directive and provided further exemptions from notification when the data controller had appointed a Data Protection Official in line with Article 18(2). As a result the Director of NSD was appointed the Data Protection Official for Research from 1 February 2003.

So far agreements have been signed between the NSD and 110 institutions, including the universities and university colleges, public and private colleges, the major national research institutes, the major university hospitals as well as several other hospitals. These agreements make NSD the mandatory Data Protection Official for all research projects within these institutions. This means that a majority of medical research projects that involve the processing of personal information, regulated by the Personal Data Act or the Personal Health Data Filing System Act, should submit their research for review by the Data Protection Official for Research.

The Data Protection Official at NSD has therefore been given very important formal tasks, reviewing and 'ensuring' compliance with the Data Protection Directive and Norwegian data protection legislation in this area. Under the Personal Data Act of 2000, the system of prior legal review outside the Data Inspectorate has been formalized by law.

### The Data Inspectorate

The Data Inspectorate is an independent administrative body under the Norwegian Ministry of Labour and Government Administration. It was set up in 1980 to ensure enforcement of the Personal Data Register Act of 1978 (now made obsolete by the commencement of the Personal Data Act of 2000). The Inspectorate deals with applications for licences and receives notifications from research projects conducted in institutions where no Data Protection Official for Research has been appointed.

### The Ministry of Health and the Directorate of Health and Social Affairs

The Ministry of Health is responsible for the Biobank Act and decides on the establishment of new biobanks. On delegation from the Ministry, the Directorate of Health and Social Affairs decides on applications for changed, extended and new use of biobank material.

Permission must be obtained from the Directorate for Health and Social Affairs when research is to be conducted on confidential information. This is the case when research is based on the non-consent alternatives provided by the Data Protection Directive and Norwegian privacy legislation. In such cases, the processing also needs to be based on exemption from the rules on confidentiality in the Public Administration Act or the Act on Health Personnel.

It should also be noted that in 1989 the Norwegian Parliament decided that all biotechnology and gene technology trials involving human subjects were to be reported to the (then) Norwegian Ministry of Health and Social Affairs before commencement. According to the Act on the Application of Biotechnology in Human Medicine, approval from the Directorate of Health and Social Affairs is necessary for certain trial projects involving biotechnology. This is the case if the projects have specific diagnostic or therapeutic consequences for the patient.

In the case of clinical trials of medical equipment, the Directorate of Health and Social Affairs shall also be notified.

## The Norwegian Medicines Agency

In the case of drug trials, notification shall be sent to the Norwegian Medicines Agency. The Norwegian Medicines Agency assesses the notifications of clinical trials in accordance with Directive 2001/20/EC on Good Clinical Practice in the Conduct of Clinical Trials on Medical Products for Human Use. The RREC will routinely send copies of letters to the project leader and transcripts of minutes of meetings to the Norwegian Medicines Agency.

## Reviewing the System for Legal and Ethical Review of Medical Research

Regulations of medical research in Norway are based on several laws and ethical standards that are not regulated by law. The legal and ethical framework within which medical research operates is becoming increasingly complex, bureaucratic and difficult to follow. Since 2000, four new laws with major impact on medical research have been implemented (the Personal Data Act, the Personal Health Data Filing System Act, The Act on Biobanks and the Act on the Application of Biotechnology in Human Medicine). Alongside these, others such as the Health Personnel Act have also been amended.

Accompanying the new regulations are fragmented institutional responsibilities, complex systems of control and forms to complete before sending applications and notifications to the different institutions reviewing medical research. This development has caused some concern and distress within the medical research community in Norway. In fact, strong voices claim that the regulations at present constitute severe and unreasonable barriers to medical and health research in Norway.

It is against this background that the Ministry of Health in 2003 appointed a committee (the Regulation of Medical Research Committee) to evaluate and propose a change or simplification to the entire system of regulation of medical research, for example the system of ethical and legal review of medical research. The work of the committee should be based on the principles laid down in the Personal Health Data Filing Systems Act, the Biobank Act and the Act on Application of Biotechnology in Human Medicine.

The committee is expected to propose actions to ensure the suitable and unambiguous regulation of medical research. According to the terms of reference, the committee will describe and compare present rules and regulations in Norway and abroad, including existing procedures for notification and licensing and the division of labour between different institutions reviewing medical research. The so-called regulation committee is also supposed to elucidate the legal definition of consent, and the data subject's right of access, in the various laws and discuss the possible impacts of established practices on medical and health research.

The committee is further mandated to assess the need for a special Act regulating medical research, and if such a need is demonstrated, to draft a new Act and propose the necessary changes in existing regulations and guidelines. The Regulation of Medical Research Committee submitted its official report in December 2004. The committee proposed a new Act on health and medical research (The Health Research Act) which is supposed to replace the Personal Data Act, the Personal Health Data Filing System Act, the Act on Biobanks and the Act on the Application of Biotechnology in Human Medicine, with regard to medical and health research. The proposal has been submitted for review by interested parties.

Chapter 20

# Research Ethics Committees and Personal Data Protection in Poland

Patrycja Bong-Połeć[*] and Paweł Łuków[†]

## The Legal Basis of RECs in Poland[1]

The Polish system of ethical review of medical research was established by Article 29 of Ustawa z dnia 5 grudnia 1996 r. o zawodzie lekarza[2] (Act on the Profession of the Physician; henceforth referred to as PP) and by Rozporządzenie Ministra Zdrowia i opieki społecznej z dnia 11 maja 1999 r. w sprawie szczegółowych zasad powoływania i finansowania oraz trybu działania komisji bioetycznych[3] (The Decree of the Minister of Health and Social Services concerning Specific Principles of the Establishment, Funding and Operation of Bioethical Committees; henceforth referred to as DMH). Further regulations can be found in Rozporządzenie Ministra Zdrowia z dnia 10 grudnia 2002 r. w sprawie określenia szczegółowych wymagań Dobrej Praktyki Klinicznej[4] (The Decree of the Minister of Health concerning Specific Requirements of Good Clinical Practice; henceforth referred to as DPK), which is one of the key elements of change to Polish law through the legislation of the European Union. In particular, DPK implements Directive 2001/20. DPK has been in effect since 1 January 2003 and it will certainly provide the institutions that are responsible for overseeing clinical trials with a better tool for the supervision of medical research.

---

[*] A GXP Auditor in a contract research organization.

[†] Ph.D, teaches philosophy in the Institute of Philosophy, Warsaw University. Specializes in ethical theory, Immanuel Kant's moral philosophy and medical ethics.

[1] The situation described in this report represents that of December 2003.

[2] Ustawa z dnia 5 grudnia 1996 r. o zawodzie lekarza (Act on the Profession of the Physician) (PP) *Dziennik Ustaw* 1997 Nr 28, poz. 152.

[3] Rozporządzenie Ministra Zdrowia i opieki społecznej z dnia 11 maja 1999 r. w sprawie szczegółowych zasad powoływania i finansowania oraz trybu działania komisji bioetycznych (The Decree of the Minister of Health and Social Services concerning Specific Principles of the Establishment, Funding and Operation of Bioethical Committees) (DMH) *Dziennik Ustaw* 1999 Nr 47, poz. 480.

[4] Rozporządzenie Ministra Zdrowia z dnia 10 grudnia 2002 r. w sprawie określenia szczegółowych wymagań Dobrej Praktyki Klinicznej (The Decree of the Minister of Health concerning Specific Requirements of Good Clinical Practice) (DPK) *Dziennik Ustaw* 2002 Nr 221, poz. 1864.

**The Establishment of RECs**

Article 29 ust. 1 of PP specifies that a clinical trial can be conducted only after being approved by an REC. The establishment of a biomedical committee is therefore vital for conducting clinical trials legally. A similar provision can be found in Article 46 of the Code of Medical Ethics of the Medical Chamber of Polish physicians. In Poland, Bioethical Committees (henceforth referred to as RECs) are established specifically for the purpose of the review of research proposals. They do not perform any other significant activities in healthcare institutions; in particular, they do not provide assistance in decision-making in therapeutic contexts. This is backed up by the current practice in healthcare institutions whereby most therapeutic decisions are made in the privacy of the patient-physician relationship; this contrasts with the proceedings of RECs that have the form of sessions, necessary for the purpose of evaluation of particular research proposals (see the section below on REC activities).

Article 29 ust. 3 of PP makes provision for three kinds of RECs; the application of each depending on the type of institution in which clinical trials are conducted:

-     committees that are established by the rectors of university-level medical schools (called Medical Academies) or by the rectors of universities with medical programmes;
-     committees that are established by the directors of medical research and development institutions;
-     committees that are established by local medical chambers.

The first two types of committee oversee clinical trials conducted in their respective institutions; the third type of committee oversees clinical trials conducted by all other institutions and organizations in which medical research is done.

REC membership is specified by §3 ust. 2 of the DMH, requiring every REC to be composed of medical specialists (practitioners with a degree in a medical speciality) and a representative of another profession, in particular: a priest, a philosopher, a lawyer, a pharmacist or a nurse. Each of these must have at least ten years' professional experience in their respective fields. Non-medical REC members cannot be employees of the institution that establishes it (§3). Additionally, DMH Art. 29 ust. 4 requires that one member of the RECs that are established at medical schools and medical research and development institutions be a representative of the local medical chamber. According to DMH §4 the number of members of a committee should be no less than 11 and no more than 15, the exact number of members being determined by the authority that establishes the particular committee.

It should be noted that while the DMH says that the non-medical members of the RECs established by medical academies and research and development institutions may not be employees of those institutions, it does not include similar requirements concerning the medical members of the REC. The lack of such a requirement may lead to a situation in which all medical members of an institutional REC may be employed by the institution they oversee. This may compromise the quality of their evaluation of research proposal.

REC members are appointed for a period of three years.[5] There is no legal possibility of discontinuation of REC membership before the end of the member's time except by their own request, or through failure to participate in the REC's proceedings.[6]

## The System of Ethical Review

In Poland RECs are part of a larger system of the supervision of biomedical research which creates a structure of direct and indirect control of the activities of particular elements of the system (see the section below on the accountability of RECs). Every study proposal must receive a permit from the Ministry of Health before the study can begin. Additionally, the study proposal must be registered with Centralna Ewidencja Badań Klinicznych przy Ministerstwie Zdrowia[7] (The Central Register of Clinical Trials at the Ministry of Health (CEBK)), which is supervised by Urząd Rejestracji Produktów Leczniczych, Wyrobów Medycznych i Produktów Biobójczych (Registration Bureau for Drugs, Medicinal and Biotoxic Products). Although the CEBK's registration does not require REC approval of a study proposal, such approvals are required by the Ministry of Health whose approval in turn is necessary for the study to go ahead legally.

The actual practice of the Ministry of Health, concerning the requirement of REC approval, has changed over time. In the past for a multi-centre study to go ahead it was necessary to send approvals to the Ministry from at least half of all RECs. Approvals from all other RECs could be sent later. Now the Ministry of Health requires approval from just one REC to authorize a research proposal. In order to register a research proposal, however, approvals from all other RECs must be sent to the Ministry of Health after they have been issued. This means that a drug can be imported to Poland (if a central warehouse is being used) even if the sponsor does not have approvals from all RECs; however the sponsor must not supply this drug to any investigators whose RECs have not yet approved the trial. If the sponsor has imported drugs to Poland, they are distributed to a particular investigator's site only when the applicable REC has granted its approval.

RECs function as a part of a research control system. Their role is to oversee clinical trials rather than provide any advice for researchers. However, in cases where an REC's approval of a study proposal is conditional on meeting certain requirements, the decision can be treated as a form of advice. Again, these requirements are typically of a legal nature and refer to a clinical trial design that does not assist clinical decision-making.

---

[5] DMH, see n. 3 *supra*, § 3 ust.1.
[6] DMH, *ibid.*, § 3 ust. 6.
[7] DPK, see n. 4 *supra*, § 10 ust. 1 pkt 4.

Although the role of RECs is to supervise biomedical research, and approval of a research proposal by an REC is mandatory, neither the PP, DMH or DPK define penalties for a failure to submit a study proposal for review. It can be supposed, however, that medical professionals who participate in research can be held responsible both professionally and legally. Physician professional responsibility is defined by the system that has been set up by Art. 41–57 of Ustawa z dnia 17 maja 1989 r. O izbach lekarskich[8] (Act on Medical Chambers) and by Rozporządzenie Ministra Zdrowia i Opieki Społecznej z dnia 26 września 1990 r. w sprawie postępowania w przedmiocie odpowiedzialności zawodowej lekarzy[9] (Decree on the Proceedings Concerning the Professional Responsibility of Physicians). According to these regulations, the professional responsibility of physicians is managed by the medical judicial system which consists of the Medical Courts of Local Medical Chambers and the Supreme Medical Court at the Main Medical Chamber. The Courts consider physicians' adherence to the principles of the Code of Medical Ethics. Medical Courts can award various penalties, the most severe of them being (temporary or permanent) revocation of the licence to practise medicine. Additionally, medical professionals can be held responsible for wrongdoings according to civil and penal laws.

In practice it is rather uncommon that an investigator is penalized. This is often because clinical trials are conducted within a system of control in which sponsors have a vital interest in assuring that the trial meets all legal requirements. Since research can only be registered with the Central Register of Clinical Trials after being approved by an REC (see above), it is unlikely that a clinical trial would be conducted without submitting a proposal to an REC. This in itself prevents investigators from engaging in serious misconduct. The ongoing supervision of clinical trials, which is designed to minimize wrongdoings during trials, is effected by the reporting requirements described below in the section on REC activities. Poland's entry into the European Union, resulting in the adjustment of Polish legislation to fit in with EU law, has recently strengthened this system of control; in particular by way of the new good clinical practice law (through the DPK).

Eastern Europe is a growing market for clinical trials, which, with Poland's joining the EU in 2004, has prompted both rapid development and the implementation of control systems. It seems as though a more centralized system of control would be vital and is likely to be implemented together with the newly introduced good clinical practice inspection programme. Starting from December 2002, good clinical practice has been made law in Poland and for this reason conducting clinical trials without REC approval is now not only a violation of good practice and principles of medical ethics, but also illegal.

---

[8] Ustawa z dnia 17 maja 1989 r. O izbach lekarskich (Act on Medical Chambers) *Dziennik Ustaw* 1989 Nr 30, poz. 158 z późniejszymi zmianami.

[9] Rozporządzenie Ministra Zdrowia i Opieki Społecznej z dnia 26 września 1990 r. w sprawie postępowania w przedmiocie odpowiedzialności zawodowej lekarzy (Decree on the Proceedings Concerning the Professional Responsibility of Physicians) *Dziennik Ustaw* 1990 Nr 69, poz. 406.

**REC's Activities and Operation**

DMH § 6 regulates the proceedings of RECs. After reviewing a study proposal, the REC's chairperson designates the members of the REC who will be responsible for drafting the REC's opinion.[10] The process is set out thus:

- The proposal is delivered to all REC members who later discuss it (DMH § 6 ust.);
- The Principal Investigator is invited to the panel in order to provide additional information and explanations (DMH § 6 ust.);
- RECs make their decisions by voting (DMH § 6 ust. 5–7). The decision is announced immediately to the institution that will conduct the trial and, in the case of multi-centre trials, to the RECs that supervise activities of these centres (DMH § 7).

As mentioned above, initiation of a clinical trial is conditional upon the approval by the investigator's local REC (PP Article 29). Together with the study protocol, the investigator must provide the REC with:

1.  information concerning insurance of the study subjects;
2.  the Patient Information Leaflet (which usually makes one document with the Patient Informed Consent Form), which should contain:
    a.  information concerning the purpose and design of the clinical trial,
    b.  information about expected medical and/or other benefits for study subjects,
    c.  risks associated with the trial;
3.  sample of the Patient Informed Consent Form which include at least:
    a.  statement of voluntary consenting process,
    b.  acknowledgement of being offered an opportunity to ask questions and having been provided answers to them,
    c.  having been informed of being able to discontinue participation in the trial at any stage,
    d.  sample of statement concerning terms and conditions of insurance,
    e.  sample of the subject's agreement to processing of his or her data that pertain to the trial (DMH § 4 ust. 1).

Among other things, the REC assures completeness of the trial documentation (DMH § 5 ust. 2).

During the trial, investigators must send safety updates to their local or institutional RECs regarding:[11]

1.  protocol amendments designed to eliminate unexpected risks to the clinical trial participants;

---

[10] DMH, see n. 3 *supra*, § 6 ust. 1.
[11] DPK, see n. 4 *supra*, § 6 ust. 3.

2.  protocol amendments that can increase the risk to subjects and significantly change the trial;
3.  all serious and unexpected adverse events caused by the investigational product;
4.  all new relevant safety information on the clinical trial. Additionally, if a trial duration time exceeds one year, investigators must send safety updates in the form of yearly reports to their RECs (DPK § 9 ust. 2).

Similar provisions apply to the study sponsor.[12] In the course of the study, the investigator's local REC can request additional documentation which may include an updated insurance policy; Unexpected Serious and Drug-related Adverse Events Reports; updated Case Report Forms; and any updates that can impact on the REC's safety assessment of an ongoing clinical trial.[13] It should be stressed that these regulations contain responsibilities of both sponsors and investigators, and that RECs do not have the right to audit an ongoing clinical trial. Despite this, theoretically speaking, it seems likely that such a review would be conducted if requested.

At the end of a clinical trial the sponsor must submit a final report that summarizes the clinical trial, patients' safety status and the trial results to the REC (DPK § 10 ust. 18). Neither the regulations nor practice provide for review of study results that are either published or considered for publication.

Considering the current legal provisions in Poland, it can be said that RECs can advise against a lawful study proposal in two situations:

-  if they conclude that the proposal is morally unacceptable;
-  if they believe that the investigator team or study site is not qualified and/or sufficiently equipped to conduct the study.

It is important to stress that the documents sent to the REC must contain information that:[14]

1.  identifies the entity (person or institution or, in the case of multi-centre studies, institutions) that intends to conduct the study;
2.  includes the name, address and professional qualifications of the person who directs, coordinates and supervises the study.

Additionally, § 5 pkt 1 of the DPK gives RECs the right to request supplementary information concerning the qualifications and professional experience of investigators. In this way approval or rejection of a particular study identifies persons who sponsor and/or conduct the study and who accept responsibility for it, as well as the site where the investigator plans to conduct the clinical trial. This responsibility is not limited to a legal one; the legality of a study proposal is just

---

[12] DPK, see n. 4 *supra*, § 10 ust. 21.
[13] ICH Harmonized Tripartite Guideline for Good Clinical Practice, First Edition, 1996.
[14] DMH, see n. 3 *supra*, § 4 ust. 1.

one of many considerations taken into account by RECs. In this context it should be noted that every REC must respect Polish law and cannot approve illegal activities. For this reason, every REC must have a legal professional among its members.[15]

It is important to note that apart from the general requirement that clinical studies be 'based on ethical principles',[16] and that RECs must make decisions 'after having considered ethical criteria',[17] the law contains no specific guidelines concerning the ethical aspect of REC activities. From professional experience in the field of clinical trial auditing, this leaves considerable room for differences of RECs' opinions within the limits of law. For example, the local REC in the city of Łódź does not approve of the use of placebos even though it is not illegal in Poland.

It is impossible, however, to make responsible generalizations concerning the actual operation, the ethical guidelines used, and the cognizance of law by REC members in Poland. We received a very poor response to a questionnaire, containing questions on the application of data protection laws in practice, prepared by the PRIVIREAL team.[18] Out of 45 Polish RECs only 12 responded, with three of them failing to fill out the questionnaire, saying the questions were not clear. The remaining nine questionnaires therefore cannot provide a basis for any scientific processing. It can only be commented that the poor response may itself be indicative of the attitude of the REC members towards the importance of their work.

## REC Accountability and Appeal

RECs are independent bodies; they do not report to any central institution or governmental agency. According to PP Article 29 ust. 5, however, appeals against the decisions of RECs are to be handled by the Bioethical Committee of Appeals, which was established by the Minister of Health following consultations with the Supreme Medical Chamber. The right of appeal is afforded to:

a.   the organization, institution or team that intends to conduct a study;
b.   the health care institution where the clinical trial is to be conducted;
c.   an REC that works in a centre that participates in a multi-centre clinical trial (DMH § 8 ust. 1).

The appeal has to be made within 14 days after an REC's decision. The ruling of the Committee of Appeals must be issued no later than two months after the appeal has been made. Details of the Committee's proceedings can be found in Regulamin

---

[15] DMH, see n. 3 *supra*, § 3.1 ust. 2.

[16] DPK, see n. 4 *supra*, § 2 ust. 3.

[17] PP, see n. 2 *supra*, Art. 29 ust. 2.

[18] The questionnaire was managed by Tadeusz Zielonka, MD, Warsaw Medical University. We would like to thank him for his kind permission to use the data presented above.

Odwoławczej Komisji Bioetycznej na podstawie zarządzenia Ministra Zdrowia z dnia 24 lipca 2001 r. w sprawie powołania oraz zasad funkcjonowania Odwoławczej Komisji Bioetycznej[19] (Rules of the Bioethical Committee of Appeals based on the Decree of 24 June 2001 of the Minister of Health Concerning the Establishment and Principles of Operation of Bioethical Committees).

At present there is no legal basis to audit the activities of an REC; however, there have been proposals to legalize such an audit. According to these proposals, RECs would be audited by the Ministry of Health if the REC agrees to being audited.

As mentioned above, the investigator or institution may object to the decision of the REC within 14 days of the decision being issued. The objection is sent to the REC that issued the decision in question, and this REC is legally obliged to pass the objection on to the Bioethical Committee of Appeals for review. Like every other REC,[20] the Bioethical Committee of Appeals is obliged to make their decision known to all local RECs in whose jurisdictions a multi-centre study had been planned to be conducted (Regulamin Komisji Odwoławczej, § 18). However, in the case where a study proposal is rejected, there is no legal obligation on any of the local RECs to consider this rejection in their review process. This allowance is taken advantage of by some sponsors who, in cases of problematic study proposals, attach to the proposal sent to one REC the approval issued by another REC. Although RECs are not obliged to consider such opinions, it seems that sponsors attempt to influence their local RECs in this way.

## RECs and Data Protection

Protection of research subjects' privacy is covered by the Personal Data Protection Act, as discussed in Paweł Łuków's 'Personal Data Protection and Medical Research in Poland'.[21] This protection is also included in The Act on the Profession of the Physician, which holds that information resulting from research can be used for scientific purposes without the subject's consent if it is impossible to identify the subject.[22] The good clinical practice regulations refer to personal data protection in DPK § 8 ust. 6, which requires that the information provided to

---

[19] Regulamin Odwoławczej Komisji Bioetycznej na podstawie zarządzenia Ministra Zdrowia z dnia 24 lipca 2001 r. w sprawie powołania oraz zasad funkcjonowania Odwoławczej Komisji Bioetycznej (Rules of the Bioethical Committee of Appeals based on the Decree of 24 June 2001 of the Minister of Health Concerning the Establishment and Principles of Operation of Bioethical Committees) *Dz. Urz.* Ministerstwa Zdrowia Nr 8, poz. 47 and Nr 134, poz. 81.

[20] DMH, see n. 3 *supra*, § 7.

[21] In D. Beyleveld, D. Townend, S. Rouillé-Mirza and J. Wright (eds.), *Implementation of the Data Protection Directive in Relation to Medical Research in Europe* (Aldershot: Ashgate Publishing Ltd, 2004), 307–318.

[22] PP, see n. 2 *supra*, Art. 28.

prospective research subjects contains guarantees of confidentiality of the part of the research documentation that could make it possible to identify the subject, and that published research results will not include the subject's personal data. These regulations are an extension of the Act on the Protection of Personal Data's requirements. It should be added that despite the fact that the Act on the Profession of the Physician makes room for proxy consent in the case of minors, the incompetent and the incapacitated, it does not compromise the protection of the subjects' personal data.

According to Ustawa z dnia 29 sierpnia 1997 r. o ochronie danych osobowych[23] (Act on the Protection of Personal Data), processing of personal data is conditional on the data subject's consent (Art. 23 ust. 1 pkt 1; cf. Paweł Łuków[24]). In agreement with this Act, § 1 ust 1 of DMH requires the investigator to include in the trial documentation a sample of the Informed Consent Form.[25] This form should also contain the subject's consent to processing of his or her personal data relevant to the trial. The data protection law allows for publication of research results only in an anonymized form; the same provision also being included in § 8 ust. 6 of DPK. Accordingly, subjects' personal data are stored with the Principal Investigator at the investigator's site.

Protection of the personal data of prospective biomedical research subjects is realized by the requirement to obtain their informed consent as a necessary condition for initiation of a study. Article 25 ust. 1 of PP provides that the investigator may only conduct a clinical trial on persons who have given their written consent (if written consent is not available, oral consent in the presence of two witnesses is required; the fact that consent was oral must also be noted in the patient's medical record). DPK § 8 ust. 1 (cf. DPK, § 10 ust. 13) also requires the subject's written and dated consent to participation in the trial. This requirement implies that by signing the Informed Consent Form the patient agrees to the review of his or her data by the study monitors, regulatory authority inspectors, and designated sponsor representatives (cf. also DPK, § 10 ust. 2). Additionally, the Informed Consent Form must be identical to the form that had been included in the research proposal presented to the REC. The amended form may be presented to the trial subjects after its prior approval by the REC (see section above on REC activities).

In practice every form includes the following statement:

> I understand that the following persons may have access to my medical information collected during the study: authorized representatives of ABC company and representatives of foreign and Polish agencies that supervise research studies and also representatives of local Ethics Committee, appropriate for the study site. I understand

---

[23] Ustawa z dnia 29 sierpnia 1997 r. o ochronie danych osobowych (Act on the Protection of Personal Data) *Dziennik Ustaw* 1997 Nr 133, poz. 883 z późniejszymi zmianami.
[24] Cf. Paweł Łuków's 'Personal Data Protection and Medical Research in Poland' (2004), n. 21 *supra*, 312–314.
[25] See also DPK, see n. 4 *supra*, § 8 ust. 1.

that information collected during the study may be analyzed in another country but confidentiality of this information will be preserved.

I agree to the transfer of my personal data, both within and outside the borders of Europe, without violating confidentiality (in compliance with Personal Data Protection Act Dz. U. 1997 Nr 133 poz. 883 z późniejszymi zmianami and Directive 8 related to Data Protection in the European Union from year 1998).

The only exceptions from the requirement of acquiring the potential subject's consent to participate in a clinical trial are included in the Act on the Profession of the Physician. These exceptions comprise of:

a.  legal minors;
b.  legally incapacitated individuals;
c.  persons who are unable to give informed consent (PP Art. 25 ust. 2, 4 and 5).

In the case of minors and the incapacitated, the consent must be obtained from the patient's legal representative. In addition to the representative's consent, written consent of the potential clinical trial subject is required:

a.  in the case of the subject who is a minor if he or she is 16 years old or under 16 but can understand his or her clinical status;
b.  in the case of an incapacitated person if he or she can understand his or her clinical status (PP, Art. 25 ust. 2 and 4).

The situation of incompetent potential subjects is regulated by Article 25 ust. 5 which requires consent to be obtained from the Guardianship Court. In cases where a patient's legal representative refuses to consent to the patient's participation in research, the investigator can seek consent from the Court.[26] The investigator can also seek the Court's decision for all three classes of potential subjects.[27]

The Act on Good Clinical Practice provides several safeguards concerning the protection of subjects' personal data. One group of safeguards refers to the trial's sponsor, whilst the other refers to the investigator. DPK § 10 ust. 16 explicitly demands that the sponsor protects the subjects' personal data according to the Act on Protection of Personal Data,[28] and § 13 ust. 1 pkt. 23 provides that the trial protocol describe the manner of coded data storage and the rules of publication of the trial's results (§ 13 ust. 1 pkt. 28). DPK's § 5 ust. 7 requires the investigator to provide protection of the subjects' data obtained in the trial and § 9 ust. 1 makes the investigator responsible for confidentiality of the participants' data. Moreover, the investigator must conduct the trial according to the study protocol[29] which usually covers a chapter devoted to patients' data protection. The sponsor and the

---

[26] See n. 2 *supra*, PP, Art. 25 ust. 6.

[27] See n. 2 *supra*, PP, Art. 25 ust. 7.

[28] See n. 23 *supra*.

[29] DPK, see n. 4 *supra*, § 5 ust. 11.

investigator are also obliged to sign a written agreement on the above-mentioned issues.[30] In addition to these safeguards, the DPK requires the investigator to inform prospective research subjects of the protection of their personal data.

Accordingly, it is the sponsor and investigator's responsibility to guarantee protection of subjects' personal data. The REC's responsibility is to make sure that appropriate measures are being proposed by the sponsor, and that the investigator has the capacity to implement these measures. For this reason coded data are not of interest to the REC. This practice seems to be grounded in the fact that the supervision of implementation of the Act on Protection of Personal Data is the responsibility of the Inspector General for Personal Data Protection.

In agreement with the broad protection provided by the Personal Data Protection Regulations,[31] RECs do not discriminate between types and forms of information. They require protection of personal and genetic information, be it in written and digitized form or recoverable from biological samples. Biological samples and other forms of clinical trial subject information (including DNA samples and blood samples) are identified by bar codes; from this moment the personal data are anonymized and this is the only form in which it is further processed. The bar codes attached to samples refer in a coded form to the identity of the protocol, the visit when the sample was taken, the procedure used for sample taking, the subject's initials, sex, and date of birth. The coding and decoding procedures are included in the study proposal that is submitted to the REC.

One safeguard of the clinical trial subjects' personal data is provided by the Personal Data Protection Regulations, which permit personal data processing only for the purpose for which it was collected and to which consent had been given. This is reflected in the Patient Informed Consent Form (which is a part of the study proposal presented to RECs) which includes a statement concerning the processing of the subjects' personal data under the condition of protecting the subjects' privacy (see above). From the point of view of these regulations it is unlikely that an REC would approve a clinical trial proposal that includes any uses of personal data that had not been consented to by the clinical trial subject.

Personal data may only be kept in personal form by the research site and it is never disclosed to the sponsor. According to Polish personal data protection law, the key element of personal data protection is authorization for the processing of such data, the anonymization of the data being of secondary importance. It can be concluded that data are considered anonymous as long as it is not available in an identifiable form to persons and institutions other than the research site. According to the requirements concerning the type of information provided to the prospective clinical trial subject, and the types of information included in the Informed Consent Form (see above on REC activities), both the investigator and the subject must be aware that the subject's source documents may be subject to independent review or audit during or after termination of the study.

---

[30] DPK, *ibid.*, § 12 ust. 1.

[31] See Paweł Łuków 'Personal Data Protection and Medical Research in Poland' (2004), n. 21 *supra*, see the section 'The Legal Basis of Personal Data Protection in Poland', 307–308.

Chapter 21

# The Constitution and Operation of Health Ethics Committees in Portugal: Rights of Patients to Personal Data Protection

Helena Moniz[†], Sónia Fidalgo[*], Rafael Vale e Reis[*] and Rosalvo Almeida[‡]

## Establishment of Research Ethics Committees

*The System for Ethical Analysis of Medical Research in Portugal*

In a very broad sense we can say that, in Portugal, all medical research is included under three levels of control. These levels correspond precisely to the three institutional levels of bioethics committees found in our country: the National Council of Ethics for Life Sciences (Conselho Nacional de Ética para as Ciências da Vida), the Centres of Reflection (Centros de Reflexão) and the Health Ethics Committees (Comissões de Ética para a Saúde).

The *National Council of Ethics for Life Sciences* is a multidisciplinary consultative body whose objective is to issue opinions on all ethical questions arising in the field of science. These opinions, generally speaking, are based on the legislative acts that regulate medical research. The National Council of Ethics for Life Sciences was created in Portugal in 1990 and functions as an independent consultative body, alongside the Presidential Council of Ministers.

The *Centres of Reflection* undertake an important role concerned with recognizing new issues and disseminating the principal guidance for reflection on open questions. These centres for bioethical studies promote a dialogue amongst people of varied backgrounds and are the main producers of specialist

[†] L.L.M, Researcher in the Biomedical Law Centre and Assistant Professor of Criminal Law, Faculty of Law, University of Coimbra: hmoniz@fd.uc.pt.
[*] Researchers at the Biomedical Law Centre, Faculty of Law, University of Coimbra.
[‡] Invited collaborator at the Biomedical Law Centre, Faculty of Law, University of Coimbra.

bibliographies. Decisions taken in other institutions are very often based on studies carried out in these centres.[1]

In response to the need to promote reflection about ethical problems, Decree-Law No. 97/95 (of 10 May) created and regulated the composition, operation and powers of *Health Ethics Committees* (hereafter CES), whose function is to 'monitor the ethical framework of medical science, in order to guarantee and protect the integrity and dignity of human subjects, as well as to analyse and reflect on issues of medical practice which involve questions of ethics' (Article 1, no. 2). It is these committees which, precisely because they function within health establishments, directly influence the ethical analysis of medical research.

In Portugal, medical research projects require the authorization of the Departmental Director and/or the Administrative Council of the hospital (on which the Clinical Director sits).[2]

In the case of carrying out clinical trials on human subjects, the CES has to give an opinion and the relevant authority (within the respective health unit) can only authorize it if the CES issues a favourable opinion. In this way, with regard to projects for carrying out clinical trials on human subjects, an unfavourable opinion from the CES is binding.[3] Since there is no specific regulation imposing a prior analysis of the technical and scientific quality of the tests, it is common for the CES to also give advice in these areas.

In the case of medical research not included within the ambit of clinical trials, the Administrative Council (and/or the Clinical Director) analyses the project and, if it believes that the project may give rise to ethical problems, submits the referred project for approval by the CES. The CES's opinion in such cases can never be binding, whether it is favourable or not.

So, in cases concerning projects involving clinical trials, the ethical analysis is truly formal—the project has to be submitted to the CES and can only be approved by the proper authority if the CES has given a favourable opinion.[4] In the case of

---

[1] For further details see M. do Céu Patrão Neves and D. Serrão, 'A institucionalização da Bioética', in *Comissões de Ética: das bases teóricas à actividade quotidiana* (2nd edn., Coimbra: Gráfica de Coimbra, 2002), 65–72.

[2] This statement is entirely correct with respect to clinical trials (new drugs or those in common use). Clinical research studies on patients currently undergoing treatment or archived cases for the purposes of conference presentations or publication in medical journals are within the internal ambit of the respective department and are made without the knowledge or required authorization of higher bodies, while studies which involve patients from other departments or bodies require higher authorization. Both clinical trials and studies carried out in hospitals but promoted or directed by external bodies require higher authorization as well as the consent of the department where they are carried out.

[3] The question of approving projects for the realization of clinical trials on human subjects will be developed in the sections below on the General Powers and General Legal Responsibilities of CESs.

[4] The general understanding is that the Administrative Council is not bound by a CES's opinion if this is favourable. The opinion of the CES in respect of the analysis of a project concerning clinical trials will only be binding if it is negative (cf. sections below on the General Powers and General Legal Responsibilities of CESs).

medical research which is outside the ambit of clinical trials, the system of ethical analysis is also formal, though more flexible. In actual fact, such research projects will only be submitted for CES approval if, at the early stages, the authorizing body felt that ethical problems may arise in the course of the project.

In Portugal there are health ethics committees in all hospitals within the public health system. However, there is no coordination between these committees, and thus they do not constitute a truly organized system. Members of the CESs work on a voluntary basis and, whether professionals from institutions or not, they are not remunerated for such work (Decree-Law No. 97/95, Article 12) and therefore only give a very small amount of their time to CES work.

There is new legislation under preparation which will transpose Directive 2001/20/EC into the national legal system, and under this an ethics committee for clinical research will be set up. This will be the only body of its kind and will have national jurisdiction. Details of its composition and operation will be published later.[5] As far as we know, the new regulation regarding the application of good clinical practice in the conduct of clinical trials for medicinal products for human use will introduce an organized system of analysis.

At present in Portugal, the analysis of medical research projects is regulated by law. In addition to Decree-Law 97/95 of 10 May, we also have Law 67/98 of 26 October regarding the protection of single individuals with respect to the treatment of personal data and the free circulation of such data. Furthermore, in the specific field of clinical trials, Decree-Law 97/94 of 9 April establishes norms which clinical trials on human subjects should respect.

Anyone submitting any clinical research project for CES approval should make available all elements necessary for the CES to reach an opinion, so that the safeguarding of human dignity and integrity is observed (Decree-Law 97/95, Article 6(1)(a)).

In the case of clinical trials, the sponsor and investigator must draw up a protocol which mentions the aims, the effective methods and the various stages of the trial (Decree-Law 97/94, Article 6(1)). The protocol should also cover the following: name, address and respective *curriculum vitae* of the sponsor, the investigator responsible for the trial as well as his or her assistants; the amount of remuneration paid to the investigator as well as any money lent or given as compensation by the sponsor to the establishments in which the trials take place; generic names of medicinal products and their composition, and the identity of the body which prepared the samples; name of the technical director responsible for the quality of the medicinal products being tested; type and definition of the clinical trial, the technique selected and its objectives; place and service in which the clinical trial is planned to take place and the respective duration; and, finally, precautions to be observed during the tests and foreseeable adverse reactions

---

[5] It is still uncertain as to how this committee will function at a national level. It is expected that its powers will be comparable to those currently enjoyed by CESs. It is hoped that there will be clarification concerning its powers to oversee authorized trials.

(Decree-Law 97/94, Article 6(2)).[6] It is this protocol which is submitted for CES approval.[7]

*Activities Covered by the CES's Analysis*

In general terms, there are two kinds of CES: the 'Comissões de Ética de Investigação Clínica' (*Institutional Review Board*) and the 'Comissões de Ética Clínica ou Assistencial' (*Institutional Ethics Committees*). The function of the former is to analyse specific questions, such as the restrictions to be imposed upon research on human subjects, namely the revision of research projects or trials of medicinal products when these involve human subjects. The latter are concerned with the ethical consideration of relationships between patients and health professionals or between fellow health professionals, aiming to resolve ethical conflicts arising within day-to-day clinical practice.

In Portugal, most CESs only give opinions when asked, although some do take initiatives proactively, above all in the area of training and collective reflection.[8] In any case, CESs constitute advisory bodies for doubtful cases proposed by institutional management bodies, and, in this way, usually focus on two functions: issuing opinions about research, and ethical advice with regard to clinical issues. Furthermore, in terms of the legislation which regulates them, CESs encompass the powers attributed to both types of committee referred to above, covering both the traditional educative functions and analysis of cases (Decree-Law 97/95, Article 6(1), (a) and (b)),[9] as well as giving opinions about protocols relating to scientific research and clinical tests (Article 6(1), (c)–(f)).[10]

---

[6] As stated in Article 7(4) of the same Act: 'Authorization cannot be conceded when the protocol does not consist of elements referred to in the former article'.

[7] Article 6 of Decree-Law 97/95 states in (c) that it is for CESs 'to give opinion on *scientific research protocols*, namely those that refer to diagnostic or therapeutic trials and experimental techniques which involve human subjects and their biological products, and which are held within the respective institution or health department' (our emphasis).

[8] Article 6(1)(b) of Decree-Law 97/95 states that it is for CESs 'to issue *on their own initiative* or by request, opinions on ethical questions in the domain of activities in the respective institution or health department' (our emphasis).

[9] Article 6(1)(a) states that it is for CESs 'to ensure that the protection and dignity of human beings within the respective institution or health department is safeguarded'. The content of (b) was referred to above in n. 8.

[10] Article 6(1) states, further, that it is for CESs 'c) to give opinion on scientific research, namely that which refers to diagnostic or therapeutic trials and experimental techniques which involve human subjects and their biological products, held within the respective institution or health department; d) give opinion regarding authorization requests for the realization of clinical trials in the respective institution or health department and oversee their execution, especially with regard to ethical aspects and to the safety and integrity of the trial subjects; e) give opinion regarding the suspension or termination of authorization for the realization of clinical trials in the respective institution or health department; f) recognize adequate scientific qualification for the realization of clinical trials in doctors of the respective institution or health department'.

CESs give opinions on the whole range of medical research projects carried out in the hospital institutions of which they form a part. Amongst these projects those outlined below should be highlighted.

*Clinical trials*   Always of external origin, promoted by large companies, and almost always multi-centred. These have clearly defined national and European rules, which are currently in the process of revision in Portugal.

*Academic studies*   End-of-course monographs by higher education students, Doctoral or Master's theses, mostly done by external researchers who want to practise research with patients or consult clinical processes in order to gather data; these are hardly ever experimental studies, and are limited to epidemiological description or classification, occasionally statistical analyses on symptom association and on cause-effect relations in various pathologies. Unlike clinical trials, observational studies or surveys do not raise issues of potential injury to participant patients, but do raise problems concerning the confidentiality of personal data. Clinic Directorates or Administrative Councils (on which the Clinical Director has a seat) always request that ethics committees review not just the study projects (school monographs, projects which require the additional transfer of patients and surveys involving patients, amongst others), but also the actual forms of obtaining consent.

*Research for conference presentations or journal publication*   Work carried out by doctors or other health professionals attached to the institution, about patients under care in the institution or archived clinical processes.

In addition to such school studies, there is also work relating to concrete clinical cases which, because they are atypical or exemplary (a kind of 'case study'), justify disclosure to the medical community for their information or teaching. Many of these projects are carried out without prior CES review, with responsibility for any eventual breach of personal data protection resting with the authors and Department Directors. Note that care is generally taken in preventing identification of patients, and even in the projection of images (of faces or where names are included) it is common practice to mask the image. Health professionals are subject to professional secrecy, but, in actual fact, breaches of secrecy or of confidentiality occurring in meetings or medical conferences are rarely reported and even less rarely punished. However, in addition to these rules (at times unapplied, as seen above) in practice self-regulation does exist since publishers or scientific conference committees will refuse any work containing data which has not been rendered anonymous. There is also an understanding that the scientific environment in which such presentations take place in itself ensures some form of protection.

## Members of the CES

CES members are designated by the Clinical Director and appointed by the Administrative Council of the health establishment and the members are persons of recognized merit (taking into account *curriculum vitae*, professional integrity and high ethical standing) who are available for such work. Article 13(c) of the Doctors' Code of Practice[11] sets out precisely the doctor's duties for which he or she was elected or designated.

The Act which regulates the composition and operation of CESs determines that they are composed of seven members and that they should be multidisciplinary (Decree-Law 97/95, Article 2), which means that, in most cases, CESs include doctors, nurses, jurists and priests, although there are cases in which they include pharmacists, social workers and members from other professions.

## The CES's Responsibility

The CES must answer to the Clinical Director of the respective institution. There is no formally organized structure at national level which coordinates or monitors the activities of CESs, a role which is in part covered by the General Director of Health by means of informative circulars.

The National Council of Ethics for Life Sciences ('Conselho Nacional de Ética para as Ciências da Vida' (CNECV)) is a consultative governmental body and has no functional relationship of any kind with CESs, but it may give its opinion on

---

[11] With regard to the legal force of the Code, Guilherme de Oliveira states: 'Codes of working practice are normally drawn up based on a legitimacy granted by a formal legislative body—in the Portuguese case, based on Decree-Law 282/77 of 5 July, which defines the Statute of the Portuguese Medical Association (Estatuto da Ordem dos Médicos) and grants it licence to draw up the Code of Practice, through the National Council of Medical Practice (Article 80).

It might have been hoped, following this prior legitimization, that the code drawn up at the beginning of the 1980s would have been approved by a formal law; if this had happened, norms of practice would have assumed the normal status of laws of state, valid not only for doctors but also for all citizens. Since the current code was published only in the *News Bulletin of the Medical Association* and not in the *Diário da República*, it cannot have the value of a formal law [Article 119 of the Constitution of the Republic requires publication, in the *Diário da República*, of formal legislative Acts]. This does not mean, however, that it does not assume significant value in a practical juridical sense; in fact, the norms are fully effective internally, within the professional bodies, with any infraction cause for disciplinary action. Furthermore, the content of the code's norms serves as a key auxiliary source for evaluating medical conduct in an ordinary Court—the Court will seek in the norms of practice the definition of the demands that can be made of a doctor in respect of diligence and care of technical preparation, and this will have effect in the judgement on the illegality and guilt of the agent; it is in this way that, for example, the provisions of norms which establish the duties of doctors can be fulfilled, in the so-called Doctors' Statute (Decree-Law 373/79, of 8 September). In other words, even though they are not considered common legal norms, norms of practice will be applied directly in disciplinary processes within the organs of the Medical Association and will be applied indirectly in processes of civil or penal liability'. Guilherme de Oliveira, 'The professional self-regulation of doctors' (Auto-regulação profissional dos médicos), *Revista de Legislação e Jurisprudência* (Coimbra n. 3923, 2001), 34–40.

matters of common concern. CESs use CNECV reports for reference and may occasionally forward more delicate issues for their consideration.

## General Powers of the CES

### The Powers of the CES

In Portugal, CESs are neither public offices nor judicial hearings (they are not legal institutions strictly speaking). Basically, they are organs of reflection which emerged in order to respond to very specific problems.

Article 7(2) of Decree-Law 97/95 is very clear in affirming that opinions issued by the CES have no legally binding status. In this way, the general understanding is that CESs give opinions to be ratified by executive bodies.[12] This is, in fact, what happens within the realm of medical research in general. However, the same Article (2) exempts from what is stated in the general system with regard to clinical trials on human subjects.[13] We will now consider what happens in such cases.

As referred to above, in the case of any medical research project, the investigator must obtain authorization from the administrative body of the respective institution. However, in the case of a project involving clinical testing on human subjects, this authorization (requested by the sponsor) is necessarily subject to prior review by the CES of the institution in question. Thus, in public institutions or health departments, the administrative body will only authorize such clinical testing on the condition that a favourable review has been issued by the ethics committee and the Director of the department where the test is to take place (Decree-Law 97/95, Article 7(1)(a)).[14,15] In the case of private health units, the authorization of the Administrative Council is subject to a favourable CES review (Decree-Law 97/95, Article 7(1)(b)).[16]

Article 8 of Decree-Law 97/94 requires that it is the CES that should respond to authorization requests for clinical trials and oversee their respective execution.

---

[12] These executive bodies are the Clinic Director and the Administrative Council of the respective health unit.

[13] Article 7 (2) of Decree-Law 97/95 determines that 'opinions issued by the CES are always in writing and have no binding status, without prejudice to what is stated in the legal system with regard to the realization of clinical tests on human subjects'.

[14] As seen above, the CES review is only binding if unfavourable and not if it is favourable.

[15] Some hospitals (such as the Instituto Português do Oncologia de Lisboa) also have a committee that gives a technical review specifically about the design of the test.

[16] In Portugal, although the possibility of holding clinical trials in private health units is legally foreseen, in practice it does not happen. Clinical trials on human subjects are usually carried out in the institutions and departments of the public health system. The reason for this perhaps lies in the fact that in private institutions doctors are less inclined to submit their patients to clinical trials. Other possible reasons to note are the relative lack of availability, and reduced number, of patients, limitations in the amount of time given to patients, or the lack of trainee doctors.

In addition to this, clinical trials cannot be authorized in institutions which do not have an ethics committee (Article 7(2)).

In this way we can see that CESs have a fundamental role with regards to clinical trials on human subjects: there has to be a CES in the institution in question in order for a clinical trial to take place, and this CES has to issue a favourable review of the project in question. Furthermore, it is the CES which has the duty of evaluating whether the scientific background is adequate for the clinical testing, as well as evaluating the experience of the investigator and his or her colleagues.[17]

CESs have the power/duty to oversee the execution of a clinical trial which they have previously approved. This idea is clearly expressed in Article 8(1) of Decree-Law 97/94[18] and in Article 6(1)(d) of Decree-Law 97/95.[19] As a matter of fact, this idea does nothing more than transpose to the national legal system part of the Helsinki Declaration which, in 'basic principles for all medical research', states that ethics committees have the right to control trials in progress (paragraph 13). However, is this right/duty being fulfilled by CESs in Portuguese hospitals? From the contact we have had with CES members we have arrived at the conclusion that they restrict themselves, in most cases, to analysing clinical trial requests and to issuing an initial opinion. In the course of clinical trials, they only receive, and this merely for information, subsequent notification relating to possible confirmed incidents (the occurrence of grave and unexpected adverse reactions—Decree-Law 97/94, Article 16(3)(a)). Consequently, they fail to fulfil their duty to oversee the execution of the test.

Under the terms of the law, CESs should also evaluate the occurrence of situations that justify the suspension or termination of the authorization previously given.[20] CESs, as well as the body charged with granting authorization, should also be informed of compensation for expenses or injury incurred by the test subjects (Article 13 of Decree-Law 97/94).

These rules, however, are soon to be altered. Under the current legislation, the National Institute of Pharmacy and Medicines (Instituto Nacional da Farmácia e do Medicamento) has to be informed only of the authorization granted by the administrative body, as well as the commencement of the tests (Article 7(5) of Decree-Law 97/94). However, the draft version of the legislation transposing Directive 2001/20/EC foresees transferring to this institute the power to authorize clinical trials on human subjects.[21] Furthermore, 'Portaria' (a regulation issued by

---

[17] Decree-Law 97/95, Article 6(1)(f) and Decree-Law 97/94, Article 8(2)(a).

[18] This Article states that 'it is the ethics committee which should give opinion regarding requests for authorizing clinical tests and oversee their respective execution, particularly with regard to ethical issues and to the safety and integrity of the clinical test subjects'.

[19] As we saw in n. 7 *supra*, this paragraph states that it is the function of ethics committees 'to give opinion regarding requests for authorizing clinical tests of the respective institution or health service and to oversee their execution, particularly with regard to ethical issues and to the safety and integrity of the test subjects'.

[20] Decree-Law 97/95, Article 6(1)(e) and Decree-Law 97/94, Articles 8(2)(e) and 18.

[21] See the addendum to this chapter for more details on the transposition of this Directive.

the Government) 1087/2001 of 6 September, which establishes the administrative principles and structural organization of the National Institute of Pharmacy and Medicines (INFARMED) as well as the powers and duties of the bodies and operational services found within it, states that it is the Directorate of Pharmacovigilance and Security of Medicines and Health Products (Direcção de Farmacovigilância e Segurança de Medicamentos e Produtos de Saúde) which 'authorizes clinical trials, *within the terms that came to be set out by law*' (Article 18(c)).

Thus, under the terms set out in the draft law referred to above, the realization of clinical trials must be preceded by a favourable CES review, which should be communicated to the applicant and to INFARMED within the space of 60 days (Article 9). However, an authorization from INFARMED (and not from the administrative body of the respective institution) must be requested before the beginning of the clinical trial (Article 12). INFARMED will decide in the shortest space of time possible, which can never exceed 60 days (Article 13).

Note that, under current legislation, in order for a clinical test to be carried out on human subjects it is necessary that the administrative body *give their authorization*, in the sense that they have to explicitly issue a positive decision. However, Directive 2001/20/EC indicates that, in most cases, the authorization can be implicit. Thus, if there was a favourable CES review and the authorization-granting authority raised no objections within the set time limit, clinical trials could commence. In conformity with the Directive referred to above, Article 13(4) in the draft legislation states that, apart from in certain special cases, authorization is considered granted if, within the space of 60 days, INFARMED has not notified the sponsor of any fundamental objections or has not issued a negative opinion.

All things considered, and in terms of the legislation currently still in force, we can see that in cases of medical research outside the realm of clinical trials, the powers of CESs are merely advisory, going no further than recommendations. However these recommendations are, in most cases, followed by the administrative body of the institution in question. It is not known for there to have been disagreements between an administrative body and a CES over a negative review. Nevertheless, if this were to occur, there would be no way for the decision to be taken out of the hands of the administrative body (the CES could only protest and/or offer to resign).

Within the domain of clinical trials, the CESs have powers which go beyond those of simply giving advice. As we have seen, a favourable CES review is necessary for the Administrative Council to authorize the research in question. In this way, CES approval of a project to carry out clinical trials on human subjects is necessary but not sufficient for the research to proceed. The CES does, in fact, have to issue a favourable review,[22] but it is the administrative organization of the institution in question that gives the authorization for the research to proceed.

---

[22] We can say that, in this concrete case, the CES's approval equates with one of the legal requirements of the clinical trial in question. However, as already stated, ethics committees are not true legal institutions, which means that under no circumstances can CES approval legalize activities which, in other forms, would be illegal.

*The Consequences for Investigators who Do Not Subject their Research to Review or who Fail to Follow what the Review Requires*

As a general rule, investigators submit their projects for CES approval. As we have seen, it is generally understood that the advice of the CES is not binding if positive, but, as far as clinical trials are concerned, it is binding if negative. The administrative body is thus not obliged to authorize a project if there is a positive CES review, but cannot authorize a project for which the CES has issued an unfavourable review.

In the case of an academic study there is no situation in which an investigator would not subject his or her research to ethical analysis since, when ethical problems are raised, it is actually the Clinical Director or Administrative Council which requests CES review not only of the project under consideration, but also of the consent procedures. As we have seen, these types of studies do not raise questions of potential injury to participant patients, but do raise the problem of confidentiality of personal data. Under the terms of Article 17 of Law 67/98, concerning the protection of personal data: 'those responsible for the treatment of personal data, as well as the persons who, in the exercise of their function, gain knowledge of personal data being handled, are *obliged to maintain professional secrecy*, even after the termination of their function'. Article 47(1) of the same Act establishes that a breach of the duty of professional secrecy is punishable by up to two years' imprisonment or by a fine of up to 240 days. Article 34 of the same Act also states that: 'any person who has suffered harm due to illegal treatment of data or any other act which violates legal previsions in the matter of personal data protection has the right to obtain reparation for damage suffered from those responsible'.

With regard to research for conference presentation or journal publication, we have already seen that many of these projects are usually carried out without prior CES evaluation since, generally speaking, these cases do no raise any ethical problems whatsoever. Problems can arise concerning the protection of personal data, and the solution calls for the norms referred to above in relation to academic studies to be invoked.

With regard specifically to clinical trials on human subjects, no cases are known of clinical trials that have not been submitted for analysis to CESs and Administrative Councils. This, of course, is due to the fact that no cases are known of clinical trials not sponsored by pharmaceutical companies.

However, if there were, hypothetically, a 'clandestine' clinical trial, this would, naturally, be cause for disciplinary procedure.[23]

---

[23] In this hypothetical case of a 'clandestine' clinical trial, we can consider two distinct situations: 1) the sponsor carries out a clinical trial without having submitted the project for CES review and without having sought the authorization of the Administrative Council; 2) the sponsor carries out a clinical trial without having obtained the authorization of the Administrative Council because the CES review in relation to the clinical trial submitted for evaluation was unfavourable. However, since the consequences for having begun the

There are two forms of disciplinary liability: administrative liability, which arises with regard to a *hierarchical relationship* (it would apply in the case of doctors, who are civil servants under the terms of Decree-Law 24/84 of 16 January[24]) and professional liability in the strict sense of the term, which arises as a result of a breach of the Code of Practice and which is dealt with by the Medical Association.

With regard to the duties of doctors (Chapter II of the Code of Practice), there is the general principle that a doctor should exercise his or her profession with the utmost respect for the right to health of patients and the community, and any practices which cannot be justified in terms of the patient's interest are forbidden (Article 6 of the Code of Practice). Chapter IV of the aforementioned code is dedicated entirely to human experimentation. Article 59 establishes, to begin with, a general principle, in which:

> human trials of new medical products and techniques, when scientifically necessary, can only be put into practice following proper experimentation on animals, and must have shown a reasonable likelihood of success and therapeutic safety. The necessary conditions of medical vigilance must have been assured and the consent, safety and integrity of the patient guaranteed.

Article 62 states that:

> clinical trials of new medical products, especially using the double concealment method, cannot deprive the patient of recognized efficient and essential treatment for the safeguarding of life and whose omission would incur disproportionate risk to the patient.

Article 63 covers ethical guarantees and states that:

> 1 – Any diagnostic or therapeutic experimentation, medical or surgical, should contain ethical guarantees, which should be examined whenever justified by the General Medical Council (Conselho de Deontologia da Ordem dos Médicos), as a source of appeal, as well as scientific guarantees controlled if possible by an appropriate independent committee. Furthermore, every effort should be made to ensure the utmost rigour in the choice of data and in the drawing up of protocols.

---

aforementioned trial in either case are not very different, we made no distinction whatsoever in the answer.

[24] Under the terms of this Act, officials and agents of the central administration are bound to a duty of obedience (Article 3(4)(c)). A violation of this duty constitutes a disciplinary offence which could lead to punishment (which could range from a mere written warning to dismissal). The duty of obedience is, furthermore, subject to the fulfilment of two requirements: orders or instructions which emanate from a legitimate hierarchical superior and in terms of service. If the order were illegal, the subordinate exempts himself or herself from liability if he or she asks for confirmation of the order or instruction in writing. If in fulfilling the order or instruction a crime is committed then the duty of obedience ceases (as covered in the Constitution of the Portuguese Republic, Article 271(3) and in our Penal Code, Article 36(2)).

> 2 – For the purposes of what is stated in the above clause, ethics committees should be created at the regional level within the Medical Association, coordinated by a representative member of the Regional Council, which is part of the National Medical Council (Conselho Nacional de Deontologia). The latter shall propose to the Regional Council the nomination of the other members up to a maximum of seven, without prejudice of appeal to the opinion of expert colleagues in the material being dealt with.

Article 66 concerns itself with the ethical limits of experimentation, stating that 'all and any kind of research likely to endanger an individual's mental life or moral conscience, or to his or her dignity and integrity is prohibited'.

Article 13 of the above-mentioned code states that it is the doctor's duty to observe the Medical Association's Statute and its respective regulations and, with regard to the 'duty to forewarn the Medical Association', the doctor should tell the Medical Association of any fraudulent behaviour or grave incompetence in the exercise of medical care of which he or she is aware (Article 95). Any doctor who covers up, even indirectly, any form of illegal medical practice commits a grave breach of the Code of Practice (Article 138). Article 139 is explicit in stating that any infraction of either the duties contained in the Medical Association's Statute[25] or of the norms contained in Code of Practice makes the doctor liable for disciplinary procedure. In turn, the Doctors' Statute[26] states in Article 7 that doctors should fulfil the obligations and functions attributed to them and which have been legally established (Article 7(a)), and that they should collaborate with the administration of departments in all things concerning the hospital service (Article 7(f)). Article 8 of the aforementioned Statute states that a breach of the duties laid down in Article 7 makes the doctor liable for disciplinary procedure, either civil or criminal, depending on the case.

In turn, the Disciplinary Statute[27] lists rebuke, censure, suspension and expulsion as disciplinary penalties (Article 12).[28] In addition to these main disciplinary penalties, the statute also includes the accessory penalties of loss of

---

[25] Decree-Law 282/77 of 18 June.

[26] Decree-Law 373/79 of 8 September.

[27] Decree-Law 217/94 of 20 August.

[28] Articles 15 to 18 set out situations in which each of these penalties should be applied: Article 15: 'The penalty of rebuke is applicable in the case of slight infringements.'; Article 16: 'The penalty of censure is applicable in cases of grave infringements to which the penalty of suspension or expulsion do not apply.'; Article 17: '1– The penalty of suspension is applicable in the following infringements: a) disobeying resolutions of the Medical Association, when these correspond to the exercise of attributed powers bound by law; b) breach of any duties authorized by law or Code of Practice and which aim to protect the life, health, well-being or dignity of persons, when this does not correspond to higher penalty; 2– Concealment of illegal medical practice is punishable by a prison term which is never less than two years.'; Article 18: 'The penalty of being struck off the Medical Association register is applicable: a) when a disciplinary infringement has been committed which also constitutes a crime punishable by a prison term of more than three years; b) when it is verified that there is clear professional incompetence, with danger for the health of patients or the community; c) when there occurs concealment or participation in the violation of the personal rights of patients.'

fees and publication of the penalty (Article 13 of the Disciplinary Statute).[29] In this way, a 'clandestine' clinical trial would lead, in principle, to the penalty of suspension (possibly accompanied by an accessory penalty), since one of the situations in which this penalty is applied is in cases of the breach of any duty authorized by law and which aims to protect the life, well-being or dignity of persons (Article 17(1)(b) of the Disciplinary Statute). In this case, there would have been a specific breach of Article 7 of Decree-Law 97/94, relating to clinical trials carried out on human subjects.[30] Expulsion could also occur if it is understood that, in a concrete case, there had been concealment or participation in the violation of the patient's personal rights (Article 18(c) of the Disciplinary Statute).

Performing clinical trials without authorization by the administrative body or a favourable CES review also constitutes an administrative offence, punishable by fine.[31]

However, it could also happen (purely hypothetically) that the CES had issued a negative opinion and the administrative council had granted authorization. In such a case, the decision (act) would be illegal (we cannot forget that the review is binding if unfavourable) and can be legally challenged (though only in the public health sector; in the private sector there would only remain, it seems, the possibility of potential civil liability in general terms).

It could occur that the sponsor or investigator had obtained a favourable CES review (and from the Departmental Director in question, if it was a trial in a public institution) and the authorization of the administrative body but, in the course of the research study, did not fulfil all the obligations to which they were bound.

The above-mentioned Article 19, which establishes the rules that clinical trials should follow, states that any breach of norms constitutes an administrative fine.

On the other hand, if the researcher does not fulfil obligations in relation to data protection and, namely, uses personal data in a manner incompatible with the determined purposes of its collection,[32] he or she commits a crime punishable by up to one years' imprisonment or a fine of up to 120 days (Law 67/98, Article 43).

---

[29] Article 20 of the Disciplinary Statute (n. 27 *supra*) sets out that 'the loss of fees consists of returning fees already received which arose from the medical act which constituted the punished infringement, or the loss of right to receive fees if they have not yet been paid'. As set out in (2) of Article 13, this accessory penalty can only be applied cumulatively with the penalty of up to five years' suspension. In turn, Article 21 of the same statute establishes that publication of the penalty consists of publishing the applied penalty in both national and regional media.

[30] These two Articles were already referred to above and explained in the section on 'Powers of RECs'.

[31] Article 19(4)(b) of Decree-Law 97/94.

[32] It should be noted that Article 10(1)(b) of Law 67/98 of 26 October concerning the Protection of Personal Data states that when the person responsible for handling the data, or his or her representative, directly gathers personal data, the purposes of such action should be indicated to the person concerned, unless he or she is already aware of them. If the person responsible for handling the data does not give such information, he or she will have

If the sponsor or investigator breaches the duty of professional secrecy by revealing or divulging personal data, in whole or in part, he or she commits a breach of the duty of secrecy, punishable by up to two years' imprisonment or by a fine of up to 240 days, with the possibility of this penalty being augmented in certain circumstances (Article 47 of Law 67/98).[33] Article 69 of the same Act allows for the further possibility of accessory penalties.

If, in a trial, the researcher commits any offence against the body or health of a participant, he or she could be punished for the practice of a crime against the participant's physical integrity (Article 143 and the Portuguese Penal Code). The question could be considered as to whether the doctor's behaviour would be covered by Article 150 of the Penal Code—'Medico-surgical interventions and treatment'.[34] Article 150 was introduced into Portuguese legislation by the Penal Code of 1982. This Article should be read as a form of normative complement to Article 156—*Arbitrary medico-surgical interventions and treatment*[35]—and with Article 157—*The duty to inform*.[36] As Costa Andrade writes, 'in short, this consists

---

committed an administrative offence punishable with a fine of between 498.79 Euros and 4987.97 Euros (Article 38 of Decree-Law 67/98).

[33] Under (2) of Article 47 of Law 67/98 the 'penalty is increased by half its maximum if the agent: a) is a civil servant, or equivalent, under the terms of penal law; b) had the intention of obtaining any patrimonial gain or other illegal benefit; c) endangered the reputation, honour and consideration or the intimacy of the private life of others'.

[34] Article 150 of the Portuguese Penal Code entitled *Medico-surgical interventions and treatment* which states the following: '1– Intervention and treatment which, according to the state of knowledge and medical experience, are considered appropriate and are carried out, in accordance with *leges artis*, by a doctor or another legally authorized person, with the intention of preventing, diagnosing, healing or alleviating illness, suffering, injury or bodily pain, or mental perturbation, is not considered an offence upon personal integrity; 2– Persons indicated in the previous clause who, by virtue of the above-mentioned aims, carry out interventions or treatment which violates the *leges artis* and, in this way, creates danger towards life or the danger of a grave offence to body or health, shall be punished with up to 2 years' imprisonment or a fine of up to 240 days, if they are not protected from more severe penalties by force of other legal provisions'.

[35] Article 156 of the Portuguese Penal Code entitled *Arbitrary medico-surgical interventions and treatment* which states the following: '1– Persons indicated in Article 150 who, by virtue of the above-mentioned aims, carry out interventions or treatment without the consent of the patient shall be punished with the penalty of up to 3 years' imprisonment or by a fine. 2– The deed shall not be punishable when consent: a) could only be obtained with a delay which endangered life or raised grave danger for body or health, or b) had been given for specific intervention or treatment, but other forms of intervention or treatment had been decided upon due to the state of knowledge or medical experience as a means of avoiding the endangerment of life, body or health; and circumstances were not verified which would permit the safe conclusion that consent would be refused. 3– if, through gross negligence, the agent falsely represents the basis of consent, he or she shall be punished by up to six months' imprisonment or with a fine of up to 60 days. 4– the criminal procedure is dependent upon a complaint'.

[36] Article 157 of the Portuguese Penal Code entitled *The duty to inform* which states the following: 'For the purposes of what is stated in the previous article, consent is only effective when the patient is informed about the diagnosis and the nature, scope and possible

of a system which has two fundamental propositions: firstly, the proclamation of a typicality of medico-surgical interventions in the area of crimes of bodily offence and homicide; secondly, the punishment of arbitrary treatment as an autonomous and specific crime against liberty'.[37]

In fact, abstractly, there are two ways of looking at cases of medico-surgical intervention and treatment:

1. To not give any differential treatment to medical acts and to define them as typical bodily injuries, whose illicit nature will later be removed both by the consent of the patient and, for the doctor, by the notion of 'exercising a right'.[38]
2. To give a differential and privileged treatment to medical acts, such that the actions of a doctor do not even amount to the legal crime of offences against physical integrity.

The wording of Article 150 of the Penal Code—'it is not considered as an offence against physical integrity'—is unambiguous regarding the criminal offence of arbitrary medico-surgical interventions in relation to corporal offences. It is seen like this in cases where medico-surgical intervention fails in its objectives,[39] regardless of whether the patient had given consent or not.[40] The legal definition of medico-surgical intervention includes a combination of subjective and objective elements: subjectively, there is a requirement both for a specific qualification of the agent (there must be a doctor or legally authorized person) and for therapeutic intention,[41] while objectively there is a requirement for medical methods according to *leges artis*.

---

consequences of intervention or treatment, except if this implies the communication of circumstances which, if known by the patient, would endanger his or her life or be susceptible to causing him or her grave damage to physical or mental health'.

[37] M. da Costa Andrade, *Comentário Conimbricense do Código Penal, Parte Especial, Tomo I* (Coimbra: Coimbra Editora, 1999), 302.

[38] For further details, see M. da Costa Andrade (1999), n. 37 *supra*, 302–313.

[39] In Portugal the production of undesired results is only overlooked as a typical corporal offence when it represents a violation of *leges artis*.

[40] Given the content of Article 150 of the Penal Code, the absence of patient consent is overlooked only for the purposes of Article 156—*Arbitrary medico-surgical interventions and treatment*—which is seen as a crime against personal liberty and not as a crime against physical integrity. (Under Article 38(1) of the Penal Code 'consent excludes the illegality of the deed when referring to freely available legal interests and when the deed does not offend good customs'. Under the same Article, consent is only relevant if it was given by a person over 14 years old and so long as that person has the necessary discernment to evaluate the sense and understanding of the declaration given at the time of it being given (3); 'consent can be expressed through any means that convey the serious, free and informed will of the titular of the legally protected interest, and can be freely revoked up until the execution of the deed' ((2) of the same Article).)

[41] Therapeutic intention is understood by Portuguese law in very broad terms, including both diagnosis and prevention.

However, given the specific context of this report, we can pose the question of whether or not experimental interventions are included in the notion of medico-surgical interventions, for the purposes of exclusion of this as a criminal offence under the terms of Article 150 of the Penal Code. The answer will differ depending on the kind of experimentation in question:

- when it is pure experimentation (human, not therapeutic, experimentation) there is a unanimous understanding that such experimentation is excluded from medico-surgical interventions;
- in the case of so-called therapeutic intervention (which is given when, in the absence of proven and corroborated scientific treatment, the doctor resorts, in the interests of the patient, to therapeutic means whose consequences cannot be anticipated or safely controlled), it is agreed that medico-surgical intervention should be carried out again.

In any case, the action of a doctor or investigator who carries out a 'clandestine' test could never be considered an action in accordance with *leges artis* and, consequently, could never be excluded from Article 150 of the Penal Code.

In the case of a therapeutic intervention (which, as we have seen, is a medico-surgical intervention), if the trial participant has not given consent, we have a situation which is subsumed within the crime of arbitrary medico-surgical interventions and treatment in which the doctor can be punished with up to three years' imprisonment or a fine.

The requirements for consent are listed, in general, in Articles 156 and 157 of the Penal Code. Under the terms of Article 157,

> ... consent is only effective when the patient has been duly informed of the diagnosis and of the nature, scope and possible consequences of the intervention or treatment, unless this implies the informing of circumstances which, if known by the patient, would endanger his or her life or would be likely to cause serious harm to physical or mental health.

In turn, Decree-Law 97/94 authorizes some specific rules relating to consent in clinical trials.[42] Paragraph (2) of Article 9, unlike the Penal Code, requires consent in *written form*. According to some Portuguese authors this norm has substantive value. This means that the requirement of written consent is not merely a formality '*ad probationem*', but rather a formality '*ad substantiam*', which means, in these

---

[42] Article 9 states the following: '1– The investigator is obliged to inform the clinical trial subject, in a simple, intelligible and true manner, of the risks, consequences and foreseeable benefits, as well as the methods and objectives. 2– Furthermore, the investigator should make available to the clinical trial subject in writing the following elements: a) Name and address of the sponsor, of the investigator responsible for the trial and his or her collaborators; b) Name of the medicinal product; c) Name of the technician responsible for the quality of the medicinal products being tested; d) Nature, duration and objectives of the clinical trial; e) Precautions to be observed in performing the clinical trial and foreseeable reactions. 3– The clinical trial subject should, also, be informed regarding the system of civil liability applicable'.

cases, no other measure of proof can be furnished unless it is a document with higher probatory force (Article 364 of the Civil Code).

## General Legal Responsibilities of CESs

### CESs and the Law

Article 6(2) of Decree-Law 97/95 is very clear in stating that in exercising their powers, 'CESs should consider in detail what is established in law, in deontological codes and in existing international declarations and directives with regard to the material under evaluation'. In this way, CESs are not authorized to approve illegal activities.

A survey was sent out to various CESs and 11 replies were received, including the largest and most important hospitals in the country. All considered that they did not feel authorized to approve activities which were against the law. With regard to the possibility of rejecting or declaring against activities permitted by law, there were five negative and five positive replies. CESs who felt authorized to prohibit activities permitted by law understood that, even if a protocol fulfils all the legal requirements, it should not be approved if it is not integrally in accordance with the rules and ethical principles.

The most relevant piece of legislation which CESs should pay attention to is, in the first instance, the Constitution of the Portuguese Republic which, in its first Article, covers the principle of respect for human dignity. Article 42 recognizes the liberty of scientific creation, which includes medical research. This Article is included in Part II of the Constitution which enshrines the *rights, liberties and guarantees* which enjoy constitutional protection, since they only acknowledge the so-called 'immanent limits', or those which arise from the necessity of respecting other constitutionally protected values such as the right to life and to physical integrity. Article 64, concerning the right of citizens to the protection of health, states that the duty of disciplining and controlling the production, distribution, commercialization and use of chemical, biological and pharmaceutical products and other forms of treatment and diagnosis is incumbent upon the State. Article 73 adds that the duty of the State is to encourage and support scientific research, establishing that which specialists define as 'a positive guarantee of liberty of creation and research'.[43,44] Furthermore, Article 81 includes within the list of priorities of the State that of 'guaranteeing scientific and technological policies which foster the development of the nation'.

This is the constitutional framework for scientific research, and, therefore, for clinical research. However, in addition to constitutional norms, a combination of norms also exists which is more or less related to the problem of medical research

---

[43] G. de Oliveira, *Temas de Direito da Medicina* (Coimbra: Coimbra Editora, 1999), 188.

[44] J. J. Gomes Canotilho and V. Moreira, *Constituição da República Portuguesa Anotada* (3rd edn., Coimbra: Coimbra Editora, 1993), 363.

and which CESs should obey in exercising their functions. Among these, we can point out:

- Decree-Law 97/94 of 9 April, which sets out the norms which should be obeyed in clinical trials carried out on human subjects;
- Decree-Law 97/95 of 10 May, which establishes the composition, the powers and operation of CESs;
- Law 67/98 of 26 October, which transposes into the Portuguese legal system Directive 95/46/EC, relating to the protection of individuals with regard to the treatment of personal data and the free circulation of such data;
- Decree-Law 30/2003, of 14 February, which altered Decree-Law 273/95, of 23 October, and which regulates medical research;
- Regulation ('Portaria') 1087/2001 of 6 September, which, since it is an internal regulation of the National Pharmacy and Medicine Institute (Instituto Nacional de Farmácia e do Medicamento) establishes the management principles and the organizing structure of this institute, as well as the attributions and powers of the bodies and operational services of which it is composed.

Directive 95/46/EC, as stated above, has already been transposed into the internal legal system by Decree-Law 67/98. Directive 2001/20/EC is still in the period of transposition into the internal legal system (it is certain, however, that Member States should have approved and published the provisions necessary to fulfil the above Directive by 1 May 2003). When the aforementioned Act is approved and published (which will revoke Decree-Law 97/94 of 9 April), CESs should also respect the norms which it establishes.[45]

As a rule, CESs devise internal regulations relating to the dates of meetings, their operating principles and occasionally the duration of mandates, all of which they should respect.

Since CESs are multidisciplinary bodies, made up of designated members including doctors, nurses, pharmacists, jurists, theologians, psychologists, sociologists and professionals from other areas of social and human sciences (Article 2 of Decree-Law 97/95), each of the members, in the course of their duties within the CES, should respect the precepts of the Code of Practice of their profession, the Statute of their professional body and the respective Disciplinary Statute, in such cases where they exist.

Portugal ratified the Convention of Human Rights and Biomedicine which came into force in Portugal on 1 December 2001.[46] This Convention, in Chapter V, refers specifically to 'Scientific Research', referring in Article 16 to 'the protection of persons undergoing scientific research'. CESs should also act in accordance with the provisions of this convention.

---

[45] See the addendum to this chapter for more details on the new Act.
[46] This was approved by a Resolution of the Assembly of the Republic, No. 1/2001, published in Series 1 of the *Diário da República*, of 3 January 2001.

Finally, international guidelines in relation to medical research are also taken into account by our legislation and by the actual conduct of CESs. This is what occurred with the Helsinki Declaration which, since it is *soft law*, its principles were transposed into internal acts and its guidelines are generally followed in clinical trials on human subjects.

## The Impact of Directive 2001/20/EC on Good Clinical Practice

As mentioned above, the transposition of this Directive into the Portuguese legal system is in the final phase of the internal legislative process. Current practice has been characterized by what is considered to be full respect for the personal data regarding patients and participants in clinical trials of medical products for human use. Clinical trials in Portugal have always been carried out with files identified by the individual's initials and a number, with the resulting observations and the records of symptoms or analyses sent to the sponsors anonymously. In the monitoring phase, the sponsor has the right for one of its representatives to review the original clinical process in order to verify if it conforms to the records sent. This review is carried out in the presence of the researcher by a person who is also bound by professional secrecy.

In the draft Decree-Law it is stated that the regulatory procedures contained in Decision 1999/468/EC regarding the principles of good clinical practice are maintained.

With regard to respect for the autonomy of trial participants, the current practice, whereupon CESs are concerned with the analysis of forms of obtaining informed consent, is also maintained in the proposed act.

## How, Disregarding Theory, CESs Take the Law into Consideration

The questions in the survey presented to CESs relating to data protection reveal some convergence of thought. There is a unanimous consensus (11 of 11) that consider conformity with the requirements of the law of data protection as a necessary condition for approval, and the majority (nine of ten) think that such requirements are not mere recommendations and declare not to ignore them.

When asked about an activity which, despite not being ethically reproachable, is against data protection law, most of the CESs (six of ten) say they would forbid it and none would give ethical approval (ten of ten). Only one CES considers ethical approval and informing researchers that it is contrary to the law and six of ten would request that legal advice is taken as a condition of their approval.

While the majority (nine of ten) of CESs interpret the conformity of requests with data protection law by themselves, some say they occasionally appeal to academic bodies (five of eight), lawyers (five of eight), the body to whom they answer to (six of eight), the National Commission of Data Protection (six of nine) or the Courts (one of eight).

CESs (eight of ten) consider themselves authorized to report transgressions, but not all (six of ten) consider themselves prepared to contact the National Commission of Data Protection regarding a violation.

Liability at law regarding their decisions is assumed by the majority of CESs (8 of 11).

The majority of CESs (eight of ten) do not consider non-conformity with the European Directive as a reason for rejection if there is conformity with the current national law.

We have seen in the section above on 'General Powers of the CES' that CESs have the right or duty to control trials in progress. We have also mentioned that, in practice, they just analyse the requests for clinical trials and give their initial opinion. Then, in the course of the clinical trial, they only receive, merely for information, subsequent notification relating to possible verified incidents, thus failing to fulfil their duty to oversee the execution of the trial.

*Legal Means that Can Be Invoked Against the CESs Concerning their Decisions*

CESs, under the terms of the law which regulates their constitution, composition and operating principles (Decree-Law 97/95 of 10 May), have above all, *consultative powers* (Article 6(1)).

In exercising their powers, CESs should consider, in particular, what is established in law, in the deontological codes and in existing international declarations and directives on the matters under review (Article 6(2)).

CES opinions or reviews are limited to the instruction of decisions taken by others, namely, the administration of the health institution to which they belong.

And what if a CES gives an unfavourable review, from *an ethical point of view*, to a research project? In fact, there is no mechanism to appeal against CES decisions on the grounds of an inopportune or inconvenient ethical decision.

But the problem can be posed in another way. In fact, it may happen that a CES gives a favourable opinion to a research project which does not take into account the principles and rules of personal data protection (which, as is known, in Portugal result from Directive 95/46/EC of 24 October 1995 and Law 67/98 of 26 October which transposed the Directive into the Portuguese legal system). In this case, the administrative and jurisdictional[47] mechanisms authorized by law will have to be put into practice not against the CES but against the body which took the decision of approving the project—even though it had been done through ratifying a favourable CES opinion. Generally speaking, we can say that when the body that makes the decisions belongs to the administrative structure (as in the case of public hospitals), the process is put into practice by administrative means in general terms. In the case of a private hospital, mechanisms of civil liability will have to be put into practice as well as the other mechanisms in the law of personal data protection.[48]

---

[47] Cf. Articles 33–49, Law 67/98 of 26 October.

[48] Those mechanisms were studied in H. Moniz and C. Sarmento e Castro, 'Report on the Implementation of Directive 95/46/EC in Relation to Medical Research in Portugal' in D. Beyleveld, D. Townend, S. Rouillé-Mirza and J. Wright (eds.), *Implementation of the Data Protection Directive in Relation to Medical Research in Europe* (Aldershot: Ashgate Publishing Ltd, 2004), 319–340.

Following this, it is clear that there are not specific mechanisms in Portuguese law which permit appeal against CES decisions or opinions for being ethically questionable, or simply for disregarding the law.

However, some complementary considerations should be put forward. Firstly, we should bear in mind that CESs have a multidisciplinary composition (Decree-Law 97/95, Article 2) in that they are composed of doctors, nurses, pharmacists, jurists, theologists, psychologists, sociologists or professionals of other areas of social and human sciences. Now, many of these professionals are compulsorily registered in public associations which regulate the exercise of their functions (such as the Medical Association) or The Bar Association ('Ordem dos Advogados'). Thus, the members of these associations are subject to strict codes of practice which constitute a strong legal restriction (even though indirectly) on the operation of CESs. A strict duty of professional secrecy normally results from these professional regulations and codes of practice. In spite of this, Article 9 of Decree-Law 97/95 reinforces the duty of secrecy of CES members. Thus, any CES member who breaches this obligation incurs not only disciplinary action, according to the rules of the respective profession, but also penal action which could be punished with the crime of breach of secrecy, according to Article 195 of the Portuguese Penal Code.

Secondly, and remembering what was said in the section above on 'General Powers of the CES', it is necessary to bear in mind what is stated in Article 7(2) of the above-mentioned Decree-Law which, underlining the written and non-binding character of CES review, provides an exemption to this for what is stated in the legal system regarding the realization of clinical trials on human subjects. This, as stated above, is contained in Decree-Law 97/94 of 9 April and makes the authorization of clinical trials dependent on the favourable review of the CES of the institution in which the trial is planned to take place.[49] As can be inferred, in this case CES review is *obligatory* (the administrative body of the institution in question cannot authorize the clinical trial without this review) and *binding* if it rejects the trial.[50]

Although we could consider public health service CESs as administrative authorities with powers of carrying out administrative acts (something which is currently not possible), it is known that the reviews are not considered as administrative acts liable to legal challenge.

---

[49] It should be noted once again that in public health institutions and departments this favourable CES review should be added to the favourable review of the department director (cf. Article 7(1)(a)). In the health establishments or units where there is no ethics committee, clinical trials cannot be authorized (cf. Article 7(2)).

[50] It also seems clear that, in the case of favourable CES review (which is added to the favourable review of the department director), the administrative body of the institution in question is not obliged to authorize the clinical trial. Thus, we are faced with a binding review but only as long as it is unfavourable. Authors characterize this type of review as 'pareceres conformes (favoráveis)' (conforming opinions (favourable)).

As is seen, Portuguese law authorizes rules directly aimed at CESs, regulating their constitution, composition and operating principles in some detail, but it does not authorize specific direct mechanisms of appeal against their decisions.

CESs are obliged to 'consider, in particular, what is established in law, in deontological codes and in existing international declarations and directives regarding the material to be reviewed',[51] but on the other hand 'they act with complete independence with regard to management bodies of the respective institution or health department'.[52,53]

It should be noted, however, that when questioned if they consider themselves liable at law for decisions or opinions issued, 70 per cent of the bodies questioned responded affirmatively.

## Specific Data Protection Matters[54]

### *The Power of CESs to Decide if Research is Justified in the Public Interest*

Out of the CESs that responded to the questionnaire, none considered that a research project in the public interest could be justified, automatically and in itself, if it requires breaches of data privacy and confidentiality.

However, the same unanimity was not found in relation to the possibility of a case-by-case analysis if the community interest in a given research project is sufficient to justify these breaches of privacy and confidentiality. In fact, only four out of seven CESs that responded believed that it is possible in a concrete case to judge if the public interest is sufficient to justify such breaches.

With regard to the question of knowing whether CESs have in themselves powers to evaluate the public interest of a research proposal which implies breaches of confidentiality and privacy and, bearing this in mind, approve or reject it, a great diversity of answers are again found. While it is true that three of nine admitted that they would reject the proposal out of an understanding that the public interest is not something they are capable of evaluating, the majority of responses accepted that CESs have the power to evaluate if the public interest justifies these exceptions. More than half the responses mentioned they would appeal to external legal review to decide.

---

[51] Cf. (2) Article 6, Decree-Law 97/95.

[52] Cf. Article 8, Decree-Law 97/95.

[53] In spite of this independence, Article 13 of Decree-Law 97/95 obliges CESs to write, at the end of each civil year, a report about their activity, to be sent to the management body of the respective institution or health department.

[54] The observations below are based on a questionnaire, made by the PRIVIREAL team and sent to the main CESs of Portugal. See the chapter in D. Beyleveld, D. Townend and J. Wright (eds.) *Research Ethics Committees, Data Protection and Medical Research in Europe – Key Issues* (Aldershot: Ashgate Publishing Ltd, 2005) on the PRIVIREAL 'Questionnaire to RECs'.

*The CES's Position Regarding Rendering Data Anonymous*

The great majority of CESs (seven of ten) consider that anonymity occurs only when no one can identify who the data belong to.

However, some consider that anonymity is maintained when the researchers (who use the data) are not able to identify, directly or indirectly, the data subject, even though those who provided the data can have access to them.

To be specific, in response to the question 'when does the committee you belong to consider that the data have been rendered anonymous, thus making unnecessary the application of the principles of data protection?', the CESs responded as follows:

-   When no one can any longer, directly or indirectly, identify who the data are about—seven positive and three negative answers;
-   When the researchers, directly or indirectly, cannot identify who the data are about, even if those (for example, clinicians) from whom the researchers have obtained the data still can—five positive and four negative answers.

In addition to this, all CESs considered that the principles of data protection should be respected in the case of researchers who intend to use obtained clinical data for the treatment of a patient, even when the data will only be used after having been rendered anonymous. All the CESs believe that patients should be informed of the process of research proposals.

*The CESs' Position on Genetic Information (DNA and Biological Material) and Data Protection Law*

All CESs considered that the use of biological material in genetic research falls within data protection law, at least in cases where the identity of the biological material donor is directly or indirectly recognizable.

CESs were also asked to analyse the following situation:[55]

Suppose that researchers wish to study the genetic component of a cancer. They propose to obtain the names and addresses of patients with this condition and their family doctors from Cancer Registries. They will then ask the doctors for permission to approach the patients (without the doctors first obtaining the consent of the patients). If the doctors give permission, the researchers will write to the patients (who will be told that their doctor has given permission to approach them and an independent ethics committee has allowed them to get their names and address from a Cancer Registry). The letter will inform the patients of the research and will ask them to fill in a questionnaire; to go to their doctor to provide a blood sample (from which DNA will be extracted); and to give the researchers the names and addresses of any of their relatives who have had cancer. (The permission of the relatives for this will not be sought.) The researchers will check what condition the relatives have/had by obtaining data from the

---

[55] This situation was taken from the PRIVIREAL 'Questionnaire to RECs', see n. 54 *supra*.

Cancer Registries (or, where the relatives have died, from databases recording cause of death).

None of the CESs accepted the proposal on the basis that there were no legal or ethical problems. Only one CES considered the proposal acceptable because it would be impractical to obtain consent in the various phases. Also only one CES considered it acceptable based on the fact that the necessity of obtaining consent at various phases would mean that consent could not be obtained from certain patients, with the result that the study would not cover 100 per cent of the cases, which would diminish the value of the research results.

The overwhelming majority of CESs considered the proposal unacceptable because various disclosures of personal information are made without the consent of patients or their relatives or (at least) without their prior consent and the possibility of refusal.

*Striking a Balance Between Data Protection and Research*

CESs were also asked if they considered that the data protection law strikes a balance between basic personal rights to privacy and the need for research, to which 9 out of 11 CESs responded in the affirmative. Two CESs believed, however, that these rights were over-protected by law.

## Addendum[56]

*Main Alterations Introduced by Law 46/2004 of 19 August Regarding the Role of the Health Ethics Committees (CES) in Clinical Tests*

In the previous system, under the terms of Article 7 of Decree-Law 97/94 of 9 April, authorization for the performance of clinical tests depended upon a favourable opinion from the ethics committee of the health institution where the tests would occur. These ethics committees (CES) are legally regulated by Decree-Law 97/95 of 10 May.

Law 46/2004 of 19 August, revoked Decree-Law 97/94 of 9 April (whilst Decree-Law 97/95 of 10 May, remains in force).

Under the terms of this new law, for tests to take place, prior authorization is required from the administrative council of INFARMED (Article 15(1)). Under the terms of Article 20(1), the 'performance of clinical tests must be preceded by a favourable opinion' from an ethics committee. In principle, this opinion will be issued by the recently created '*Ethics Committee for Clinical Research*' (CEIC) (Article 18(5)).

However, under the terms of Article 18(6), 'the CEIC may appoint a CES to issue the opinion, when the specific nature of the tests so requires, or if there is

---

[56] Rafael Vale e Reis, Researcher in the Biomedical Law Centre (Faculty of Law, University of Coimbra), October 2004.

some other justification, and this decision should be communicated to the promoter'. The criteria to be used for the appointment of the ethics committee (CES) that is to issue the opinion, are regulated by an Administrative Rule from the Minister of Health (Article 20(5)).

The opinion must be issued within 60 days of the date of receipt of the application by the CEIC. This period may be suspended or extended under the terms of Article 21.[57]

Thus, the CESs will continue with their regular ethical analysis of clinical practice, but *they are no longer the main body for the issuing of ethical opinions concerning clinical trials*. The CES will only act in this regard in a subsidiary capacity, when appointed to do so by the CEIC.

The CEIC has technical and scientific autonomy, and its composition, financing and rules of functioning are established by an Administrative Rule from the Minister of Health.

The CEIC is answerable to the Minister of Health, alongside INFARMED, and is responsible for:

a.  Defining the material and human resources required by the health ethics committees in order to be able to issue opinions when required to do so by the CEIC;
b.  Issuing the opinion laid down in Article 20, without prejudice to the provisions of Article 19;
c.  Receiving and validating applications for opinions made by promoters;
d.  Monitoring the activity of the health ethics committees, in matters concerning clinical tests;
e.  Drawing up the annual report of activities and submitting it to the Minister of Health.

Applications for opinions are presented by promoters to the CEIC, in accordance with the detailed instructions to be established by the administrative council of INFARMED.

---

[57] Note that opinions about tests involving medication used for xenogenetic cellular therapy is not subject to any time limit—Article 21(5).

# Chapter 22

# Bioethical Review in Romania

Octavian Doagă[*†1]

## Introduction

In the context of contemporary scientific development, bioethics must offer an answer to the scientific challenges that usually cross moral or juridical boundaries. Scientific research, always being driven by the concepts of utility and efficacy, may result in an awareness of the conflict between risks and benefits in an expert's attitude and in public opinion; in particular between what is positive and what is negative for society. In any case, research on human subjects must respect the natural, sacred dimensions of human dignity.

In a society where the options are often endless, science needs ethics that evolve, and are open and dynamic, whilst more than ever being focused on the sacred right of the human being to be him or herself. In this respect, bioethics has to overrule the law, as well as scientific resolutions or conventions, in such a way that science will not affect the human integrity at any level.

The initial goal of science and technology was to ultimately contribute to the evolution of humankind[2] toward a more civilized and stable state. In this regard, bioethics has the role of preventing science from changing the concept of being 'human' into something else, something that will jeopardize 'neo-human' rights entirely.

In the life science and healthcare domain, medicine is evolving very fast, basically because of the incredible explosion of technological achievements. The faster the process, the harder it is for the society to engulf and digest the 'tasty muffin'. Even though there is a lot of hunger out there, medicine must evolve like

[*] M. D., Department of Biophysics, 'Carol Davila' University of Medicine and Pharmaceutics, Bucharest, Romania. Member of the National Bioethical Committee, Ministry of Health, Romania.

[†] *Acknowledgements:* The professional support of Prof. Dr. Serban Palade, President of the National Ethical Committee, Ministry of Health, Romania and Dr. Liana Ples, Head of the Juridical Department of the College of Physicians, Bucharest, Romania is gratefully acknowledged.

[1] The situation described in this report represents that of December 2003.

[2] Gh. Scripcaru, A. Ciuca, V. Astarastoae and C. Scripcaru, *Bioetica—Stiintele vietii si drepturile omului* (Bioethics—Life sciences and human rights) (Bucharest: Polirom, 1998), 12–45.

respect for human rights; thus national regulations must be open to European Directives since all European nations will be united (sooner or later), and European citizens must all have the same mobility and rights.

Obtaining the unification of diverse national bioethical systems is a difficult task, primarily because ethics or bioethics, by definition, are very much influenced by the local customs, common-laws and religious beliefs of each country.

The PRIVIREAL project may prove to be salutary in this attempt to provide an overview of the bioethical systems in the European Union and future candidate countries. The following is an overview of the bioethical system in Romania, a country that is required to fulfil all the requested standards to become part of the European Union in 2007 or 2008.

## The National Bioethical System

In Romania there is a well-defined system for ethical review dedicated to medical research with human subjects (clinical trials), regulated specifically since 1997. The ethical review system of clinical trials on medicinal products for human use (MPHU) has more specific regulations than other types of clinical trials. In each medical institution, one Institutional Ethics Committee is responsible for the ethical aspects of the medical activities (clinical practice, research or, where it applies, clinical trials on medicinal products for human use). There is a Committee for Medicinal Products within the framework of the Ministry of Health, which keeps the records of all clinical trials on MPHU approved by the Institutional Ethics Committees.

For dealing with other bioethical matters not covered by the laws, the Ministry of Health also has a Bioethical Committee that holds a national advisory role.

The people involved in the review process are not paid for these activities, and secretarial support and travel costs for the REC members' activities are supported by the local institution. Therefore the system, although regulated, works on an informal basis. However, if formal purely means that the RECs' activities and composition are regulated by law, then RECs in Romania are formal. On the other hand if formal means the people involved are receiving a fee for their involvement, the RECs in Romania would not be formal, rather working on a 'pro bono' basis.

The performance of clinical trials is regulated by an Order of the Ministry of Health[3] which introduces the Rules of Good Practice in Clinical Trials into Romania. This is in line with European Directives and includes the Declaration of Helsinki and other international guidelines. These rules define the activities of the Ethics Committees. For a clinical institution to be allowed to host clinical trials on MPHU it has to obtain a specific authorization from the Ministry of Health.[4] Although research in general, meaning research in every domain, is regulated by a specific Act[5] of the Romanian Government, medical research is also regulated by

---

[3] Order No. 858 of 19 October 1997.
[4] Regulated by Order No. 579 of 28 August 2001.
[5] Order No. 57 of 16 August 2002.

another Act of the Ministry of Health.[6] Research financed by governmental grants is reviewed by the Medical Science Academy. There are other laws and regulations concerning organ transplants and biological product manipulation,[7] and on patients' rights.[8]

There are some other provisions stated in the Ethical Code elaborated by the College of Physicians in 1997. These rules are mandatory for physicians, including those involved in clinical research. The rules are stated in Section D, Articles 127 to 132, and their main concern is to establish some ethical rules with regard to experiments on humans.

There are two different types of ethics committees: those that review ethical aspects in all clinical trials, including those on MPHU, and those that can only review ethical aspects in trials that do not involve MPHU. In order to gain the ability to review clinical trials on MPHU, the Institutional Ethics Committee (IEC) must obtain accreditation from the National Ethical Committee (NEC) and the Medical Science Academy. At the institutional (local) level, the same ethics committee is responsible for usual clinical practice and clinical trials. At the central level there is a separate system for each.

The activities of these committees include the following:

- evaluation of the trial protocols;
- evaluation of the team members;
- evaluation of the written and verbal information presented to the subjects or their legal representatives or the consent given with or without a witness;
- the means for obtaining the consent of the subjects;
- the compensatory measures in case of complications after or during the trial;
- approval or denial of the study;
- continued observance of the trial once it has begun.

## The Constitution of Local Ethics Committees

The members of the National Ethical Committee for Clinical Trials are nominated by the Romanian Medical Science Academy, the Physicians Council, the Physicians' Federative Chamber, the Pharmacists' Council, the Department of Cults, the Office for Customer Protection, The League for Human Rights and the Psychology Faculty of the University of Bucharest. For the Institutional Ethics Committee the Scientific or Administrative Council of the institution nominates the members. The minimum number of members is five and there are never more than 17. At least two have to be medical doctors, preferably one with good experience in medical research and the other with good experience of medical practice; both from outside the clinic that is being reviewed. The committee must also include a pharmacist, a medical assistant, a jurist and, if possible, a person with a licence in

---

[6] Order No. 215 of 29 March 2002.
[7] Law No. 2/1998.
[8] Law No. 46/2003.

religious science. There are also recommendations that there should be a broad representation of different age groups and that both genders must be represented. Also, in a region where a national minority predominates, there must be representatives of this minority in the committee. Finally the members have to be well educated and have strong moral integrity.

The national committee is accountable to the Ministry of Health through the Committee for Medicinal Products and the Bioethical Committee. The institutional committees are accountable to the national committee. Both IECs and the NEC (collectively RECs) must complete an annual report.

**General Powers of the Ethics Committee**

The ethics committee's activities concern all ethical aspects of the medical activities in healthcare units, including current medical practice or clinical trials. The committee, whilst able to advise and make recommendations, also has the power to approve or reject applications. The approvals of the National Ethical Committee and the Committee for Medicinal Products are necessary and sufficient for a clinical trial on MPHU to go ahead. For other clinical trials (including phase IV trials of MPHU), IEC approval is enough.

The consequences (penalties, disciplinary action, and so on) for researchers who do not submit their research for review, or fail to follow what the review requires, are also regulated. Qualified personnel involved in clinical trials on MPHU that do not respect all the regulations of the Rules of Good Practice in Clinical Trials in Romania risk the penalty of imprisonment for three to six months or a fine of 10 to 30 million Lei (300 to 900 Euros).[9] Please note that these penalties are *only* available for the trials on Medicinal Product for Human Use (MPHU). For trials on MPHU, the National Agency of Medicinal Products informs the Courts. For other kinds of medical trials, the REC informs the College of Physicians of violations of the deontological and ethical rules, who decide the disciplinary penalties. These penalties include reprimanding, a disciplinary warning and, the most severe, cancellation of a physician's licence.

There are some interesting concerns about the circumstances in which the committee's approval may render lawful activities that would otherwise be unlawful. In general no such circumstances were reported in Romania. We understand that the decisions of RECs must include the 'uncovered' (by law) aspects of clinical research. Therefore if there is a situation where the activities may be regarded as unlawful because there are no precise regulations on that specific case, the REC can decide whether that practice can go ahead or not; however, they cannot declare if this is legal or illegal. In those cases, where the laws are in contradiction to the ethical decision of the committee, the committee must report this to the authorities so as to initiate the legal procedures to change the laws accordingly. However, the committee can still only make decisions from an

---

[9] Emergency Order No. 152, 14 October 1999, of the Romanian Government, Article 99.

ethical point of view. We consider that RECs cannot have attributes so as to certify the 'legal' status of a clinical trial.

We strongly believe that the implementation of the European Directive will increase the ability of RECs to make the correct decisions, with these decisions having lawful power. This will help to eliminate some ambiguous situations. In every case, RECs are supposed to obey the laws and regulations concerning bioethical review in Romania. These regulations must correlate as much as possible with international agreements. To obtain a general overview of the ethical 'quality' of REC decisions, we initiated an action at the national level, with the support of the Ministry of Health, in the frame of PRIVIREAL.

We think that, in making decisions, RECs should not rely too heavily on the written law but on the ethical guidelines that include all aspects to consider (religious, social, cultural, and so on). In that sense, RECs must be sensitive to international bioethical agreements (such as the Helsinki Declaration).

Usually an REC will make recommendations that must be followed during the project. However, there are cases where applications are rejected because an REC considers that there is no way for the project to go ahead without breaking ethical rules. In such cases, the different forms of legal action that can be taken against an ethics committee on the basis of its decision are different depending on the type of clinical trial in question. In the case of trials on MPHU the investigator or sponsor can resubmit the application within one month following the rejection of a project. There are no other legal actions that we know of that can be used against the NEC or the Committee for Medicinal Product of the Ministry of Health. For usual clinical trials, the decision of an IEC can be contested to the NEC, or directly to the Ministry of Health, through the Bioethical Committee.

In Romania, Law 677/2001 introduced specific regulations concerning personal data protection during different kinds of procedures or activities, including medical research with a human subject. Among others, the Law refers to those activities declared to be in the public interest of the community; however it does not specify whether such bodies, such as RECs, have the power to decide if a research activity is justified in this respect or not. We consider these decisions to be reserved for the Ministry of Health in consultation with the Bioethical Committee. RECs can only make recommendations in this fashion for those trials where the consent of the data subject is too difficult to obtain, and the benefits exceed the inconvenience. During the processing procedures of data concerning sensitive information about the health status of individuals, we believe that the reason for coding is to randomize (not 'anonymize') the information. Anonymization means that there is no other chance to re-identify a person when faced only with the data record. The data subjects must be informed about all the processing intended, even though data are rendered anonymous before or after the processing. In our opinion, the data rendered anonymous for the purpose of processing are not actually rendered anonymous, because there is a chance for someone to identify the data subject. For example, although those who are processing the data cannot identify the data subjects, the data does still exist in personal form in the hands of those who obtained it from the data subjects.

**Concluding Remarks**

In countries attempting European Union integration, having a bioethical review system holds importance proportional with the level of their national medical research. In these countries, we should expect aspects of medical research that are on the bioethical borderlines only to appear occasionally. The development of modern medical technologies is always expensive and is closely related to the economic power of the country; thus the social impact of RECs activities will be more relevant in countries with good economic conditions. Bioethics must provide the regulatory interface between the newest achievements of science and social acceptance. At the national level, there will always be differences in the way society accepts and implements bioethical rules. Law, instead, must and can be the same, and in Romania the legislation is already modified to fit the European Directives. All European countries, with a strong or weak biotechnological status, must adapt their legislation to the European Directives ensuring the free mobility of people across Europe, and the formation of the future European citizen. The implementation of different 'bio'-solutions will eventually affect the entire world, and so all countries must be prepared.

# Chapter 23

# Research Ethics Committees in Slovakia

Jozef Glasa[*] and Jane Miller[†]

## Establishment of Research Ethics Committees[1]

Ethical review of research began in the Slovak Republic after the Czech-Slovak 'velvet revolution' of 1989 and was driven by scientists, bioethicists and the Good Clinical Practice (GCP) requirements of pharmaceutical companies. This was part of a general reform of the health and biomedical research systems at the time, that aimed to decentralize such research systems and integrate the Slovak Republic with 'pertinent European structures'.[2,3] Committees considering medical ethics were established initially in research institutes, major teaching hospitals, medical faculties and medical societies, and by 1993 there were 70 local ethics committees in the country. There was some decline during the mid-1990s because of a lack of authorities' interest and insufficient funding; however, this has been reversed and there is now much more support for ethical review.

The first set of guidance dealing solely with ethics committees was written by the Central Ethics Committee and issued by the Ministry of Health in June 1992.[4] This dealt with the establishment and practice of ethics committees both in a healthcare and research context. These guidelines are to be replaced by new

---

[*] Associate Professor Jozef Glasa, M.D., Ph.D. is a physician and clinical researcher, and teaches at the Slovak Medical University in Bratislava. He is the present chairman of the Central Ethics Committee based at the Ministry of Health and the Director of the Bratislava Institute of Medical Ethics and Bioethics n.f. (IMEB).

[†] PRIVIREAL coordinating co-worker, Sheffield Institute of Biotechnological Law and Ethics, UK.

[1] The situation described in this report represents that of October 2004. It is worth noting that since this date there have been six new laws enacted, changing some aspects of the REC system.

[2] J. Glasa, J. Bielik, J. Ďačok, M. Glasová and J. Porubský, 'Ethics Committees in the Slovak Republic' in J. Glasa (ed.), *Ethics Committees in Central and Eastern Europe* (Bratislava: Charis/IMEB Fdn., 2000), 229–238, 266.

[3] J. Glasa, J. Bielik, J. Ďačok, M. Glasová and J. Porubský, 'Ethics committees (HECs/IRBs) and health care reform in the Slovak Republic: 1990–2000' (2000) No. 4 *HEC Forum* 12, 358–366.

[4] Ministry of Health (Bratislava), 'Guidelines for ethics committees in health care facilities and biomedical research institutions' (1994) 1 *Medicínska Etika and Bioetika* No. 2, 6–8.

regulations which the Ministry of Health will issue with regard to 'clinical investigation of drugs and GCP' and 'ethics committees'.[5]

There are two laws which refer to research ethics committees—Law No. 277/1994 on Health Care, and Law No. 140/1998 on Drugs and Health Equipment—both of which have been amended since their introduction and which at the time of writing are going through further amendments. The changes to these laws, and the other four laws pending, will further strengthen the position of ethics committees.[6]

The present laws set out requirements that are 'rather general and simple'.[7] Law 277/1994, in §40 para (4), requires that 'the health care facilities (that review, comment and approve the clinical investigations) ... should establish independent committees for review of ethical questions (ethics committees)'. Law 140/1998 states in §16 that 'an opinion of an ethics committee of the facility where the clinical drug investigation is to be performed is required'. However, amendments made in December 2003 introduced further provisions—for example §16 now also lists the items required to be submitted to the REC, includes time-limits for the issuing of an opinion, adds that a single opinion is needed in the case of multi-centre trials, and provides other requirements regarding the suspension and inspection of trials and the reporting of serious adverse effects.

## Structure and Function of RECs

There are two levels of ethical review at present, with a probable third to be introduced with the review of the REC system in late 2004.

The Central Ethics Committee (CEC) was established by the Ministry of Health in 1990 to act as an advisory body on bioethics. Its support of local ethics committees (both for research and clinical ethics review) only extended to guidance or recommendation, and no hierarchical relationships were introduced. In 2002, the Ministry of Health issued amended statutes and appointed a new CEC to revitalize its work. The Statutes gave the committee the remit to advise the Ministry of Health, and other ministries, on 'ethical questions connected with health care, medicine and biomedical research, in particular on the new legislative proposals in these specific areas'.[8] It 'only exceptionally performs the ethical

---

[5] J. Glasa, 'Legislation in the Field of Ethics in Biomedical Research in the Slovak Republic' (Luxembourg: Office for Official Publications of the European Communities, 2004 (in press)).

[6] J. Glasa, 'K problému revitalizácie etických komisií v Slovenskej republike' (Problem of revitalization of ethics committees in the Slovak Republic) (2002) 9 *Medicínska Etika and Bioetika* No. 3–4, 10–15.

[7] Cf. n. 5 *supra*.

[8] J. Glasa, 2004—minutes of the meeting with the European Commission on 'Ethics in New Member States' available online at http://europa.eu.int/comm/european_group_ethics/docs/synthesnewnec.pdf, last accessed 18 May 2005. This is a report by The European Group on Ethics in Science and New Technologies to the European Commission EGE Secretariat—June 2004.

review of projects or protocols for a specific research project (when for example, there is no other relevant or responsible ethics committee for the specific project)'.[9] The CEC also answers queries from local ethics committees.

'Local ethics committees are established by directors of health care facilities or biomedical research institutions, to review protocols of clinical trials or biomedical research projects planned to be performed in that facility/institution'.[10] In addition, they provide follow-up of any research protocol they approve. According to the 1992 guidelines, these ethics committees are in place to give advice; it is the director of the institution where the research will take place that makes the final decision on the research. As previously mentioned, the 1998 Drugs Law makes the opinion of an ethics committee on drug clinical trials a mandatory requirement.

The State Institute for Drug Control (SIDC) is responsible for the authorization of drug clinical evaluations (Section 15(2), 1998 Drugs Law). Since January 2004, after further amendment of the Drugs Law, the SIDC also carries out inspections of good clinical practice and good manufacturing practice (Section 16(e)). Applications for phase I–III clinical trials, and the notifications of phase IV trials, should contain an opinion from an ethics committee.

At present, 'the unfavourable (negative) opinion of an ethics committee is able to prevent the realisation of a research project (or drug clinical trial) in a given health care facility or biomedical research institution (or stop it; especially in the cases of non-compliance or serious adverse events)'.[11]

Ethics committees thus have a standing in law at present, and this will be greatly enhanced by the new, more extensive laws. These laws will give 'more detailed provisions' concerning local committees as outlined above. They will also allow for the establishment of regional ethics committees whose role will be to 'review and follow up multi-centre clinical trials and multi-centre biomedical research projects (with the exception of the review of the "local aspects" of research projects)'.[12]

## Activities Covered by Ethical Review

The Law on Health Care (277/1994) defines biomedical research projects that require ethical review in §40 ind. 1, as an 'investigation aimed at confirmation of a previously formulated hypothesis, which is necessary for obtaining new medical knowledge, elaboration of new methods or hypotheses, or for clinical investigation (trial) of drugs or medicinal devices or health equipment in the interest of preservation or improvement of people's health'.[13] It then states in Section 40(4)

---

[9] Cf. n. 5 *supra*.
[10] *Ibid.*
[11] *Ibid.*
[12] *Ibid.*
[13] *Ibid.*

that an independent committee should review this research, and it should also monitor the performance of clinical investigations.

In addition, §40 states that an ethics committee 'has at least 3 members and is composed of health care professionals and at least one lawyer'. It excludes from membership 'any person, who has ordered the investigation; any person who is close to or an employee of the former person; and for any researcher'.[14] Consensus of all committee members is required for ethical approval, although this is to be amended to provide for a majority voting procedure as an alternative.

Law 140/1998 on Drugs and Health Equipment in §16(2) ind. j requires an 'opinion on the clinical trial given by the ethics committee of the facility, where the clinical trial is to be performed'.[15] The objectives of a drug clinical evaluation are to evaluate the therapeutic efficacy of the investigational product, its safety, contra-indications, interactions, adverse reactions, and to obtain new scientific knowledge (Section 15). This law also makes it a requirement that documentation regarding the trial, including ethical approval, is sent to the SIDC whose authorization is necessary for the trial to proceed.

The 1992 guidance for the establishment of ethics committees mentions membership in Article 3, stating that the membership number should be uneven and the members multidisciplinary. Members may include: healthcare workers and specialists, pharmacists, nurses, researchers, lawyers, specialists in medical ethics (philosophers or theologians), psychologists, and patient representatives. The Chair should be a physician. The basic tasks of ethics committees depend on whether the committee in question is in a healthcare facility or a research institute (Article 7). Those in healthcare facilities should: provide advice on clinical ethics problems; 'examine ethical issues raised by the medical and legal aspects of the diagnostic and therapeutic procedures used in the health care facility';[16] review biomedical research protocols (of which clinical research should *always* be reviewed); consult and advise on the medical-ethical questions raised by healthcare workers or other workers; and provide advice on resource allocation. Those committees in research institutes should review ethical issues raised by the medical and legal aspects of biomedical research (both initially, during the research and on publication), and also perform the tasks of healthcare committees, should the facility provide healthcare services.

## Implementation of Directive 2001/20/EC

Law No. 140/1998 was amended in December 2003 to include, among others, this Directive. In particular §16 was extended to include a timescale for the decision of

---

[14] Cf. n. 5 *supra*.

[15] *Ibid.*

[16] *Ibid.*

an ethics committee, a list of required documentation to be submitted for review, and the need for a single opinion in the case of multi-centre trials.[17]

## Attention to the Law

In practice local ethics committees 'respect the relevant international requirements and standards (especially those of the GCP) as reflected in the ethics committees' statutes and standard operating procedures (SOPs) on a voluntary basis'.[18]

The 1992 guidelines, in Article 5, state that ethics committees should principally be guided by the Helsinki Declaration when making their decisions. They also outline that they should be 'guided by' the laws of the Slovak Republic, and the regulations and guidelines issued by the Ministry of Health, in addition to having the freedom to refer to any existing literature or other resources on medical ethics. In Article 7, outlining the basic tasks of the ethics committees, it states that they should 'review ethical issues raised by the medical and *legal* aspects of biomedical research projects' (our emphasis). It should also be noted that it is possible that a lawyer would be present on the committee. The 1992 guidance will, however, be superseded by the new Ministry of Health regulations, which will provide more extensive provisions relating to ethics committees.

## Matters Related to Data Protection

The protection of personal data is covered by Law No. 428/2002[19] which amended previous laws and transposed 'relevant international instruments on personal data protection (including the Directive 95/46/EC)'.[20] Section 3 defines personal data as 'data relating to an identified or identifiable natural person, where such a person is one who can be identified, either directly or indirectly, in particular by reference to a generally useable identification number or to one or more features or attributes specific to his physical, physiological, mental, economic, cultural or social identity'.

Section 4 also gives explicit definitions of these important notions, which are used in the law:

---

[17] J. Glasa, 'Challenges for ethics committees in the new EU member states. The approach in the Slovak Republic' in *An EMEA/EFGCP Workshop on Ethics in Clinical Development—From Legislation to Implemetation* (London: EMEA, December 11–12, 2003).

[18] Cf. n. 5 *supra*.

[19] Personal Data Protection Law of 3 July 2002. An English translation is available through the Slovak Office for Personal Data Protection at http://www.dataprotection.gov.sk /buxus/docs/act_no_428.pdf (last accessed on 18 May 2005).

[20] Cf. n. 5 *supra*.

a.   personal data processing;
b.   provision of personal data;
c.   providing access to personal data;
d.   making personal data public;
e.   liquidation of personal data;
f.   imposing a block on personal data;
g.   information systems;
h.   purpose of personal data processing;
i.   consent of the person;
j.   transborder flow of personal data;
k.   anonymized data;
l.   address;
m.   general identifier;
n.   biometric data;
o.   audit of the information system safety.

It also defines the controller, processor, authorized person, the data subject, and the user.

Anonymized data are defined as 'data modified to a form in which it cannot be associated with the data subject'. The only other legal provision is stated in §7(4)b, that the consent of the person is not required if 'the processed personal data are used for statistical purposes; in these cases personal data have to be made anonymous'.[21]

There are a few exemptions provided for in Law No. 428/2002 where consent of the data subject is not required for additional processing. This is the case for the 'further processing of personal data for historic, statistical and scientific purposes', which will not be considered as incompatible with the initial purposes (§6(1)b). This is also the case for processing 'exclusively for the purposes of scientific, artistic, and literary works, ... and also historic or scientific purposes' and with the provisos that the data will not be made public and that it will be processed by the original data collector.[22]

The amendments that are currently being made to the Health Law are envisaged to have 'more specific wording on personal health data ... with regard to biomedical research'.[23]

Although there is no specific law on human genetics in the Slovak Republic, it is felt that the Law on Protection of Personal Data covers genetic information. Additionally, 'insofar as genetic information may be considered as an integral part of the personal health information' there are provisions in the Health Law concerning confidentiality, privacy and access that would be pertinent to genetic information.[24]

---

[21] Cf. n. 5 *supra.*
[22] *Ibid.*
[23] *Ibid.*
[24] *Ibid.*

## Conclusion

Ethical review of clinical trials and biomedical research is well established in the Slovak Republic and this will be strengthened by the revision of health legislation occurring in late 2004. It is thought that it will introduce some very positive and systemic changes in the area of ethics committees, a welcome move for bioethics in Slovakia.

Conclusion

Chapter 24

# Research Ethics Committees in Slovenia

Joze Trontelj[*]

## Establishment of Research Ethics Committees (RECs)[1]

Since the 1960s there has been a formal system for ethical review of medical research in Slovenia. Although there is no specific law regulating biomedical research on humans the Oviedo Convention[2] has been in force since 1 December 1999. This important legally binding international instrument contains rather detailed provisions on biomedical research. There is also a long-standing practice, of over 40 years, of ethical review of medical research. There are currently several binding internal regulations that are observed:

- All research on human subjects funded by public money must be reviewed for ethical acceptability and approved by the National Medical Ethics Committee (NMEC), by regulation of the Ministry of Education, Science and Sports.
- All biomedical research in the framework of theses for M.Sc. or D.Sc. degrees, as well as students' scientific research, must gain previous approval by the NMEC (by regulation of the Medical School).
- Ethical approval is required by the Slovene Directive on Clinical Drug Trials[3] for all clinical trials of pharmaceutical products. Slovenia has also started to implement the provisions of the European Directive 2001/20/EC on the application of Good Clinical Practice in the conduct of clinical trials on medicinal products for human use.
- Any scientific paper reporting on biomedical research submitted for publication in a Slovene medical journal must be accompanied by the documented approval of an REC.

[*] Dr. Joze Trontelj, The National Medical Ethics Committee of Slovenia.
[1] The situation described in this report represents that of December 2003.
[2] Convention for the Protection of Human Rights and Dignity of the Human Being With Regard to the Application of Biology and Medicine (1997, Council of Europe ETS No. 164), 1–12.
[3] Pravilnik o kliničnem preskušanju zdravil (Directive on Clinical Drug Trials), UL RS 28. 7. 2000, No. 67: 8372–8385.

-   Slovenia has signed and is expected to ratify the Additional Protocol to the Convention on Human Rights and Biomedicine, on Biomedical Research.[4] This should provide a basis for the new law on biomedical research, regulating among other things, ethical *review* of research in great detail.

The NMEC takes care of the large majority of all ethical review of research. The ethical committees within the regional hospitals are authorized to review local studies not presenting any serious risk or burden, for example, non-invasive and observational research. An ethics committee of the Institute of Oncology advises on oncological research; however, an approval still has to be obtained from the NMEC.

Ethical review is required for all research involving intervention on, or interaction with, human beings. Additionally, it is required for all research on personal medical data, and biological material of human origin is also covered.

The Health Minister appoints members to the NMEC from a selection of reputed experts nominated by the Medical School, the National Health Council, and the Slovene Medical Chamber.

The NMEC, as an independent body, is not formally accountable to any supervising authority. According to Article 8 of the Act on the NMEC,[5] its decisions cannot be appealed. If a different view is adopted by the CDBI of the Council of Europe or the World Health Organization, the NMEC is obliged to reconsider its decision. Regional RECs are responsible to the NMEC.

**General Powers of RECs**

In general an approval by an REC is sufficient, and necessary, for the research to go ahead. However, in clinical drug studies (phase I–III), an approval of the Agency for Medicinal Products (of the Ministry of Health) is also required.

Occasionally researchers have failed to submit research for which they wrongly assumed that review is not required, often because in their opinion it did not present any ethical problem. When such cases come to light, a careful retrograde review is obtained; so far the evaluation has never been negative. Cases of intentional non-compliance have, so far, not been recorded. If they were, disciplinary action would follow with potentially serious consequences for the researcher, for example, revocation of the licence.

There are no circumstances under which RECs will approve activities, rendering them lawful, that would otherwise be unlawful.

---

[4] Additional Protocol to the Convention of Human Rights and Biomedicine concerning Biomedical Research (30 June 2004) Council of Europe, CETS No. 195.

[5] Ministerial Decree on the Constitution, Terms of Reference and Procedures of the National Medical Ethics Committee (in Slovene) *Uradni list Republike Slovenije (Official Gazette of the Republic of Slovenia)* No. 30, 2 June 1995, 2149–2150.

## General Legal Responsibility of RECs

RECs may reject or advise against activities that are lawful. This is because not everything that is ethically unacceptable is prohibited by the law. In principle RECs cannot approve activities that are unlawful. However, legislation in certain areas lags behind the developments in science as well as medical practice. Therefore the NMEC, as an exception, may authorize research on corpses or materials removed from them in certain cases where this could be a punishable offence according to the existing law (for example, where there is intervention without explicit consent of the person before their death).

Formal *legal* guidance at the national level does not exist. However, the NMEC in its deliberation relies on the provisions of the Oviedo Convention[6] and its Additional Protocol on Biomedical Research,[7] as well as on established international guidelines such as the Helsinki Declaration. The NMEC has also adopted and published a guideline for researchers developing a research project involving human beings. This has been largely based on the Protocol, supplementing the Convention on Human Rights and Biomedicine, on Biomedical Research.

### The Impact of Directive 2001/20/EC on Good Clinical Practice

Most provisions of Directive 2001/20/EC on Good Clinical Practice have already been incorporated into the Slovenian regulation of clinical studies. The Slovenian Directive on Clinical Drug Testing,[8] regulating good clinical practice in the field of pharmaceutical research and research on medical appliances, is based on this Directive. In addition, the rather detailed provisions of the Protocol on Biomedical Research have been observed by both the RECs and the scientific community since these guidelines have been in use.

### The Law in Practice

The law sets out minimum requirements; in sensitive cases, therefore, the NMEC enforces higher standards of protection where rights of the human subjects are concerned. The NMEC takes great care to ensure that privacy of sensitive personal data is properly observed. In the case of the NMEC, its decisions are final according to the law. However, the NMEC is obliged to reconsider its decisions if the appropriate forum of the Council of Europe adopts a different stance on the subject. On the other hand, civil legal actions against an REC that approved a research project in which subjects have suffered undue damage are conceivable; however, such cases have so far not occurred.

---

[6] See n. 2 *supra*.
[7] See n. 4 *supra*.
[8] See n. 3 *supra*.

**Specific Data Protection Matters**

When consent has not been obtained from the data subject, RECs do have the power to make decisions about when research is justified in the public interest. Where unreasonable effort would be necessary to contact the data subjects, the potential risk of damage to the data subject appears remote, and the study is expected to provide important new scientific information, the NMEC may exempt the research proposer from the duty to seek consent.

Other exemptions from the data protection rights of the data subject are also allowed. For example, where research on data or biological samples identifies potentially serious, and preventable, risks to health of the data subject; the individual's identity may be uncoded and appropriate action taken to initiate the necessary preventive measures or treatment.

Coded data are only considered to be rendered anonymous when the data controller's code, which can be used to discover the identity of the data subject, is irreversibly erased. The NMEC insists on information as to anticipated or intended processing of personal data to be given to data subjects, whether or not the data are rendered anonymous. RECs do not consider data as being anonymous for the purposes of processing when it still exists in personal form in the hands of those who obtained the data from the data subject. In fact in cases of particularly sensitive information, the NMEC requires both assurance from the researchers that links to an identifiable data subject be irreversibly destroyed and for details of the actual procedure to be used to be provided.

The collecting and analysing of genetic information is considered to be a situation where data protection rights may easily be violated. The NMEC's practice is to inform the proposers of molecular genetic studies that an approval is only granted for the *particular* study submitted, and that any new study on the same material is subject to a new review. The donors of the material must also be so informed. They must have a choice to give their consent only to the present study (as opposed to all future studies), and in case of any new study, to be asked for a new consent. A request for blank advance consent for any future studies is in principle only acceptable for irreversibly anonymized material.

# Chapter 25

# Research Ethics Committees in Spain

Carlos Maria Romeo-Casabona[*] and Pilar Nicolás[†]

## Establishment of RECs

*System of Ethical Review for Medical Research*

Review of the ethical aspects of scientific research is compulsory when we are dealing with a clinical trial involving medication. Clinical trial means any research with human beings to determine or confirm the clinical, pharmacological or other pharmacodynamic effects and/or to detect adverse reactions, and/or to study the absorption, distribution, metabolism and excretion of one or more medications in research with the goal of determining their security and/or effectiveness.

Considering other scientific research, the criteria established in the health legislation must be followed, but generally, no review of the ethical aspects of the research is required by an established system, although there are some specific rules for research in certain areas.

*General criteria*  The Spanish Constitution recognizes the right to free scientific research in Article 20(1)b. Also, according to Article 44.2 of the Spanish Constitution, the Government has a duty to promote science and research for the general interest, and this is a leading principle of economic and social policy.

The limit to this right is the respect for fundamental human rights. There are some rights that have a special relevance such as the right to life and integrity (Article 15) and to honour and intimacy (Article 18). In the same way, the Spanish Constitution considers as fundamental rights personal freedom (Articles 1 and 17) and dignity (Article 10.1).

General Health Law and Law 41/2002 (on Respect for the Patient's Autonomy and the Regulation of Clinical Documentation) establishes the patient's rights that must be respected. We should point out that according to Article 10.4 of the National Health Law, the patient has the right to be warned if any diagnostic, predictive or therapeutic procedure may be used in research, and the patient has to give his or her written consent for this.

---

[*] Professor of Criminal Law, Director of the Inter-University Chair BBVA Foundation-Provincial Government of Biscay in Law and the Human Genome, University of Deusto, University of the Basque Country.
[†] Member of the Inter-University Chair, Research Assistant at the University of Deusto.

Finally, the principles established in the Declaration of Helsinki have to be respected, since Spain has signed it and according to Article 96 of the Constitution, once published officially in Spain, international treaties will comprise of the internal ordering.

*Some specific criteria*   Law 35/1988 on Assisted Reproduction Techniques and Law 42/1988 on the Donation and Use of Embryos and Foetuses or their Organs, Tissues or Cells, established some specific rules for research with pre-embryos,[1] embryos or their tissues, organs or cells. The first law underwent a reform recently through Law 45/2003, and Royal Decree 176/2004 of 30 January established the National Centre for Transplants and Regenerative Medicine. Through the Royal Decree 2132/2004 of 29 October, the requisites to research with human pre-embryos are also regulated.

*A Formal or Informal System?*

Article 64 of Law 25/1990 (20 December) on Medicinal Products establishes the review of clinical trials by Research Ethics Committees. According to this law, no clinical trial shall be commenced without the previous report of a Clinical Research Ethics Committee. The committee will assess the methodological, ethical and legal aspects of the proposed protocol, as well as consider the balance of the trial's anticipated risks and benefits. This condition was developed by Royal Decree 561/1993, which established the Requirements for the Accomplishment of Clinical Trials involving Medicinal Products.

Law 53/2002 of 30 December, on Administrative and Fiscal Measures and Social Order, introduced several changes to Law 25/1990 with the goal of eliminating the differences between this law and Directive 2001/20/EC on Good Clinical Practice. Royal Decree 223/2004 of 6 February develops this regulation and regulates Clinical Trials with Drugs, in the place of Royal Decree 561/1993, and incorporates the Directive to the Spanish juridical framework.

The new rule, whose entry into force was 1 May 2004, has a Chapter (number III) dedicated to Clinical Research Ethics Committees. The coordinating centre for such committees is created, and its functions, minimum accreditation, composition, requirements with respect to goals, infrastructure and general operating rules are established. In the following Chapter (IV), the procedure to obtain the corresponding opinion is regulated.

*Clinical Ethics*

The research review system is separate from the system of Medical Attendance Ethics Committees, who are in charge of reviewing the daily activity of the health centres and above all operate when there is a conflict in relation to clinical ethics. They are just advisory committees and their reports and decisions do not have

---

[1] This term is used in Spanish law for an embryo which is less than 14 days old.

obligatory force, unlike the RECs. Moreover, their existence is not compulsory; it is just a recommendation in order to achieve maximum quality in the assistance health service.

Nevertheless, there is a connection between both committees. Article 13.3 of Royal Decree 223/2004 states that in the cases where a Medical Attendance Ethics Committee exists, it is necessary that one of its members be part of an REC.

*Activities Covered by the Research Review*

The research review covers the evaluation of the legal, ethical and methodological aspects of clinical trials, evaluation of the changes in authorized clinical trials and the control of the trial from the beginning until the final report (Article 10 of Royal Decree 223/2004).

The committee will evaluate the protocol, the research instructions and the whole documentation and will take a decision considering the following points (Article 17 of Royal Decree 223/2004):

a. The suitability of the clinical trial considering the actual knowledge.
b. The suitability of its design to obtain conclusions based on the adequate number of subjects related to the objective of the study.
c. The criteria to select and retire the subjects, as well as the equitable selection of the sample.
d. The justification of the foreseen risks compared with the expected benefits for the subjects, other patients and for the community, considering the principle of protecting the subjects of Article 3.
e. The justification of the control group (even if it is a placebo or an active treatment).
f. The provisions to control the trial's development.
g. The suitability of the researcher and his or her collaborators.
h. The suitability of infrastructures.
i. The suitability of written information provided to the subjects and the procedure to obtain their informed consent, alongside the justification of research with people not able to consent.
j. The insurance or financial guarantee provided for the trial.
k. The quantities and, where needed, forecasts of payments for research subjects or researchers and any other relevant aspect of the contract between the promoter and the centre that must appear in the contract (as provided by Article 30).
l. The planning for selecting subjects.

*REC Membership Requirements*

There must be at least nine members of an REC. The number and composition of members in the committee assures its independence, capacity and the experience to review the methodological, ethical and legal aspects of the investigation, the pharmacology and clinical practice in hospital and extra-hospital medicine. There are doctors as members of the committee—one of whom will be a clinical pharmacologist; one a pharmacist of a hospital, and a university graduate in infirmary. At least one member will have to be independent of the centres in which the projects are carried out, and in which they require the committee's ethical evaluation. At least two members must be people not having a health-related profession, one of which will have to be licensed in law. This will simultaneously guarantee a system of reformation of members that allows new incorporations regularly, and adds to the experience of the committee.

As established by Article 4 of Law 25/1990 (20 December) on Medicinal Products; being a member of a Clinical Investigation Ethics Committee is incompatible with any class of interests derived from the manufacture and sale of medicines and sanitary products (Article 12 of Royal Decree 223/2004).

In addition, in the case that the Commission of Investigation or the Committee of Welfare Ethics exists, the REC will have to include a member of each (Article 14.3 of Royal Decree 223/2004).

*Responsibility and Accountability*

RECs are accredited by the competent health authority in each area, initially and after membership changes. The initial and any following accreditations of RECs will be notified to the Spanish Agency of Medicine and Sanitary Products and to the Coordinating Centre of Ethical Committees of Clinical Investigation. There is, however, no provision concerning the specific responsibility of RECs or the revision of its decisions by any authority. RECs are independent institutions.

**General Powers of RECs**

*Approval and Authorization*

To begin a clinical trial, the previous favourable decision of the Clinical Research Ethics Committee is required, as well as other authorizations (Article 15 of Royal Decree 223/2004).

Furthermore, RECs have the possibility to advise the health authorities of the Autonomous Communities (regional areas with their own governments and powers) to suspend a trial, when it is unlawful, the conditions the trial was authorized under have changed, the ethical requirements are not fulfilled or it is necessary to protect the subjects or public health. The health authorities of the Autonomous Communities will communicate this to the Spanish Medicine and Sanitary Products Agency, which will have to judge the case (Article 26.3 of Royal Decree 223/2004).

*Sufficiency of approval*   Apart from the favourable decision of the REC, it is necessary that the Directors of all centres where the trial is going to be held give their conformation and also that an authorization is obtained from the Spanish Medicine and Sanitary Products Agency (Article 15 of Royal Decree 223/2004). The process of providing the authorization is described in Articles 20 to 27 of Royal Decree 223/2004.

Authorization by the Spanish Medicines Agency is also necessary for clinical trials (Article 65, Law 25/1990).

*Necessity of approval* As previously mentioned, the prior decision of a Clinical Research Ethics Committee is necessary to undergo a clinical trial (Article 15 of Royal Decree 223/2004). The procedure is outlined in Articles 16 to 19 of that Royal Decree. If it is a multi-centre trial, that is, when two or more Spanish centres take part, it is required that only one decision be enacted by the 'reference' committee independently from the number of RECs. Each REC will send a report to the reference committee, which will be considered in the final decision, which has to be specially explained if it disagrees with the opinion of any of the other RECs on any part of the trial. However, the local aspects in these reports are the only mandatory feature (Article 19 of Royal Decree 223/2004).

*Failure to Submit Research for Review or to Follow the Review's Judgment*

Royal Decree 223/2004 points out that Article 108 of Law 25/1990 on Medicinal Products outlines some administrative infractions, sanctioned according to Article 109. Law 25/1990 does not refer specifically to the review of the RECs, but it does refer to administrative authorization, and according to Article 15 of Royal Decree 223/2004, one of the requisites of said authorization is to attach the review of the REC together with the application.

So, the only way of avoiding review by an REC is not to submit it to an administrative authority, which will itself constitute an administrative infraction. Article 108 on infractions states:

2. The infractions specified next will constitute administrative faults and shall be sanctioned in the terms provided in the next Article: ...

... b. Serious Infractions ...

... 10) Make any clinical tests without the previous administrative authorization.

So not submitting the research for review by an REC will constitute a serious administrative infraction. Such infractions will result in the following sanctions:

- Minimal degree: from 500 001 to 1 150 000 pesetas.[2]
- Medium degree: from 1 150 001 to 1 800 000 pesetas.
- Maximum degree: from 1 800 001 to 2 500 000, it being possible to exceed the above mentioned quantity until reaching the quintuple of the value of the products or services which are the object of the infraction.

On the other hand failing to comply with the reviewed protocol will be considered a very serious infraction:

---

[2] The fixed conversion rate is 1 Euro to approximately 166 Pesetas, figure taken from www.xe.com on 16 February 2005.

6.  Making clinical tests without adjusting the protocols that have allowed the authorization; or without the consent of the subject or his or her legal representative, or a substantial breach of the duty of informing the subject about the clinical test in which he or she takes part.

Very serious infractions result in the following sanctions:

- Minimal degree: from 2 500 001 to 35 000 000 pesetas.
- Medium degree: from 35 000 001 to 67 500 000 pesetas.
- Maximum degree: from 67 500 001 to 100 000 000, it being possible to exceed the above mentioned quantity until reaching the quintuple of the value of the products or services which are the object of the infraction.

The body responsible for imposing these sanctions will be either the State Health Administration or the Autonomous Community Health Administration (Article 109.3, Law 25/1990).

It is really surprising that the law considers it more serious not to comply with the protocol than to administer a medical test without authorization. Maybe the legislator considers this as a formal breach, as long as the hypothetical non-authorized test is able to fulfil the legal and ethical requirements. It could be considered that there is a bigger risk of endangering a subject's health when a protocol is not fulfilled because they could be breaking specific requirements of the test.

Apart from these administrative sanctions we should mention the possibility of civil liability (and even criminal) in the case of damage to the subjects of the clinical trials. Article 1902 of the Civil Code sets down that whoever causes damage to another by an action or an omission being negligent or guilty, will have to repair the said damage. Not submitting the research for review or failing to follow what the review requires will aggravate the guilt or negligence in the case of damages and civil liability.

*Circumstances in which REC Approval will Render Activities Lawful that would Otherwise be Unlawful*

Decisions made by RECs do not have any formal role in rendering lawful activities that would otherwise be unlawful. According to the RECs' responses to the questionnaire as part of the PRIVIREAL project, the Committees are not permitted to do so.

**General Legal Responsibility of RECs**

*Attention to the Law*

Article 10 of Royal Decree 223/2004 establishes that RECs will examine the methodological, ethical and legal aspects of the clinical trial protocols sent to them.

According to this, RECs would be able to reject lawful activities based on ethical principles and unlawful trials cannot be approved. We must consider that at least one member of each REC must be a lawyer (Article 12.2 of Royal Decree 223/2004), and that the trial will be stopped if the law is broken (Article 26 of Royal Decree 223/2004).

RECs can require that the health authorities of each Autonomous Community temporarily suspend a trial if the law is broken, its authorization conditions have changed, the ethical requirements are not fulfilled, or it is necessary to protect the subjects or public health (Article 26.3 of Royal Decree 223/2004).

To conclude, we can say that the linkage of REC decisions to the law is total, and the legal suitability of the trial is the first criterion to be considered within the examination.

Article 64.2 of Law 25/1990 states that '2. The Committee will consider the methodological, ethical and legal aspects of the proposed protocol as well as the test's anticipated risk and benefits balance'. According to this, RECs would be able to reject lawful activities on the basis of ethical principles.

Article 60 makes it obligatory to comply with some concrete ethical hypotheses, and therefore, by means of this Article, incorporates them into the legal framework. The second paragraph of this Article includes the more general obligation of following the Declaration of Helsinki, and also the successive declarations updating it, with regard to the respect of fundamental rights.

These conclusions have been confirmed by the committees' responses to the PRIVIREAL questionnaire.[3]

On the other hand, RECs must respect the law and they cannot approve unlawful activities—consulted RECs confirmed this. Apart from the previously mentioned Article 64.2 that obliges RECs to consider the legal aspects, Law 25/1990 (Article 64.3) and also Royal Decree 223/2004 (Article 12.2) set down the membership requirements of RECs and establish that at least one of them must be a jurist: 'ethics committees will be formed by an interdisciplinary team composed of doctors, hospital chemists, clinical pharmacologists, nurses and non-medical personnel with at least one lawyer'.

This compulsory presence of a jurist seems to reflect an implicit legal requirement for the RECs to reject unlawful activities.

Article 65 also states that the Spanish Medicines Agency can interrupt a clinical trial or demand protocol modifications if the law is broken.

*The Implementation and Impact of Directive 2001/20 EC on Good Clinical Practice*

Directive 2001/20/EC has made it necessary to change the current Spanish legislation. Law 53/2002, of 30 December, on Fiscal, Administrative and Social Measures, has introduced several changes into Law 25/1990 on medicinal products

---

[3] See the chapter in D. Beyleveld, D. Townend and J. Wright (eds.), *Research Ethics Committees, Data Protection and Medical Research in Europe – Key Issues* (Aldershot: Ashgate Publishing Ltd, 2005) on the PRIVIREAL 'Questionnaire to RECs'.

with the goal of eliminating the differences between this rule and the EC Directive. The legal framework needed has been given by a new rule approved by Royal Decree 223/2004 of 6 February which regulates clinical trials with medications, replacing Royal Decree 561/1993, bringing the Spanish juridical framework into line with this Directive.

Article 125 of Law 53/2002 introduced the following changes in Law 25/1990 dealing with RECs. Firstly, the definition of clinical trial is written again (important changes are not introduced), and observational studies are excluded from this law. Article 59 of Law 25/1990 on Medicinal Products is substituted by the following:

1. Within this law, a clinical trial is considered to be all research with human beings with the goal of confirming or assuring the clinical, pharmacological and/or other pharmacodynamic effects and/or to detect the adverse reactions and/or study the absorption, distribution, metabolism and elimination of one or more medications in research with the goal of guessing its efficacy and/or safety.

2. Observational studies will not fall under this chapter's scope. An observational study is one where medications are given in a normal way, according to the usual conditions of medical practice. The assignment of a patient to a concrete therapeutic strategy will not be decided prior to the trial by a trial protocol, but it will be determined by the common practice of medicine, and the decision of giving a certain medication will be clearly dissociated from the decision of including the patient in the study. Any intervention, either diagnostic or control, that is not common in clinical practice will not be applied to the patients, and epidemiological methods will be used for the analysis of the gathered data.

Secondly, the content of Article 60 of Law 25/1990 on Medicinal Products is changed. The most significant changes appear in the information and consent provisions that will now fall under Law 41/2002 on Patient Autonomy. The current Article 60 is:

Article 60. Respect of ethical principles
All trials will be subject to the administrative authorization foreseen in Article 65, also in respect of the following demands:

1. No clinical trial will be started as long as there is not enough scientific data and in particular, pharmacological and toxicological trials on animals, which guarantee that the risks involved to the human subject are acceptable.

2. Clinical trials will be carried out with respect to the person's fundamental rights and ethical postulates that affect the biomedical research where human beings are affected, using the contents of the Helsinki Declaration and successive declarations that update such postulates.

3. With the purpose of avoiding obsolete or repetitive research, it will only be possible to begin clinical trials to show the effectiveness and security of the proposed therapeutic modifications, whenever there are reasonable doubts.

4. The trial subject will give his free written consent, after receiving information on the nature, importance, implications and risks of the clinical trial. If the trial subject cannot write, he will be able to give, in exceptional cases, a verbal consent with a witness.

In the case of people who cannot give their free consent, their legal representative will give it after receiving instructions and explanations about the goal and risks of the trial. It will also be necessary to have the agreement of the subject if conditions allow him to understand the nature, importance, goal and risks of the trial.

5. The previous section will be understood without damage to what is foreseen in Section 2 of Article 9 of Law 41/2002, of November 14, regulating the patient's autonomy and of rights and obligations in the field of information and clinical documentation, in the terms determined by law.

6. In the case of clinical trials without therapeutic interest for the research subject, the payment established by contract will be paid anyway, but it will be reduced according to the subject's participation in the experimentation in the case that it is not finished.

Thirdly, the first paragraph of Article 62 of Law 25/1990, of 20 December, on medicinal products is modified. Insurance is needed for any trial, and not only for those products in the research phase, but also for new indications of tests on authorized medication or when there is no therapeutic interest for the subject. It is written as follows:

1. It will only be possible to carry out a clinical trial when the necessary criteria on insurance or compensation have previously been adopted which cover the damages that the subject may suffer as a consequence of the trial.

Fourthly, administrative intervention in the procedure of authorizing trials will only be undertaken by the Spanish Medicines Agency according to a new procedure. This is written as follows:

Article 65. Administrative intervention
1. Clinical trials with medications in research will be under the authorization of the Spanish Medicines Agency, according to the procedure established by rules.
2. The Spanish Medicines Agency will be able to interrupt the clinical trial at any moment or demand the introduction of changes in its protocol, in the following cases:

   a. If the law is broken.
   b. If the conditions that led to the authorization change.
   c. If ethical principles gathered in Article 60 are not fulfilled.
   d. To protect the research subjects.
   e. To defend public health.

3. Health related Administrations will have inspection abilities regarding clinical trials, even being able to investigate the individual clinical records of those research subjects, always keeping their confidentiality. They will also be able to do a preventive interruption of the trial due to any of the causes pointed out in the previous point, immediately communicating it to the Sanity and Consumption Ministry.
4. Health related Administrations will look after the execution of the Good Clinical Practice rules.

5.  The main researcher of a trial will immediately notify the promoter of any serious problems which have arisen through the trial, except for when the problems are specified in the protocol which do not require an immediate communication. The promoter will keep a detailed record of all the problems notified to him, the communications to the Health related Administrations and the Clinical Research Ethics Committee will be done as is established by law.
6.  The favourable or unfavourable results of each clinical trial, whether the trial is finished or not, will be communicated to the Spanish Medicines Agency, without influencing the communication to the corresponding Autonomous Communities.

Royal Decree 223/2004 has taken into account the basic principles for clinical trials with human beings based on the protection of human rights and dignity regarding the application of biology and medicine, as shown in the Declaration of Helsinki and in the Convention on Human Rights and Biomedicine,[4] as well as all the other rules for the adequate protection of personal data. On the other hand, new administrative procedures have been developed to authorize clinical trials by the Spanish Central Administration, which intend to increase the speed and simplify the currently existing steps, harmonizing the different regulations in this field of the EU Member States and allowing the mutual recognition among the sanitary authorities of these states regarding the results of clinical trials.

In relation to the evaluation of the clinical trial, and with regards to the Clinical Research Ethics Committee, apart from establishing deadlines for this evaluation, it is necessary that no more than one decision is enacted even where more than one REC is involved. In this sense, in the multi-centre clinical trials, where two or more Spanish centres take part, a 'reference' committee will be designated among the different ethics committees involved, to enact the only decision. This makes it necessary to create a coordinating body called the Clinical Research Ethics Committees Coordinating Centre. It is compulsory to comply with the good clinical practice principles, which are referred to: first, the responsibilities of the sponsor, the investigator and the monitor (who is a person linking the sponsor and the investigator); second, the publications; and third, the registry of the documentation of the clinical trial. The fulfilment shall be verified by the Spanish Agency on Medical Products, which shall inform the European Agency (Articles 34 to 40 of Royal Decree 223/2004). Many requirements are indispensable to justify the participation of human beings in clinical trials, including: the verification of the use of good clinical practice rules, data and information controlling; the production of documents needed to check that they have been produced, recorded and communicated, as well as the rules of correct production, import and labelling of medications in research; the surveillance of the security of medications; and the communications between the competent authorities in this field. Finally, this Royal Decree is complemented with good clinical practice rules and the instructions on how to run clinical trials in Spain, and the guidelines of the

---

[4] Convention for the Protection of Human Rights and Dignity of the Human Being with regard to the Application of Biology and Medicine: Convention on Human Rights and Biomedicine, Oviedo, 4. IV.1997.

European Commission that will be published by the Ministry of Sanitary Health and Consumption.

## RECs and the Law in Practice

In Spain, RECs are aware of the obligation to review each trial in relation to data protection rules. The new Royal Decree points out this requirement specifically in Article 3.2, according to which clinical trials will be carried out under conditions with respect to the subject's rights and the ethical rules that affect biomedical research with humans. Clearly, it will be necessary to safeguard the physical and mental integrity of the subject, as well as his or her intimacy and the protection of his or her data in accordance with Organic Law 15/1999 of the 13 December on the Protection of Personal Data. The freely expressed and informed consent of each research subject will be obtained and documented before his or her inclusion in the trial. The law on data protection and research subjects is therefore left to Organic Law 15/1999, but also to Law 41/2002, on Respect for the Patient's Autonomy and Regulation of Clinical Documentation (which is pointed out in Article 60 of the recently changed Law on Medical Products, as we mentioned previously).

The principles that should be respected according to these rules are, to summarize, the necessity of express consent to use health data (which includes their collection) giving some previous information on the conditions of data treatment; the obligation of confidentiality and fulfilment of security requirements in relation to the treatment; and the recognition of the right of the data subject to access data at any moment and cancel them. However, this last right can be limited because research data maintenance is mandatory, as stated in Article 39 of Royal Decree 223/2004.

RECs review these questions to authorize a trial, and they reject it if respect to these principles is not guaranteed. The committee carries out this study. Nevertheless, if respect of personal data protection requirements are not appropriately justified in a trial in which future benefits are foreseen for the patient, the REC usually requests an external opinion.

## Legal Action Against RECs

There are no legal provisions that establish any legal action against an REC or its members. Furthermore, according to the answered PRIVIREAL questionnaires, RECs do not believe that the committees have any liability at law in relation to their decisions with regard to research proposals.

We do not know of any judicial resolutions referring to an REC's decisions.

## Specific Data Protection Matters

### RECs and Public Interest Judgments

The RECs themselves do not authorize exemptions to data protection rights. They would make an approval subject to a competent external legal opinion that the public interest justifies those exemptions and not obtaining the consent of the subject.

### RECs and 'Anonymized' Information

*Coded data*   The committees hold the view that data have been rendered anonymous when researchers cannot directly or indirectly identify who the data are about, even if those (for example the clinicians) from whom the researchers have obtained the data still can.

We should point out some differences on the regime of dissociated data between the Organic Law on Personal Data Protection and Law 41/2002. In the Organic Law, dissociated data falls inside its scope when anyone can associate it to a person and it cannot be disclosed without the subject's consent. However, in Law 41/2002, clinical record data can be used for research goals if they are provided without any identity. That is, if researchers receive any dissociated and coded data, and cannot associate them to a person, the principles of data protection will not be applied, even though other people can do this operation (the identifying). We must understand that this is the law that must be applied because it is more recent and more specific than the Organic Law on Personal Data Protection, but the contradiction between the two laws must be pointed out.

*Further processing after anonymization*   In the case that data are anticipated or intended to be used for further processing after they are rendered anonymous, it is not necessary to inform the subject because the data have previously been rendered anonymous.

### DNA Samples (Biological Materials), Genetic Information and Data Protection Rights

RECs consider that at least when identification of the human source is directly or indirectly possible, processing human biological material for genetic research falls within the scope of data protection law.

Chapter 26

# The Swedish System for Ethics Review of Biomedical Research and Processing of Sensitive Personal Data

Elisabeth Rynning[*]

## Introduction

In Sweden, there has been a system for ethics review of medical research involving humans in operation since the late 1960s.[1] The World Medical Association (WMA) had adopted the Helsinki Declaration in 1964,[2] laying down a requirement for ethics review of biomedical research involving humans. Another, perhaps even more important, reason for the development of research ethics committees (RECs) in Sweden was the decision made in 1966 by the US National Institutes of Health (NIH) that ethics review would be a mandatory prerequisite for financing. Quite a number of Swedish researchers were funded by the NIH, and thus had strong incentives for adapting to this new requirement. The first Swedish RECs were established by individual faculties of medicine; a nationwide system was then developed in cooperation with the Swedish Medical Research Council and the Ethics Delegation of the Swedish Society of Medicine. As for research in the area of social sciences and humanities, there was previously no comprehensive REC

---

[*] Professor of Medical Law at the Faculty of Law, Uppsala University.
[1] For a description in English of the old Swedish REC system, see: The Swedish Medical Research Council, *Guidelines for ethical evaluation of medical research involving human subjects. The policy and organization of research ethics in Sweden* (Stockholm: Medicinska Forskningsrådet, MRC report 2 1996, English translation 1999); and E. Rynning, 'The Regulation of Neonatal Research in Sweden' in S. Mason and C. Megone (eds.), *European Neonatal Research—Consent, ethics committees and law* (Aldershot: Ashgate Publishing, 2001), 167–183, at 176–178. For information in Swedish, see: Government bill *Regeringens proposition 2002/03:50 Etikprövning av forskning*, 37–40; and E. Rynning, 'Etisk granskning av medicinska humanforskningsprojekt—lagstiftning behövs!' (Ethics review of biomedical research involving humans—a call for legislation!) (1997) *Läkartidningen*, 1771–1774.
[2] World Medical Association Declaration of Helsinki: Ethical Principles for Medical Research Involving Human Subjects (adopted by the WMA General Assembly in 1964, revised in 1975, 1983, 1989, 1996 and 2000), as available from the webpage: http://www.wma.net/e/policy/b3.htm, last accessed 18 May 2005.

system. Ethics review was carried out within some research councils, more or less restricted to projects funded by the council in question.[3]

The international attention afforded to the important role of RECs, in the protection of the *legal* rights of research subjects, has increased during the past few decades. Although the voluntary ethics review was considered to function quite well, the need for a legally based system was recurrently discussed in Sweden.[4] Among the more recent areas of concern were both new developments regarding genetic analysis, and the processing of personal data in research.[5] As the Government started preparations for bringing Swedish law into conformity with the standards of the Council of Europe Convention on Human Rights and Biomedicine (1997),[6] it became evident that certain changes in the system for ethics review of research were necessary.[7] Although the need to implement the Good Clinical Practice Directive[8] also contributed to this development, the particular changes required for the implementation of the Directive were not really considered during the preparation of the Act on Ethics Review of Research; they were prepared separately at a later stage.[9] Unfortunately, the minimal coordination regarding the preparation of new legislation in the areas of biobanking, ethics review and clinical drug trials has resulted in a more complex (and partly inconsistent) legal situation than should have been necessary.[10]

---

[3] Government bill 2002/03:50, 41–45.

[4] Government bill 2002/03:50, 30–37; see also E. Rynning, n. 1 *supra*, (1997) and (2001).

[5] See the terms of reference for the Commission *Forskningsetik (Dir. 1997:68)*.

[6] Convention for the Protection of Human Rights and Dignity of the Human Being with Regard to the Application of Biology and Medicine: Convention on Human Rights and Biomedicine (1997, Council of Europe ETS No. 164).

[7] For example Government bills *Regeringens proposition 2000/01:3 Forskning och förnyelse*, 94; and Government bill 2002/03:50, 28. Sweden was one of the states that signed the Convention in 1997, but has not yet ratified it.

[8] Directive 2001/20/EC of the European Parliament and the Council of 4 April 2001 on the Approximation of the Laws, Regulations and Administrative Provisions of the Member States Relating to the Implementation of Good Clinical Practice in the Conduct of Clinical Trials on Medicinal Products for Human Use, *Offical Journal L* 121/34, 1 May 2001; see Ministerial Report *Ds 2001:62 Etikprövning av forskning som omfattar människor* (Stockholm: Ministry of Education, 2001), 198–200.

[9] Government bill 2002/03:50, 178 and the separate Government bill *Regeringens proposition 2003/04:32 Genomförande av EG-direktivet om kliniska prövningar av humanläkemedel*. The implementation as such has not led to any material changes in the Act on Ethics Review of Research. Instead, a number of complementary provisions have been added to the Medicinal Products Act (mainly concerning clinical trials involving minors and incapacitated adults). The Directive requirements for single opinion concerning multi-centre trials, the time frames for the ethics review, as well as the requirements for particular expertise in the review boards have been regulated in Ordinance (2003:615) on Ethics Review of Research Involving Humans, which complements the Act on Ethics Review.

[10] See E. Rynning 'Offentligrättslig reglering av biobankerna—en utmaning för lagstiftaren' (Public law regulation of the biobanks—a challenge to the legislator) in S. Wolk (ed.) *Biobanksrätt* (Lund: Studentlitteratur, 2003), 116–118, 124–125 and 168.

On 1 January 2004 a new, legally regulated system for ethics review entered into force in Sweden. The provisions are found in the Act (2003:460) on Ethics Review of Research Involving Humans, complemented by several ordinances and regulations.

## The Old Swedish REC System

*Coverage of the Old System*

The old Swedish REC system was legally unregulated and in principle, with some exceptions, formally voluntary. Even so, it was generally considered to guarantee a good coverage of biomedical research on humans conducted in Sweden.[11] No public healthcare provider would allow clinical research, no financing would be granted from research councils, and results would not be accepted for publication without the approval of an REC.

Approval by an REC thus was not a general legal prerequisite for lawful medical research involving humans; however, in most practical cases it was still necessary in order for the research to go ahead. Before 1 January 2004 there was only one type of research where ethics review was a mandatory requirement explicitly laid down in a statute enacted by Parliament. This concerned certain uses of human biological material for research purposes, in accordance with the rather recent Act (2002:297) on Biobanks in Health Care, which entered into force on 1 January 2003.

This Act does not cover all human biological material, but is limited to such material as has been originally collected within the professional activities of a Swedish healthcare provider (see Chapter 1, Section 3, of the Act on Biobanks). Furthermore, only biological material that can be traced to an identifiable human being or foetus is covered. The scope of the Act also has other limitations.[12] There are two types of activity that explicitly require ethical approval under the Act on Biobanks: the setting up of a biobank for the purposes of research or clinical trials, and the use of biobank samples for a *new* purpose (that is, a purpose other than that/those for which the samples were collected and stored), if that new purpose is research or a clinical trial (see Chapter 2 Section 3, and Chapter 3, Section 5, paragraph 3, of the Act on Biobanks). In the latter case, the REC decides on the information and consent requirements for using the samples for the new purpose. The Act on Biobanks does not, in fact, lay down any formal requirement for ethical

---

[11] The Swedish Medical Research Council, *Guidelines for ethical evaluation of medical research involving human subjects. The policy and organization of research ethics in Sweden* (Stockholm: Medicinska Forskningsrådet, MRC report 2 1996, English translation 1999), 51; Government bill *Regeringens proposition 2002/03:50 Etikprövning av forskning*, 38.

[12] See E. Rynning, 'Public law aspects on the use of biobank samples—privacy versus the interests of research' in M. G. Hansson and M. Levin (eds.), *Biobanks as Resources for Health* (Uppsala: Uppsala University, 2003), 91–128, at 106–107 and 115–116.

approval of each individual research project or clinical trial where samples of human biological material are used. Nevertheless, it is quite clear from the *travaux préparatoires* that such a review is expected to take place.[13] It is also required under the guidelines previously issued by the Medical Research Council's National Board for Ethics in Research.[14]

In Sweden, DNA samples and other human biological material have not been considered to be covered by general data protection rights such as these are laid down in the Personal Data Act.[15] Information gained from such materials is covered by the Personal Data Act (1998:204), as are data concerning the donor. With regard to the handling of the biological material as such, guidelines were first issued in 1999 by the Medical Research Council's National Board for Research Ethics.[16] The new Act on Biobanks in Health Care did not follow until 2003.[17] The relationship and borderline between the two, the Biobanks Act and the Data Protection Act, as well as the difference between identifiable human biological material and personal data, still remain rather unclear.[18] Digitalized DNA would fall under the Personal Data Act, whereas DNA in its natural state would fall under the Act on Biobanks.

There existed, however, some other regulations from which it seemed obvious that ethics review was certainly expected to take place. One of the prerequisites for clinical drugs trials, laid down in Section 13 of the Medical Products Act (1992:859), was that the trial must be *ethically justifiable* in order to be approved by the Medical Products Agency. According to the *travaux préparatoires*, this meant that review by a regional REC would normally be mandatory,[19] and the Medical Products Agency's regulation on clinical trials explicitly required all trials

---

[13] Government bill *Regeringens proposition 2001/02:44 Biobanker i hälso- och sjukvården*, 48–50 and 53. One could even get the impression that the Government believes ethics review already to be a legal prerequisite in these situations.

[14] Swedish Medical Research Council (MFR) *Research ethics guidelines for using biobanks, especially projects involving genome research*, adopted in June 1999, (Dnr 1999-570), revised by the Swedish Research Council in 2002.

[15] The Swedish Government has thus declared that DNA samples and other parts of the human body should in principle be considered to constitute personal data, provided that the material can be traced to identifiable living persons, see Government bill 2001/02:44, 31. The Government argues, however, that the mere keeping of samples in a so-called biobank does not fall under the definitions of such partly automated or manual processing of data as is regulated in the Personal Data Act. Since the keeping of biobanks still constitutes a particularly sensitive activity, which should be subject to similar high standards for the protection of privacy and personal integrity as is required under Directive 95/46/EC, a special Act on Biobanks in Health Care is called for.

[16] MFR guidelines, cf. n. 14 *supra*.

[17] See E. Rynning (2003), n. 12 *supra*; see also U. von Essen, 'Focusing on personal integrity violation—legal guidelines for ethical practice' in M. G. Hansson and M. Levin (eds.), *Biobanks as Resources for Health* (Uppsala: Uppsala University, 2003), 129–148.

[18] See E. Rynning (2003), 'Public law aspects on the use of biobank samples—privacy versus the interests of research', n. 12 *supra*; and E. Rynning (2003), 'Offentligrättslig reglering av biobankerna—en utmaning för lagstiftaren', n. 10 *supra*, 86–89.

[19] Government bill *Regeringens proposition 1991/92:97*, 94.

to be approved by an REC.[20] However, it was still pointed out that the RECs were only advisory bodies in relation to the Medical Products Agency. Another example of a statutory provision concerning ethics approval could be found in Section 19 of the Personal Data Act; an alternative to notifying the Data Inspection Board of certain processing of personal data for research purposes without the consent of the data subject.[21]

## *The Review*

Even though the individual RECs were formally independent of each other, a certain harmonization and coordination was provided for by the Swedish Medical Research Council's 'National Board for Ethics in Research'. This is a multidisciplinary board, consisting of experts in law and ethics, as well as representatives from the National Board of Health and Welfare, the Medical Products Agency, and the Swedish Society of Medicine. The Board also included two lay members.[22] All ten regional RECs were represented on the Board, normally by their Chairpersons who formed the main body of the Board.[23] The views of the Board were thus always directly accessible to the RECs. Throughout the years, this National Board issued general recommendations and guidelines,[24] although these were not formally binding and no appeal could be made to the Board in an individual case. In 2000, the Medical Research Council was merged with several other research councils to form the Swedish Research Council. The National Board for Ethics in Research remained active within this new Council, as the Working Group for Research Ethics in Medicine, up until the introduction of the new review system in 2004.

In their review of a research project, the old RECs were expected to consider the following aspects:[25]

a.   the scientific reliability/validity of the project;
b.   the possible risks of harm or discomfort for research subjects;

---

[20] Part 3, Section 1, of the Medical Products Agency's provisions and guidelines (LVFS 1996:17) on the clinical trials of medicinal products; and Section 10 (LVFS 2001:6) on Medical Devices, together with appendix 8.

[21] See E. Rynning, 'Processing of Personal Data in Swedish Health Care and Biomedical Research' in D. Beyleveld, D. Townend, S. Rouillé-Mirza and J. Wright (eds.), *Medical Research and the Implementation of Data Protection across Europe* (Aldershot: Ashgate Publishing Ltd, 2004), 381–402.

[22] All in all, however, since one of the laypersons was a physician, only a small minority of two or three people out of the 18 members were neither researchers in biomedicine nor qualified health professionals.

[23] *Guidelines for ethical evaluation of medical research involving human subjects. The policy and organization of research ethics in Sweden*, n. 11 *supra*, 53.

[24] Government bill 2002/03:50, 39.

[25] *Guidelines for ethical evaluation of medical research involving human subjects. The policy and organization of research ethics in Sweden*, n. 11 *supra*, 58–59.

c.  the anticipated value of the knowledge that the results of the project will provide;
d.  the balance between the risks of harm or discomfort (according to b) and the benefit of the project (according to c);
e.  the information and consent procedures.

Risks of integrity infringements were considered under b) and d), and information concerning the processing of data under e). If the risks could be reduced, this should of course be done.

### Composition of the Old RECs

The membership requirements of RECs in the old system were laid down in the individual rules of procedure of each committee; accordingly they were not identical. The RECs had about 10–16 regular members, out of whom two or three were required to be lay persons (with the exception of one REC, where 6 out of 12 members were lay persons).[26] This means that the requirements for lay representation varied widely, from about 15 to 25 per cent, and in one case 50 per cent. Furthermore the lay persons, who were usually appointed by the county councils, were sometimes nurses, politicians actively involved in decisions regarding healthcare services or persons otherwise connected to the medical profession; however, they could also include clergymen and the occasional lawyer. In general, however, there were no legal experts on the RECs, although some of them consulted with legal expertise when the committee itself recognized a legal problem. There was in fact no requirement for any expertise other than medical, pharmaceutical and odontological. The researchers elected by the faculties of medicine thus constituted a strong majority in most of the committees. The main reason for having a majority of medical experts on the RECs has been quoted as being the requirement of the Helsinki Declaration that research must be carried out on a sound scientific basis, which presupposes the professional evaluation of various medical aspects.[27] In some of the RECs, the medical experts were thus explicitly required to be 'active researchers, not below the level of associate professor' or 'well established researchers'.[28]

Although the old RECs cannot be said to have had any intention of disregarding the law, they often lacked the expertise required in order to review the lawfulness of individual research projects. Despite the educational efforts of the Data Inspection Board, this was probably true in particular with regard to data protection law and the rather complicated Swedish rules on medical records,

---

[26] E. Rynning (1997), n. 1 *supra*. See also *Guidelines for ethical evaluation of medical research involving human subjects. The policy and organization of research ethics in Sweden*, n. 11 *supra*, 54–56.
[27] *Guidelines for ethical evaluation of medical research involving human subjects. The policy and organization of research ethics in Sweden*, n. 11 *supra*, 54.
[28] Government bill 2002/03:50, 38.

confidentiality, secrecy and official documents. The observations made by the Data Inspection Board certainly seem to indicate as much.[29]

## The New Swedish System for Ethics Review of Research

*The Introduction of a New System Based on Law*

With the entry into force of the new Act on Ethics Review of Research Involving Humans, on 1 January 2004, ethics approval has become a mandatory legal requirement for certain types of research on humans. The purpose of the Act is to protect, in relation to research, individual human beings and the respect for human dignity (see Section 1, paragraph 2, of the Act). A framework of basic principles for justifiable research is laid down in the Act, including traditional requirements concerning respect for human dignity, risk/benefit assessment, and informed consent. The review is performed by a new organization of independent, regional boards for ethics review of research. These boards are all chaired by a judge, but the majority of the members are still researchers. All members are appointed by the Government. A novelty is the possibility to appeal against decisions rejecting research projects. Such appeals are tried by the new Central Board for Research Ethics.

The Act on Ethics Review is supplemented by a number of further regulations: the Ordinance (2003:615) on Ethics Review of Research Involving Humans, the Ordinance (2003:616) with Instructions for Regional Boards for Ethics Review, the Ordinance (2003:617) with Instructions for the Central Board for Ethics Review, and forthcoming regulations from the Swedish Research Council.[30] So far, no English translation of the new Act on Ethics Review in Research has been made available.

*Coverage of the New Review System*

In the new system, the regional boards are required to review certain types of scientific research, as well as scientifically based development projects (see Section 2 of the Act on Ethics Review of Research). The Act is only applicable to research performed in Sweden (see Section 5) but it is not limited to *biomedical* research alone. The review thus covers two main groups of research described in Section 3–4 of the Act: firstly, research involving the processing of certain types of personal data without consent and, secondly, research involving physical interventions, physical or psychological manipulation or studies on biological material from identifiable dead or living humans. These types of research may only

---

[29] See the report of the Data Inspection Board, *Behandling av känsliga personuppgifter i forskningen* (Processing of personal data in research) (Report 1, Stockholm: Swedish Data Inspection Board, 2003).

[30] See Sections 39–41 of the Act on Ethics Review and Section 12 of the Ordinance on Ethics Review.

be carried out after the required ethics approval has been obtained (see Section 6). It does not matter if the research is conducted in the private or in the public sector.

Thus, ethics review is explicitly mandatory for processing certain types of personal data without consent. According to Section 6, paragraph 1 of the Act on Ethics Review, research may only involve the processing of such personal data as indicated in Section 3 if this processing has been approved. Section 3 mentions the processing of two types of personal data without consent. The first concerns sensitive personal data under Section 13 of the Swedish Personal Data Act (implementing Article 8.1 of Directive 95/46/EC), thus including any health-related information. The second concerns certain types of personal data regarding criminal offences, coercive measures in criminal procedures, and administrative detention, under Section 21 of the Personal Data Act (implementing Article 8.5 of the Directive).

Conversely, however, no ethics approval is required for research that involves processing of sensitive personal data *with* the consent of the data subject (or in some cases his or her competent representative). Since such research is not normally required to be notified to the Data Inspection Board,[31] it will be up to the researchers themselves to assess whether or not valid informed consent is really obtained in compliance with the requirements of the Personal Data Act. Judging by the reports of the Data Inspection Board, not all researchers have sufficient knowledge about the data protection legislation.[32] The researchers will also decide by themselves whether or not it is at all ethically justifiable to approach the data subjects concerned to ask for their participation.

Ethics review is also not required for research on human biological material that is considered to be anonymous, even if the material is of a sensitive kind, such as tissue from aborted foetuses or human embryos.

The views taken by the former RECs concerning anonymization of data and biological material probably varied, especially in the early years of the Personal Data Act. It still seems to be quite common for researchers in general to consider coded data as anonymous.[33] This view may also have been shared by some RECs, but in the later years of the old system there was an ongoing discussion about these issues in the coordinating National Board for Ethics in Research. Initiatives to provide REC members with education concerning the implications of the Personal Data Act were also taken by the Data Inspection Board. As regards the new review

---

[31] With the exception of automated processing of personal data concerning hereditary disposition, derived from a genetic investigation, which is to be notified to the Data Inspection Board for preliminary review not later than three weeks in advance, see Section 10 of the Personal Data Ordinance. The requirement does not apply to such processing of personal data as is governed by specific regulations in a statute or an enactment.

[32] See the reports of the Data Inspection Board, *Personuppgifter i genforskning—uppföljning av förhandskontroller* (Report 4, Stockholm: Swedish Data Inspection Board, 2002), 12–14; and *Behandling av känsliga personuppgifter i forskningen* (2003:1), n. 29 *supra*, 12–23.

[33] See the reports of the Data Inspection Board, *Personuppgifter i genforskning—uppföljning av förhandskontroller* (2002:4), n. 32 *supra*, 6–7; and *Behandling av känsliga personuppgifter i forskningen* (2003:1), n. 29 *supra*, 5–6.

boards, the presence of legal expertise would seem to guarantee a better knowledge of Swedish data protection law.

The rather narrow scope of the Act on Ethics Review has been rightly criticized, not least with regard to research involving sensitive data concerning vulnerable groups such as psychiatric patients.[34] A Commission appointed to prepare the details of the new system was also given the task of considering whether any additional types of research should require ethics review.[35] However, the only extension made so far relates to a provision in Section 2 of the Ordinance with Instructions for Regional Boards for Ethics Review, authorizing the boards to give advisory opinions concerning such research involving humans as is not covered by the Act.[36]

*The New Organization for Ethics Review*

As already mentioned, the main task of reviewing research projects is now performed by regional boards for ethics review of research. There are six such boards, situated at the universities of Gothenburg, Linköping, Lund, Umeå and Uppsala, as well as at the Karolinska Institute in Stockholm.[37] Since the new system does not only cover medical research, every board has at least two separate departments; one for reviewing medical research and another for non-medical research.[38] Each regional board has its own geographic area of jurisdiction.[39] Multi-centre studies are reviewed by the board responsible for the area where the main principal of the research project is located.[40] If the principal is located abroad, the application is reviewed by the board responsible for the area where the main part of the research is to take place.

A new feature of the formally regulated review system is the possibility of appeal. There is thus a Central Board for Ethics Review of Research, with the task of reviewing appeals from researchers as well as applications that are referred from regional review boards (see Section 31). Such referral is made when the regional board is unable to reach a unanimous decision, provided that it is requested by a

---

[34] Government bill 2002/03:50, 102–103.
[35] See the terms of reference for the Commission, *Ny organisation för etikprövning av forskning (Dir 2003:43)*.
[36] In the old system, the REC's review was expected to cover all medical research projects involving human research subjects, from both scientific and general ethical viewpoints. The scope of REC activities was not very clearly defined, but would seem to have included research on human biological material as well as health-related data, at least when the data or material could be traced to identifiable individuals. To a certain extent, research on anonymous human material has also been reviewed.
[37] See Sections 1 and 6 of the Ordinance with Instructions for Regional Boards. Basic information (in Swedish) about the new organization as well as contact information regarding the individual review boards can be found at the web page http://www.forskning setikprovning.se, last accessed 18 May 2005.
[38] Section 25 of the Act on Ethics Review; and the Government bill 2002/03:50, 150.
[39] See Section 3 and Annex 1 to the Ordinance on Ethics Review.
[40] Section 3, paragraph 3 of the Ordinance on Ethics Review.

certain number of the board members.[41] Otherwise the decision follows the opinion of the majority. The Central Board also has certain responsibilities regarding the monitoring of research that falls under the Act on Ethics Review (see Sections 34–35). The secretariat of the Central Board is situated at the Swedish Research Council in Stockholm.[42]

Although the secretariats of the boards are located within other public authorities, they are considered to be independent agencies, both financially and operationally.[43] The regional boards are expected to be fully financed by fees from applicants, whereas the Central Board is run with government funding.[44] The fees for ethics review vary between 5 000 and 16 000 SEK (approximately 550 Euros and 1 750 Euros), depending on the type and scope of the project.[45]

*Composition of the New Boards for Ethics Review*

In the new system the departments of the regional boards for ethics review all consist of a Chairperson and 15 other members, out of whom five represent public interests (see Section 25 of the Act on Ethics Review). The remaining ten members are required to have scientific expertise. All board members have personal replacements, whereby if they have to be absent from a meeting there is a specific person appointed to replace them.[46] The Government appoints the members; however, candidates to be scientific experts are presented by the universities concerned. The members of the review boards are all paid for their services, although the amounts are fairly modest.[47]

The Chairperson, as well as his or her replacement, must be (or have been) a qualified judge. This is primarily in order to guarantee the independent position of the review board, and the legal rights of individuals concerned.[48] A judge is also well trained to make decisions concerning widely differing factual matters. He or she is experienced in the act of balancing conflicting interests and is used to making sure that all relevant facts are presented. The presence of a judge furthermore provides a guarantee of legal expertise on the boards.

---

[41] Normally at least three board members, but if only nine members are present such a request should be granted if posed by two members, see Section 29 of the Act.

[42] Section 2 of the Ordinance with Instructions for the Central Board.

[43] See Government bill 2002/03:50, 146. This means that the review boards will be more independent in relation to the faculties of medicine, although perhaps not in relation to the Government.

[44] Government bill 2002/03:50, 187–191. See also Sections 10–11 of the Ordinance on Ethics Review.

[45] Appendix 2 to the Ordinance on Ethics Review.

[46] Section 9 of the Ordinance with Instructions for the Regional Boards.

[47] The present amount for an ordinary member is 1 450 SEK (about 150–160 Euros) per meeting day, see the final report of the Commission on the New Organization for Ethics Review of Research (*Utredningen om ny organisation för etikprövning av forskning, U 2003:05*), Dnr U 2003:05, 120, 19 December 2003.

[48] Government bill 2002/03:50, 153.

The five members representing public interests are expected to reflect a wide cross-section of the public, helping to broaden and deepen the ethical evaluations with their different types of experience.[49] This experience could consist of just ordinary life experience and knowledge of human nature. The representatives of the public should be able to see the applications from a different perspective compared to that of the researchers, which is considered necessary in order to obtain a more comprehensive review. They should not be professionally active in, or have a scientific education corresponding to, the area of research that is to be reviewed.[50] They should, however, have some local or regional connection to the geographic area in question. The Swedish Federation of County Councils proposes candidates.[51]

The composition of the scientific board members varies depending on the type of research the department in question is set up to review. Regarding medical research it is explicitly stated in the *travaux préparatoires* that the most frequently occurring specialities should always be represented, and that the field of medicine has become so specialized that there is no room for any other type of scientific expertise on the boards reviewing such research.[52] When it comes to research in the areas of humanities and social sciences for example, the review is mainly focused on the protection of personal integrity (privacy). This type of consideration is not thought to require the same kind of expertise in the particular scientific discipline of the research project that is being reviewed. It is thus recommended that non-medical research be reviewed by a board where the expertise of the scientific members is very broad, representing a variety of disciplines. With regard to the departments for reviewing medical research, however, it could be questioned if the composition meets the requirements for a multidisciplinary review; laid down for example in Article 16 of the Convention on Human Rights and Biomedicine and Article 9 of the Additional Protocol on Biomedical Research (2004).[53] The latter Article specifies that the ethics review shall 'draw on an appropriate range of expertise and experience adequately reflecting professional and lay views'. In order to provide a multidisciplinary review, observing ethical as well as legal, social and economic aspects of the research, it would perhaps not seem adequate that the only professional expertise required is medical and legal (the Chairperson). The members representing public interest could of course provide such complementary expertise in various disciplines, but as has been described above, this would not seem to be a requirement.

---

[49] Government bill 2002/03:50, 202.

[50] Government bill 2002/03:50, 153.

[51] See the final report of the Commission on the New Organization for Ethics Review of Research, n. 47 *supra*.

[52] Government bill 2002/03:50, 152.

[53] Additional Protocol to the Convention on Human Rights and Biomedicine, concerning Biomedical Research, adopted by the Committee of Ministers on 30 June 2004, CETS No. 195. The Protocol, together with an Explanatory Report, can be viewed at the Council of Europe webpage: http://conventions.coe.int, last accessed 18 May 2005.

It is not discussed in the *travaux préparatoires* what kind of composition would be appropriate for the review of issues concerning the processing of sensitive personal data without consent, when such processing takes place within a medical research project. If the project does not involve any other biomedical interventions that require ethics review (such as surgical interventions, medication or analysis of samples from identifiable individuals), the data processing could be reviewed by the more broadly composed board just mentioned. However, these boards probably do not have the qualifications for fully assessing the scientific soundness and perceived scientific value of, for example, an epidemiological study. On the other hand, the boards composed for reviewing medical research projects may not have the equivalent qualifications for performing a risk/benefit assessment regarding data protection rights and privacy infringements. This latter shortcoming may prove especially problematic with regard to mixed research projects, which include both processing of sensitive personal data and physical interventions or studies on human material. It would seem likely that all such projects will be reviewed by the boards with only medical scientific expertise, regardless of whether or not the review also entails the processing of sensitive personal data without consent.

The Central Board for Research Ethics is also chaired by a judge (see Section 32 of the Act on Ethics Review).[54] This board has only six other members, of whom four are scientific experts and two represent public interests. Here, the composition does not vary depending on the type of research to be reviewed; however, the Board is expected to make sure it has a satisfactory basis for its decisions, for example by means of advisory opinions from the Swedish Research Council.[55] It is stated in the *travaux préparatoires* that it is particularly important that the Central Board should consist of members with a broad experience of research ethics assessments which are also outside of their own areas of research.[56] Candidates for the scientific member positions are proposed by the Swedish

---

[54] The present Chair is a member of the Swedish Supreme Court.

[55] Government bill 2002/03:50, 161–162.

[56] At present, the four scientific members are all professors. However, perhaps somewhat surprisingly, three of them come from the area of biomedicine (the fourth is a professor of philosophy). Even though the Chairperson is a high judge, the qualifications of this group to also assess scientific research in the area of social sciences does not seem altogether satisfactory. It could be noted that one of the two representatives of the public's interests is a physician, and so is the personal replacement of the other lay representative. It may thus happen that the Committee at certain meetings will be constituted of five people who are either researchers in biomedicine or healthcare professionals, complemented by one professor of philosophy and the Chairperson possessing legal expertise. Even for reviewing biomedical research such a composition does not seem ideal. It is explicitly stated in the Council of Europe Explanatory Report to the Additional Protocol on Biomedical Research, Article 9, that 'the participation of laypersons is important in ensuring that the public can have confidence in the system for oversight of biomedical research. Such laypersons will be neither healthcare professionals nor have experience in carrying out biomedical research'.

Council for Research; the representatives of the public positions by the Red Cross and the organization Doctors Without Borders.[57]

## Prerequisites for Ethics Approval in the New System

*General Requirements*

In order for a research project to be approved under the Swedish Act on Ethics Review, certain basic prerequisites must be fulfilled. It is required that the research can be carried out with respect for human dignity, and that human rights and fundamental freedoms will be observed (see Sections 7 and 8 of the Act). However, it is highlighted that the interest of new knowledge, which may be developed by research, should also be taken into consideration at the ethics review. Nevertheless, the well-being of humans shall be given precedence over the needs of science and society. These Sections of the Act are clearly influenced by Articles 1 and 2 of the European Convention on Human Rights and Biomedicine. In the *traveaux préparatoires*, it is stressed that respect for human dignity not only involves protection of the interests of research subjects directly concerned by the research, but also consideration of the further implications of the research; for example damage to future generations.[58] Such deliberations could speak both in favour of the research and against it.

A basic requirement is that the research should also be scientifically sound. The project must have the potential of generating well-founded and important knowledge, by the use of reliable research methods.[59] It must be expected that the results of the research could be useful to society and humanity as such. This assessment of the scientific soundness and expected value of the research is necessary for the following balancing of risks and benefits related to the project; considered to be one of the most central elements of the review, alongside the evaluation procedures for informed consent.[60] Section 9 of the Act on Ethics Review thus prescribes that research may only be approved if the risks involved are counterbalanced by its scientific value; with regard to the health, safety and personal integrity of the research subject.[61] Furthermore, the research must not be approved if the expected results could be achieved by other means, involving less risk to the health, safety and personal integrity of the research subjects (see Section 10). It is explicitly prescribed that processing of personal data, in accordance with

---

[57] Information provided by Professor Gisela Dahlqvist, member and scientific secretary of the Central Board.

[58] Government report 2002/02:50, 98.

[59] *Ibid.*, 98–99.

[60] *Ibid.*, 99.

[61] It could be noted that this risk/benefit assessment does not mention the possible risks to society or future generations. Such considerations are only indirectly regulated by the more general prerequisites laid down in Sections 7–8.

Section 3 of the Act, may only be approved if it is necessary in order for the research to be carried out.

The need for scientific soundness is also expressed by the prerequisite that research may only be approved if it is to be carried out under the supervision of a researcher with appropriate scientific competence (see Section 11 of the Act). In the *travaux préparatoires* it refers to the Council of Europe Protocol to the Convention on Human Rights and Biomedicine, on Biomedical Research.[62] Article 8 of the now-adopted Protocol deals with scientific quality; requiring all research covered by the protocol to be carried out 'under the supervision of an appropriately qualified researcher'. In the Explanatory Report it is stated that the suitability of the person supervising the research must be assessed in relation to the particular project concerned.[63] Under the Swedish Act on Ethics Review, 'appropriate scientific competence' is understood to presuppose a doctoral degree (for example a Ph.D. or the equivalent).[64] The supervising researcher should thus be experienced in working independently, and applying recognized and ethically acceptable scientific methods.

*Information and Consent*

The Act on Ethics Review lays down a number of requirements regarding information and consent (see Sections 13–22). However, these provisions are not applicable when special provisions on information and consent in research can be found in another regulation (see Section 13). Such special provisions exist, for example, with regard to clinical drug trials and certain research involving the use of identifiable human tissue.[65] It should also be remembered that processing of personal data for research purposes only falls under the Act on Ethics Review as regards sensitive personal data processed *without* the consent of the data subject. Accordingly, no personal data processing would seem to fall under the provisions on information and consent in Sections 13–22 of this Act. Such issues are instead covered by the data protection legislation, primarily the Personal Data Act. However, whether or not the various relevant information and consent requirements are met will still be a matter for the review board to consider in their assessment of the risks to the personal integrity of the research subject. Concerning the situation where a research subject withdraws his or her consent to participation

---

[62] Government bill 2002/03:50, 197.

[63] Explanatory Report, n. 53 *supra*, point 31.

[64] Government bill 2002/03:50, 100.

[65] See Sections 13 a–g of the Medicinal Products Act and Chapter 3 of the Act on Biobanks in Health Care. These consent provisions are not quite the same as those in the Act on Ethics Review. The new consent requirements in the Medicinal Products Act, after the implementation of Directive 2001/20/EC, are thus stricter than those in the Act on Ethics Review when it comes to trials involving minors or incapacitated adults. The Act on Biobanks is even more restrictive with regard to storage and use of biological materials from incapacitated adults, whereas this Act provides the most generous rules on informed consent from mature minors (stating no formal age limit at all).

in the research project, it is expressly stated in Section 19 of the Act on Ethics Review that data collected before this withdrawal may still be processed in the research.[66]

Section 16 of the Act on Ethics Review gives a general description of the information that should be disclosed to research subjects, but it is expected that the Government or the Swedish Council for Research will issue further regulations on this matter.[67] The requirements laid down in Section 16 include: information on the overall plan of the research project; the methods to be used; the consequences and risks that the research may involve; who is the principal of the research; the fact that participation in the project is voluntary; and that the research subject may at any time withdraw his or her consent. This list meets some of the requirements laid down in Article 13 of the Council of Europe Additional Protocol on Biomedical Research, though certainly not all of them. For example, there is no mention of information regarding the opinion of the ethics committee; the arrangements to ensure respect for private life and the confidentiality of data; any foreseen potential further uses, including commercial uses of the research results data or biological material; or the source of funding for the research project.[68]

As regards research projects involving physical interventions, psychological manipulation or the use of human biological material, under Section 4 of the Act on Ethics Review, consent will normally be required. It is prescribed in Section 14 that such research may only be approved if it can be expected that the applicable provisions on information and consent will be followed; or if the special prerequisites for research without consent laid down in Sections 20–22 are met. The main rule, under Section 17, is thus that the research subject himself or herself should freely consent to participation in the project; this after having received information in accordance with Section 16. It is required that the consent be explicit and specific to certain research. Normally consent should be given in writing, but if for some reason it is given orally, it must be appropriately documented by a sufficiently competent researcher taking part in the project.[69]

With regard to minors, that is persons below the age of 18, there are special provisions in Section 18. It is thus prescribed that a research subject who has reached the age of 15, and understands the implications of the research, may give informed consent on his or her own behalf. Otherwise, informed consent shall be obtained from the custody holders of the minor. The minor shall then as far as possible be informed about the research, and if he or she understands the implications of the research, it must not be carried out against his or her will.

---

[66] This provision matches the rule on withdrawal of consent that is found in Section 12 of the Data Protection Act.

[67] Government bill 2002/03:50, 130. So far, no such further regulation has been issued.

[68] Some obligations to provide information on these issues may of course be regulated elsewhere, whereas other issues are not regulated at all. It is still a problem that there is so far no comprehensive description of the information requirements accessible to researchers and review boards in the form of legal regulation or guidelines.

[69] Government bill 2002/03:50, 132.

The situation regarding incapacitated adults in Swedish law is more complicated, since there are no general rules on proxy decision-making in healthcare and research.[70] Such legislation is under preparation but cannot be expected to enter into force for several years.[71] Due to this unclear legal situation, the Government chose a very strict line in the Act on Biobanks in Health Care, making it virtually illegal to store and use samples taken from incapacitated adults within the activities of healthcare providers.[72] Under Sections 20–22 of the Act on Ethics Review, however, research on incompetent adults may take place without consent, provided certain special conditions are met. The requirements are similar to those in Article 17 of the Convention on Human Rights and Biomedicine, but not the same. The research should thus be expected to render knowledge that cannot be achieved by research involving persons who are capable of giving consent, whilst having the potential to be of direct benefit to the research subject. If there is no potential for such direct benefit, the research may still take place if it has the aim of contributing to a result that can be of benefit to the research subject, or somebody else who is suffering from the same or a similar disease or disorder, providing the research only entails an insignificant risk of harm and an insignificant burden to the research subject. Additionally, the research subject shall as far as possible be personally informed about the research, and consultation shall take place with his or her relatives as well as with the special representative or administrator concerned. The research must not be carried out if the research subject or any of the other persons consulted objects.

The fact that research-related provisions on information and consent can be found in a number of different laws and regulations, varying with regard to their content, unfortunately makes Swedish law in this area both unclear and partly inconsistent. For example, the use of a tissue sample from a minor or an incapacitated adult for research purposes will entail the application of one of three different sets of prerequisites. If the project is a clinical drug trial, the strict new rules of the Medicinal Products Act will apply. Otherwise, the use of the samples will fall under the consent requirements of the Act on Ethics Review; *unless* they have been collected in the professional activities of a healthcare provider, in which case the consent requirements are found in the Act on Biobanks in Health Care. Furthermore, the processing of personal data in the research project will entail the application of general consent requirements laid down in the Personal Data Act (which contains no specific provisions at all regarding minors and incapacitated adults). Handling a legal situation of such complexity will indeed constitute a

---

[70] Government bill 2002/03:50, 139–143; see also E. Rynning, 'Rättssäkerhet och rättsskydd i vården av icke beslutskompetenta vuxna' (Legal protection in healthcare for incompetent adults) in L. Vahlne Westerhäll (ed.), *Rättssäkerhetsfrågor inom socialrätten* (Stockholm: Norstedts Juridik, 2002), 267–301.

[71] See terms of reference for the Commission *Förmyndare, gode män och förvaltare (Dir. 2002:55)*. A report with proposals for legislation was due to have been presented during autumn 2004.

[72] Government bill 2001/02:44, 42. See also E. Rynning (2003), 'Offentligrättslig reglering av biobankerna—en utmaning för lagstiftaren', n. 10 *supra*, 120–125.

challenge both to researchers and to the boards for ethics review. As concerns proxy decision-making for incapacitated adults, it is hoped that the future legislation on proxy consent in healthcare and research will provide a simpler and more comprehensive regulation of the area.

## Specific Data Protection Matters

As mentioned above, the Swedish boards for ethics review, just like the old RECs, may decide that research involving the processing of sensitive data is justified in the public interest, without the consent of the data subject. In the old system this authorization was regulated in Section 19, paragraph 2 of the Personal Data Act. Paragraph 1 of the same section stipulated that sensitive personal data could be processed for research and statistics purposes without the consent of the data subject, provided the processing was necessary[73] and the interest of society in the project was manifestly greater than the risk of improper violation of the personal integrity of the data subject. The provision thus contained an exemption from the consent requirement based on Article 8.4 of Directive 95/46/EC (substantial public interest and the provision of suitable safeguards). According to paragraph 2, the prerequisites under paragraph 1 should be deemed satisfied if the processing had been approved by an REC.[74] However, it was not until the entry into force of the Act on Ethics Review that such approval of a board for ethics review became a *mandatory* requirement. Before 1 January 2004 the data controllers could choose to perform the balancing of interests themselves, but in that case, notification to the Data Inspection Board for prior checking was required under Section 10 of the Personal Data Ordinance. Today, this option is no longer open to the data controllers.

Under Sections 3 and 6 of the new Act on Ethics Review of Research, a research project that involves the processing of certain types of personal data without consent *must* be submitted for ethics review. A research project involving

---

[73] Necessary in the manner stated in Section 10 of the Personal Data Act, implementing Article 7 of the Directive.

[74] If an REC chose to give an opinion on this issue, it would not, however, seem to have been intended for the REC to be under any obligation to apply the particular balancing test described in paragraph 1 of Section 19, see the Parliamentary Report (SOU 1997:39) *Integritet—offentlighet—informationsteknik* (Stockholm: Fritzes, 1997), 298–301. Even so, no alternative criteria for the balancing of interests are mentioned in the *travaux préparatoires*. It is merely stated that the ethics review can be expected to provide sufficient guarantees that sensitive personal data will only be processed without consent in such exceptional cases where this is really justified by the public interest of the research being performed. Whether or not any information should be provided to the data subjects in these cases is also considered to be a matter well handled by the research ethics committees. It is stressed in the report that the RECs are highly qualified and include members representing public interests. Nevertheless, as already mentioned, the observations of the Data Inspection Board seem to indicate that the old RECs did not have sufficient knowledge of the data protection rights laid down in the Personal Data Act. See the report of the Data Inspection Board, *Behandling av känsliga personuppgifter i forskningen* (2003:1), n. 29 *supra*.

such processing may be carried out only if the processing has been approved. The basic criteria for the risk/benefit assessment under the Act on Ethics Review are explicitly intended to match the criteria previously laid down in Section 19, paragraph 1 of the Personal Data Act.[75] Even so, while the Personal Data Act required the interest of society in the research project to be *manifestly greater* than the risk of improper violation of the personal integrity of the data subject, Section 9 of the Act on Ethics Review finds it sufficient that the risks to the health, safety and personal integrity of the research subject be *counterbalanced* by the scientific value of the research.

Other exemptions from the data protection rights of data subjects, or from the duties of data controllers, have not been explicitly regulated with regard to general decision-making by the old RECs or the new boards for ethics review. However, the RECs were thought to be well suited to decide about exemptions from the duty to inform.[76] With regard to the further use of human biological material for new purposes, under the Act on Biobanks in Health Care, the boards for ethics review are entrusted with deciding the information and consent requirements for such use of the samples. The same applies with regard to identifiable stored samples that do not fall under the Act on Biobanks (see Section 15 of the Act on Ethics Review).

### Legal Implications of the Ethics Approval

*The Lawfulness of Research Activities*

As mentioned above, the old RECs only possessed advisory power.[77] Nevertheless, in practice their recommendations have by necessity been followed—at least officially—to such an extent that the voluntary nature of the old system could certainly be questioned. From the ethical point of view, unlawful research activities would normally be considered *prima facie* unethical. The Helsinki Declaration expects researchers to be aware of ethical as well as legal and regulatory requirements for research on human subjects in their own countries.[78] According to their own codes of procedure, the old Swedish RECs were expected to follow the principles of this Declaration as well as the guidelines of the Medical Research Council's National Board for Ethics in Research.[79]

In the new system for ethics review, the decisions of the review boards are formally binding. Approval is a mandatory legal prerequisite for research projects that fall under the Act on Ethics Review; carrying out a project that has been

---

[75] Government bill 2002/03:50, 119 and 196.
[76] Parliamentary Report (SOU 1997:39) *Integritet—offentlighet—informationsteknik* (Stockholm: Fritzes, 1997), 298.
[77] Government bill 2002/03:50, 38.
[78] Principle A.9 of the Helsinki Declaration, revised version of 2000.
[79] This is clear from the rules of procedure of most RECs, and is also stated in the guidelines of the National Board; see *Guidelines for ethical evaluation of medical research involving human subjects. The policy and organization of research ethics in Sweden*, n. 11 *supra*, 12.

rejected is thus unlawful. Ultimately responsible for the procurement of the necessary ethics approval is the principal for the research project, normally a public agency or private company carrying out the research.[80] More seldom, the research principal may be a natural person running a research project. When the principal is a juridical person, for example a university or a pharmaceutical company, it is expected that there will be an internal organization appointed to fulfil the requirements concerning applications—abidance by the terms of the ethics approval and so on. If there is no documentation regarding the delegation of these responsibilities to certain officials, the board of directors may be held personally accountable for any such breaches against the Act on Ethics Review.[81] Even so, it is stressed in the *traveaux préparatoires* that individual researchers themselves should of course always reflect on the ethical issues that arise in their work.[82]

Even though ethics approval is a mandatory legal prerequisite for certain types of research, this does not mean that otherwise unlawful activities will become lawful just because the project has been approved by a board for ethics review. It is explicitly stated in Section 6, paragraph 3 that an ethics approval in accordance with the Act does not imply that the research may be carried out if the research is unlawful by any other statute of law. It is underlined in the *travaux préparatoires* that the ethics review does not include any general assessment of the lawfulness of the project in relation to all other legal rules that may be applicable to the project.[83] Nevertheless there must be a rather strong assumption that in a *post factum* judicial assessment of the lawfulness of a certain medical experiment, or risky clinical research project, the existence of ethics approval would not be insignificant. For example, under Swedish criminal law, consent does not exempt from liability much more than minor battery;[84] whereas the additional existence of what is called 'social adequacy' may render ordinary or even aggravated battery lawful. The risk/benefit assessment performed as a part of the ethics review, and the following approval or rejection of the project, would certainly be considered to give an indication of the social adequacy of a particular research project.

## Additional Authorization Required

In many areas of research the approval of the competent regional board for ethics review is sufficient for the research to go ahead. The research must be started within two years of the decision of the review board, otherwise the approval will no longer be valid. Naturally, if the research is to take place within the premises or

---

[80] See Sections 2 and 23 of the Act on Ethics Review, and the Government bill 2002/03:50, 92–94 and 101.

[81] Government bill 2002/03:50, 94.

[82] *Ibid.*, 101.

[83] *Ibid.*, 195.

[84] See Chapter 24, Section 7, of the Penal Code and Government bill *Regeringens proposition 1993/94:130 Ändringar i brottsbalken (ansvarsfrihetsgrunder m.m.)*, 37–39 and 42–43.

activities of a healthcare provider, the authorization of the principal of this institution is also required.

For certain types of research, however, such as clinical trials for medicinal products and medical devices, the additional formal authorization of the Medical Products Agency is needed (see Section 14 of the Medicinal Products Act (1992:859), Section 8 of the Act (1993:584) on Medical Devices and Section 6 of the Ordinance (1993:876) on Medical Devices).[85] The use of tissue from an aborted foetus requires the authorization of the National Board of Health and Welfare (see Section 11 of the Transplant Act (1995:831)). There is no similar requirement for centralized authorization regarding other types of tissue, not even for the use of human embryos. If, however, biological material taken from a living person is of a non-regenerative kind, or if the intervention can otherwise entail considerable harm or discomfort to the donor, it may be *removed* for a medical purpose other than transplantation only by permission of the National Board of Health and Welfare (see Section 9 of the Transplant Act). So far this rule may also be applicable to the removal of human biological material for research purposes, but it has been proposed that such additional authorization should not be needed with regard to research that has received ethics approval.[86]

Although not a requirement for additional formal authorization, it should also be remembered that automated processing of personal data concerning hereditary disposition, derived from genetic testing, must be notified to the Data Inspection Board for prior checking no later than three weeks in advance.

It is important to remember that despite their task of reviewing research projects involving the processing of certain personal data without the consent of the research subjects, the review boards do *not* have any authority to grant exemptions from the general rules on confidentiality and secrecy. This is explicitly stated in Section 12 of the Act on Ethics Review, which prescribes that personal data may only be disclosed to be used in research if this does not constitute any violation of provisions on secrecy and confidentiality. Thus, regardless of an ethics approval, researchers in many cases still face the problem of actually gaining

---

[85] As of 1 May 2004, certain changes have been made in the Medicinal Products Act as a result of the implementation of Directive 2001/20/EC. Clinical trials that have been duly notified to the Medical Products Agency may thus normally be started without any formal authorization from the Agency; see Section 14 of the Medicinal Products Act.

[86] It could be argued that the removal of human ova for research purposes would require the authorization of the National Board of Health and Welfare in accordance with Section 9 of the Transplant Act, but so far such removal of ova solely for research purposes would not seem to have taken place in Sweden. See the Parliamentary Report (SOU 2002:119) *Rättslig reglering av stamcellsforskning* (Stockholm: Fritzes, 2003), 79–80. In the preparation of new legislation regarding certain research involving fertilized human ova, it is explicitly proposed that the removal of human ova for research purposes should *not* be subject to authorization under Section 9 of the Transplant Act, since the research project will require the approval of a board for ethics review. See the Government bill *Regeringens proposition 2003/04:148 Stamcellsforskning*. This rule should also be applied with regard to other removal of human biological materials to be used in a research project that has been approved by a review board.

access to the data in a lawful way. Access to official documents such as medical records within the public healthcare sector, or public health data registers, is decided upon by the agency keeping the data and not by the board for ethics review.[87] Even so, in practice the rules on secrecy and confidentiality are given a very generous interpretation as regards access to sensitive data for research purposes.[88] If the project and the planned data processing have been approved by a review board, this will definitely be of significance to the access issue also. If the agency keeping the sensitive data requested, finds it to be clear that the disclosure will not constitute any harm to the person concerned, or to his or her close ones, the data will be disclosed. The data subject has no right of appeal against such a decision, and may never have been consulted in the first place.[89]

## Supervision and Sanctions

*Supervision of Research Activities*

During the preparation of the new legislation on ethics review the task of monitoring research projects was discussed. The old RECs performed no monitoring or quality control activities, although exceptionally the committees may have requested a report of the study's outcome.[90] It was at first suggested by the Ministry of Education that the regional boards for ethics review should supervise the projects they approved;[91] however, in several responses to the consultation report this was deemed unsuitable.[92] It was thus decided that the Central Board for Research Ethics shall monitor research activities that fall under the Act on Ethics

---

[87] See Chapter 2, Section 14 of the Freedom of the Press Act and Chapter 15, Sections 6–8 of the Secrecy Act (1980:100).

[88] See E. Rynning (2004), 'Processing of Personal Data in Swedish Health Care and Biomedical Research', n. 21 *supra*; and E. Rynning, 'Patientuppgifter som forskningsresurs—om intresseavvägningar och integritetsskydd' (2003) *Förvaltningsrättslig Tidskrift*, 95–126. There has been an ongoing public debate in Sweden concerning the correct interpretation of the law in this area, due to some recent Court cases where researching doctors have been ordered to reveal confidential information obtained from patients/research subjects, to other researchers wishing to review the source materials (Gothenburg Administrative Court of Appeal, for example cases no. *5741–2002* and *6208–2002*, decided on 6 February 2003).

[89] See the decisions by the Administrative Supreme Court, *Regeringsrättens Årsbok* 2003, ref. 18.

[90] See *Guidelines for ethical evaluation of medical research involving human subjects,* n. 11 *supra*, 71. According to the views of the Medical Research Council's National Board for Ethics in Research, it was also expected that significant complications and serious adverse events, occurring in a research project that had been approved, be reported to the responsible REC (with the exception of clinical drug trials, where such reports are instead provided to the Medical Products Agency), see the guidelines above, 65–66.

[91] Ministerial Report (Ds 2001:62) *Etikprövning av forskning som omfattar människor,* 183.

[92] Government bill *Regeringens proposition 2002/03:50 Etikprövning av forskning,* 163.

Review, though only to the extent that such supervision is not already the responsibility of any other supervisory body, for example the National Board of Health and Welfare, the Medical Products Agency or the Data Inspection Board.[93] Supervision of research projects will therefore require a considerable amount of coordination and cooperation between the different agencies concerned.

The Central Board has certain powers with regard to its supervisory duties (see Section 35 of the Act on Ethics Review). These powers include right of access to information, documents and research premises. At the request of the Board, the principal of the research shall offer such assistance as is needed for the oversight to be carried out. The Board is also authorized to issue such injunctions and prohibitions as are required to uphold the legislation on ethics review of research. If there is reason to suspect a criminal breach of the Act on Ethics Review, the Board shall notify the Office of the Public Prosecutor.

*Liability for Breaches of Research-Related Requirements*

In accordance with Section 38 of the Act on Ethics Review, intentional breaches of the requirement for ethics approval, as well as intentional breaches of any conditions laid down in such an approval, now constitute a criminal offence. The penalty is a fine or imprisonment for a maximum time of six months. Negligence is not criminalized and in petty cases, no sentence shall be imposed. If the action is criminal under a provision in another statute, that provision should be applied instead. In order to answer the question of *who* may actually run the risk of personal criminal liability, it is necessary to consider the internal organization of the institution or company carrying out the research.

Under the old review system, the possible legal consequences for researchers who did not submit their research for review, or failed to follow the recommendations of an REC, would seem to have depended largely on the type of research and the employer of the researcher.

Each employer may of course administer disciplinary sanctions in accordance with labour law and relevant agreements.[94] With regard to professional activities performed within the area of health and medical services, Swedish healthcare personnel fall under a special type of administrative disciplinary liability, regulated by statutory law.[95] This liability also covers activities within clinical trials (involving patients or healthy volunteers), but no disciplinary sanction can be imposed unless there has been an intentional or negligent breach of a statutory provision that is of importance to the safety and security of patients or research subjects.[96] Matters concerning disciplinary sanctions (warning or admonition) are

---

[93] Section 34 of the Act on Ethics Review. See also Government bill *Regeringens proposition 2002/03:50 Etikprövning av forskning*, 163–165.
[94] See Ministerial Report, n. 91 *supra*, 67–68.
[95] See Chapter 5 of the Act (1998:531) on Professional Activities in Health and Medical Services.
[96] See Chapter 5, Sections 2–3 of the Professional Activities Act.

decided by a national authority, the Health and Medical Services Liability Board (*Hälso- och sjukvårdens ansvarsnämnd, HSAN*).[97]

The Swedish patient insurance and pharma-insurance schemes both cover research activities and clinical trials, but only on the condition that the project has been approved by the competent board for ethics review and is carried out in compliance with the conditions stated in the approval.[98] If the conditions are not fulfilled, however, any damages that are incurred may prove costly to the institution or company responsible for the project. As employees, individual researchers only risk personal liability in tort under exceptional circumstances, related to the character of their actions, the position of the employee, the interests of the injured party and other circumstances as set out in Chapter 3, Section 10 of the Damages Act (1972:207).

## Accountability of the Review Boards

### The Exercise of Public Power

The legal standing and accountability of the RECs in the old system was somewhat unclear, although they undeniably formed a part of the Swedish public administration. As such they were bound to obey the general provisions and principles applicable to the administration, laid down for example in the Instrument of Government and ordinary statutes of law. One of the primary principles governing the administration concerns legality. Chapter 1, Section 1 of the Instrument of Government thus prescribes that '[P]ublic power shall be exercised under the law'. Furthermore Courts and public authorities, as well as others performing tasks within the public administration, shall have regard in their work for the equality of all persons before the law and shall observe objectivity and impartiality.[99] There are also a number of provisions in the Administrative Procedure Act (1986:223), concerning for example the service duties of public agencies, general requirements with regard to the handling of matters and disqualification due to bias. In addition to the monitoring performed in their respective areas of competence by different supervisory agencies such as the Data Inspection Board, the National Board of Health and Welfare and the Medical Products Agency, the public administration is also under the surveillance of the

---

[97] See Chapter 7 of the Professional Activities Act. This Board also decides about revocation of licences for healthcare personnel, on application by the National Board of Health and Welfare. Presumably, misconduct in research would have to be quite grave in order for the licence of the healthcare personnel in question to be revoked.

[98] As regards patient insurance, see Section 1, paragraph 2 of the Terms of Indemnity of the County Council's Mutual Insurance Company (*Landstingens Ömsesidiga Försäkringsbolag, LÖF*), adopted 1 January 1995, available at http://www.lof-forsakring.com/, last accessed 18 May 2005.

[99] See Chapter 1, Section 9, of the Instrument of Government.

Parliamentary Ombudsmen and the Government's Chancellor of Justice.[100] The Ombudsmen supervise the Swedish public administration, in order to make sure that the treatment afforded by public authorities to individual citizens is lawful and appropriate.[101] Supervision is exercised both by the assessing of complaints and by means of inspections and such other inquiries as the Ombudsmen may find necessary.

When administrative activities involve the exercise of public power (*myndighetsutövning*), which is an important concept in Swedish public law, certain additional provisions and requirements apply. The concept can be defined as a public activity that entails the 'exercise of power in order to decide a benefit, right, duty, disciplinary measure, termination of employment or other comparable relationship'.[102] In general, the activities of the old RECs were not regarded as an exercise of public power, due to the fact that the review was formally voluntary and the decisions only advisory, although in practice this could certainly be questioned.[103] Especially with the new requirements for ethics review laid down in the Act on Biobanks, as of 1 January 2003, it would seem difficult to deny that the RECs did in fact exercise some public power. Regardless of this issue, any Swedish public agency would be expected to act in accordance with applicable laws and regulations. It would not be considered acceptable for representatives of the public administration to approve of activities that they know to be unlawful. Not all cases where representatives of the administration prove to be lacking in their general knowledge of the law need to be considered negligent. However, it would certainly be desirable that administrative decision-making bodies have access to sufficient expertise in order to provide them with knowledge of the laws relevant to their particular area of responsibility.

The new review boards, operating under the Act on Ethics Review, are clearly exercising public power in the way described above.[104] This means that a number of additional provisions in the Administrative Procedure Act are applicable to their decision-making and handling of matters.[105] Furthermore, the principle of proportionality is often given as a general norm in the exercise of public power.[106] This principle, implying that an intervention by a public authority should never go beyond that which is necessary to protect the interest at risk, might of course be understood to indicate that the review boards should not, without good reason, reject a project that involves no unlawful activities. On the other hand, the lawfulness of a research project is now dependent on the appraisal made with

---

[100] See the Act (1975:1339) on Supervision by the Chancellor of Justice.

[101] See the Act (1986:765) with Instructions for the Parliamentary Ombudsmen.

[102] F. Sterzel, 'General Public Law' in H. Tiberg (ed.), *Swedish Law—a survey* (Stockholm: Juristförlaget, 1994), 43–93, at 88.

[103] E. Rynning (1997), 'Etisk granskning av medicinska humanforskningsprojekt—lagstiftning behövs!', n. 1 *supra*, 1771–1774.

[104] Government bill 2002/03:50, 146.

[105] These provisions concern, for example, explanatory reasons for decisions, and communication with the parties.

[106] F. Sterzel (1994), n. 102 *supra*, 88.

regard to the general prerequisites of the Act on Ethics Review, concerning, for example, respect for human dignity, human rights and fundamental freedoms (see Sections 8–9 of the Act), risk/benefit assessment (see Section 10) and risk minimization (see Section 11). The boundaries of lawful research in the individual case is thus, to a certain degree, at the discretion of the competent board for ethics review and it is stressed in the *traveaux préparatoires* that it is intended for the boards to be relatively free in their evaluation.[107]

*Legal Liability*

The exercise of public power is also of decisive importance with regard to criminal liability for the members of an ethics committee. In order for a civil servant to commit the criminal offence of a 'breach of duty' (*tjänstefel*), under Chapter 20, Section 1 of the Penal Code, there has to be some connection to the exercise of public power; this would not have been the case with the old RECs. In the new system, the boards for ethics review do exercise public power and may consequently fall under penal liability for 'breach of duty' if they intentionally, or negligently, disregard what their task requires of them (see Chapter 20, Section 1 of the Penal Code). The penalty for this crime is a fine or imprisonment for a maximum of two years (or, if the circumstances are aggravating, up to six years). In petty cases, no sanction may be imposed.

As regards the possibility of obtaining compensation for damages in cases where the public administration has acted erroneously, there are general provisions laid down in Chapter 3 of the Torts Liability Act (1972.207). This liability falls on the State, and the individual members of a board for ethics review would only be personally liable under exceptional circumstances (see Chapter 4 Section 1 of the Torts Liability Act).

**Conclusions**

The introduction of a new, legally regulated system for ethics review of research involving humans is certainly an important step in Swedish research policy. We now have a legal requirement for ethics approval of certain types of research, and the role of the review boards has become substantially clearer. This increased clarity applies both to formal matters, such as the composition, procedure and general powers of the review boards, and to the basic factual prerequisites that should be met in order for a research project to be approved. All in all, the new system is better equipped to protect the rights of both researchers and research subjects, as well as the interests of society. Swedish law has also been brought closer to conformity with EU law and Council of Europe standards.

Nevertheless, there is still reason for concern on a number of points. Although the composition of the new boards for ethics review is broader than that of the old

---

[107] Government bill 2002/03:50, 101.

RECs, for example now including legal expertise, the boards for reviewing biomedical research still do not seem ideally equipped for the assessment of issues regarding the processing of sensitive personal data in biomedical research.[108] The scope of the Act on Ethics Review also gives cause for criticism; for example, as long as consent is obtained, the Act does not cover research projects that involve processing of sensitive personal data from vulnerable research subjects. Certain concepts that are of decisive importance to the scope of the legislation, such as 'identifiability', remain unclear.

The balancing of privacy rights against public interests, with regard to the processing of sensitive personal data without consent, would now only seem to require that the scientific value of the research *counterbalances* the risks to the research subject; whereas previously the Personal Data Act prescribed that the interest of society in the research must be *manifestly greater* than the risk of improper violation of the personal integrity of the data subject. The reassurance in the *travaux préparatoires*, providing that no material change is intended,[109] is not satisfactory.

The most serious problem concerns the very complex regulation of *inter alia* information and consent requirements for research, especially with regard to minors and incapacitated adults. The relationship and interaction between different relevant statutes is far from clear. By way of cross-references and exemptions, Swedish law thus provides an intricate hierarchy of varying prerequisites to be met, depending both on the type of research and on other circumstances. Important societal qualities such as legal transparency and predictability are thereby lost, at least with regard to the majority of researchers and research subjects. Future comprehensive rules on proxy decision-making in healthcare and research may provide some improvements in this area; however, there would also definitely seem to be an urgent need for further revisions of the regulatory framework.

---

[108] As stated at n. 56 *supra*, this applies also to the present composition of the Central Board for Ethics Review.
[109] Government bill 2002/03:50, 119.

Chapter 27

# Research Ethics Committees and the Law in the UK

Stephen Baker[*], Deryck Beyleveld[†], Susan Wallace[‡] and Jessica Wright[**]

## Introduction

This report discusses the Research Ethics Committee (REC) system in the UK, with special reference to the responsibilities that RECs have to attend to legal requirements generally, and data protection laws in particular, when they review research proposals. The UK has implemented Directive 2001/20/EC on Clinical Trials, through Statutory Instrument 2004 No. 1031, the Medicines for Human Use (Clinical Trials) Regulations. This entered into force on 1 May 2004. New standard operating procedures (SOP) for RECs were issued in March 2004, which apply to all National Health Service (NHS) RECs, not just clinical trials ethics committees.[1] There is much that is controversial in the new regulations. However, not all of this is directly relevant to the role of RECs in relation to protecting data protection rights specifically, and for the most part we have not commented on (or even drawn attention to) such aspects.[2]

---

[*] Director of Prescribing, Sheffield Teaching Hospitals NHS Foundation Trust.
[†] Director of the Sheffield Institute of Biotechnological Law and Ethics and Professor of Jurisprudence, University of Sheffield.
[‡] Policy and Projects Officer (Humanities), Cambridge Genetics Knowledge Park, Cambridge.
[**] PRIVIREAL coordinating co-worker and Doctoral student at the Sheffield Institute of Biotechnological Law and Ethics, University of Sheffield.

[1] COREC (2004) *Standard Operating Procedures for Research Ethics Committees in the UK* available on the COREC webpage: www.corec.org.uk (last accessed 18 May 2005). Version 2 were issued in October 2004, containing no fundamental changes to the operating system outlined in version 1, but clarification and guidance on certain points. Reference in this paper will be to version 2.

[2] Notable examples are the provisions lowering the age of consent for research in England and Wales from 18 to 16 (Part 1 para. 1), and those permitting the hospital to nominate anyone they choose (including a doctor not primarily responsible for the patient's treatment) to be the legal representative of a patient unable to give informed consent (Schedule 1, Part 1, paragraph 2(ii)).

## The Establishment and Regulation of Ethical Review of Medical Research in the UK

RECs have operated in the UK NHS since the mid-1960s.[3] Until 2004 there were two kinds of NHS RECs—local research ethics committees (LRECs) and multi-centre research ethics committees (MRECs). Where research was to be conducted in multiple locations, applications were made to an MREC. LRECs or MRECs could be responsible for single-site research conducted in their local area, and if a multi-centre trial was to take place within their jurisdiction, LRECs could review the MREC-approved application for 'locality issues'.

The names 'MREC' or 'LREC' still exist, but a new system is now in place for grading RECs. All RECs in the UK are now either 'recognized', including those which can review clinical trials involving medicinal products for human use or any other research, or 'authorized', covering RECs which *cannot* review the aforementioned clinical trials, but can review other research. Recognized RECs are broken down into type I, II or III committees. Type I committees are recognized for review of phase I trials in healthy volunteers throughout the UK, typically including either NHS or private committees. Type II committees are recognized for the review of clinical trials of investigational medical products (not including phase I on healthy volunteers) taking place at sites within an area defined by the geographical remit of their own appointing authority, these only include LRECs. Type III committees are recognized to review the same trials as Type II, but they can be taking place at any site within the UK. This type includes all previous MRECs, and some LRECs—the difference between MRECs and LRECs thus being that *all* MRECs are now type III, which is not the case for LRECs.

Other agencies apart from the NHS, such as the Medical Research Council (MRC), may act as an 'appointing authority' and create independent RECs to review in-house projects. Similarly, UK universities[4] and the pharmaceutical industry have established RECs for their own purposes. These now all fall under the new REC grading system described above. However, NHS RECs review the majority of medical research conducted in the UK, and unless stated otherwise, the NHS REC system in general forms the basis for the remainder of this report.

Until recently, the REC system was voluntary. The LREC system in England and Wales was only formalized under Department of Health (DH) guidance in 1991, almost 30 years after RECs began to operate, while Scottish LRECs came under formal guidance in 1992. The MREC system was created in 1997. New guidance covering both LRECs and MRECs, Governance Arrangements for NHS

---

[3] Royal College of Physicians of London *Committee on the Supervision of the Ethics of Clinical Investigations in Institutions Report* (London: Royal College of Physicians, July 1967).

[4] See the Nuffield Foundation *University Research Ethics Committees: Their role, remit and conduct* (London: Nuffield Foundation, 2004).

Research Ethics Committees (GAFREC), was published in 2001.[5] In addition, the Department of Health published its Research Governance Framework for Health and Social Care (RGF) in 2001.[6] The latter document also gives guidance to RECs, and there are similar framework documents for Scottish, Welsh and Northern Irish RECs.[7]

In 2002, the first legislation giving explicit statutory duties to RECs came into effect with the Health Service (Control of Patient Information) Regulations 2002 and the Adults with Incapacity (Ethics Committee) (Scotland) Regulations 2002. However, for RECs, the situation in the UK changed even further with the implementation of Directive 2001/20/EC. The Medicines for Human Use (Clinical Trials) Regulations 2004 (hereafter the 'CT regulations') include detailed rules for RECs, and have instigated changes in the REC system. But the regulations, like Directive 2001/20/EC, only cover trials involving medicinal products for human use. They do not cover, for example, trials using medical devices (unless used to deliver a medicine), or 'non-interventional trials' (even if these concern medicinal products for human use), although there remains some uncertainty as to what precisely is meant by a 'non-interventional trial'. Therefore RECs will only be governed by statutory law when they review studies that are covered by Directive 2001/20/EC. When reviewing research projects not under the CT regulations, RECs will continue to follow existing guidance, the SOP. However, according to the Department of Health, and as stated in the SOP, the conduct and performance of RECs under its control will be governed and assessed, in general, as if all research under their review fell under the CT regulations (SOP, Introduction).

## RECs and Clinical Ethics

RECs do not provide clinical ethics advice in the UK. Instead, over the last ten years, there has been a growth of separate clinical ethics committees (CECs) to provide this service. Currently, the UK Clinical Ethics Network consists of 63 CECs.[8] They are located in individual institutions and are usually formed on the initiative of interested parties. There are no formal guidelines dictating

---

[5] DH (2001) *Governance Arrangements for NHS Research Ethics Committees*, available online at. http://www.dh.gov.uk/assetRoot/04/05/86/09/04058609.pdf (last accessed 18 May 2005). There is also Governance for NHS Research Ethics Committees in Scotland.

[6] A second edition of the RGF was published in 2005. It incorporates changes related to the implementation of Directive 2001/20/EC. RGF references in this paper refer to the 2005 version.

[7] See the Research Governance Framework for Health and Social Care (Scotland), Research Governance Framework for Health and Social Care in Wales. The Northern Ireland Framework is currently under consultation.

[8] See the UK Clinical Ethics Network webpage which contains a list of all clinical ethics committees known to it, at: http://www.ethics-network.org.uk/Committee/list.htm (last accessed 18 May 2005). For more information on CECs, see D. Beyleveld, R. Brownsword and S. Wallace, 'Independent Ethics Committees in the United Kingdom' in G. Lebeer (ed.), *Ethical Function in Hospital Ethics Committees* (Amsterdam: IOS Press, 2002).

membership requirements or the activities in which CECs should engage; these vary from committee to committee.

## The Criteria for REC Review

According to the RGF, paragraph 2.2.2,

> The Department of Health requires that all research involving patients, service users, care professionals or volunteers, or their organs, tissue or data, is reviewed independently to ensure it meets ethical standards.

Specifically, research that must be reviewed by an REC is defined in GAFREC, paragraph 3.1, as:

> any research proposal involving:
>
> a.   patients and users of the NHS
> b.   individuals identified as potential research participants because of their status as relatives or carers of patients and users of the NHS...
> c.   access to data, organs or other bodily material of past and present NHS patients
> d.   fetal material and IVF involving NHS patients
> e.   the recently dead in NHS premises
> f.   the use of, or potential access to, NHS premises or facilities
> g.   NHS staff—recruited as research participants...

According to the SOPs, the types of research to be reviewed are the same as those stated in GAFREC (SOP 1.65–1.68). GAFREC (paragraph 9.7) states that RECs need to review projects

> with special attention given to the nature of any intervention and its safety for participants, to the informed consent process, documentation, and to the suitability and feasibility of the protocol.

The research sponsor, on the other hand, 'is responsible for ensuring the quality of the science' (GAFREC 9.8). GAFREC also states that the purpose of REC review 'is to protect the dignity, rights, safety and well-being of all actual and potential research participants' (GAFREC 2.2), but 'they should also take into account the interests, needs and safety of researchers' (GAFREC 2.3). However, this should be of secondary importance to the concerns of the research participants.

This stated, the CT regulations do provide a list of matters the REC should consider, which includes weighing foreseeable risks against benefits (Schedule 1, part 2(2)). Schedule 1 also outlines the conditions and principles of good clinical practice, and states that these principles apply to all clinical trials. However, it is not stipulated that the REC take these into account, except for the weighing of risks against benefits. The SOPs do not mention the principles of good clinical practice, and state that guidance on the matters to be considered within ethical review can be found in GAFREC (SOP 3.4).

## REC Membership Requirements

Membership requirements differ between the Scottish RECs and RECs from the rest of the United Kingdom. Non-Scottish RECs must not have more than 18 members, one third of which must be lay members with the remainder being expert members. Additionally,

> at least half of these lay members must be persons who are not, and have never been either health or social care professionals, and who have never been involved in carrying out research involving human participants, their tissue or data (GAFREC 6.7).

Schedule 2, Section 3(5)b(iii) of the new CT regulations reflects this, and adds that the lay members should never have been a chairman, member or director of: aa) a health service body, or bb) any other body providing health care.

If necessary, RECs may obtain advice from outside experts on clinical and scientific matters where the REC is lacking expertise in that area. Such trials include those involving minors or incapacitated adults unable to give informed consent.[9]

Unlike the rest of the UK,[10] Scotland has in place the Adults with Incapacity (Scotland) Act 2000. The purpose of this Act 'is to provide for decisions to be made on behalf of adults who lack legal capacity to do so themselves because of mental disorder or inability to communicate'.[11] Therefore, additional requirements are needed for reviewing research proposals that might include adults covered under the Act. The Adults with Incapacity (Ethics Committee) (Scotland) Regulations 2002 also require Scottish RECs to have no more than 18 members; however, Section 3.3 requires,

> The membership of the Committee shall, so far as practical, include at least—
>
> a.  one person who has experience in relation to the treatment of adults who are incapable;
> b.  one medical practitioner who provides personal, or general, medical services under sections 17C or 19 of the National Health Service (Scotland) Act 1978;
> c.  one registered nurse or registered midwife;
> d.  one registered medical practitioner having experience in clinical pharmacology;

---

[9] See the CT regulations, 15.6 and 15.7.
[10] The Mental Capacity Act 2005, extending to England and Wales, has recently been enacted. The Act is in force, except for Sections 30 to 41 of the Act, which will come into force when the relevant orders are made. .
[11] See the Explanatory Notes for the Act.

e. one registered pharmaceutical chemist as defined by Section 24(1) of the Pharmacy Act 1954 or a registered person as defined by Article 2(2) of the Pharmacy (Northern Ireland) Order 1976;

f. one registered medical practitioner who holds the position of hospital consultant;

g. one registered medical practitioner having experience in the field of public health medicine;

h. one member who is registered as a member of a profession to which the Professions Supplementary to Medicine Act 1960 applies; and

i. three lay members.

With this membership, the Scottish RECs will have the expertise needed if research involving incapacitated adults is considered.

As per Section 51(3)(c) of the Adults with Incapacity Act (Scotland) 2000, any research conducted in Scotland on adults with incapacities must be approved by an ethics committee approved by Scottish Ministers under Section 51(6) of the Act (which in essence means one of the Scottish RECs).

## Accountability of RECs

Prior to the latest reorganization, LRECs were responsible to the Strategic Health Authority[12] that established or inherited them, while MRECs were directly responsible to the Secretary of State for Health. However, from 1 March 2004, COREC assumed the responsibilities of these health authorities in relation to the operational procedures for all RECs. Under the CT regulations, relevant RECs come under the direct authority of the United Kingdom Ethics Committees Authority (UKECA). Only those recognized by UKECA (termed officially 'recognized RECs') will be able to review clinical trial research using medicines in humans.[13]

The Secretary of State for Health; the National Assembly of Wales; the Scottish Ministers; and the Department for Health, Social Services and Public Safety for Northern Ireland will be the ruling officials for UKECA. However, it is expected that they will devolve their responsibilities to other staff as necessary. For

---

[12] GAFREC uses the term health authority; this was changed through the National Health Service Reform and Health Care Professions Act 2002 to Strategic Health Authority.

[13] It is important not to confuse UKECA with the 'Competent Authority' referred to in Directive 2001/20/EC. The latter body in the UK is the Medicines and Healthcare Products Regulatory Agency (MHRA), which licenses medicines and regulates medical devices. The role given to UKECA is strongly criticized by the editor of the *Bulletin of Medical Ethics* in his editorial to the April 2003 issue of the *Bulletin*, on the grounds that it threatens to politicize the decision-making of RECs. In our opinion the role given to COREC was also questionable as it was an arm of NHS R&D, creating an intrinsic conflict of interest, the role of R&D being to facilitate research, not to protect patients' rights. The recent (1 April 2005) move of COREC to the National Patient Safety Agency, following the DH's review of arm's length bodies, shows that the DH may have recognized this problem. However, whether this will be an improvement over NHS R&D remains to be seen. In our opinion, the REC system should be run by an independent commission answerable only to Parliament.

example, COREC is continuing to function after the establishment of UKECA. However, its exact role is yet to be determined. It currently monitors compliance with the SOP through the Offices of RECs (ORECs) and administers the Central Allocation System (the method used for booking in, allocating and distributing research proposals). COREC is also authorized by the DH to exercise UKECA's statutory function in relation to appeals (SOP 7.10). The situation may become clearer in the future following the implementation of the UK Government's review of 'arms length bodies'. Under this review, the National Patient Safety Agency will take the national lead in supporting the development of NHS RECs, and has already taken over responsibility for COREC from the Department of Health.[14] Similarly, the NHS Appointments Commission will take on functions necessary to guarantee the independent appointment of REC chairmen and members as required by Directive 2001/20/EC.

UKECA is responsible for establishing, recognizing and monitoring all RECs involved in the review of clinical trials in place at the time the CT regulations came into effect. In addition, UKECA can recognize as ethics committees even those bodies under other authorities, for the purposes stated in the CT regulations. UKECA may determine what research projects an REC will review or the area in which it will work, and can abolish a committee if necessary. UKECA may also monitor RECs and provide advice and assistance as necessary.

## General Powers of RECs

### Approval

RECs have the power to approve or reject applications within their remit; but, while REC approval is necessary for research to proceed, it is not sufficient for the research to go ahead. For example, under the RGF (paragraph 3.12.6) final approval from the host NHS institution is also needed. Additional regulatory approvals may also be needed for certain categories of research. For trials regulated under the CT regulations (regulation 12) no one is able to begin a clinical trial or recruit subjects for a trial without the approval of the REC. The regulation also requires that the principal investigator obtain appropriate authorization from the licensing authority.

### Penalties for Non-Compliance

According to RGF, paragraph 5.8, if an institution or staff member does not comply with the framework requirements, the situation will be dealt with 'through normal management channels'. This could include not submitting a proposal to an REC for review prior to beginning the research. The RGF does not specify penalties for offences.

---

[14] Department of Health, *Reconfiguring the Department of Health's Arm's Length Bodies*, 2004, available on its webpage, www.dh.gov.uk (last accessed 18 May 2005).

RECs themselves have no power to penalize those found committing an offence; however, they may file reports to the institutions or appropriate regulatory bodies detailing any relevant findings. Doctors and others may be disciplined under the rules of their own regulatory body. For example, in the case of Dr. Jyoti Argawala, the General Medical Council (GMC) found him guilty of 'serious professional misconduct'[15] when he was found to have forged REC approval for his research. As a result, the GMC struck him off the medical register.

Under the CT regulations, failure to follow some specific provisions will result in penalties. For example, any person who begins a trial without authority from the Medicines and Healthcare Products Regulatory Agency (MHRA—the licensing authority) or an REC will have committed an offence. Likewise, any person who provides false or misleading data to an REC or the MHRA in the course of the application or conduct of a clinical trial will have committed an offence. Other restrictions apply to those involved in the sale, manufacture or distribution of the investigational medicinal products used in the trials. Individuals committing an offence may face a fine or imprisonment depending on the severity of the crime. Penalties will be enforced through the licensing authority, not the REC.

Although the CT regulations make no mention of this, it is arguable that it is also possible for REC members to commit offences. For example, presumably because of workload issues, the SOP states that applications may be given to a 'lead reviewer' who then may present a summary of the application to the Committee (SOP 2.20–2.23). Hypothetically, if that member wilfully provided incorrect or incomplete information to the other committee members in the process of that review, perhaps to mislead them into believing the trial is safer than it is, then that member might be held to be guilty of an offence.

Under Regulation 8 of the Health Service (Control of Patient Information) Regulations 2002, if the investigator does not process the medical information in the manner approved, or acts without approval of the REC or the Secretary of State for Health, he or she may face a fine of up to £5 000. Once more this is not determined by the REC but the Secretary of State.

*Legal Consequences of REC Decisions*

Section 60 of the Health and Social Care Act 2000 empowers the Secretary of State to pass regulations to render lawful the processing of confidential personal health data without the consent of the subject, where certain conditions are fulfilled: namely the regulations are in the interests of improving patient care or in the public interest (s.60(1)); it is not reasonably practicable to achieve the purposes of the regulations by obtaining consent (s.60(3)); and the purpose of the regulations is not solely or principally to determine the care or treatment of particular individuals (s.60(5)). The specific effect of the regulations is to render the processing of personal health data lawful despite any obligation of confidence owed (see s.60(2)(c)). According to Section 60(6), the regulations must be consistent with the

---

[15] D. Carnall, 'Doctor struck off for medical fraud' (1996) 312 *British Medical Journal* 399–400.

Data Protection Act 1998; but this does not affect the effect of Section 60(2)(c). It should be noted that Section 60(2)(c) is ambiguous. On one interpretation it states that the regulations will render the processing of confidential information lawful. On another interpretation, it states only that the regulations will render the processing of personal data not unlawful on account of the processing breaching an obligation of confidentiality. The latter interpretation is surely correct, for, on the former interpretation, Section 60(6) states that the regulations could render the processing of some personal data lawful despite being in breach of the Data Protection Act 1998. This cannot be right, because the Data Protection Act 1998 stands in lieu of the Data Protection Directive in UK law, satisfying the conditions sufficient for the regulations is not sufficient to guarantee conformity with the data protection law, and, according to the doctrine of the supremacy of EC law, the UK Parliament cannot legislate in contravention of an EC Directive while the UK remains part of the EU.

Using these powers, the Health Service (Control of Patient Information) Regulations 2002 have been passed. Two of the regulations provide for the involvement of RECs. Regulation 2 permits confidential information on patients referred for diagnosis or treatment of neoplasia (which includes cancer) to be used, disclosed or obtained for medical purposes. This includes medical research approved by an REC by persons approved as individuals or a class by the Secretary of State (in practice the Patient Information Advisory Group 'PIAG' set up by Section 61 of the Health and Social Care Act 2001), and the person lawfully in possession of the information. This is provided (see regulation 7) that the person is a health professional or a person acting under an equivalent duty of confidentiality in the terms of the Data Protection Act 1998, and certain security measures are satisfied.

Regulation 5(a) permits confidential patient information to be processed in circumstances laid out in the Schedule to the regulations, on the condition that this is approved by an REC and the Secretary of State (again, in practice PIAG), the procedure being that an REC must first approve the activities involved in research, and then the proposal must be submitted to PIAG. In view of the position taken on the legal responsibilities of RECs by the DH (see below), the idea behind this arrangement is quite possibly that the REC acts solely as ethics filter, while PIAG considers the legality and public policy aspects of the proposed processing.

Apart from these cases, decisions made by RECs do not have any formal role in rendering lawful activities that would otherwise be unlawful. However, it is not beyond the bounds of possibility that the Courts would treat REC approval as a mitigating factor of an action the Court rules to be unlawful when it considers what penalties to impose on researchers or what damages to award against them. This raises the question of the responsibilities of RECs themselves to attend to the law in their decisions. For it is arguable that the more likely it is that Courts will treat REC approval as a mitigating factor in actions brought against researchers, the more important it becomes that the RECs themselves be accountable for their decisions in relation to the law, if the rights of research subjects are to be adequately protected.

**General Legal Responsibility of RECs**

The RGF, at 3.12.7, states,

> It is not the role or responsibility of NHS research ethics committees to give legal advice, nor are they liable for any of their decisions in this respect. Irrespective of the decision of a research ethics committee on a particular application, it is up to the researcher and the NHS or social care organisation who have the responsibility not to break the law.

If RECs have concerns 'that implementation of a research proposal might contravene the law' (RGF 3.12.7), they may inform the researcher submitting the application and the appropriate authority of their concerns. The researcher and the authority should then seek legal advice.

Under GAFREC,[16] at paragraph 2.6, it is made clear that RECs are 'required to have due regard to the requirements of relevant regulatory agencies and of applicable law', and this has been reiterated by the DH and COREC in a joint publication.[17] This is reinforced by the fact that the Annex to the RGF lists relevant laws (including the Data Protection Act 1998) as ethical principles that RECs should apply. However, the DH/COREC document states in its Annex B(7) that 'the governance arrangements make it clear that it is not for RECs to interpret regulations or laws', which faces RECs with the conundrum of having to give due regard to regulations and laws they are not permitted to interpret. What might be intended is that RECs are not to interpret *unclear* laws and regulations, the DH taking the view that some laws are clear and do not require interpretation. If this is so, then the statement is still unhelpful because it is notoriously the case that the import of a law or regulation can seem perfectly clear to one person, yet receive a different interpretation from another person who also regards the provision as transparent.

We are not aware of any legal reason why RECs may not reject proposals that are *lawful* on the grounds that they consider the proposals to be nonetheless unethical (unless specific laws provide to the contrary, though currently there are none such that we are aware of). However, the DH guidance does not positively rule out, and may even be taken to positively suggest, that RECs may approve proposals that they believe are *unlawful* if they consider the proposals to be nonetheless ethical. This is because it neither requires (as against permits or at most recommends) RECs to draw actions they have legal concerns about to the attention of researchers or their employers, nor makes the provision of positive legal advice by the researchers or their employers a condition of REC approval.

---

[16] The SOP direct one back to GAFREC for guidance on the matters to be considered in ethical review (SOP 3.4).

[17] Department of Health/COREC *The use of human organs and tissue: An interim statement. Annex B(2)* (London: DH Clinical Ethics and Human Tissue Branch, April 2003).

This is highly controversial because there are a number of legal considerations that indicate that RECs must make lawfulness a condition of ethical approval.[18]

As far as the law is concerned, it is arguable that RECs are public authorities under UK statutory and common law. This is for several reasons. Their source of power comes from a statutory body; they perform public functions and they have responsibilities under statutory law, these being the standard criteria used by the Courts to determine which bodies are public. In the first instance, public authorities are liable to judicial review of their decisions under the common public law. Judicial review is the protection granted individuals from the potential abuse of the power given to public authorities. An individual can request from the Courts leave to apply for judicial review of a decision made by a public authority. If granted, the Court will then review the circumstances of the case to see if there are grounds for judicial review of the decision. If the decision is reviewed, the Courts will prescribe actions to be taken by the public authority to redress the mistakes made in the original decision.

RECs are also, arguably, public authorities or 'emanations of the state' under EC law, in which case they must obey EC law over any contradictory domestic law. The European Court of Justice in *Foster v British Gas plc*[19] (at 3348), gave this description of emanations of the state:

> A body, whatever its legal form, which has been made responsible pursuant to a measure adopted by the State, for providing a public service under the control of the State and has for that purpose special powers beyond those which result from the normal rules applicable in relations between individuals is included in any event among the bodies against which the provisions of a directive capable of having direct effect may be relied upon.

RECs are under the control of the State, through the Department of Health, and they have special powers to act in the public good. These powers are laid out in statute and supervised by the State. In consequence, if, for example, the UK Data Protection Act 1998 does not properly implement Directive 95/46/EC on Data Protection, RECs must obey the Directive over the domestic law. If they do not, they may be open to judicial review procedures.

Bearing in mind that the RGF (2.2) specifies the role of RECs as, *inter alia*, to protect the rights of research subjects,[20] it is significant that RECs (assuming them to be public authorities) must also act in accordance with the UK Human Rights Act 1998 (HRA), which extensively, if not completely, implements into UK law the European Convention on Human Rights (ECHR) (specifically Articles 2–12 and 14, Articles 1–3 of Protocol 1 to the ECHR, and Articles 1 and 2 of Protocol 6

---

[18] It should be noted that, in its now superseded Notes for Guidance to researchers making application to an MREC, COREC stated that MREC approval is conditional upon researchers observing all legal requirements. This statement did not fully square with the statements in the RGF, and the 'New Operational Procedures for NHS Research Ethics Committees: Guidance for Applicants to RECs' (COREC, April 2004) do not mention this.

[19] *Foster v. British Gas plc* [1990] ECR I-3313.

[20] The CT regulations and the SOP are silent on the role of research ethics committees.

to the ECHR, which are to be read with Articles 16–18 ECHR, subject to any derogations or reservations per Sections 14 and 15 of the HRA (see Section 1)). Specifically, the HRA forbids public authorities from acting incompatibly with the 'Convention rights' unless primary legislation makes it impossible for them to comply with the Convention rights (see Section 6(1) and (2)), and to act incompatibly with the Convention rights includes failure to act compatibly with the Convention rights (see Section 6(6)). Section 6(3) of the Act defines public authorities as:

a.   a Court or tribunal; and
b.   any person certain of whose functions are functions of a public nature.

During the passage of the Act, the Home Secretary declared that public authorities fell into three groups: standard public authorities, functional public authorities, and Courts and tribunals.[21] Standard public authorities are those governmental in nature, including 'bodies which are self-evidently of a public nature, such as the police, government departments, the Probation Service, local authorities'.[22] Functional public authorities, on the other hand, are those that have both private and public functions. The Courts have used many tests to determine whether a body is a public authority: for example, function, authority, public funding, statutory basis, public interest and the jurisprudence of the European Court of Justice (ECJ).[23] RECs have a public function; their authority is a Government body; their funding comes from the NHS; they have statutory duties; they exist to act in the public interest and they are surely emanations of the State under EC law. On this basis, RECs appear to be standard public authorities and, if so, they must protect the rights of individuals accorded by the HRA when performing their functions.

As is pointed out in the 'Overview of International Materials Regarding the Role of RECs' in an accompanying volume,[24] Directive 2001/20/EC also appears to require EC Member States to give a specific role to RECs in interpreting data protection law. Specifically, reading Article 3(2)(c) with Article 6(3)(g) and 6(4) of the Directive 2001/20/EC implies that RECs have a responsibility to safeguard subjects' data protection rights under Directive 95/46/EC that may not be devolved elsewhere (including to the researcher, the researcher's employer, or even to PIAG—whose role under the Health and Social Care Act 2001 is, in any event, intrinsically in relation to confidentiality not data protection law as such, though it

---

[21] See, for example, the House of Commons debate on the Human Rights Bill, 17 February 1997, col. 773.

[22] H. Fenwick, *Civil Liberties and Human Rights* (3rd edn., London: Cavendish Publishing, 2002).

[23] D. Oliver, 'The Frontiers of the State: Public Authorities and Public Functions Under the Human Rights Act' (2000) Autumn *Public Law* 476–493.

[24] See D. Beyleveld, D. Townend and J. Wright (eds.), *Research Ethics Committees, Data Protection and Medical Research in Europe – Key Issues* (Aldershot: Ashgate Publishing Ltd, 2005).

must be borne in mind that *unlawful* breaches of confidentiality in processing personal data are breaches of the first data protection principle of the Data Protection Act 1998). However, the CT regulations make no mention of this.[25] The CT regulations do state that the condition that 'the rights of each subject to physical and mental integrity, to privacy, and to the protection of the data concerning him in accordance with the Data Protection Act 1998 are safeguarded' applies to all clinical trials, but does not mention who will ensure this (CT regulations, Schedule 1, Part 2, Section 15).

An interesting point in relation to whether or not the REC takes into account the law when reviewing a protocol also arises when considering research using human tissue. The Human Tissue Act 2004 includes stipulations that research using human tissue from a living person can go ahead without consent, on the condition that it is both ethically approved and the researcher cannot identify, or possibly identify, the person the tissue originates from. The requirements are the same for the use of the results of DNA analysis for research. The RECs will surely have to take these provisions into consideration in the future when reviewing relevant protocols, as it mentions ethical approval explicitly.

Finally, it should be noted that RECs are also not responsible for any ongoing monitoring of research; again it is the responsibility of the sponsor and the principal investigator to ensure 'that a study follows the agreed protocol' (RGF 3.12.8). The CT regulations state that a

> ... trial shall be initiated only if an ethics committee and the licensing authority comes to the conclusion that the anticipated therapeutic and public health benefits justify the risks and may be continued only if compliance with this requirement is permanently monitored (Schedule 1, part 2, section 14).

It does not mention who should monitor this. The SOP outlines that the main REC has no responsibility for the 'proactive monitoring' of research studies, the accountability for which lies with sponsors and employing organizations (SOP 9.3). However, the main REC should receive progress reports on the research at least annually, which they should use to keep their ethical opinion under review. The ethics committee may request a meeting to discuss ethical concerns, and it may review its favourable opinion at any time (SOP 9.4, 9.52).


**Practice of RECs**

In view of the DH's advice, it should not be surprising that RECs will pay different amounts of attention to an applicable law, such as the Data Protection Act 1998, according to the awareness, insight, and expertise available within the membership and the administrative officer(s) of the individual REC.

---

[25] The ambivalence of the Department of Health to legal responsibilities of RECs in the period leading up to the RGF is discussed in D. Beyleveld, 'Law, Ethics, and Research Ethics Committees' (2002) 21 *Medicine and Law* 1, 57–75.

A PRIVIREAL questionnaire was sent[26] to RECs in the UK to determine what their actions may be when confronted with a) a protocol which is unlawful but *otherwise* ethical, and b) a protocol which is unethical but *otherwise* lawful. This brief survey also asked if the respondents believed that RECs should give advice on purely ethical considerations, independent of legal ones.

Two MRECs responded, both with the view that they believe they would approve a proposal which is unlawful, if it is otherwise ethical, reflecting the opinion that they should give advice on purely ethical grounds. One MREC stated its members sometimes regard the law as unethical and judge on ethical grounds alone, and when a proposal could be illegal but is otherwise ethical, they would approve it and comment on this possible illegality. The same MREC mentioned that interpretation of the Data Protection Act can itself cause problems, for example when considering what is and is not a matter of national interest, a decision which could cause some aspects of data protection to be sidestepped.

The other MREC outlines that the committee is not able or expected to give legal opinions, including whether or not a proposal infringes the law, and judges a protocol only on whether is it ethical or not. This committee also mentions that on some occasions, a proposal could be illegal but ethical, and gives the example of the cannabis study, a collaboration with the Home Office where, as information was required for governmental purposes, the subjects were guaranteed that prosecution would not follow. In the spirit of helpfulness, this committee would point out any action it believes to be against the law to the investigators, who would be responsible for taking any action to avoid breaking the law, and who would be responsible for the consequences. This committee in general believes that it is not the responsibility of the committee to interpret the law.

A local REC responded to these questions and stated that the committee would reject proposals which are either unlawful and otherwise ethical, or unethical and otherwise lawful, perhaps reflecting the opinion that proposals should be both ethical and legal. The divergent views between the MRECs and LREC show that within the UK, what matters are taken into consideration during ethical review are far from standardized.

## Liability of RECs Under Common Law[27]

As we have opined, RECs have public law responsibilities under Statute and common law. As yet there is no UK case where an REC has been brought to Court under private law proceedings because of a decision it has made. However, if it does happen in the future, there is Canadian case law that may be taken into

---

[26] This survey was completed in mid-2003, before the CT regulations came into effect, therefore the respondents are termed MREC and LREC, within the meaning of the old system.

[27] We wish to thank our colleague Dr. Shaun Pattinson for his comments and advice on this section. We, however, remain solely responsible for its contents.

account. In *Weiss c. Solomon*[28] a man, W, agreed to enter a research study on the use of ophthalmic drops. The procedure consisted of the participant being administered the drops, then undergoing a fluorescein angiography to judge the results of the treatment. After being injected with the fluorescein, W suffered cardiac failure and died. It was known at the time of the procedure that W suffered from a heart condition, but this information did not lead to him being excluded from the trial. In addition, the room in which the procedure was carried out was not equipped with resuscitation equipment, which might have been used to save his life. The plaintiffs claimed that the physicians and the hospital were negligent in their duty because they did not properly inform W of the possible risks involved with the procedure, they did not exclude patients with heart conditions from the study, and they did not provide resuscitation equipment. The defendants were found liable. Specifically, the hospital, through its research committee, was found negligent for not ensuring that the information given to the prospective trial participants adequately explained the possible risks of the research procedure.

UK judges may consider this case when determining a judgment against an REC. However, it is possible that the reasoning used in this case would not be persuasive. The judges might instead rely on the *Bolam*[29] test as used in *Sidaway*,[30] in relation to which it could be argued that a reasonable REC would have provided the same information as was provided to W. If this argument failed, as Brazier notes, '[h]ow would a court decide whether a reasonable ethics committee would/should have noted the potential illegality in the trial?'[31] The Department of Health states in GAFREC at 9.11,[32] that 'RECs need to take into account the potential relevance of applicable laws and regulations'. However, as we have seen, in the RGF, at 3.12.7,[33] it states that '[i]t is not the responsibility of NHS research ethics committees to give legal advice, nor are they liable for any of their decisions in this respect'.

The REC is responsible for contacting the researcher or sponsor if there are potential legal concerns regarding the study, but this is the end of their responsibility. The researcher and/or sponsor are responsible for seeking legal advice.[34] RECs are not provided with legal assistance in order to make their decisions; therefore they might not know if a trial might result in injury to a patient. However, as noted, as public authorities, RECs are required to implement EC law as well as UK statutory law and the DH states that they must be aware of

---

[28] *Weiss c. Solomon* [1988] RJQ 731.

[29] *Bolam v. Friern Hospital Management Committee* [1997] 1 WLR 582.

[30] *Sidaway v. Board of Governors of the Bethlem Royal Hospital* [1985] AC 871.

[31] M. Brazier, 'Liability of ethics committees and their members' (1990) 6 *Professional Negligence* 188.

[32] DH *Governance Arrangements for NHS Research Ethics Committees* (2001). Available to download from the DH website www.dh.gov.uk (last accessed 18 May 2005).

[33] DH *Research Governance Framework for Health and Social Care* (2nd edn., London: Department of Health, 2005).

[34] *Ibid.* at 3.12.9.

the law and potential illegalities. However, if they used their best knowledge to come to a decision, this might prove sufficient to avoid private law claims.

The UK Courts have historically proven reluctant to hold public authorities liable in negligence for their actions,[35] although current case law shows that this is beginning to change. For example, in the case of *Hill v. Chief Constable of West Yorkshire*,[36] the plaintiff sought to appeal a lower Court judgment dismissing the claim that the police had been negligent in their duty to protect her daughter from being murdered. As other murders had been occurring in the area that the daughter frequented, the crime should have been foreseeable and the police under a duty of care to prevent it. Their Lordships based their judgment, amongst other reasoning, on whether there was a special relationship between the defendant and the deceased that would create a duty of care that would hold the police responsible for preventing the attack on the deceased. The appeal was dismissed as Their Lordships found that there was not a special relationship, that the police had a general duty to protect the public but not to protect specific individuals. In addition, they agreed that if a precedent was set by finding the police negligent, other cases would be brought and time and manpower would be spent dealing with litigation, rather than on crime detection and prevention.

This second 'public policy' reasoning can be applied directly to RECs. Many RECs review a large number of proposals for research studies every month.[37,38] If cases were brought against RECs for even a fraction of these projects, RECs would be forced to spend more time and money defending their actions than on reviewing protocols. Therefore, a case can be argued for not finding RECs liable in negligence.

However, while this public policy defence is still in place, there has been a retreat from giving public authorities blanket immunity for their actions. As noted, in *Hill,* one question was whether or not there was a duty of care placed on the public authority. In order to prove a duty of care, the Courts look for three features, as stated in *Caparo plc v. Dickman*[39] at 617:

> ... [I]n addition to the foreseeability of damage, necessary ingredients in any situation giving rise to a duty of care are that there should exist between the party owing the duty and the party to whom it is owed a relationship characterised by the law as one of 'proximity' or 'neighbourhood' and that the situation should be one in which the court considers it fair, just and reasonable that the law should impose a duty of a given scope upon the one party for the benefit of the other.

---

[35] Palmer Company Law Challenging the FSA's decisions. *UK Palmer 11.008*, 2001.

[36] *Hill v. Chief Constable of West Yorkshire* [1988] QB 60.

[37] R. Nicholson, 'A study of local research ethics committee annual reports' (June/July 1997) *Bulletin of Medical Ethics* 13–24.

[38] J. Blunt, J. Savulescu and A. Watson, 'Meeting the challenges facing research ethics committees: some practical suggestions' (1998) 316 *British Medical Journal* 58–61.

[39] *Caparo plc v. Dickman* [1990] 2 AC 605.

In *Kent v. Griffiths and Others*,[40] the issue of proximity was questioned. In this case, K, a woman, was suffering from an asthma attack. An ambulance was called. However, it was delayed in its arrival. Before arriving at the hospital, K suffered a respiratory arrest resulting in brain damage. The claimant brought an action against the ambulance company alleging negligence for failing to arrive promptly. The appeal brought by the defendant was dismissed as the judges agreed that a duty of care existed in this case. Proximity was established when the call was accepted by the ambulance service. In addition, it was foreseeable that K would suffer if the ambulance did not arrive promptly and there were no circumstances to preclude a duty of care from existing.

Could this issue of proximity relate to RECs? If an REC approved a research study, and subsequently a patient was harmed, could the REC be held liable in negligence? The answer would perforce depend on the circumstances. If the individual harmed was known to the committee because he or she was, for example, identified in the protocol for the study, then proximity might be proved and there might be a case to argue. However, it is extremely unlikely that the individual persons recruited into a study will be known to an REC (at least in its capacity as an REC), making proximity establishing a duty of care difficult to prove.

Another consideration is whether UKECA, as a third-party responsible for RECs, could be held liable for their supposed negligent actions. Again, based on prior cases, such an action is unlikely to succeed. In *Yuen Kun Yeu and Others v. Attorney-General of Hong Kong*,[41] the plaintiffs sought to appeal a lower Court decision dismissing their claim that the Commissioner of Deposit-taking Companies should be held negligent for not ensuring that the companies under his responsibility properly safeguarded the assets of depositors. The plaintiffs had deposited funds into such a company, which went into liquidation resulting in the loss of the plaintiffs' money. The Court, as in *Hill*, considered whether there was a special relationship such that the Commissioner owed a duty of care to members of the public. The Court dismissed the appeal, finding that there was not such a duty of care owed. As Lord Keith of Kinkel stated, at 195 of the judgment,

> The commissioner did not have any power to control the day-to-day management of any company, and such a task would require immense resources. His power was limited to putting it out of business or allowing it to continue. No doubt recognition by the company that the commissioner had power to put it out of business would be a powerful incentive impelling the company to carry on its affairs in a reasonable manner, but if those in charge were determined upon fraud it is doubtful if any supervision could be close enough to prevent it in time to forestall loss to depositors.

This reasoning can be used regarding RECs under UKECA. While UKECA is the umbrella body over RECs, it does not have day-to-day responsibilities for REC activities. UKECA does not have the power to overrule REC decisions. Therefore,

---

[40] *Kent v. Griffiths and Others* [2000] QB 36.
[41] *Yuen Kun Yeu and Others v. Attorney-General of Hong Kong* [1988] AC 175.

the relationship will not be close enough to impose a duty of care on the participants in research projects approved by the REC. However, interesting questions would arise if UKECA were to require RECs to follow regulations that in turn caused the REC to act in such a way that research participants were harmed in some way. Unfortunately, space precludes us from pursuing this thought here.

Next is the question of whether individual REC members can be held liable for their decisions. Because most RECs discuss proposals in confidence[42] it would be difficult to place blame on individuals. If, for instance, a researcher claimed that an REC member was biased against them and deliberately led the committee to refuse their application, unless 'inside information' was obtained, it would be very difficult for an outsider to know what was said and by whom. If an individual can be named, the CT regulations, as noted earlier, can impose penalties in specified cases on those who wilfully mislead an REC in their decision-making regarding trial falling under the regulations. In other situations, if the individual at blame is an NHS staff member, the person complaining would most likely be instructed to follow 'normal [DH] management channels and disciplinary procedures' as indicated in the RGF at 5.8.

Liability coverage is provided for NHS staff. The National Health Service (Liabilities to Third Parties Scheme) Regulations 1999 and the National Health Service (Liabilities to Third Parties Scheme) Amendment Regulations 2000 provide liability coverage for third-party loss, damage or injury for NHS trusts, health authorities, primary care trusts and special health authorities. These would cover the expert members. As for lay members, GAFREC states, at 4.14, that

> [t]he appointing Authority will take full responsibility for all the actions of a member in the course of their performance of his or her duties as a member of the REC other than those involving bad faith, wilful default or gross negligence.

In addition, at 5.9, GAFREC states that, '[t]he appointing Authority shall provide each appointed member with a personal statement regarding the indemnity provided, and its conditions'. Therefore, members are provided with information as to the coverage provided for them.[43]

## Concluding Remarks

In this report, we have argued that RECs have specific legal responsibilities to protect data protection rights of research participants, in the main public law responsibilities, responsibilities under the UK Human Rights Act 1998 and Directive 2001/20/EC. DH guidance and the way in which the UK has implemented Directive 2001/20/EC at best plays down (and often obscures these

---

[42] R. Ashcroft and N. Pfeffer, 'Ethics behind closed doors: Do research ethics committees need secrecy?' (2001) 322 *British Medical Journal* 1294–1296.

[43] This sits rather oddly with the guidance that RECs bear no responsibility for their decisions in relation to the law.

responsibilities), and may even be held to deny them. Legislation on confidentiality might also be interpreted to be in breach of the Data Protection Directive insofar as it suggests that the conditions to render actions that are in breach of confidentiality not unlawful on this count are to be considered lawful even if they breach the UK Data Protection Act 1998. Apart from issues of legality that all this gives rise to, it is also questionable from an ethical point of view. This is because of the particularly vulnerable position of research subjects in relation to protection of their data protection rights. Unless RECs play an active role in protecting these rights, they are unlikely to be protected effectively, but the DH guidance (in large part because of the conflicting and unclear way in which it is couched) and the new regulations at best do nothing to positively encourage RECs to take data protection seriously, and it is clear that at least some RECs interpret the DH guidance to mean that the protection of legal rights to data protection is none of their business.

# Index